KU-077-382

A guide to London's churches

Mervyn Blatch

Constable London

First published in Great Britain 1978
by Constable and Company Ltd
3 The Lanchesters
162 Fulham Palace Road
London W6 9ER
Copyright © 1978 Mervyn Blatch
Second edition 1995
ISBN 0 09 474630 3
Set in Linotron Times
by CentraCet Ltd, Cambridge
Printed in Great Britain by
BAS Printers Ltd, Wallop

A CIP catalogue record for this book
is available from the British Library

Author's Note

The dedication section is omitted in the cases of the better-known saints. To avoid cross-reference, in other cases it is shown separately for each church.

* Asterisks indicate features of special interest.

Contents

Maps

Acknowledgements

I am grateful to the National Monuments Record for permission to reproduce the illustrations on pages xxi and 151, and to Miss D. M. Niblett of St Ursula's Hostel for the illustration on page 285.

Thanks are also due to Mr Francois Prins, archivist of All Souls', Langham Place for the photographs on pages 198, 199 and for the Nash cartoon (page 197) as well as for the drawing of St Peter's, Vere Street (page 258).

A special word of appreciation must go to Mrs Holsman of the Winston Churchill Memorial and Library, Fulton, Missouri for sending me the guide and photograph of St Mary the Virgin, Aldermanbury (page 189), and to Mrs Arlene Cusuman of Christ Church, Philadelphia for the photograph of the font in which William Penn was baptised (page 5)

I must also give credit to Prebendary Gerard Irvine for the drawing made available to me of the new St Matthew's, Great Peter Street, Westminster: to the Rector of Stepney for the excellent picture of the rood at St Dunstan's and to Mr Tony Thomas for the photograph of St Helen's, Bishopsgate showing the church stripped out for restoration work.

To my publishers I am appreciative of the free hand I have been given to write as I feel would be most helpful to 'visitors' and in a form which I hope will enable them to pick out quickly what particularly interests them. I have aimed at encouraging the church-lover to wander off the beaten track, even if this means making special arrangements to see interiors.

I would like to acknowledge the help given me by my two grandsons but, above all, my sincere thanks go to my wife for her support and encouragement. I am deeply grateful to her.

Preface

Two questions arose when I came to write this book: 'Which parts of London?', and 'Which churches?' The Greater London Council area today extends from Kingston-upon-Thames in the south to Barnet in the north, and is altogether too diffuse and varied a region to construct a coherent picture of Metropolitan places of worship. The 19th century saw an enormous growth of churches to meet the needs of an increasing and largely church-going population; many of these buildings are of little or no interest to the lover of churches.

It seemed to me that a proper compass would be the City of London, the City of Westminster and the eleven enlarged inner boroughs formed in 1965 and roughly corresponding with the boundaries of the pre-1965 London County Council area, and that I should restrict myself to pre 19th century buildings plus those later churches of special architectural, historical or social interest. I have only exceeded these geographical limits in the case of St John the Evangelist, Upper Norwood, a notable Victorian building in the Borough of Croydon; and two churches once in the City but transferred elsewhere: All Hallows, North Twickenham, and St Mary Aldermanbury, now at Fulton, Missouri, USA.

Non-Anglicans will deplore the omission of churches ranging from the Italianate Baroque splendours of Brompton Oratory to the quiet seclusion of St Mary's, Holly Place, Hampstead, the great Free Church centres such as Wesley's chapel and the City Temple; others may regret the lack of any reference to the grandeur of the Catholic Apostolic Church in Gordon Square and the architectural richness of royal or institutional places of worship like the Queen's Chapel or Wren's Royal Hospital Chapel. I can only plead that to go beyond what I have covered would have made the book unmanageable and excessively weighty to carry around. The same considerations apply in the cases of St Paul's and Southwark Cathedrals, and Westminster Abbey.

I have been indebted to many incumbents for giving up time to show me round their churches and correct my descriptions. Many work in difficult conditions and yet have achieved remarkable successes. And it is to the incumbents of London churches that I dedicate this book.

The guide-books, sometimes written by them and often by local historians, have been an unfailing source of information, some, like those of All Hallows by the Tower, St Bride's, St Clement Danes,

St James's, Piccadilly, St Mary-le-Bow, St Margaret's, Westminster and the Tower of London Chapels are beautiful productions.

Of more comprehensive studies, I must single out the *Buildings of England* volumes on London by Sir Nikolaus Pevsner, *Parish Churches of London* by Canon Basil Clarke, *Old London Churches* by Elizabeth and Wayland Young, *The Old Churches of London* by Gerald Cobb and *A London Steeplechase* by R. G. Ellen. The drawings in the glossary came from the delightful engravings in Parker's 'A Concise Glossary of Architecture', published in 1846.

The debt which lovers of the English architectural heritage owe to Pevsner is incalculable; he guides us with unrivalled architectural scholarship and experience through the well-known buildings, leads us to lesser-known places and draws our attention to others we never knew existed. The comprehensive and informed accuracy of Basil Clarke and the imaginative approach of the Youngs have illumined my path, whilst Gerald Cobb is without equal on City churches. R. G. Ellen has provided most helpful historical data in his clear lucid style.

Except where I have quoted from other writers the opinions are my own, based upon visits made to each church.

London's churches through the ages

'London' is probably derived from a Celtic word 'londo' meaning 'wild, bold', and we have every reason to believe that before the Romans came there were no permanent settlements and only a few huts where London now stands. But with their unerring eye for a good site the Romans saw the possibilities of the two hills above the high-water mark of the Thames (later to become known as Ludgate Hill and Cornhill) and they noted the natural harbours on the Fleet and Walbrook which made it easy for them to bring in supplies by river from their main port at Rutupiae (Richborough, Kent). For good measure, they saw that there was suitable building material to hand and that the soil around was well adapted to cultivation. So, within a few years of the Roman occupation of Britain, Londinium displaced Camulodunum (Colchester) as the focal point of Roman administration.

There is in consequence – as Roger Wilson points out in his guide to Roman Britain – much to see in London dating from Roman times but, although it is known that Restitutus, Bishop of London, attended the Council of Arles in AD 314, one will not find the remains of any Christian place of worship. It was no Christian church but a pagan temple that hit the headlines in September 1954 and caused a stir, when the lower courses of the Temple of Mithras were discovered near Walbrook during the digging of the foundations for a modern office block. These can still be seen, uprooted, beside the main entrance of Bucklersbury House in Queen Victoria Street.

Throughout the country Christian churches from Roman times are rare, despite the fact that Christianity was well established many years before the end of Roman rule. The little chapels at Lullingstone in Kent and Silchester in Hampshire are all that we have to tell us what the buildings looked like. The Lullingstone church formed part of a villa which at one time celebrated and continued to celebrate a pagan cult; the Silchester church measured only 42 by 33 feet over all, with an apse containing the altar at the western end of the nave, and aisles, transepts and narthex. The altar seems to have been of wood and the priest celebrated facing west with his back to the congregation.

As with other sides of life in this country, a curtain descends upon our knowledge of what happened after the departure of the legions and it may well be that for a time London, as other great cities in Britain, was abandoned altogether – some like Calleva Atrabatum

(Silchester) and Verulamium never to rise again. The Anglo-Saxon Chronicle records that Britons of Kent fled to London from the invaders, but it is not until 604 that history picks up the story. In that year St Paul's Cathedral – at the request of King Ethelbert – was founded by Mellitus, Bishop of London.

The Saxons were tillers of the soil and grouped themselves round the log hall of the lord. We do not know how soon London became a great city again but Bede, early in the 8th century, calls it the capital of the East Saxons with much trading activity. We know that, after the Danes sacked the city in the middle of the 9th century Alfred the Great restored the walls, and London fulfilled his hopes as a bastion against attack when the Danes were on the warpath again a hundred years later. Despite being sacked for a second time in 982 it became a centre of power, wealth and independence – a position which it has never lost, and although Winchester was the *de jure* capital, London became the *de facto* capital. There was a great Saxon market in East Cheap which J. Sydney Taylor called 'this mart where Commerce had raised her throne', and the Saxon kings had a palace in the City until Edward the Confessor moved to Westminster (the palace was taken over by the Ealdormen – hence Aldermanbury).

The reflection of these developments in churches is hard to follow. We must assume that places of worship multiplied in later Saxon times even if many may have been made of wood. There is practically nothing to see in London from that epoch today: only the arch of a Saxon church at All Hallows by the Tower, founded about 675, parts of crosses in the same church, a Danish gravestone found in St Paul's Churchyard (now at the Museum of London), and a fine rood at St Dunstan's, Stepney. All Hallows would appear to have been an aisleless church in which Roman bricks were used to a large extent.

It seems that William the Conqueror did not trust Londoners for he set up his palace (the Tower of London) to the east of the City, where he could both guard it from river attack and at the same time secure himself against uprisings from within the City itself by 'the vaste and fierce populace'.

There was no Domesday Survey of London so that we start the mediaeval period at a disadvantage. From the Norman period there remain the Chapel of St John in the Tower, the crypts of St Mary-le-Bow and St John's Clerkenwell, and parts of what is left of St Bartholomew-the-Great – and we can trace the transition to Gothic styles in the Temple Church, but the picture is far from clear in the early Middle Ages. Too much was swept away by subsequent rebuilding or destroyed by fire. William Stephen, writing in 1186 in the reign of Henry II, records that there were about 126 churches in London, of which it is unlikely that more than a dozen lay outside the walls. This at least shows that London, in developing as a city of merchants, had already become a city of churches. About 1192, the city was granted the status of having its own Mayor and Aldermen.

As the time gap narrows, the mist clears and we have 17th century engravings by W. Hollar, C. J. Visscher, and a more conjectural series of drawings by H. W. Brewer published in 1921 to show us what the City looked like in early Tudor times. It was a mass of small congested streets with revealing names like Blow Bladder Street (now Newgate Street) and Stinking Lane. A forest of steeples with more spires than today was dominated by the soaring 500-foot lead-sheathed spire of Old St Paul's. (The engravings do not include the spire because it was destroyed by fire in 1561.)

Around the edges of the City were many monastic establishments – the Augustinian Priory of St Mary Overie (now Southwark Cathedral), the Cluniac Abbey of St Saviour, Bermondsey, the Cistercian Abbey of St Mary Graces, Spitalfields, and Carthusian Charterhouse, not to mention the great Benedictine royal foundation of Westminster, together with many lesser establishments. Within the City were the Priory of Augustinian Canons of Holy Trinity Aldgate, Augustinian St Bartholomew's and the Benedictine nunnery of St Helen's. The Friars, too, built their houses in towns. They favoured long naves for public sermons and these were over 200 feet at the Franciscan house north of Newgate Street (Greyfriars) and the Dominican house at Blackfriars, compared with a maximum of 120 to 130 feet in the churches. There were also the Austin Friars, the nave and aisles of whose church were made over to Dutch and French refugees in 1550 with the aim of encouraging Protestant worship in London. These were all suppressed at the Dissolution, although the churches of Westminster Abbey, part of St Bartholomew-the-Great, the nuns' church at St Helen's, and the part of Austin Friars mentioned above were saved.

There can have been few such concentrations of ecclesiastical buildings in such a small space anywhere in the country and they had to be fitted in where space could be found. Apart from the monastic establishments and St Paul's Cathedral there were no stately places of worship such as St Mary Redcliffe in Bristol or St Peter Mancroft in Norwich, but relatively small and architecturally modest buildings, as can be seen by the few that survived the Great Fire of 1666. London in mediaeval times consisted of the City, Southwark and the Royal precinct of Westminster. The population in the one square mile of the City grew slowly and only increased from about 35,000 (Poll tax return) in 1377 to 50,000 in 1530 just before the Reformation. It is unlikely, therefore, that all these churches were required for parish purposes and even when they were, the parishes were sometimes very small; St Helen's comprised only a few houses. As T. D. Atkinson points out, many churches were very tiny affairs built in all sorts of odds and ends of places, over gateways and the like, and some were semi-private chapels.

The survivors of the Great Fire, mainly in the north and east of the City, are basically 15th and early 16th century and, therefore, late mediaeval. St Helen's, Bishopsgate, which was associated with the Benedictine nunnery of St Helen's, is the most considerable. But by and large, interesting as they are for what they tell us of mediaeval church-building in London, they are not especially notable and not greatly dissimilar from many in the south of England. Their furnishings, however, were probably a great deal more elaborate than the simpler and more decorous ones designed for Protestant worship that took their place later. No doubt there was a certain rivalry between neighbouring churches, and wealthy parishioners would make fine gifts and vie with one another in an effort to outdo their neighbour. Screens, above which was the crowning rood, the focal point of mediaeval worship, stained glass and statues would have made the interiors richer and more colourful than the inside of a post-Reformation place of worship.

All this was swept away by the zealous Reformers and with the dismantling of the monasteries London must have presented a sorry sight in the middle of the 16th century – crumbling monasteries, churches being stripped of their treasures and in some cases, like St Mary-le-Strand, actually being removed to make way for secular buildings – in this case, a nobleman's palace.

Between 1530 and the end of Queen Elizabeth's reign (1603), the population rose from 50,000 to over 200,000, but much of this increase was outside the City despite repeated attempts to stop the influx of poorly-off citizens from the country to the outskirts. Nevertheless, and although attendance at church was compulsory, no more ecclesiastical buildings were founded in London during this period. We have an admirable picture of what the City looked like in John Stow's *Survey of London.*

This lull continued with few exceptions (Queen's Chapel, St Katherine Cree, St Paul's Covent Garden, St Luke's Charlton) during James I's and Charles I's reigns. Growing dissensions between king and people leading to Civil War did not encourage church-building. And the Puritans certainly did not favour the erection of Anglican places of worship (St Matthias' Chapel, Poplar, dating from 1654 and All Hallows tower [1659] are rare examples).

But, at 2.00 a.m. on Sunday 2nd September 1666, a fire broke out in the shop of John Farynor, the king's baker, in Pudding Lane towards the east of the City. Samuel Pepys, who lived in Seething Lane further east, saw nothing to alarm him when he looked out of the window during the night and even the next morning, but this was the beginning of one of the greatest conflagrations this country has ever known. A strong wind blew from the south-east, an unusual quarter, and fanned the flames across and through the City like a great swath, destroying all in its path and continuing throughout three days. By the end of this time, approximately four-fifths of the City lay waste, including 86 churches and a badly damaged St Paul's Cathedral.

Fortunately, with the Restoration of the Monarchy in 1660, a wealth of talent had been released and a galaxy of great men appeared in the worlds of philosophy, science and the arts, including the son of a Wiltshire parson, not trained as such but becoming one of the most skilled and productive architects ever to have worked in England. Sir Christopher Wren was responsible for a new St Paul's and for rebuilding 51 of the City churches, each with differing needs and on every shape of site.

Wren's churches were, with the exception of St James's, Piccadilly outside the City, rebuildings, as even by 1700 the total population of London (including the outer areas) which had been decimated by the Plague, responsible for 100,000 deaths, was only about 600,000. But, by the beginning of the 18th century, London began to expand mainly around the Strand and towards the East. To cater for the eastward growth, Nicholas Hawksmoor built his monumental churches of Christ Church at Spitalfields, St Anne's at Limehouse and St George-in-the-East. These were erected under the Fifty Churches Act of 1711 after the Marlborough Wars 'for the building of Fifty New Churches in the Cities of London and Westminster or the suburbs thereof'. The target of fifty was never approached but although the quantity was meagre, the quality was excellent. Some of London's finest churches, which had

St Mildred's, Bread Street. Destroyed in war

to be of stone and have steeples, were built under this Act, such as the Hawksmoor churches mentioned above, St George's, Bloomsbury and St Mary Woolnoth (both Hawksmoor buildings), St Mary-le-Strand (James Gibbs) and St Paul's, Deptford (Thomas Archer).

This was followed by a further lull in church building and only twelve went up between 1750 and 1800.

By 1800, however, the population had mounted to nearly a million and, with the building of the docks, it shot up to two million by 1840, mainly in the poorest areas of the east end. The authorities were anxious that these areas should be protected from the moral dangers of their environment by an adequate supply of places of worship and, as a hundred years earlier, victory in battle was followed by a resurgence of church construction. Under the Church Building Act of 1818, one million pounds, later increased to one and a half millions, was set aside by Parliament – ostensibly as thanksgiving for victory at Waterloo – for this purpose, in which London's needs figured high. Many of the so-called 'Waterloo' churches were erected on the cheap but others like Holy Trinity, Marylebone and St Peter's, Walworth were buildings of quality, and the Commissioners were conscientious Churchmen anxious to do their best. In the next ten years 38 new churches were consecrated in the Diocese of London so that, if the quality was often not high, the quantity was much greater than under the 1711 Act.

Other efforts were made by the Church itself. Bishop Blomfield, and after him Bishop Tait, raised money through separate special Funds for church construction, and although the sums raised fell short of their expectations they were able to build or help to build 78 additional churches under Bishop Blomfield and another 41 under Bishop Tait.

But by this time the City was being affected by the building of railways. A process of moving out, first to the inner suburbs and then further afield, presented the Church authorities with a problem which has continued ever since – that of catering for a shifting population. Generally speaking, the City reached a peak in its number of residents during the middle of the 18th century, the inner ring (e.g. Battersea and Lambeth) in 1901 and the outer ring (e.g. Camberwell, Deptford, Fulham and Hackney) in 1921, since which dates there has been a decline, especially marked in the City (from 112,000 in 1861 to 5,000 in 1951), except in one or two favoured areas such as Hampstead and Kensington. In the City, a process of demolition began involving 20 churches between 1841 and 1908, as can be seen from the Corporation of the City of London's blue plaques placed on the sites, some like St Antholin's, Watling Street, being of architectural merit. Money realised from the sale of sites was diverted to new churches elsewhere (e.g. St Michael's, Camden Town). The Luftwaffe in the 1939–45 War did much, although indiscriminately (St Alban's, Wood Street and St Mildred's, Bread Street were grievous losses) to correct the imbalance of churches, and the situation in the City has since been adjusted by rebuilding some only and turning others over to Guild activities.

Many churches that survived Victorian demolition were subjected to the attentions of Victorian architects, insensitive to work of earlier ages and determined to introduce changes suited to the ritual prescribed by the Oxford Movement. In particular, the introduction of choirs, also new organs and stained glass which Wren did not favour, seriously affected the atmosphere of his churches.

The War and bombing hastened the exodus from London, and today commuters live far away from the metropolis so that the inner suburbs have suffered from the same decline of population as occurred earlier in the central areas. They, too, suffer from reduced congregations and difficulties in making ends meet.

At the time of writing (end 1994), an ominous cloud has descended upon the future of the City churches by the proposals submitted to the Bishop of London by the Commission headed by Lord Templeman in their January 1994 report.

There is undoubtedly a problem in putting all the 36 churches to good use and finding the wherewithal to maintain and run them. But the Templeman strategy to have only 4 super-parishes in the north and east of the City (St Bartholomew-the-Great, St Giles Cripplegate, St Helen Bishopsgate and All Hallows by the Tower) instead of the 22 existing parishes, with 8 churches as their satellites, and to leave the remaining 24 to fend for themselves (classified as 'reserve' churches), ignores the complex growth of the City and the special character of each individual church. The boundaries of the 'super-parishes' appear to have been drawn on arbitrary lines without regard to their specific spiritual needs.

Each of the City churches has its particular associations (historical, musical, literary and artistic) and many of them are performing valuable ecumenical functions.

Each has close links with the particular area in which it is situated and they are the setting for the holding of Livery Companies' annual services, house Regimental Chapels, etc.

This is quite apart from their architectural interest (one has only to think of St Stephen's Walbrook as a superb example of how Sir Christopher Wren converted a plain rectangle into a building of exceptional architectural inspiration.

Among other great assets is the variety and quality of the woodwork to be found in them. It has been said that a history of English church woodwork could be written from what survives in the City places of worship.

It may be that some of them may have to find the finance to maintain them and a non-stipendiary minister or reader to care for their spiritual needs but one would hope that the City with its great resources would come to the rescue where necessary.

If the Templeman report is implemented in full, we shall be throwing away a vital part not only of the City's but also of the nation's heritage and it is devoutly to be hoped that 'A More Excellent Way' can be found.

I am much indebted to the Introduction of Pevsner's *London – except the Cities of London and Westminster* in the 'Buildings of England' series for information contained in the above, and especially for the population tables towards the end of it.

City of London

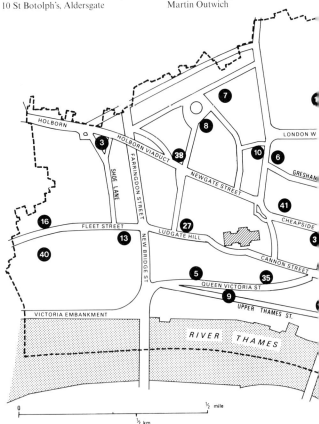

City of London

1 All Hallows by the Tower with St Dunstan in the East

Dedication

'All Hallows by the Tower' is now the usual title of this church, although until recently, and because of the link with the Abbey of Barking, it was often known by the more high-sounding name of 'All Hallows Berkyngechirche by the Tower.' St Dunstan in the East, severely damaged in the bombing, was not rebuilt but turned into a garden and the parish joined to All Hallows. (See separate description)

History

The existence of a Saxon church in London is often largely surmise but here we are on firm ground. It is known that sometime before 675 AD, Erkenwald (Eorconwald), Bishop of London, founded a Christian community at Berkynge (Barking), seven miles down river, and made his sister Ethelburga first Abbess. The Abbey had a large estate near All Hallows and the church was probably used by its tenants and representatives.

The 1940 bombing revealed a substantial Saxon arch with Roman bricks incorporated, probably the entrance to a church which may have been as wide as the central part of the present church. The bombing also exposed the remains of a Saxon shaft inscribed with the name 'Werhenworrth'; later in 1951 half the circular wheel-head of a cross, also inscribed in Anglo-Saxon, was found under the floor. These remains, except for the rood at St Dunstan's, Stepney, and a Danish gravestone in the Museum of London, are the only works of pre-Conquest ecclesiastical art in the capital to come down to us.

The Norman church which succeeded the Saxon building was constructed some ten years after the Tower of London next-door. This later place of worship, now represented by one isolated pillar embedded in the wall of the vestry and fragments in the crypt, had aisles. In the 14th century the chancel was renewed and a vicars' private burial vault (now a columbarium) built below the sanctuary.

Earlier, in the middle of the 13th century, a chapel dedicated to the Virgin Mary was built on the other side of the road to the north. Attached to this chapel was a Guild or Fraternity which was raised to the status of a Royal Chantry by Edward IV in 1465. The foundation disappeared at the Reformation.

All Hallows by the Tower

The tower was shaken by an explosion in 1650 and was rebuilt in 1659, a rare example of church building in London in the Cromwellian period.

Seven years later, All Hallows narrowly escaped destruction in the 1666 Fire and was only saved by Admiral Penn (father of William Penn) having houses in the area destroyed to halt the fire.

All Hallows was repaired in 1813–5 by D. A. Alexander and restored extensively by J. L. Pearson in the 1890s when the two-storey porch was built.

In December 1940 two air-raids left the church in a state of ruin from which it was restored by Lord Mottistone and Paul Paget. Reconsecration took place in 1957.

Exterior

Unlike many City churches, All Hallows is not hemmed in by buildings and stands freely on a commanding island site forming a striking group from the west with the Tower of London. The red brick tower survived the bombing and, set at a picturesque angle to the church, makes an attractive focal point, now enhanced by a Scandinavian-type spire of Columbian pine sheathed in copper.

Interior

Although much of the walling remained and the style of the present building is basically Perpendicular, the restoration has not attempted to reconstruct the old church. Instead, the ceiling is of reinforced open concrete. The new piers are made of Painswick (Gloucestershire) limestone, a more attractive material, reinforced by Pittsburg steel on the north and Texan steel on the south side. A gallery with theatre-box projections runs along the top of the arches. The plain rectangular east window has five cusped lights, and there is no division between chancel and nave. Lord Mottistone has succeeded in making the rebuilt church 'larger inside than outside'.

In the south aisle is the Mariners' Chapel with a crucifix made of wood from the famous tea clipper 'Cutty Sark' and a 15th century Spanish figure of Christ in ivory.

A 15th century figure of St James of Compostela and a slightly later one of about 1510 of St Roche are placed beside the nave columns, third from the east end. There is also a figure of St Anthony of Egypt at present in a wall alcove where stairs went to the rood loft; this is a 16th century figure with a high headdress.

The undercroft below the nave now houses a Roman tessera

Font in which William Penn was baptised at All Hallows by the Tower (now at Christ Church, Philadelphia, U.S.A)

pavement and a museum full of fascinating finds – a showcase of Roman artefacts, Roman tombstone to Demetrius, plus the Saxon shaft and wheel-head (see History).

Furnishings

The furnishings, other than the exquisite Grinling Gibbons font cover (which was removed to safety during the 1939–45 War), sword rests, parts of the lectern and some of the altar-rails, all disappeared in the bombing. There are now:

*Font In the south-west baptistry, a new font made of Gibraltar limestone by a Sicilian prisoner-of-war with the Grinling Gibbons cover (for which Gibbons was paid £12). It has cherubs, dove minus olive branch, leaves, flowers, wheat-ears, fir-cones etc. During restoration, it was found to have been made from more than 100 separately carved pieces, fixed in place by steel pins and glue. It dates from 1682.

Organ This is a new instrument built by Harrison & Harrison Ltd. in 1957 at an approximate cost of £20,000 to replace the much altered organ originally made by Renatus Harris in the late 17th century. A second instrument (Mirfield Organ) in the south aisle was installed as a temporary organ for use in the Porch Room after the bombing.

Royal Arms The Royal Arms in front of the organ-loft are those of Charles II.

Stained glass The modern glass in the south aisle is by Reginald Bell. The well-designed windows in the baptistery are by Keith New.

Pulpit This is a Wren furnishing from St Swithun's, London Stone, with thick garlands and segmental pediments. It is supported on a slender stem and has a staircase with delicately-turned balusters.

Lectern The rails, which survive from the original lectern, date from 1613 and are made of Sussex iron; they were most skilfully restored after the war damage.

Altar-table and rails The table is a replica of the old Jacobean table; the brass rails which surround it on three sides incorporate some of the original 18th century work which survived.

Mural The modern mural behind the altar-table depicting the Last Supper is by Brian Thomas.

Tate altarpiece The four panels used as an altarpiece in the north aisle are a precious survival from the chapel built by Sir Robert Tate (alderman) on the north side of the chantry chapel (see History). The four panels are all that remain of a winged altarpiece dating from the end of the 15th century.

Monuments

Alderman John Croke A tomb-chest monument with canopy to Sir John Croke, who died in 1477, has been restored by Cecil Thomas, who carved the bronze memorial next to it.

Hieronimus Benalius Further west in the north aisle is an attractive wall monument to Hieronimus Benalius (d. 1584) showing this Italian parishioner kneeling in a square frame with coat-of-arms above.

Brasses All Hallows has the largest set of brasses in the City. There are 17 in all, ranging from the most ancient (William Tonge, 1389) to the finest (Andrew Evyngar, a salter, with wife and children, 1530, Flemish). These are mostly in the sanctuary area.

Associations

All Hallows has rich associations.

Toc H The church, which is their Guild church, will long be remembered for its association with the Toc H movement founded by the Rev. Tubby Clayton, who became vicar in 1922. The tomb of John Croke (see *Monuments*) houses a casket containing the Lamp of Maintenance given by the Prince of Wales in 1922 as patron in memory of friends lost in the War and the north aisle in which the tomb lies is known as the Toc H Chapel. At the east end of the undercroft is an altar table built of stones from a Crusaders' castle at Athlit below Mount Carmel in Palestine; this contains the columbarium. Alongside is the Oratory of St Clare which became the oratory of Toc H Women's Association with the Association's 'Lamp of the Magnificat' behind a grille.

Victims of Execution The headless bodies of the saintly Bishop Fisher, the poet Thomas Howard, Earl of Surrey, Lord Thomas Grey (Lady Jane's father) and Archbishop Laud were all brought to the church after execution before being buried elsewhere.

William Penn William Penn was given his elementary education in the parish school room which stood somewhere near the Porch Room and he was also baptised in All Hallows (plate p. 5).

John Quincy Adams John Quincy Adams, sixth President of the USA, was married in the church in 1797. His father was the second President.

Knollys Rose A charming ceremony takes place each year under the auspices of the Watermen and Lighterman's Company when payment of a rose is made as quit-rent levied in 1391 for permission granted to Sir Robert Knollys and his wife to build a bridge ('haut-pas') across

Seething Lane. The red rose is plucked from a garden owned by the Corporation of London near the site of Sir Robert's garden.

General
Although there is not much left of the mediaeval atmosphere, the associations and the recent discoveries make All Hallows a place of very great interest.

2 All Hallows', London Wall

Dedication
The dedication of All Hallows' (All Saints'), London Wall reminds us that it once stood on the old boundary of London. Moorfields open waste land where archery was practised, lay just beyond.

History
The shape of City churches was frequently dictated by the form of the plot on which they were built. The All Hallows' site was a fringe of land next to London Wall and the buildings erected on it had to be long and narrow. The semi-circular vestry actually rests on a bastion of the old Roman wall.

Evidence shows that the earliest of three churches constructed here goes back at least to Henry I's reign (1100–35) for it is referred to as having been linked by his Queen, Matilda, to Holy Trinity Priory, Aldgate. The second known place of worship on this site dating from the 13th century and consisting of nave and aisle, was raised well above street level behind a retaining wall. It had Perpendicular windows and a weather-boarded tower surmounted by a bell-turret. There was an anchorite's cell in the church, known locally as the 'Anker Hole'.

All Hallows' survived the Great Fire but, by the 18th century, the parish had become one of the most densely populated parts of the country and, as the church had fallen into decay, it was decided to build a new place of worship.

The successful applicant for the job of architect was George Dance the Younger, son of the designer of the Mansion House and St Botolph's, Aldgate. He was only 24 years old at the time and this was his first major commission.

He produced between 1765–7, at a cost of £3,000, a building of great charm which, although nearly put under the axe in Victorian times

All Hallows', London Wall

because the style was out of fashion, has been saved by its quality despite severe damage during the air-raids. The interior was restored by Sir Arthur Blomfield in 1891.

Few parishioners remained after the war but, after lying derelict for over 20 years, a new use was found for All Hallows' under the Guild Churches Act of 1952 and it was sensitively restored by David Nye, being eventually reconsecrated on 9th July 1962. The building was the headquarters of the Council for Places of Worship, which advises on all matters concerning the preservation, repair, and furnishing of churches all over the country. The Council moved to other premises in December 1994. Religious services are still held in the chancel and the Carpenters' Company continue, as they have done for over 600 years, to hold their annual Election Day Service in the church. The parish has been united with that of St Botolph's, Bishopsgate.

Exterior
The bare, plain brick walls give no hint of the beauty within. Semicircular lunettes high up are the sole concession to window space and the only noteworthy features are the rounded apse at the east end, the circular cupola in stone and the Tuscan west doorway with frieze and pediment which looks out into the wider section of London Wall. The tower projects from the main body of the church.

Interior
One is immediately captivated by the beauty and grace of the interior. Despite the western half being given over to the library and offices of the Council for Places of Worship, the redecoration is fresh and lively, and faithfully follows the old pattern where it could be traced. George Dance, the architect, was reacting against the rather heavy Hanoverian style prevailing before he built All Hallows' and introduced delicate but vigorous plaster motifs to the tunnel vault of the nave and a delightful pattern of lozenges and rosettes over the apse. The absence of projecting transverse arches further increases the effect of lightness. Fluted attached Ionic three-quarter columns carry the vault.

The west gallery still remains and the effect of a settlement of the south wall during the period before the restoration can be detected in the slope of the west gallery and the lintel of the door below.

Furnishings
Royal Arms The Royal Arms on the west gallery are those of George III, who had just come to the throne at the time All Hallows'

was built. They date, however, from later in his reign (between 1801 and 1816).

Font This came from St Paul's Cathedral.

Organ This is a small 19th century chamber instrument which had been found to accord perfectly with the needs of the building. It was originally built about 1880 for a private house (Highbury Barn) in Islington and came to All Hallows' from Islington Parish Hall in 1960.

Chandelier Originally one of a pair given by a parishioner who shortly afterwards went bankrupt. It is inscribed with the date 1766 and the names of the incumbents and churchwardens.

Pulpit Once a three-decker until Victorianised, the remaining top stage is placed midway along the north wall. It is unusual in that it can only be reached by going out of the church and through the vestry.

Painting The painting in the apse is a copy of an early 17th century Italian painting by Pietro Berretini di Cortona showing St Paul receiving his sight. The copy was made by the architect's brother.

Monuments

Joseph Patience He was an architect who died in 1797. The memorial is in the form of a bust on a plinth with circular relief, standing on a sarcophagus.

William Beloe A tablet on the wall above the steps leading down to the crypt commemorates William Beloe, died 1817, who translated Herodotus.

Incumbents

In addition to William Beloe, who was rector, it is of interest to note that S. J. Stone, who composed the hymn 'The Church's one Foundation', was vicar here and that, at his own expense in 1891, he renewed the interior.

General

All Hallows' holds its secret until on entering one is reminded once again of the wealth of splendid 18th century ecclesiastical architecture which London possesses.

3 St Andrew's, Holborn

Dedication
According to tradition, the apostle Andrew – the patron saint of
Scotland – suffered martyrdom on a diagonal or X-shaped cross, which
became his emblem.

History
There is mention of a St Andrew's church in a charter of King Edgar
dated AD 951 concerned with the boundaries of Westminster.
Whatever Saxon church existed was succeeded by a stone Norman
building which, in turn, grew into the later mediaeval church of which
the tower was erected about 1446. It had many chapels for the Inns of
Chancery in the neighbourhood, who contributed generously to the
church's maintenance.

St Andrew's escaped the Great Fire but, by that time, was so
decayed that, like those destroyed, it had to be rebuilt under Wren (in
1684–7). He kept the base of the tower and the west end, of which the
Gothic arches and window remain, and in 1704 refaced the tower in
Portland stone and heightened it. Serving a very large parish, the new
place of worship was built on the lines of St James's, Piccadilly, to
enable as many people as possible to see and hear the preacher, and
was in fact the largest of Wren's churches after St Paul's Cathedral.

Altered in 1818, the drastic treatment St Andrew's received later in
1871–2, at the hands of the Victorian architect, S. S. Teulon, is now
obliterated by the destruction wreaked by the War and the subsequent
rebuilding by Seely and Paget in 1960–1. Teulon had shown his usual
insensitivity by interfering with the organ gallery and case, altering the
sanctuary, mounting the pulpit on what Elizabeth and Wayland Young
describe as 'a kind of Byzantine wedding-cake', removing the christening
pew from near the font covering the walls, columns and roof with
polychrome decoration and installing dark glass. The only gain was that,
by tampering with the organ gallery, he exposed the old Gothic arches.

The bombing in 1941 destroyed the church and all its contents,
leaving only the tower and walls standing, but the rebuilding is a happy
achievement which gives the visitor much to enjoy. The reconsecration
was on 25th October 1961.

Exterior
At one time St Andrew's stood at the top of what was Holborn Hill
but the building of Holborn Viaduct between 1867 and 1869 left it

below the level of the pavement. The approach (now down instead of up) is from the south through imposing iron gates decorated with a figure of St Andrew bearing his cross emblem.

On the north wall is a Resurrection carving (cf St Giles-in-the-Fields and St Mary at Hill) which used to stand over the entrance to the burial ground (now built over; more than 3,000 of the parishioners died in the Plague).

The sides, terminating in balconies, have two tiers of windows large round-headed above and smaller segmental-headed below. At the slightly projecting east end are two vestries with domes. At the west end, opened up in 1968 by demolition of buildings and now with a little garden in front are two figures of charity children (see later). The tower is flanked by flat-topped constructions built to contain the staircases to the galleries.

The dominating feature is the west tower, which has elaborate belfry windows. The pronounced cornice above the balcony and clumsy pinnacles looking like Roman altars with pineapples on top but unfortunately no longer with vanes, give the steeple a top-heavy appearance.

Interior
Despite Teulon, the pre-war interior was much admired and the restorers have reproduced it as faithfully as possible, making it fresh and bright in the process. The attractive elliptical ceiling is decorated with green plaster panels in gilt frames, the wide aisles have groined ceilings.

Side galleries are supported on panelled Doric piers which turn to Corinthian columns at gallery level. There is also an organ gallery at the west end.

Built into the 15th century vestibule at the west end is a charming small chapel.

The lack of monuments and the width give a spacious interior undimmed by excess of stained glass and brightened by all the new woodwork.

Furnishings
St Andrew's has succeeded in obtaining many excellent furnishings to replace those lost in the bombing.

Organ From the old Chapel of the Foundling Hospital. A Renatus Harris instrument altered and enlarged in a case of great beauty, grey-brown, lavishly gilded and having flat tops with cornices. Handel helped in its design and gave recitals on this instrument. Boards with the Creed, Lord's Prayer and Ten Commandments from an old reredos are fixed to the gallery walls on either side.

Font A chaste furnishing of white marble, also from the old Chapel.

Chapel Statue The statue of the Virgin Mary at the entrance was specially bought for the church.

Chapel Reredos An English Baroque furnishing with pedimented and coffered lintel, all lavishly gilded and with delicately wrought iron Communion rails. This furnishing came from the ruined church of St Luke's, Old Street.

Chapel stained glass The panel of the Holy Dove giving a *trompe-l'oeil* effect is by Brian Thomas, who also designed the windows at the east end.

Pulpit Another furnishing from the old Chapel. Hexagonal on massive stem decorated with demi-Corinthian fluted columns on the angles and Roman arches with keystone. Use is also made of a bead ornament.

Lectern The charming gilt lectern is of wrought-iron.

Reredos The segmental-headed altar-piece has a cherub in the head and garlands at the sides. In the front are free-standing Doric columns. The pre-war church had a 17th century altar of porphyry.

A statue of St Augustine of Canterbury is placed near the high altar.

The fine ornaments on the left of the sanctuary were given in memory of Comar Wilson of the Anglo-American Corporation.

Candlestick The large and beautiful veined marble paschal candlestick beside the font came from St Mary's Abbey, West Malling, Kent.

Stained glass A grievous loss from the bombing was the fine glass from 1718 by Joshua Price in the two-tier east Venetian window. The subject of the three lower lights was the Last Supper and of the upper three, the Ascension. There was also – on the north side – a window with the Royal Arms of Queen Anne and – on the south – those of Thavies Inn (John Thavies was a great benefactor). These were some of the only surviving glass from the Wren period. All have been reproduced by Brian Thomas.

At the west end is some old glass in a floral pattern.

Embroidery The banner of the Crucifixion, with the light of Easter beyond, is the work of Molly Arnold.

Monuments

Thomas Coram The tomb to Thomas Coram, founder of the famous 18th century Foundling Hospital for abandoned children in

Bloomsbury, has been placed in a recess at the west end. This also
came from the Hospital Chapel. The weeping child came from the
monument to Thomas Manningham, rector and later Bishop of
Chichester who died in 1722, as also did the charming cherubs placed
on the wall above the tomb. The incised tablet from the Manningham
memorial can be seen on the wall above the low door leading to the
stairs of the tower. On the wall within the chapel is another delightful
monument which survived the bombing.

Associations
The associations of St Andrew's are many and varied.

Charity children The two figures of a boy and girl outside the west
front used to be on the wall of the parochial school in Hatton Garden,
now turned into business premises but where two more can be seen.
There are others in St Bride's, Fleet Street, and on the wall of the old
parish school – now the parish hall – behind St Botolph's Bishopsgate.
Yet another pair are to be seen opposite St Mary's, Rotherhithe.

Henry Sacheverell This controversial character was put on trial for
preaching what was considered a seditious sermon in St Paul's
Cathedral against the 1688 Revolution which brought William III to
the throne. With the help of Dean Swift he became rector of St
Andrew's from 1714 until his death in 1724, when he was buried under
the high altar. An oval tablet of cherry wood, by John Skelton,
inscribed with fine white lettering, commemorates him. He did much
to beautify the sanctuary, including the installation of the Price glass.

Henry Wriothesley, Earl of Southampton (father of the patron of
William Shakespeare) was baptised here in 1545 with Henry VIII as
godfather.

William Marsden, a local doctor, founded the Royal Free Hospital as
a result of finding a young woman dying on the steps of St Andrew's
one winter's night in 1827. A memorial tablet, designed by John
Skelton, and erected by the Cordwainers' Company, can be seen on
the wall opposite Coram's tomb.

Samuel Wesley, father of John and Charles Wesley, was ordained
priest in the church by Bishop Compton of London, in 1689.

Marc Brunel, engineer of the first tunnel under the Thames and
father of the more famous engineer, Isambard Kingdom Brunel, was
married here in 1799.

William Hazlitt, the essayist, was married here in 1808 with Charles
Lamb present and with his sister, Mary Lamb, acting as bridesmaid.

Benjamin Disraeli, the famous Victorian Prime Minister, was christened here at the age of 12 on 31st July 1817. His father, Isaac, was incensed at being fined for refusing the office of warden at Bevis Marks Synagogue in the City and came to St Andrew's to have the child christened in protest.

Henry Addington, Prime Minister unfavourably compared with Pitt in 'Pitt is to Addington, As London is to Paddington' was baptised here (date unobtainable).

General

This is a fine church, better inside than out, and most fortunate in the furnishings found for it and in the work of the post-war restorers and craftsmen.

No longer a parish church – the parish has been divided between St Alban's, Holborn and St Bride's, Fleet Street – St Andrew's is now a Guild church and the administration centre for the Archdeaconry of Hackney, the Stepney area lay training programme and the various St Andrew's charities. It is also the headquarters of the Royal College of Organists.

4 St Andrew Undershaft

Dedication

According to tradition St Andrew, one of the apostles, suffered martyrdom on a diagonal or X-shaped cross, which became his emblem.

'Undershaft' almost certainly refers to a shaft or maypole which, on May Days, rose above the steeple in front of the south door but which, after a riot directed against aliens by apprentices on 1st May 1517 in which many were killed, was hung up on hooks in Shaft Alley. There it remained until an impassioned sermon in 1550 at St Paul's Cross against pagan practices led the residents in the Alley who had wined and dined well to cut it up and burn it.

History

First mentioned in the 12th century, the church was referred to in 1268 as 'St Andrew juxta Alegate'. It was rebuilt in the early part of the 14th century and again, apart from the lower parts of the tower, in 1520–32. The second rebuilding was at the expense of the Lord Mayor and parishioners, some of whose arms are to be seen in the aisle windows.

There was a restoration in 1634 and repairs in 1723–5, when it was elaborately decorated with monochrome painting. A more thoroughgoing restoration by Sir Arthur Blomfield and Ewan Christian took place in 1875–6, when glass from the east window was transferred to a new west window, most of the 1723 paintings removed, the position of the organ changed and the Tijou altar rails consigned to the boiler room. (The fine Wren-period reredos was demolished about 1820). Further restoration took place in 1930.

St Andrew's is one of only four places of worship in the City to have escaped serious damage both in the Great Fire and in the 1939–45 War but, apart from a bad fire in the heating system in 1976, it suffered considerably from the IRA terrorist bombs which exploded outside the Baltic Exchange on 10th April 1992 and the Bishopsgate bomb of 24th April 1993.

A great deal of damage was done to the roofs, most of the windows lost their glass (only a short time before, £20,000 had been spent on replacing the glass and renovating the east window) whilst the north-east corner had to be rebuilt. The work, however, of repairing the church was put in hand as soon as possible and it was reopened for worship on Tuesday, 14th September 1994. It can now be used for the services which cannot be held at St Helen's Bishopsgate until it is restored.

Exterior

Apart from the 19th century top of the south-west tower with its stair-turret the plain exterior is mostly Tudor. Situated at the corner of Leadenhall Street and St Mary Axe, entrance to the church is either from the south-west through iron gates or the north-west doorway, the former having a fine 16th century door and interesting sanctuary knocker. The aisle windows have four and the clerestory windows three lights all without tracery. At the east end the chancel projects.

Interior

A typical late Perpendicular design with nave of six bays, aisles and clerestory. The arcades have slender four-shaft-four-hollow columns with capitals on the shafts only and depressed arches in the spandrels which are decorated with the remaining part of the 1723 painting, showing scenes from Christ's life on earth. There is no division between nave and chancel.

The almost flat panelled roof was rebuilt in 1949–50 and the 125 carved and gilded oak bosses put back. Considerable repair was needed to make good the bomb damage. The slightly cambered beams rest upon corbels, on one of which the date 1532 can be discerned. The aisle roofs have also needed major repair.

This interior is lofty and light, well suited to its present use, for which the pews have been removed and replaced with chairs.

Furnishings

Font Plain marble octagonal font with baluster stem by Nicholas Stone, master-mason to James I and Charles I. It dates from 1631 but the cover is later. It is enclosed in rails with baluster stems.

Pulpit A notable Wren-period furnishing.

Organ A particularly good instrument, being from the workshop of Renatus Harris and enclosed in a fine case of 1696 with two seated figures on top. The bomb damage has been repaired by Rushworth & Draper Ltd.

Communion Rails Although by Jean Tijou (dating from 1704), these rails were thrown out by Blomfield and are now very properly reinstated.

Stained glass One of the most regrettable casualties of the bombs was the brightly coloured, mainly golden glass in the west window – formerly in the east end. Sometimes referred to as the 'Protestant' window because it included figures of Edward VI, Elizabeth I, James I, Charles I and William III, it may be that, for this reason, it was moved from the east end as perhaps being unsuitable to have above the altar. The bomb damage was considerable.

The replacement east window depicting the Crucifixion and Ascension of Christ was repaired with new glass as recently as 1993; more new glass was needed to restore that damage by the IRA St Mary Axe bomb.

Some 16th-century armorial glass remnants have been found and fitted into the apices of some of the aisle windows. The arms are those of parishioners who had contributed to the 1530–32 rebuilding.

Monuments

There is much to see, due to the number of parishioners who were men of note, some becoming Lord Mayors.

Sir Thomas Offley (d. 1582) and wife (d. 1578). They are shown with three sons as kneeling figures facing one another across a prie-dieu.

John Stow (d. 1605). St Andrew's was the church of this painstaking and detailed chronicler of Elizabethan London, to whose survey we owe so much and to whom reference is frequently made in this book.

He lived to the age of about 80 but died in poverty. The monument of Derbyshire marble and alabaster in the north-east corner shows him, bald-headed, writing a book at a table, flanked by square pillars richly decorated with ribbonwork lions' heads, books and crosses. He holds a quill pen in his right hand and rumour has it that, during some confusion caused by the bomb, a biro pen replaced the quill pen but the chronicler is happily once again properly equipped. Near the anniversary of his death on 5th April, the Ward Alderman (formerly the Lord Mayor) renews his quill pen and presents a copy of Stow's book to the writer of the best essay on London received that year.

Alice Bray (d. 1616). She had three husbands, all stationers, and is commemorated by a small pedimented monument high up on the north wall; she is wearing a ruff and is kneeling at a prie-dieu under an arch flanked by richly decorated square piers.

Sir Hugo Hammersley (d. 1636). He was Lord Mayor in 1627. A large wall monument about ten feet high, with kneeling figures under curtains, shows him in armour with his wife behind him and there are two mourning soldiers outside the flanking columns.

Peter Vansittart (d. 1705). The tablet placed high on the south wall is decorated with skulls and cherubs' heads.

Sir Christopher Clitheroe (d. 1642), who gave some of the west window glass, was Lord Mayor in 1635 and Governor of the East India Company. There is a simple tablet to him.

Hans Holbein, the painter, is believed to have resided in the parish and is commemorated by a brass tablet on the south wall.

Fabian Stedman. A recent addition to the memorials is a metal bell-shaped tablet in the south porch lobby on the west wall. Stedman was one of the originators of the art of change ringing of church bells. He was the publisher of 'Tintinnalogia or the art of Ringing' in 1668 and the author of 'Campanologia or the art of Ringing improved' dated 1677. Stedman was buried at St Andrew Undershaft on 16th November 1713.

Brasses. Amongst the brasses are two to be noted, one to *Nicholas Lewson* (d. 1539), his wife, eight sons and ten daughters, shown as kneeling figures facing one another, and the other to *Simon Burton* (d. 1593 at the age of 85) with his two wives, one son and three daughters.

General

Stow's 'fair and beautiful church of St Andrew the Apostle' is an important survivor of a larger City mediaeval church. Subsequent

alterations have not obscured its Tudor character and it is now
pursuing an active ministry amongst the younger workers in the City.

5 St Andrew by the Wardrobe with St Ann's, Blackfriars

Dedication
According to tradition, St Andrew – the patron saint of Scotland –
suffered martyrdom on a diagonal or X-shaped cross which became his
emblem. 'Wardrobe' refers to the department of the royal household
in which the king' stores, including arms and ceremonial clothing, were
kept. It was moved from the Tower of London to Wardrobe Place,
north of the church, about 1361 and remained there for more than 300
years until the building was destroyed in the Great Fire of 1666.

St Ann's, Blackfriars was the church for those living within the
precincts of the Blackfriars Dominican monastery but it was not
rebuilt after the Fire and the parish was united with that of St
Andrew's. In a corner of one of St Ann's two churchyards is to be seen
the only fragment of the great priory to survive above ground.

History
As with many churches, it is not known when worship first began on
this site; it may have been that St Andrew's was founded at the time
when the Fitzwalters took possession of the mediaeval mansion of
Baynard Castle nearby. The church was sometimes referred to as St
Andrew-juxta-Baynard Castle. First written mention is in a St. Paul's
Cathedral manuscript dated 1244.

Victim of the Great Fire, St Andrew's was rebuilt by Sir Christopher
Wren during the years 1685 to 1695 and some of the furnishings date
from that time, although not originally made for St Andrew's.

A west gallery was added in 1774 and many alterations were made
early in the 19th century; the usual practice, however, at this period of
substituting open benches for the existing box pews was not followed
but these were altered in the 1889 restoration. The church was burnt
out again in December 1940 – this time by fire-bombs – and, during the
subsequent sensitive restoration by Marshall Sisson between 1959 and
1961, he removed some of the fussy 19th century embellishments,
including the balustraded parapet on the south wall and the vanes on
the corners of the tower. He also partitioned off the north aisle and,
for the sake of symmetry, the south aisle was similarly treated.

St Andrew's now has an enlarged parish which includes the pre-Fire

parishes of St Nicholas Cole Abbey, St Nicholas Olave, St Mary
Somerset, St Mary Mounthaw, St Benet's Paul's Wharf and St Peter's
Paul's Wharf as well as portions of other parishes.

In 1986 the parish became a plurality with St James's, Garlickhythe.

Exterior
Despite its unassuming exterior, the completion of Queen Victoria
Street in 1871 gave St Andrew's, perched up on its slope, a
commanding position. The tower, which projects from the south-west,
and the south wall with once more a plain brick parapet, survived the
bombing and, stripped of their 19th century accretions, look much as
Wren left them. The other walls also survived. What remained of the
courtyard after the construction of the street was landscaped as a
garden and memorial gates were added in 1902, in memory of Banister
Fletcher. The south portal dates from the same year. The crucifix by
Walter Tapper was dedicated in 1937.

The weather-vane on the tower came from St Michael's, Bassishaw
(demolished in 1900) after spending some time in the then Lord
Mayor's garden at Sydenham.

Interior
Although the enclosure of the aisles has reduced ground-floor space
and the old box pews have been replaced by benches in light-toned
oak, the interior, with the aid of furnishings which have found their
way here by circuitous routes, retains its Wren character.

The galleries on three sides are supported by Doric piers.

Emblems on the tunnel vault of Wren's ceiling have been
reproduced as far as possible, the rest, including the groined vaults of
the aisles, being white except for the gilded caps of the pillars.

Furnishings
Pulpit This was originally the pulpit of St Matthew's, Friday Street, a
church built by Wren at the same time as St Andrew's but demolished
in 1885. It came via St Peter's, Fulham. The sounding-board and back
piece have gone whilst the base, stem and stairs have had to be
replaced.

Font The marble font and attractive cover with cherub's head
decoration also came from St Matthew's but via St Clement's, Fulham.
St Andrew's has another font cover which was once on the font of All
Hallows, East India Dock Road and, when that was bombed, went to
All Saints, Poplar.

Organ The organ in the west gallery was originally built in 1769 for Lord Hatherton of Teddesley Hall, Stafford. It was loaned to St Bartholomew-the-Great in 1953 by Noel Mander, from whom it was purchased for St Andrew-by-the-Wardrobe in 1961.

Royal Arms The Stuart Royal Arms at the west end of the south gallery were originally at St Olave Jewry (demolished except for tower in 1888). After a spell in the rectory of St Margaret's, Lothbury, they were presented to St Andrew's.

Reredos Boards from the former reredos were preserved. The present altar-piece was designed by Marshall Sisson with carving by A. J. Eyres. The oak altar in St Ann's Chapel came from St Nicholas Cole Abbey and fits the space perfectly. It is decorated by four gilded cherubs' heads.

Chandeliers The chandeliers are of early 18th century date and, although similar, are not a matching pair. They are made of latten (a compound of zinc, lead and tin) and have twelve lights in two tiers.

Figure of St Andrew The figure of St Andrew with his diagonal cross in the sanctuary dates from about 1600.

Sanctuary chair The sanctuary chair dates from 1687. A second one dated 1690 was stolen.

Painted/stained glass The panel of glass depicting the conversion of St Paul at the west end is painted glass of the 18th century. The four modern windows on the south side which include two in St Ann's Chapel depicting the marriage of St Ann (the Virgin Mary's mother) and St Joachim and St Ann teaching the Virgin Mary to read are stained glass by Carl Edwards.

Monuments
Memorials in oak and limewood to *William Shakespeare* (1564–1616) POET PLAYWRIGHT PARISHIONER (he had a house in Ireland Yard) and *John Dowland* LUTANIST SINGER COMPOSER, described in the church guide as the 'greatest of English song-writers', flank the window in the west gallery. Each figure is shown kneeling at a faldstool on a stage with the curtain drawn back by cherubs, Shakespeare on the south side and Dowland on the north. The memorials were designed by Peter Foster and executed by A. Cooper.

General
St Andrew's is still a parish church holding regular weekday services, running an advanced Sunday School including lectures by eminent churchmen on Sunday afternoons.

The Indian Orthodox Church use St Andrew's for their services every Sunday morning at which time St Andrew's parishioners hold their services at St James's Garlickhythe.

6 St Anne and St Agnes

Dedication
The double dedication, first mentioned in 1467, is unique in the City. The church was once known as St Anne-in-the-Willows although, even in Elizabethan times, there were no signs of willows.

St Anne was the mother of the Virgin Mary; St Agnes shares with St Pancras the honour of being amongst the Church's youngest martyrs, for she was only thirteen when she died for her faith in Rome about 350 AD (possibly earlier).

History
Dates vary from about 1200 to 1291 for first mention of the church. The old church had a Norman tower, repaired in 1629–30; before this, the whole structure had been badly damaged by fire in 1548, although soon repaired. Despite being further away from the seat of the Great Fire than some churches, St Anne and St Agnes was, except for part of the tower, completely consumed and Wren rebuilt it between 1676 and 1687, his eleventh reconstruction. The church next door, St John Zachary (Zachary was St John's father), was not, however, restored and the parish was joined to St Anne and St Agnes in 1670.

Internal alterations were made by W. M. Brooks in 1838–9 and by Ewan Christian in 1888–9. Badly damaged by bombs in December 1940, the church went through a period of neglect until Braddock and Martin-Smith took restoration in hand between 1963 and 1968. They had to take down and rebuild much of the walls and the rest was a careful reproduction of what the church had been before the outside was stuccoed in 1820–1.

Exterior
The exterior has gained greatly both structurally and in its setting from post-war work. The removal of the stucco has exposed the pleasant red brick of the walls on the north, south and east sides, which are symmetrical, each with a large round-headed window under a pediment and flanked by two smaller ones, all with rusticated surrounds. Both the churchyards of St Anne and St Agnes, and of

St Anne and St Agnes. Bell turret with weather vane

neighbouring St John Zachary have been turned into gardens affording an unimpeded view from the south-east.

The small, simple 14th century west tower is capped with a pretty slightly leaning bell turret, terminating in a gilded weather-vane with a capital letter 'A' on top (plate opposite)

Interior

Only 53 feet square, structurally the interior is nevertheless one of Wren's most interesting designs, similar to that of St Mary at Hill and of St Martin-within-Ludgate. All three were clearly based on the plan of the Nieuwe Kerk at Haarlem, Netherlands, a plan which goes back to very early Christian days. It is a cross in a square with the four arms of the cross having high tunnel vaults and meeting to form a groin-vaulted centre section. The corner spaces between the arms of the cross have low, flat ceilings, whilst the lines of the cross are emphasised by an entablature which goes right round it. The central area of St Anne and St Agnes is marked by four fine columns on high pedestals with gilded Corinthian capitals.

The ceilings have restrained and beautiful plaster decoration, the corner ones having circles enclosing flowers and fruit with attractive cornices and egg and dart decoration, whilst the arches opening out into the centre have gilded and coffered rosettes, and panels. The groined vault is coloured blue.

There is no stained glass and there are no galleries, giving a light and spacious effect to this small interior. In accordance with Lutheran tradition (St Anne and St Agnes is now a Lutheran church) the building is so centrally planned that the space which goes right round the pews is plain to the point of bareness. The walls are panelled up to a height of over eight feet and the colour of the high, modern pews matches that of the walls.

Furnishings

The reredos and west doorcase belonged to St Anne and St Agnes, but most of the furnishings came from other churches.

Doorcases A fine south-west doorcase with broken pediment supported on attached Corinthian columns and crowned by a gilded angel gives access to the interior. There is another doorcase at the west end, plainer but carrying a figure of Father Time, complete with gilded wings, sickle and hour-glass, given by Benjamin Williams in 1682–3.

Royal Arms A fine Charles II Royal Arms came from St Mary's Whitechapel (war casualty).

Organ The moveable Noel Mander organ made in 1962 has been sold and replaced with an instrument of two manuals and 19 registers with pipework dating from 1790, rebuilt in the church in 1991. It merges English and German tonal resources while retaining the 'straight' pedal board from 1889.

Font The tall, circular font of white veined marble standing on an elegant pedestal was made after the War to replace one which came from St Mildred's, Bread Street and is a copy of it, except for the decoration. The cover is carved in high relief with leaves and rosettes, and has a gold and red crown.

Pulpit The hexagonal pulpit, without tester, contains three inlaid panels from St Augustine's, Watling Street (burnt 1940). It is further decorated with foliage and winged heads of cherubs, one of whom looks very startled. The gilded lion nearby and the unicorn by the lectern were also in St Mildred's, Bread Street.

Lectern In the form of a brass angel supporting the reading shelf and standing under a dormered dome. It came from St Mary's Rotherhithe.

Reredos The notable reredos (unfortunately stained black) contains paintings of Moses and Aaron in carved frames and came from St Michael's, Wood Street via St George's, Southwark. The open scrolled pediment carries a lamp with a flame on top and gilded cherubs. There are also carved swags and Corinthian pilasters.

Sanctuary Chairs Well carved sanctuary chairs are decorated with affronted birds having long wide sharp beaks, and intricate foliage, whilst the arms terminate in lions' heads.

Other items On the sill of a south window are two elevated busts, one of which may represent Sir Christopher Wren; in the middle of the north wall is a crown above two mitres, symbolic of the monarch being Head of the Church.

General

St Anne and St Agnes has been used by Lutheran congregations, ever since it was restored after the 1939–45 War. Ownership of the church remains Anglican, although it was rebuilt with contributions from the international Lutheran community for use by Lutherans. St Anne's Lutheran Church, an international English-speaking congregation, holds three services and two lunchtime concerts in the church each week. Services in Latvian, Estonian and Swahili are also held regularly.

N.B. The church is open from 10 a.m. to 4 p.m. on Mondays, Wednesdays and often Fridays, and from 9 a.m. to 9 p.m. on Sundays (Telephone 0171-373 5566.)

St Anne and St Agnus. West end with Charles II Royal Arms

7 St Bartholomew-the-Great, Smithfield

Dedication

Bartholomew was one of the Apostles. He is said to have preached the
Gospel in India and there to have been flayed alive by those opposed
to his teaching. His emblem is a flaying knife.

'Smithfield' comes from Smoothfield, a largely marshy area in
mediaeval times.

History

Rahere forsook the easy life of an obsequious courtier to become a
pious monk in the reign of Henry I as a result of a pilgrimage to Rome
and after being struck down by malaria. As thanksgiving for his
recovery, and on the strength of a vision when St Bartholomew came
to his rescue, he obtained a grant of land in Smithfield from the King
and there founded simultaneously his hospital (affectionately known
today as 'Barts') and a priory. Work on both probably started about
1103. The more usual date of 1123 associated with the foundation is
more likely to be nearer the year of consecration of the eastern parts
of the priory.

These were completed in his lifetime and his successor added the
transepts and eastern part of the nave, the latter of ten bays being
completed in the 13th century. The chancel originally ended in an
apse, but about 1330 this was made square and a Lady Chapel added,
which increased the over-all length of the church to 349 feet, longer
than some of the smaller cathedrals like Bristol, Chester and
Rochester.

Prior Bolton, prior from 1500 to 1532, installed the charming oriel
window on the south side of the chancel to enable him to participate in
masses without leaving his lodgings. He was succeeded by Prior Fuller,
who compliantly handed over the Priory at the Dissolution on 25th
October 1539 and was granted a pension.

After the Dissolution, the chancel was retained as the parish church
but the nave was pulled down and only the old gateway to the south
aisle left, plus the first nave bay largely concealed by the organ. The
large central tower had already disappeared before the Dissolution but
in 1622–8, the present red brick south-west tower with its pretty
lantern was built and the chancel repaired.

Thereafter, this impressive place of worship was allowed to fall into
a deplorable state, and despite restorations in 1789 by George Dance
and in 1791 by Thomas Hardwick, the parts of the church not wanted

St Bartholomew-the-Great. Prior Bolton's oriel window

were let off for various secular uses; a blacksmith's shop was installed in the north transept, a school in the triforium, stables in the cloisters, whilst in the Lady Chapel there were first tenements then a printing shop and later a fringe factory. In addition, a fire in 1830 destroyed the chapter house and south transept. It was not until the 19th century that a start was made in clearing these encroachments, terminating in the careful restorations of Sir Aston Webb at the end of the 19th century. He finally got rid of the troublesome fringe factory and rebuilt the Lady Chapel. Later, eight bays of the east walk of the cloister were restored and opened in 1928.

The interests of the Prior and the Corporation did not always coincide in the Middle Ages and the Priory's ownership of Bartholomew Fair was a particular source of friction. On the other hand the sub-Prior appears to have been disgracefully treated in 1250, when the Queen's uncle, who had not even been ordained, made a visitation in armour as Archbishop of Canterbury and all but crushed the protesting sub-Prior to death.

There were rights of sanctuary from early times at the Priory.

Exterior

St Bartholomew's is still surrounded by small streets as it was in the Middle Ages, and hides itself behind the entrance gate from Smithfield, above which is a restored mediaeval timber house. This gate was the original 13th century south entrance to the nave.

Beyond is a path through the churchyard, to the right of which is part of the former outer south aisle wall. Beyond – also on the right – is the east walk of the cloister.

The porches are all 19th century; the northern one has a statue of St Bartholomew outside, whilst the main entrance has a statue of Rahere. The exterior is harshly refaced in flint and Portland stone.

Interior

One enters by the south side of the crossing and is presented with a magnificent example of rugged early Norman architecture, vigorous and uncompromising. Massive drum columns support the unmoulded round arches, which are compressed at the apse, restored by Sir Aston Webb at the end of the 19th century. Above runs a triforium with four bays and blank tympanum under an encircling arch to each bay of the chancel; in the apse there are two-light blind arches. There is a minimum of decoration – scalloped capitals and an outer ring of billet moulding. The clerestory windows are late 14th century.

It is possible to study the transition from Norman to Gothic in the crossing, which has round arches on the east and west sides and pointed ones (perhaps the earliest in London) on the north and south sides.

The transepts are a sadly truncated version of those originally built and are crammed up against the crossing, only the arches to the chancel aisles and the south nave aisle being mediaeval. On the south side, entry is gained to the east walk of the cloister, rebuilt in the 15th century, of which the old vault springers and two doors to the former chapter house remain but of which most is 20th century rebuilding. The cloister originally had 36 bays and the eight bays now restored are used as a choir vestry.

*Prior Bolton's oriel window with canted sides is over the south ambulatory of the chancel and is a delightful feature. In the centre panels below the glass is his rebus – an arrow (bolt) piercing a wine tun.

Beyond in the south-east corner is the Chapel of Knights Bachelor.

Behind the apse, the rebuilt Lady Chapel extends eastwards up a slope. To the left of the entrance to the Chapel, access to the former mortuary chapel has been opened up for use as a meeting place for the congregation. The south side is largely Aston Webb's restoration of 1897, but the character of this 14th century addition has been retained, with its three large lancet windows under an arch at the east end and two separate single lancets at the sides.

Furnishings
Of minor interest, except for monuments. The church is unique, however, in having five pre-Reformation bells.

Font A plain stone 15th century octagonal font, one of only two pre-Reformation examples left in London. The cover, shaped like a pyramid, has eight carved ribs which terminate with heads of tonsured monks.

Organ Purchased in 1886 from St Stephen's, Walbrook for which it was made in 1765 by George England. The instrument was restored in 1931.

Screen to Lady Chapel The work of a fine Victorian craftsman, J. Starkie Gardner, dating from 1897. Of wrought-iron, it consists of five bays with gates in the central bay, on either side of which are two candle brackets, whilst the uprights of the screen are carried slightly above the hammered iron frieze as single candlesticks.

Monuments

Rahere On the north side of the chancel and dating from the 15th century, 300 years after his death. He is shown recumbent in the black habit of the Augustinian Canons on a tomb chest under a canopy, his tonsured head resting upon a tasselled cushion. At his feet are two kneeling bedesmen and a larger angel holding a shield. The back wall is pierced, enabling pilgrims to make offerings from the ambulatory.

Percival Smallpiece, died 1558 and wife, died 1588. On the south side of the sanctuary in brown marble. Two frontal busts separated by a mullion and between side pilasters.

Sir Walter Mildmay, died 1589 and wife. He was Chancellor of the Exchequer and founder of Emmanuel College, Cambridge. On the north wall of the choir. Large wall-monument in Italian marbles with pediment and columns, but no effigy.

Sir Robert Chamberlane, died 1615. On north wall of chancel. A small memorial with kneeling figure and two standing angels holding open two curtains.

Elizabeth Freshwater, died 1617. On the east wall of the south transept. Another small monument with kneeling figure. She is shown under an arch.

James Rivers, died 1641. *Edward Cooke*, died 1652. On the south wall of the ambulatory. Both are frontal busts and each figure holds a book.

Brass On the south side of the south ambulatory floor is a brass to John Deane, first rector (1539–44).

Associations

Benjamin Franklin worked in the printing shop in the Lady Chapel in 1724.

William Hogarth, the painter, was baptised here in 1697.

City of London Squadron, RAF, whose Battle Honours standard is there, have their War Memorial in the Lady Chapel and hold a special commemorative service in the Chapel each May.

City of London Yeomanry ('Roughriders') memorial is in north transept. They hold their annual service in October.

John Wesley preached here in 1747.

Butchers' Company hold their annual service here.

General

Although only a shadow of its former self, St Bartholomew's is the most considerable Norman church in London. It is dark but compelling and one must be grateful for the sensitive and loving work, though not agreeing with some of it, which was put into the restoration by the Victorians.

8 St Bartholomew-the-Less

Dedication

Bartholomew was one of the 12 Apostles. He is said to have carried the Gospel to India, and there to have converted a king to Christianity by healing his mad daughter. The hostility aroused by his teaching amongst priests who served the local idols led to his being flayed alive. The emblem of his martyrdom is a flaying knife.

History

Henry I's courtier Rahere founded St Bartholomew's Hospital in 1123 at the same time as the Priory next door and there was a chapel attached to the hospital from the very beginning, although on a different site. It was moved to where it now stands in 1184 but despite the substantial Norman remains at St Bartholomew-the-Great, the earliest construction within the hospital area is the 15th century tower of the chapel. At the Dissolution, when it was known as the Chapel of the Holy Cross, it became the parish church for the hospital and has remained so ever since.

By the end of the 18th century the walls were in a crumbling state and the architect George Dance the Younger removed the interior and substituted a wooden octagon which extended above the roof and beyond the east wall, one of the few major church constructions in the 60 years between 1760 and 1820.

The wooden octagon decayed and in 1823–5 Thomas Hardwick replaced it with the nave of stone and iron we see today, said to resemble closely its predecessor. At the same time, he rebuilt the walls in brick. Forty years later in 1865, the architect's grandson P.C. Hardwick, remodelled the sanctuary and added tracery to the upper part of the windows.

Badly damaged during the 1939–45 War, St Bartholomew-theLess was restored by Seely (Lord Mottistone) and Paget, being reopened in 1951. A major restoration, including reroofing in lead and cleaning the exterior, was started in 1990 and completed in April 1994.

St Bartholomew-the-Less. Tower

Exterior
The church is tucked away on the left after entering the hospital precincts. It is a strange mixture with the lantern of its 19th century octagon sticking up above the surrounding walls and unbuttressed 15th century west tower; the latter is stark and bare but has an unusual south-west stair turret on top with pretty ogee cap. The parapet is of brick.

Interior
Entrance is through the tower and on the left the vestry retains its original floor with two brasses (see *Monuments*), the arches are 15th century. The interior of the tower has recesses and is embellished with banded columns.

The vestibule opens out into the octagon of the nave with starshaped plaster rib vault and a roof made of iron. Triangular chapels fill the spaces between the sides of the octagon and the rectangle of the walls.

Geometrical tracery in the clerestory lunette windows and post-war glass by Hugh Easton do not help the interior but otherwise the Gothic style of the octagon, now painted grey and white, is pleasantly original and bright.

The walls are lined with memorials to surgeons and others connected with the hospital.

Furnishings
The pews and fittings are mostly Victorian but there are some interesting monuments. The right window of the apse has representations of St Bartholomew and the hospital founder, Rahere.

Monuments
John Freke and wife On the west wall of the tower is a 16th century altar-tomb with canopy and inscribed slab to John Freke, surgeon who died in 1756, and his wife Elizabeth, who died in 1741.

Lady Elizabeth Bodley On the north wall of the nave is a monument to the wife of Sir Thomas Bodley, founder of the famous library at Oxford.

John and Mary Darker Tablets by John Bingley to John Darker died 1784 and Mary, his wife, died 1773 are to be seen on the west wall, left of the organ loft. The tablet to John has putti by an urn.

Brasses Two nicely incised brasses in the vestry are of William Markby, who died in 1485, and his wife. They are shown in civil dress.

Associations

Wat Tyler Although not specifically linked with the church, it is of interest to record that Wat Tyler, leader of the Peasants' Revolt in 1391, was carried into the hospital after being mortally wounded by Sir William Walworth, Lord Mayor of London, and it is said that Tyler was later dragged out of the building and beheaded.

Inigo Jones The great architect of the early Stuart period was baptised here in 1573.

General

There are other hospital chapels in London such as the attractive one at Guy's, built by Richard Jupp in 1780, with its outstanding monument to Thomas Guy by John Bacon (see plate opposite). But St Bartholomew-the-Less is different in that it is a parish church. It is an architectural oddity, but with much of interest, and its special function is evidenced by the new doorway opened in 1969 at the south end of the east wall for invalid chairs.

9 St Benet's, Paul's Wharf (now the Metropolitan Welsh Church)

Dedication

'Benet' is a shortened form of Benedict, the Italian monk who, after living in a cave as a hermit, realised that monks sharing in a community could serve God more fully than as solitary individuals. He thus became the founder of the western form of monastic institution. He was born in AD 480 and died in 543. The full name of Benedict was often used for the church until the early part of the 19th century.

'Paul's Wharf' was owned by the Dean and Chapter of St Paul's Cathedral; stone for the rebuilding of the Cathedral after the Fire was unloaded there.

History

The church was first mentioned in 1111 as *'Sancti Benedicti super Tamisiam'*. Stow, in Elizabeth's time, called it St Benet Hithe.

Destroyed in the Great Fire, St Benet's was rebuilt by Wren between 1677 and 1683; its neighbour St Peter's, Paul's Wharf – also destroyed – was not rebuilt and its parish joined to St Benet's. Since that time, St Benet's has survived, singularly free of later alteration. Beautified and repaired in 1836, it escaped bomb damage in the 1939–45 War, although a post-war restoration was carried out by

Guy's Hospital. Monument to Thomas Guy by John Bacon, 1779

Godfrey Allen in 1946. Its luck slightly ran out in 1971 when a small fire damaged the east end of the north gallery.

The church was in danger of being scrapped in 1854 but, in 1879, when the parish was united with that of St Nicholas Cole Abbey, it was taken over by the Welsh Episcopalian Church and is still the Metropolitan Welsh Church within the Church of England London diocese, beautifully cared for by them. The services are conducted in the Welsh language.

The College of Arms have used the Church as their chapel since 1555 under a charter of Philip of Spain and Queen Mary. They have their named seats on either side of the altar. There is also an entire set of their banners hanging in the Church completed by that of the Earl Marshal, the Duke of Norfolk. The Heralds use the Church on a regular basis.

A major restoration costing half a million pounds is in progress.

Exterior

A delightful harmony in dark red and blue brick with Portland stone quoins, very Dutch in feeling. Roadworks have left St Benet's in a conspicuous position but somewhat isolated from the main thoroughfare of Queen Victoria Street. The roof of the north side facing the street is hipped. In contrast to the homely red and blue chequerwork, there are stone festoons over all the round-headed windows on the north and south sides and, over the middle bay of the east wall, a fine cherub's head.

The charming north-west tower projects slightly from the north aisle and has the same decorative treatment of modillion cornice, together with alternative courses of brick and stone quoins at the angles as the rest of the church. Faced with stone at the base, the mainly brick tower is crowned with a lead-sheathed curved dome lit with eight oval lucarnes on top of which is a small lantern and a short lead spire. The contrasting curves of the dome and spire are captivating, described by Gerald Cobb as 'a little work of art – quite perfect'.

Interior

The interior is just as appealing. The dimensions are only 41¼ by 51¼ feet, the extra width from south to north being occupied by the north aisle. This is separated from the main body of the church by Corinthian columns with panelled bases supporting a gallery; there is no division between nave and chancel.

The gallery carries on the front the arms of the Archbishop of

St Benet's, Paul's Wharf

Canterbury, the Royal Arms and the Fouled Anchor of the Court of Admiralty. It is decorated with carvings of fruit. This gallery was occupied until their institution was dissolved in 1867 by the ecclesiastical lawyers of Doctors Commons. Among its many and complex activities this institution could provide facilities for hasty marriages which probably accounts for the fact that 13,423 marriages were celebrated at St Benet between 1708 and 1731.

The gallery at the west end is divided by the organ. Beneath this, a panelled screen shuts off the western half of the nave from the rest, thus forming a vestibule.

The walls are panelled and the ceiling is flat. The church retains its old stone floors with many ledger slate monuments.

Curious features are the substitutes on the north wall, consisting of palm-branches, shells and cherub-heads, for the Corinthian capitals of pillars and pilasters round the rest of the walls.

Furnishings
Doorcase and Royal Arms Opening out from the tower lobby is a splendid doorcase with a finely carved and painted Royal Arms of Charles II above. Cherubs' heads, which abound in the church, are carved in the spandrels. These Arms are on the balcony of the Royal Box, St Benet being the only City church to possess one. They were given by the king, who was present at the opening of the church in 1683.

Stalls and pews The pews have been lowered and are made of wood from the old box-pews. Old wood was also used for the stalls, which have carved frieze-panels and capping on their backs.

Pulpit Richly carved of hexagonal form. Stairs, stem and base are all modern but the royal cypher C. R. Donum 1683 can be faintly traced on several panels. The sounding-board has been removed and is now used as a ceiling at the base of the tower; the panelled standard which supported the sounding-board is mounted on the front of the reading desk.

Reredos The altar-piece of wood with pierced and inlaid segmental pediment and urns on top has the usual gilding and panels with Ten Commandments, Lord's Prayer and Creed.

Communion rails Reputed to be the work of Inigo Jones, the rails have scrolled twisted balusters. The Laudian altar from the same period is now in the north aisle.

Altar-table A sumptuous piece with top upheld by angels as legs and a fine figure of Charity sitting on the stretcher. The top is of inlaid woods. Cherubs' heads at the corners and a text at the edge with a modillion cornice encircle the top. The table was made in Belgium in 1660 and bought by Grinling Gibbons for the church.

Poor-box The poor-box in the vestibule with moulded top and base on stand made up of four twisted balusters is – as are the communion rails – reputed to be the work of Inigo Jones.

Organ The Bishop organ, which retains its original pipes, has been restored.

Monuments

Of the many attractive monuments, including several from the 18th century, a number commemorate members of the College of Arms and of Doctors' Commons.

Inigo Jones This great architect, whose paternal grandfather was Welsh and who carried out a restoration of the church probably in the 1640s, was buried in 1652 beneath the chancel of the old St Benet's. A small tablet on the east wall of the present church records the original inscription and was put up in 1878.

An even earlier Welsh link goes back to the reign of Edward I, who brought Welsh masons to repair the tower. Presumably they were no longer needed for building castles.

Mark and Alice Cottle A curious large monument consisting of a shield of arms beneath a draped canopy and below a sphere commemorates these two. Mark died in 1681 and Alice in 1698. The memorial is made of black and white marble.

Sir Robert Wyseman He was Dean of the Court of Arches. He died in 1684 and was buried in the chancel. This large memorial of white marble is in the form of a portrait medallion of good workmanship in a foliated frame with a looped curtain.

John Charles Brook A tablet north of the reredos commemorates in glowing terms this member of the College of Heralds who was killed in 1797 when the floor of the Haymarket Theatre gave way. The Royal Family was present when this happened.

Associations

Twelfth Night St Benet's is referred to in a scene from *Twelfth Night*, no doubt performed at the adjacent Black Friars Theatre. The scene is outside Olivia's house and her servant, the Clown, who has received two pieces of gold from the Duke who was visiting Olivia, tried to obtain a third piece with the words: 'The bells of Saint Bennet, Sir, may put you in mind; one, two, three.' But the duke replied: 'You can fool no more money out of me at this throw.'

There are three bells from Shakespeare's time, the largest of which has been cleaned and rehung; it is now used as a calling bell.

Henry Fielding Henry Fielding, the novelist, married his first wife's former maid here in 1747.

General
This is the most homely and lovable of all Wren's churches and one of the least altered. There are few which can better be appreciated in their entirety both outside and in.

N.B. Not normally open except during services or by prior arrangement with the Vicar (telephone no. is on outside board).

10 St Botolph's, Aldersgate

Dedication
One of three churches still standing in London dedicated to this 7th century Saxon abbot who became the patron saint of travellers.

History
In 1068, William the Conqueror confirmed the patronage of St Botolph's on the Dean of the Priory of St Martin's-le-Grand. First referred to as 'St Botulph without Aldredesgate', there were probably two churches before the present one, the first lasting from about 1050 until 1350, and the second, with nave and aisles plus three east windows, until the middle of the 18th century.

Two, and possibly three, brotherhoods were instituted in mediaeval times: the brotherhood of the Trinity in 1374 and another dedicated to St Fabian and St Sebastian in 1377; but these two may have been the same, merely changing the name at the later date. Another to St Katherine was existing in 1389, although no date of foundation is known.

Much of the steeple was rebuilt in 1627. The whole church escaped the worst of the Great Fire, being protected by London Wall from the fate of nearby St Anne and St Agnes. Apart from St Botolph's, Billingsgate, the 'gate' churches survived the conflagration but, like St Botolph's, Aldgate and St Botolph's, Bishopsgate, it fell into disrepair.

Many petitions for money were made. Partial repairs were carried out in 1754 but a complete rebuilding, except for the east wall, took place during the latter part of the 18th century, completed in 1791 under the direction of Nathaniel Wright, District Surveyor for this part of the City.

In 1831 the east end was set back eight feet for the purpose of improving the approach to the new General Post Office in St Martins-le-Grand. Since that time, various internal alterations have been made, especially in 1874 when the present pews, replacing the old box-pews, were installed.

St Botolph's ceased to be a parish church in 1954, the parish being divided between that of St Giles, Cripplegate and St Bartholomew-the-Great, Smithfield. Instead, it became a Guild Church, and was until recently the Servicing Centre of the Industrial Chaplaincy of the Diocese of London.

Exterior

The brown brick exterior (grey stucco at the east end) is formidably plain, only relieved by an engaging wooden cupola at the west end and a Venetian window between coupled Ionic columns, and a pediment with clock, at the east end. However the view from the south-west is greatly helped by the charming little Postman's Park (see Plate 44), where there is a Memorial Cloister recording the names of those concerned with little-known acts of heroism. The park is largely made up of the churchyards of St Botolph's, Christ Church, Newgate, and St Leonard's, Foster Lane.

Interior

After the dull exterior, going inside is an exciting surprise, for the interior is a well-preserved structure of the late 18th century, with coffered apses constructed inside the walls at each end and a charming organ gallery curving forward in elegant manner. The yellowish-brown of the marbling in the sanctuary and of the nave piers/columns is offset by the delightful Wedgwood blue of the beautiful plaster ceiling.

High lunette clerestory windows are cut into the barrel-vaulted nave in the same manner as at All Hallows', London Wall. Square piers support galleries on the north and south sides, below which are delicate plaster friezes. At gallery level, the piers change to columns, with gilded capitals supporting entablatures, above which rises the ceiling with its decoration of large plaster rosettes resembling flattened Prince of Wales feathers.

The half-domed east end apse is coloured blue and gold whilst,

St Botolph's Aldersgate, from Postman's Park

below the fine window (see *Stained glass*), are sanctuary panels of the four Evangelists.

Extra seating round the side walls is fitted with cast-iron screens below.

A vestry in the south-east corner has been converted into a small chapel.

Furnishings
Organ The organ in a case standing on Ionic pillars was made by Samuel Green in 1778. It was rebuilt and added to in the 19th century.

Pulpit This is a fine hexagonal late 18th century example of simple design in inlaid mahogany supported on a pedestal in the form of a palm tree. The former sounding board was given by a previous vicar to St Paul's Cathedral.

Stained glass The east end window is a unique work of 1788 in the form of a transparency by James Pierson after a picture by Nathaniel Clarkson, representing the Agony in the Garden, with the rare feature of moulded plaster curtains coloured purple enfolding.

Many of the other windows, including two smaller works of Pierson, were destroyed by 1939–45 bombing. The post-war glass on the south side, by M. C. Farrar-Bell, depicts various events in the history of the church and surrounding district, including the original confirmation of patronage on the Dean of the Priory of St Martin's-le-Grand (see History).

Altar-rails and tables The rails are Victorian, but the table in the chancel decorated with Jacobean arches underneath dates from 1639. The Chippendale table in the sanctuary was used in its place between 1787 and 1872.

Monuments
Many survive from the old church.
Lady Anne Packington A recessed table-tomb in the south-east corner with panelled coving commemorates this noted benefactress of her day. At the back are brass figures of herself, husband and child. The inscription, incised and painted black, red and gold, records that her husband, Sir Joseph, was 'Chirographer' (nearest modern equivalent might be 'conveyancer') of the Court of the Common Pleas. The monument dates from 1563.

Anne Branch, died 1611. By the side of the Junior Warden's pew under the organ gallery there is a brass to Anne Branch.

Elizabeth Smith, who died in 1750 at the age of 15. The monument by L. F. Roubiliac is a cameo bust and has a simple epitaph.

Zachariah Foxall Near the entrance door is a monument to Zachariah Foxall who died in 1758. Putti hold a medallion and behind is an obelisk.

Catherine Mary Meade, who died at the age of 21 in 1791, the daughter of George Meade of Philadelphia. According to the inscription, she was 'transferred from Pennsylvania's friendly coast' to die on 'Albion's sea-girt shore'.

Associations

John and Charles Wesley On the gateway of the churchyard is a tablet commemorating the conversion of John and Charles Wesley in Aldersgate Street in 1738 when John felt his heart 'strangely warmed' – an event which led to the great Wesleyan Revival Movement.

Ironmongers' Company and Plaisterers' (Plasterers) Company St Botolph's is the Guild Church of these two Livery Companies.

Post Office Rifles The Roll of Honour of the 8th Battalion, City of London Regiment (the Post Office Rifles) is kept in a case with a glass top, affixed to the end of the choir-stalls, and a memorial tablet is placed against the column nearest the font on the north side of the chancel.

General

There can be few contrasts more striking in City churches than that between the stark, barrack-like dullness of the exterior and the delightful late 18th century atmosphere of the interior.

11 St Botolph's, Aldgate

Dedication

Very little is known about this Saxon abbot who died in AD 655. His name has come to be associated with travel of which he became the patron saint.

In order that those on a journey could pray on arrival and departure from London, no fewer than four churches situated near gates to the City have been dedicated to this English 'St Christopher'. One at Billingsgate has disappeared but the other three (Aldersgate, Aldgate, and Bishopsgate) remain.

History

The earliest reference to a church here is 1125. This first building, of which the foundation goes back to Saxon times, was enlarged in 1418 but completely replaced in Tudor times. Brewer's drawing of Aldgate as it was in Henry VIII's reign shows a building with a handsome tower crowned by flying arches supporting a small lantern and spirelet like the pre-Fire St Mary-le-Bow; it also had three gables of equal height. The drawing shows what an animated scene the area round the church must have presented. It lay just outside Ald (old) Gate, within which stretched the great Holy Trinity Priory of Augustinian Canons, the most important monastic building in London after Westminster Abbey and to which St Botolph's Church belonged. The road traversed the east courtyard of the priory and there was a constant traffic of travellers in and out of London. A canon from Holy Trinity conducted the services of the church until the priory was dissolved in 1531.

Although St Botolph's escaped the Great Fire, it later fell into decay and the church that we see today was erected in its place by the architect of the Mansion House, George Dance the elder, and consecrated in 1744.

Considerable alterations were made by the Westminster Cathedral architect, J. F. Bentley, in 1889. He made the carved ceiling and added decorative plasterwork, created the chancel by adding the side screens, replaced the gallery fronts with a pierced balustrade and substituted the large box-pews with the present seating. Despite receiving a severe shaking in the 1914–18 War and having a bomb which did not explode through the roof in the 1939–45 War, the church survived, only to be badly damaged by fire in 1965. This was made good by Rodney Tatchell and J. S. Comper who greatly improved and enriched the interior, notably by the creation of the baptistry in the space under the tower.

The parish of St Botolph includes the former parish of Holy Trinity, Minories, the two being united after Holy Trinity was closed in 1899. Originally the latter was the place of worship of the 'Poor Clares' or 'Sorories Minores', who gave their name to Minories.

Exterior

The church is one of three in London which are aligned south to north instead of west to east. It is of red brick with stone dressings and there are Venetian windows on three sides. The tower rises on the south or entrance side and is completed with a pierced obelisk type of spire;

St Botolph's, Aldgate

there are domed entrances on each side. The façade of the fabric proper has a pediment, thus separating it from the tower. The building lies in a small churchyard.

Interior

To reach the nave one passes through the octagonal baptistry. It has glass doors at each end and it now houses the font and some of the more interesting monuments.

The nave has aisles on each side which are placed under low sloping galleries supported by square pillars. One enters under another gallery at the south end. All have high balustrades. The interior space is comfortably and attractively furnished but the 19th century figured ceiling in a mauve colour by Bentley does not lie easily with the 18th century architecture of Dance and one may perhaps wish that the plaster standing angels with their shields in the coving and the bands of square boss-like leaves were not so obtrusive.

The chancel is attractively furnished although the east window is highly coloured.

A reading area has been fitted out in the eastern part of the north aisle.

Furnishings

St Botoph's is fortunate in its decorous furnishings which include a fine organ and a piece of wood-carving of exceptional interest.

Font Now in the new baptistry. Dating from the 18th century, it is circular and has an attractive octagonal domed cover.

Organ The original Renatus Harris instrument in the west gallery, given by Thomas Whiting to 'the whole Parrish' in 1676, is particularly notable. It is the oldest church organ in London.

*Wooden Carving Probably the outstanding feature of this church is the sumptuous carving of the south wall, brought here from the destroyed St Mary Matfelon, Whitechapel. It shows King David, surrounded by musical instruments. It is in high relief.

Pews These are a nice feature with their scrolled arms.

Pulpit The oak pulpit dating from about 1745 is plain but has interesting inlaid panels with various symbolic designs.

Altar-rails The fine gilt wrought-iron altar-rails are decorated with a winged angel on the gate.

Reredos By Bentley and handsomely adorned with pilasters and Corinthian columns. The three panels, made in a method of batik using dye and wax resist, were designed by Thetis Blacker in 1982.

St Botolph's, Aldgate. King David wood-carving

Using as her inspiration St John's account of the Holy City seen
through the Gate of Heaven (Revelation ch. 21) she has placed the
Tree of Life in the centre panel. From the roots of the Tree flows the
River of Life. The foundations of the city are coloured according to
their stones. In the side panels are angels guarding the Gate, holding
Alpha and Omega, symbolising the beginning and end of creation.

Pyx The stoneware ceramic pyx holding the Blessed Sacrament was
designed and made in the shape of a dove by Juliet Pilkington.

Altar pall this was made by Barbara Sansoni.

Stained glass The east window is an enamelled glass copy of Rubens'
'Descent from the Cross' and was given in 1857. Most of the other
windows mark Aldermen of the Ward who have also been Lord
Mayors of London.

Monuments

Thomas Lord Darcy and Sir Nicholas Carew On the north-east side of
the baptistery is the monument to the two Catholics executed by
Henry VIII for rebellion – Thomas Lord Darcy and Sir Nicholas
Carew – together with members of their families. The memorial is in
the form of a recumbent, emaciated figure between Corinthian
columns, and dates from 1560–70.

Robert Dowe In the south-east corner is the Robert Dowe
monument which has been recoloured. It shows his bust with 'Geneva'
cap in a niche and dates from 1612 (repaired 1675).

Sir John Cass In the opposite corner, there is the bust of Alderman

Sir John Cass (1661–1718) whose schools and Foundation still work closely with the church.

William Symington Inside the church, under the south gallery, is a tablet to William Symington, who constructed the *Charlotte Dundas*, the first steamboat that could be put to practical use. But the invention was not taken up and he died in poverty.

Benjamin Pratt Another tablet commemorates Benjamin Pratt who 'affected to end his days in celibacy' and died 3rd May 1715.

Thomas Bray Founder of the Society for Promotion of Christian Knowledge (SPCK) and the Society for Propagation of the Gospel (SPG), Thomas Bray is commemorated by a memorial tablet unveiled by the Queen in March 1980.

Associations
Chaucer lived in the parish in 1374.

Edmund Spencer was married in St Botolph's and has left a harrowing description of the Great Plague of 1665, when over 5,000 victims were buried in two pits dug in the churchyard.

Duke of Suffolk After execution, the head of the Duke of Suffolk (Lady Jane Grey's father) was brought to Holy Trinity, Minories, and, when this church was united to St Botolph's, the head was removed to the churchyard and can no longer be seen.

General
St Botolph's still lies on a frontier dividing Inner and Outer London between the bowler-hats of the City and the small shops of the East End. Many of its parishioners today are Jewish and St Botolph's is the headquarters of the Diocesan Council for Christian/Jewish understanding. It conducts in the crypt a mission for homeless men and women (The St Botolph's Project). The statue of the Virgin Mary looking at the crypt through the suffering of the Crown of Thorns shows two aspects of life in this church; it is by Connie Cook. It was given by her and stands on the pillar opposite the pulpit.

St Botolph's is a place of worship cared for and caring, and the feeling that it gives on entering is one of warmth and welcome.

12 St Botolph's without Bishopsgate

Dedication
St Botolph's is one of three London churches, all outside the old City gates, which are dedicated to this Saxon abbot who became the patron

St Botolph's, Bishopsgate. Steeple from south-east

saint of travellers. The church was beyond Bishopsgate hence the name given of St Botolph's Without. A fourth St Botolph's (Billingsgate) was destroyed during the Great Fire.

History
During the building of the present place of worship, the foundations of the original church, which may have been erected by the Saxon bishop Erkenwald, were uncovered but the earliest mention of a church on this site was in 1212 when it was called 'Sci Botulfi exa Bissopeg'.

In 1247 land north of St Botolph's was given to found the Priory of St Mary of Bethlehem; this was converted after the Suppression into the Bethlehem Hospital for Lunatics (Bedlam).

At one time, an anchoress (female hermit) was attached to the church – she received 40s a year from the Sheriffs of the City.

In Elizabeth's reign the building adjoined the town ditch but, the historian Stow adds, was 'inclosed with a comely wall of brick'.

Although surviving the Great Fire, the building later became ruinous and was demolished in 1724. A new church was erected at a cost of £10,400 by James Gold and consecrated in 1728.

No fewer than seven restorations have been carried out since but St Botolph's, except for the destruction of the west windows, survived the air-raids of the 1939–45 War. During the Victorian period, the numbers of parishioners increased so much that a daughter church – All Saints, Skinner Street, (demolished in the 1860s) – had to be built and towards the end of the 19th century the living was considered to be one of the richest in London if not of the whole country.

The parish hall to the west of St Botolph's was built in 1861, in the same style as the church. It is sometimes used by the Fan Makers' Company. The charming charity children in Coade stone came from an earlier building.

St Botolph's suffered considerable structural damage from the IRA terrorist bomb which exploded in Bishopsgate on the morning of 24th April 1993.

The entire roof particularly suffered and most of the stained glass was severely damaged. Happily, fragments of the east window have been retrieved and pieced together with new glass to restore the window. The windows on the south side have been replaced with plain glass at ground level but some stained glass was recovered for the gallery level. The west window, which was by Hugh Easton and depicted the Resurrected and Ascended Lord, cannot be restored and will be replaced with plain glass.

The structural damage to the roof and windows has been made good but the organ, which was devastated, has yet to be restored.

Exterior

St Botolph's is exceptional in having a tower at the east end. Being the principal façade towards Bishopsgate, this has been given a handsome stone face, decorated with coupled Doric pilasters, frieze and pediment. The sides are more modestly built of brick and have two tiers of windows. The square tower with gallery is crowned with a circular cupola, ogee cap and urn.

Interior

The interior, surrounded by galleries on three sides, has a coved ceiling and tall plastered Corinthian columns on oak plinths which stand above the Victorian pews. The frequent restorations have altered the original character but the insertion of a dome with lantern in 1828 has helped to lighten an interior which would otherwise be dark. Aisles and galleries are in classic style.

The 1878 restoration led to the remodelling of the chancel, which has marble panels on the walls. The east window dates from 1869. The south-east chapel is the memorial chapel of the Honourable Artillery Company (HAC).

The aisle vaults are nicely tricked out with crowns and mitres whilst, at the base of the galleries, the names of every incumbent back to 1323 are inscribed in gold lettering – an interesting variant to the usual list on a board. A quotation from Hebrews VII 23–24 underlines our temporary state and the permanence of Christ: 'And they truly were many priests, because they were not suffered to continue by reason of death: But this man, because he continueth ever, hath an unchangeable priesthood'.

The chancel arch is decorated with medallions of roses.

Furnishings

Pulpit and Lectern St Botolph's retains its original pulpit and lectern. The pulpit has a staircase with nicely turned balusters. The lectern has console feet and is embellished with cherubs and plaques.

Organ The organ, first erected in 1764, was rebuilt in 1912 but severely damaged by the Bishopsgate bomb in 1993.

Monument

Sir Paul Pindar A plain tablet above the staircase leading to the north gallery commemorates Sir Paul Pindar, one of the church's most famous parishioners, who was British Ambassador to Turkey in 1611 and was buried here in 1650. The facade of his house in Bishopsgate was moved to the Victoria and Albert Museum in South Kensington.

Associations
Edward Alleyn, founder of Dulwich College, was baptised in the church in 1566.

John Keats, the poet, was baptised in the church in 1795.

John Cornwell A memorial cross honours John Cornwell, of HMS *Chester*, whose heroic conduct at the Battle of Jutland in 1916 earned him a posthumous VC.

The Honourable Artillery Company has its Book of Remembrance in St Botolph, which is the Regimental church.

London Rifle Brigade This famous brigade is remembered by a tablet in the south aisle and a Book of Remembrance below.

General
Although built only 20 years earlier than its companion at the other end of Houndsditch, St Botolph's without Bishopsgate is not at all the same architecturally. The Bishopsgate place of worship is stately, the Aldgate church more homely, but both provide warmth of welcome and are part of the rich repertoire that London has to offer the lover of churches.

13 St Bride's, Fleet Street

Dedication
Until the beginning of the 19th century St Bride's was referred to as St Bridget's. This is the only church in London dedicated to her.

She was born about AD 453 and is second in fame amongst Irish saints only to St Patrick with whom she was almost contemporary. She founded the first Irish nunnery at Kildare. Amongst miraculous powers, she is credited with changing well water into beer.

History
Nowhere else in London can one follow more closely the development of a church from its earliest beginnings. It is possible that this was the first place in the capital where Christ was worshipped. The building lasted until the 10th century, when it was replaced by another, possibly because the earlier church had been destroyed by the Danes. Fire in

1135 may have swept this later building away, for it was followed by yet another building, which had an impressive tower from which rang one of London's four curfew bells. In this church the Curia Regis, principal court of the realm, was held in 1205 and, in 1210, King John granted a charter there.

Church number four was erected in the 15th century and it was here that St Bride's long association with printing and the press began. Many prelates had settled outside the walls between the City and Westminster because land there was cheaper and they trusted that their spiritual station would protect them from the risks of violence run by rich merchants. The clergy at that time had almost a monopoly of literacy and, therefore, they were the printers' best customers. William Caxton lived, died and was buried in Westminster but his Alsatian apprentice, Wynkyn de Worde, who acquired the press, brought it to a place alongside St Bride's and made a commercial proposition of it. Wynkyn was buried in St Bride's.

The 15th century place of worship lasted until the Great Fire. St Bride's was in the thick of it and virtually nothing was saved. As so often in the City, Wren came on the scene and between the years 1670 and 1675 designed the building we see today, one of the earliest to be rebuilt by him. The famous tower and wedding-cake spire followed in 1701–3. Victorian attentions were confined to the decoration of the sanctuary by Basil Champneys and the installation of new glass in the east window. The church was gutted by incendiaries in December 1940 but structurally was restored to its previous state and rededicated in 1957. Considerable changes, however, were made to the furnishings, principally with the substitution of open collegiate-type seating for the old box-pews and the removal of the galleries.

All this is most imaginatively displayed in an exhibition housed in the crypt, which alone makes a visit worthwhile. Survivals of tesselated pavement and walls from Roman times can be seen and the many and varied links with newspapermen and notable residents are also shown.

Exterior

St Bride's is hemmed in on all sides and the celebrated steeple can only be enjoyed from a distance. The main entrance is approached along a little alley from Fleet Street. The well from which Bridewell took its name was in the south-east corner of the crypt, but is now dried up.

*Although perhaps not reaching the architectural heights of St Mary-le-Bow's steeple, the one at St Bride's, despite being struck three

times by lightning, which in one case led to eight feet being taken off
it, exceeds it in actual height measurement (226 feet). Without the
variety of forms which at St Mary-le-Bow carries one easily from stage
to stage, nevertheless the series of diminishing octagons with open
arches and pilasters, whilst repetitive, is full of subtleties. The top
stage, for instance, has square and not round-headed openings. As Sir
John Summerson points out, although the arches and pilasters get
smaller as one mounts, the pedestals get taller, and musical and bell-
pealing analogies have been drawn from the various proportions, so
that it is not without reason that William Henley described it as 'a
madrigal in stone'. The belfry stage, moreover, is skilfully and
beautifully designed.

Interior
Here, the post-war changes are strikingly evident and, although some
may regret the loss of the Wren furnishings, there is a freshness and
brightness which give an air of vitality. Structurally, the restorations by
Godfrey Allen have been faithful to the old and we can see again the
Tuscan columns (coupled sideways rather than lengthwise) and the
tunnel vault with penetrations for the clerestory windows as they were,
newly decorated with gilded rosettes in panels along the transverse
arches of the ceiling and the nave arcades. Furthermore the view
westwards is no longer impeded by the organ and we can now see
'Wren' vistas which have been hidden for nearly 300 years, including
the old minstrels' gallery. A splendid freestanding oak reredos
dominates the view looking eastwards with a *trompe-l'oeil* mural above
making the flat wall resemble an apse, all by Glyn Jones.

Large figures of St Bride and St Paul by David McFall are perched
above the entrance piers.

The floor consists of black marble from Belgium and white from
Italy.

Furnishings
Charity children Many pairs of charity children which used to be
placed outside schools are to be seen in London (e.g. the charming
pair in Coade stone outside the parish hall of St Botolph's
Bishopsgate). The St Bride's pair in the south-west corner used to
stand outside the Bridewell Hospital, formerly the Bridewell Palace.

Royal Arms The Royal Arms, in the balustrading of the minstrels'
gallery, are carved in a single block of Beer (Devon) stone weighing
nearly two tons.

Stalls The modern, open stalls are finely carved and given emphasis by the large screens behind with massive Corinthian piers supporting an entablature divided at regular intervals by roundheaded pediments carrying shields.

*Reredos This memorial to the Pilgrim Fathers (Edward Winslow, one of the leaders, was a parishioner) has coupled Corinthian columns and carries eight flambeaux above. On the reredos is an oil painting of the Crucifixion, above which is an oval stained-glass panel of Christ in Glory.

Associations

As at St Margaret's, Westminster, the associations of St Bride's are too numerous to mention in detail. It was the first church to use the Book of Common Prayer; over 2,000 parishioners died from the Plague; Samuel Pepys, as well as his eight brothers and sisters, was christened in St Bride's; Dryden, Milton, Izaak Walton, Johnson, Boswell, Garrick, Joshua Reynolds, Goldsmith, Burke, Addison, Pope, Hogarth and Mrs Siddons all lived within 100 yards of the church. Later, Charles Lamb, Wordsworth, Keats and William Hazlitt came to this area whilst today the associations with the Press as recorded on the stalls and on many new and restored memorials are legion.

It must also be added that the parents of Edward Winslow, one of the leaders of the Pilgrim Fathers and three times Governor of Plymouth, Massachusetts, were married in St Bride's and he himself was a boy apprentice in Fleet Street. Perhaps the most significant incident, in view of what followed, was the argument between King George III and Benjamin Franklin over what form of lightning conductor to use after the spire had been struck by lightning in 1764. George III had called in Benjamin Franklin to advise him and the latter had recommended pointed ends. The King insisted on blunt ends which led to comments about 'good, blunt, honest King George' and 'those sharp-witted colonists'.

A plaque installed by the Overseas Press Club of America commemorates American journalists who have died on overseas service.

The University of Southern Illinois has a broken angel, retrieved from a former St Bride's church after it was destroyed, incorporated into one of its buildings.

John Taylor, who became vicar in 1543, named 'Cardmaker', was burned at the stake at Smithfield on 30th September 1555 for opposing the Catholic reaction under Queen Mary.

William Rich (1755–1811) came to London as apprentice to a pastry cook at 3 Ludgate Hill and married his master's daughter. Rich achieved fame in his business, not least for the wedding cakes modelled on St Bride's steeple which he could see from his window. One secret was the use of the best French brandy, 'even when it cost one guinea a bottle'.

Bridewell Sermon In 1959, an annual service was revived to receive the Bridewell Governors and children into the City. It is held on the second Tuesday of March and includes a sermon, which has come to be known as the 'Bridewell Sermon'.

General

The moving out of the newspapers from Fleet Street since the mid-1980s has inevitably loosened the ties between St Bride's and the press. However, the parish still deals regularly with them, holding weddings and memorials for their employees, and St Bride's is still very much the 'journalists' church'.

N.B.: Further Reading: *Phoenix of Fleet Street* by Dewi Morgan.

14 St Clement's, Eastcheap

Dedication

St Clement was a 'fellow-labourer' of St Paul and was the third Bishop of Rome after Peter. The story about his being cast into the sea with an anchor round his neck is more likely to be legend than fact and there is some doubt as to whether he was actually a martyr.

Eastcheap, until King William Street and the approach to London Bridge was opened up, used to run further west and the church was on the street instead of being tucked round the corner in Clement Lane.

History

St Clement's appears in a charter of 1067, confirming grants of livings by William the Conqueror to Westminster Abbey. This may not be authentic, the first known rector being Stephen de Southlee (about 1308), but the abbot held the living throughout the mediaeval period. In the 13th century, the church was called 'St Clement Candlewickstrate'.

In 1349, a Lady Chapel was added.

This church, which Stow (the Elizabethan) commented was 'a very small church', was one of the first to be consumed in the Great Fire, being only a few yards from where it started in Pudding Lane, but the Wren rebuilding was a fairly late one of 1683–7.

In 1834 there was a proposal to demolish St Clement's which was defeated, but in 1872 William Butterfield ran amok in it; in Elizabeth and Wayland Young's graphic words 'he underwent a crise de nerfs'. Apart from the usual disfigurements, 'he tore apart the lovely triple altar-piece, flinging the two wings of the triptych on to side walls and leaving the centre mean and pointless where it was'. The reredos, which Sir Ninian Comper put in its place in 1933, is a doubtful asset, but some of the harm was corrected in 1936 when the organ, after reconstruction, was restored to its old position.

In 1925 the ceiling was taken down, the replacement being modelled on the previous one.

Relatively unscathed from the 1939–45 War there was further work in 1949–50 and redecoration in 1968.

Exterior
Very retiring and unassuming. The west front is stuccoed except for the upper parts of the south-west tower where the brick is exposed. The tower follows the curve of the street and is therefore on a different plane from the rest. It is unadorned except for a balustrade and stone quoins.

Interior
Lofty in proportion to the size of this small church, none of the walls are regular. As a result, the south aisle tapers inwards from west to east; it is separated from the main body by two tall Corinthian columns on high pedestals painted a rather incongruous blue. The clerestory on each side has small segmental-headed windows, those on the north with indifferent glass and the others clear The walls are panelled to a height of 8 feet.

The most attractive feature structurally is the ceiling, flat with a large oblong in the centre and squares at the corners and made most ornamental with its plaster wreath of fruit and flowers in gilt panel. It has a red and gilded cornice.

Furnishings
Organ Originally Renatus Harris, still with its front casing but enlarged. When St Clement's was shaken by bombs one night, the rector played 'Rule Britannia' on it the following morning.

Font The octagonal marble font is 17th century and has a very pretty cover enclosing a dove holding an olive branch and capped with gilded flames (no doubt as a reminder of the Fire). It is said that the great 19th century statesman, William Gladstone, liked it so much that he brought his friends and grandchildren to see it.

Bread-shelves On the south wall is an example of the 'dole' cupboards used for distributing bread to the poor according to specific benefactions. The Royal Arms on the cupboard are Stuart.

Doorcase A finely-carved doorcase with broken segmental-headed pediment and decorated with cherubs' heads lies in the north-east corner.

*Pulpit An exceptionally fine and large example with a very big tester. Adorned with standing cherubs and swags, it is hexagonal, of Norwegian oak and has oval panels.

Reredos The Comper reredos consists of three main sections each enclosed with two Corinthian fluted columns, the outer pair pedimented and the main central section segment-headed. These heads alternate with smaller pediments (two in the centre section) and segment heads below. The four panels depict the Annunciation (outer pair), St Clement, wearing the papal tiara and with anchor, and St Martin of Tours (inner pair).

Although this fine piece of craftmanship might appear well in a Mediterranean setting, it does not harmonise with the furnishings of a 17th century place of worship nor, it is safe to say, would Wren have approved of such an injection of colour.

Associations

Lovers of St Clement's claim that this is the 'Oranges and Lemons' church on the grounds that this was a rhyme for City churches only and that the mediaeval orange market was on the steps of London Bridge near the wharf where the Spanish oranges were unloaded. It seems, however, that St Clement Danes may have established the stronger claim.

General

St Clement's, the church of Candlewickward, is the smallest parish church in the City. The conflict between the colour of the reredos and of the columns with the decorous furnishings may disturb but this does not diminish the quality of the latter.

The church of St Martin Orgar was not rebuilt after the fire and the parish was joined to St Clement's, Eastcheap. ('Orgar' may refer to

Ordgarus the Dane, in which case it is interesting that two churches at the opposite ends of Old London Bridge had Danish dedications, the one on the south side being St Olave, Tooley Street.) The tower remained but was replaced by a curious brick construction in 1852–3 which can still be seen in Martin Lane (off Cannon Street) nearby, with its wooden clock dated 1853 on a bracket.

15 St Dunstan in the East (Ruin)

Dedication
St Dunstan was Archbishop of Canterbury in the 10th century and did much to restore monastic life after the Danish raids. Amongst his many skills, he was musician, manuscript illuminator and metalworker.

History
The mediaeval church was one of the wealthiest in the City. In 1632, the walls were repaired in Portland stone and these stood up to the Great Fire. Wren therefore had only to rebuild the tower and spire and, in 1697 (or possibly earlier), showing his great versatility, erected one of striking originality and grace, only exceeded in height in the City by the dome of St Paul's Cathedral. Flying arches support the spire on the principle used at the pre-Fire church of St Mary-le-Bow and at Newcastle-on-Tyne and Edinburgh Cathedrals.

Small stepped buttresses are placed at the base of the spire. The tower has tracery in the upper windows and large pinnacles at the corners; broad horizontal divisions break it up into stages. The south and west doorways have crocketed hood-moulds.

In the Regency period, the walls were found to be out of true and the rest of the church was rebuilt by the architect David Laing between 1817 and 1821 in Georgian Perpendicular style, an early example of the Gothic Revival.

St Dunstan's was gutted in the 1939–45 War and has been left as a ruin to show what the City suffered. The walls, however, have been encased in cement, the mullions of the windows restored, Wren's railings made good and the whole laid out most imaginatively as a garden with trees and shrubs, flower-beds and a fountain. This won a Landscape Heritage Award in European Architectural Heritage Year (1975).

General
The tower houses a private chapel for the vicar of All Hallows by the
Tower whose residence is alongside. The bells now ring out from a
winery over the Napa Valley in California, USA.

16 St Dunstan in the West

Dedication
Churches dedicated to St Dunstan occur at opposite ends of the City,
although only the steeple and walls of St Dunstan in the East near the
Tower remain. It was St Dunstan who, as the powerful Abbot of
Glastonbury, did so much to restore monastic life after the Danish
raids of the 9th century and later became Archbishop of Canterbury.

History
It is probable that a Saxon church existed here because Lanfranc the
first Norman Archbishop of Canterbury, forbade dedications to Saxon
saints for new churches.

The mediaeval church – first mentioned in the 1180s – passed from
monastic hands to the Crown in 1237 but reverted to monastic control
in 1386 when the Rectory of St Dunstan was bestowed on the
Premonstratensian Canons' Abbey of Alnwick in Northumberland to
compensate for the loss of property caused by Scottish raids over the
border. The Crown, however, continued actually to make
appointments to the living until 1403. Patronage remained, however,
with the Abbey until 1536 when, at the Dissolution of the Monasteries,
it once more passed to the Crown. St Dunstan's holds the original
charter of King Charles II restoring the Anglican incumbent in 1662.
Between 1643 and 1662 there were 'intruded' Commonwealth
ministers.

The building was considerably altered in 1701 when the nave
arcades were removed and a flat roof replaced the previous arched
one, so that the interior became an open panelled rectangle, with a
large pulpit next to the altar at the east end as focal point. These
alterations appear to have weakened the structure, so that it was found
necessary to pull down the old church and build in 1829–33 the present
one on a site further to the north to permit of road widening.

During the early part of the 19th century, an additional church – St
Thomas in the Liberty of the Rolls – was erected to cater for the

St Dunston in the West

growing population, which now accounted for 12,000 parishioners. This was pulled down in 1886.

Damaged in 1944 when the lantern of the tower was set alight with incendiaries, the church was restored in 1950.

Today, St Dunstan's no longer has parish status, but in 1952 became a Guild Church concerned with the work of the Church of England Council on Foreign Relations. One of the chapels has been made over to the Rumanian Orthodox congregation who brought in from Rumania the ornate screen to the west of the chancel.

Exterior

The building, which – like St Botolph's, Aldgate and St Edmund, King and Martyr, Lombard Street – is orientated north and south, is octagonal in design. The tower, with its clock on a massive and elaborate bracket and, further to the right, the statue of Queen Elizabeth, makes an arresting group when viewed from across Fleet Street. The architect, John Shaw, died twelve days after the outer walls were finished but his work was appreciated to the extent of a commemorative tablet being placed over the south door by grateful parishioners: a rare tribute.

The stone tower is on the south side – the rest of the building is constructed of brick and is modelled on the tower of All Saints Pavement at York. It has long unglazed Perpendicular windows in the upper part, forming a lantern, and a straight top with pinnacles.

The statue of Queen Elizabeth, together with the figures of King Lud and his two sons below in the vestry porch, comes from the west wall of Lud Gate which was pulled down in 1760. Dating from 1586, it is probably one of the oldest representations in stone of the great Queen.

Clock

The clock, with its gold and black bracket, was made by Thomas Harrys in 1671 for £35. When the old church was pulled down, the Marquis of Hertford moved the clock to his villa in Regent's Park, which took its name of St Dunstan's Lodge from the church. This house eventually passed into the possession of Sir Arthur Pearson, the founder of St Dunstan's Organization for the Blind. The clock was returned to the church in 1936 by Viscount Rothermere. The way in which the two giants strike out at the bells and turn their heads at the sounding of the hours and quarters is similar to the action of the figures in the clock at St Mark's Square, Venice. It was the first clock in London to have a minute hand.

Interior

The octagonal interior is a surprise in London. The building is not centrally planned with an altar or pulpit in the middle, but there are seven recesses and the chancel and altar are placed in the north bay. The recesses are vaulted.

Furnishings

Screen The richly decorated icon screen, designed and painted at the beginning of the 18th century, shuts off the Rumanian Orthodox chapel from the rest of the church; it came from the Antim monastery in Bucharest and was installed in 1966.

Stained glass The north-west window, which can be glimpsed through the screen, is by Kempe and depicts Izaak Walton, the angler, and the subjects of his 'Lives'. He held the offices of 'Scavenger, Quistman and Sidesman' in St Dunstan's from 1629 to 1644.

The north window is a reconstruction after the air-raid damage although the upper lights containing dark reds and blues by Henry Williment survive. The main lights depict four famous church leaders of the Saxon and early Norman period – St Dunstan, Lanfranc, Anselm and Stephen Langton. St Dunstan, according to the legend associated with him, is seizing the devil by the nose with his hot tongs; the devil had come to tempt him whilst he was making a golden chalice for his church.

A window on the west side commemorates John Fisher. He was a Cordwainer, and the church has a Cordwainers' service in his memory in mid-July.

Altar and Reredos These are early 17th century in Flemish flamboyant style from Antwerp; they are elaborately carved in oak and have canopies. The altar-rails are made from fragments of 17th century pierced carving from old stalls.

Organ Frequently altered, it still contains some material from the Renatus Harris organ of 1677. The organists included Frederick Oakeley, who translated and wrote the music for 'Adeste fideles'.

Monuments

Many monuments from the old church remain. These include:

Henry and Elizabeth (died 1530) Dacres A brass shows them both kneeling with labels protruding from their mouths.

Gerard Legh Died 1563. The well-made tablet is flanked by standing figures and there is a long Latin inscription.

Hoare family The banking family of Hoare is remembered by a tablet of 1725 to Sir Richard and more substantially with a sarcophagus on the east wall (1754) to another Sir Richard who, while Lord Mayor of London, presented in 1745 the wrought-iron sword-rest which is placed in front of the pews. The Hoare vault is below. This family have provided churchwardens since the second Sir Richard's death.

Edward James Auriol Drowned in the river Rhone in 1847 at the age of 17. A white marble bust showing him lying on a pillow as if asleep is placed in an arched recess apart from the memorial.

Hobson Judkin A touching inscription commemorates 'The Honest Solicitor. Who departed this Life June 30 1812'. and adds 'This Tablet was erected by his clients as a token of gratitude and respect for his honest, faithful and friendly conduct to them through Life. Go reader and imitate Hobson Judkin.'

Associations

William Tyndale Translator of the Bible was curate here.

Dr John Donne Donne, whilst Dean of St Paul's Cathedral, held the living between 1624 and 1631, the year of his death.

Heads of Tyndale and Donne can be seen on the west and east sides of the entrance arch.

Rachel Walton Rachel, the first wife of Izaak Walton, was buried in St Dunstan's in 1640.

American pioneer ancestors A framed list on a rear pew records famous names associated with American history:

Thomas West, Baron de la Warre, was married in St Dunstan's in 1596. He was a member of the Virginia Company and became first Governor of the State of Virginia in 1610. Delaware Bay, River and State are named after him.

George Calvert, 1st Lord Baltimore, was buried here in 1632. He promoted a charter for the foundation of the state of Maryland. The colony was started by his eldest son, Cecil, who became the 2nd Lord Baltimore. The City of Baltimore is named after him.

Lawrence Washington was buried in St Dunstan's in 1617. His sister Anne and brother, also Lawrence, who was first Governor of Maryland, were baptised here in 1621 and 1622 respectively. They were ancestors of George Washington.

Charles Dickens St Dunstan's eight bells were the chimes of Dickens's 'Christmas Carol'.

'Praise God' Barebones Barebones, after whom 'Barebones' Parliament was named, was parish constable and married in the church in 1648 .

Samuel Pepys Pepys records in his Diary how he made a pass at a young lady sitting near him during Divine Service, but was repulsed with a hat-pin.

General

Although just within the City boundaries, St Dunstan's is far removed in style from a typical Wren City church. Lantern tower, clock and Queen Elizabeth statue, familiar to Fleet Street journalists and Temple lawyers alike, combine with its octagonal interior to make it a highly individual building distinct from any other London church.

17 St Edmund, King and Martyr, Lombard Street

Dedication

Born in Saxony about AD 840, Edmund became King of East Anglia in 855 at the age of fifteen. He was defeated in battle by the invading Danes in 870 and, refusing to deny his Christian faith or to treat with his opponents, he was tied to a tree, used as an archery target and finally beheaded at Hoxne, Suffolk. The great mediaeval Abbey of Bury St Edmunds grew up over the burial place of his remains.

The church of St Edmund, King and Martyr is the only one now dedicated to him in the City of London.

History

Most of the early history is surmise. Records show that Matilda, the wife of Henry I, bestowed the living on the Priory of Holy Trinity, Aldgate and that in 1150 'Daniel the Priest' was rector. At this time, known as St Edmund Grasschurch, it stood in the London grass market established for the sale of hay, herbs and vegetables. Other than this, nothing is known of the mediaeval church which probably had a shrine dedicated to St Edmund. The building was destroyed in the Great Fire.

There is some doubt as to whether Wren himself or his surveyor assistant, Robert Hooke, designed in whole or in part the new church; also whether the north/south orientation was due to the exigencies of

St Edmund the King. Font

the site or the desire – as Gerald Cobb suggests – to capitalise from the sale of leases on the west and east sides. The demand for space was illustrated in later years by part of the small frontage on one side of the entrance door being let for a gunsmith's shop and part on the other side being used as a shed to house the parish fire engine. Work on the post-Fire building lasted from 1670 to 1676, the spire following and being completed in 1706.

Subsequent repairs and alterations were numerous, including fairly gentle treatment by William Butterfield in 1864. St Edmund's was unlucky to be the recipient of a bomb in the 1914–18 War (one of the few churches in the City), which brought the roof down and necessitated its reconstruction. Damage from incendiaries in May 1941 caused the loss of stained glass and, more important, the Queen Anne Royal Arms. Restorations were carried out by Rodney Tatchell in 1957, who also rebuilt the vestry and enlarged it to provide offices in 1968.

Exterior

St Edmund's narrow stone frontage is divided into three bays with arched windows and quoins, the centre pedimented tower bay slightly projecting. The windows have cherub's head keystones and are surmounted (the main entrance door also) by a horizontal lintel supported on console brackets.

The parapet of the tower, which has a prominent cornice, is embellished with urns and pineapples. Above is a lead lantern and concave spire capped by gilded ball and vane. The whole steeple is a most agreeable composition made more satisfying by the way in which the belfry stage of the tower is linked Italian-fashion by concave side pieces to the corners, which are decorated with large urns. At one time there were four more urns at the base of the spire and eight further up – a sad loss.

A handsome clock projects on a bracket.

Interior

A plain small rectangle without aisles, which with its richly-decorated and carved furnishings looks, as commented by T. Francis Bumpus, rather like the private chapel of a nobleman's house. The design is strongly Dutch in character. The ceiling is flat and makes an awkward join with the semi-dome, painted with a figure of Christ over the altar.

At the south end, unusual recessed side galleries with metal rails flank the organ.

Furnishings

Font A small furnishing dating from Wren's time, of good quality and with the unusual feature of having a semi-circular balustrade round it and of being placed in the south-west corner. The cover is decorated with gilded figures of four of the apostles out of the original twelve. (See plates p. 69 and 72).

Organ The organ is also unusual in having its case divided into two, one part at the south end and the other on the west wall. The south end casing came from St Dionis Backchurch (see 'General'). It was originally a Renatus Harris instrument but is much changed. The arms are Stuart Arms.

Churchwardens' Pews There are two high carved churchwardens' pews on each side of the south entrance.

Hatchments On the east wall are three hatchments (coats-of-arms in lozenge-shaped frames), one of which has the arms of Princess Charlotte, only daughter of the Prince Regent who became George IV.

Fresco On the wall of the vestry hall is an old fresco, depicting a Dominican friar, discovered on the site of St Nicholas Acons' Church (destroyed in the Great Fire).

Sword-rest Dates from 1753 and was ordered by the church to mark the election of one of their parishioners, Edward Ironsides, as Lord Mayor.

Pulpit Without tester but enriched with much fine carving.

Lectern Made up of re-used panelling.

Choir-stalls Enriched with pierced panelling and urns.

Altar-rails The altar-rails have turned balusters of unusual shape.

Communion table The Wren-period Communion table has elaborately carved legs.

Reredos A richly-decorated furnishing with six gilded panels and gilt lettering on a dark red background. The panels contain the Ten Commandments, the Lord's Prayer and the Creed together with figures of Moses and Aaron painted by William Etty in 1833. Behind is a segmental pediment with urns.

Doorcases At the sides of the reredos are two handsome doorcases with broken segmental pediments decorated with urns emitting flames.

Stained glass The strongly-coloured east window was originally intended for St Paul's Cathedral and was made in Munich but objection was taken to the angels being coloured red and it lay in the Cathedral crypt until eventually presented to St Edmund's as a memorial to the Duke of Clarence who died in 1892. (See also Royal Fusiliers in *Associations*.)

A contemporary font of Wren type – in Willen Church, Buckinghamshire for which Robert Hooke was the architect

Monuments
Edward Ironside, Lord Mayor 1753. Died during his year of office. Marble monument on east wall with oval plaque to his wife, Anne, beneath.

Dr J. Milles, Dean of Exeter, who died 1784. This marble monument by the elder Bacon is on the east wall and shows the figure of Hope resting on an urn. The memorial also includes Edith, his wife, who died at the age of thirty-five. Dr Milles was rector for forty years.

Rev Geoffrey Studdert-Kennedy On the west wall is a wooden tablet to Rev G. Studdert-Kennedy, 'Inspired Preacher, Writer and Poet', who was an army chaplain in the 1914–18 War, nicknamed by the troops 'Woodbine Willie' and rector here from 1921–9.

Charles Melville Hays President of the American Grand Trunk Railway, who was drowned in the Titanic disaster, is remembered by a brass tablet on the west wall.

Associations
Joseph Addison, poet and essayist, was married here to the Dowager Countess of Warwick on 9th August 1716, his next-door neighbour.

German bomb In a glass case are fragments of the German bomb which fell at 10.00 am on 7th July 1917 and caused so much damage – a sad memento!

Royal Fusiliers Stained glass 'Victory' window on the east side commemorates this Regiment. Below is a simple battlefield cross with the names of ten men killed on 25th October 1918.

General
St Edmund's is a modest church but, like most of the City churches, highly individual. Its steeple makes an attractive addition to Lombard Street and its projecting clock blends well with the banking signs which are so much a feature of this thoroughfare.

After the Great Fire, the parish of St Nicholas Acons (not rebuilt) was joined to St Edmund's. Later additions were St Dionis Backchurch (demolished 1878) and All Hallows Lombard Street (demolished 1938 but tower and furnishings removed to Twickenham) bringing with it St Benet Gracechurch Street (demolished 1867) together with its own parochial attachment, St Leonard Eastcheap (not rebuilt after the Great Fire).

In 1988, St Edmund, King and Martyr was linked in plurality with St Mary Woolnoth to form the parish of St Edmund, King and Martyr and St Mary Woolnoth, Lombard Street.

18 St Ethelburga-the-Virgin within Bishopsgate

Dedication
There have been many Ethelburgas, but the one to whom this once
charming little church was dedicated was almost certainly the sister of
Bishop Erconwald of London who appointed her Abbess of Barking,
which later became the largest Benedictine abbey in the country.

It is unlikely, as some believe, that these two were children of Offa,
King of Mercia, although Offa did have a daughter who became an
abbess, but there was no apparent connection with London.

This is believed to be the only Anglican church in the whole country
with this dedication.

History
It is impossible to say when the first church on the site was built. It
may have been Saxon, it may have been Norman, but the first
reference to St Ethelburga's Church was in 1250 and a rector, Robert,
son of Robert of Merstham, is mentioned in 1304. It is probable that
they ministered in an Early English church which would have been
pulled down in the 14th century and some of the materials used in the
present church. From 1366 it was in the hands of the prioress and
convent of St Helen in the adjoining parish until the Dissolution of the
Monasteries when Henry VIII seized it. In 1569 Queen Elizabeth
granted it to the Bishop of London where it has since remained.

In 1629, a west gallery reserved 'only for the daughters and
maidservants of the parish to sit in' was installed. In 1662, presumably
because there was no longer a need for such accommodation, this was
removed.

Two shops, dating from 1570 and 1614, were permitted to cling to
the wall on each side of the entrance porch on the west wall (as one
sees today in the Netherlands) with later a connecting upper storey
which almost completely hid the 14th century window. These were not
removed until 1932.

Just before the 1914–18 War, a thoroughgoing restoration was
carried out and many of the fittings dated from that time, including the
screen and the west gallery upon which was situated the organ, a small
Harrison built at that time. The stone flooring and the dark oak
woodwork were to the designs of Sir Ninian Comper.

Apart from damage to the roof and ceiling, St Ethelburga's survived
the 1939–45 War but, on 10th April 1992, an IRA terrorist car bomb
exploded outside the Baltic Exchange in St Mary Axe causing damage

to the church hall. Far worse, however, was to follow for, in the morning of 24th April 1993, a massive IRA terrorist lorry bomb exploded in Bishopsgate a few yards from the church. It smashed in the west wall, blew off the roof and caused immense damage. It seemed as though nothing was left, but when the rubble and mess was cleared up, it was found that the memorial tablets on the north and south walls and Hans Feibusch's mural on the east wall were virtually unscathed. In fact, the greater part of the building survives and there are hopes of restoration.

Fortunately, the painting by Peter Coeke van Aelst, the 16th century Flemish painter, of Christ healing the blind beggar was on loan to St Paul's Cathedral, whilst the mid or late 16th century font with its delightful ogee-shaped cover, which came from St Swithin's, London Stone, is reparable; this font has on its upper surface a brass motto in Greek round the bowl in the form of a palindrome which translated reads: 'cleanse (my) transgression, not only (my) outward appearance' This fitted in well with the motto which had been let into the floor: '*Bonus Intra Melior Exi*' ('Come in good, go out better'). Other smaller treasures have also come through, including the 1767 bailiff's staff surmounted by the famous silver figure of St Ethelburga and Tudor chalice dating back to 1560 which was almost certainly the one used when Hudson and his men received Communion before embarking on their historic voyage to Canada in 1607 (see below).

Furnishings
Among the casualties were Sir Ninian Comper's chancel screen and rood-loft above, also the organ casing designed by him. All the stained glass was lost including the three windows of considerable interest by Leonard Walker referring to incidents connected with the voyages of Henry Hudson. The first, on the south side and the gift of the Hudson Bay Company, showed him and his crew taking Holy Communion at St Ethelburga's on 19th April 1607, four days before setting out to discover a route to Japan and China via the North Pole. The second, also on the south side and the gift of USA citizens, depicted him sailing up the Hudson River and the third, on the north wall beside the pulpit, donated by British Empire citizens,showed him on his ill-fated voyage in 1611 cast adrift by mutineers.

Associations
John Larke Among the incumbents was John Larke, a friend of Sir Thomas More, who was hung, drawn and quartered on 7th March 1544.

Other notable rectors These included William Bedwell (1601–1632) who was one of the translators of the Authorised Version of the bible, John Evans who became Bishop of Bangor from 1702–1716 and W. F. Geikie-Cobb (1900–1914), noted for his unorthodox views on a number of subjects, including the remarriage in church of divorced persons, presiding over dozens of these ceremonies during the 1930s into the 1940s.

John Wesley John Wesley preached in the church in 1785.

General

What is to be the future of this unique little church, the smallest in the City, measuring internally 56 feet in length and 30 feet in height? The present situation (14th November 1994) is that, on the instructions of the Diocese of London, an informal development competition will be organised. The Friends of St Ethelburga, whose chairman is Viscount Massereene, a Bishopsgate stockbroker, will submit an entry. Their approach will not start from a commercial base, but will be a true conservation project restoring this historic building so that it can once again be used as a quiet place with its garden for prayer and meditation.

It is sincerely to be hoped that this modest but once beautiful building will continue to be – as Sir John Betjeman described it – 'a sole and typical survivor, an intimate little place with the atmosphere of mediaeval London.'

19 St Giles' without Cripplegate

Dedication

Tradition states that St Giles, born of royal parents in Athens, went to France about AD 666 and became a hermit, living in a cave. In a stone carving above the north door of the church he appears with a hind which, according to legend, he saved from hunting dogs. St Giles includes blacksmiths, beggars, cripples and maternity in his patronage.

'Cripplegate' may indicate that more cripples gathered here than at other gates or it may refer to the Saxon word 'crepel', a burrow or underground passage.

History

Although St Giles' was one of the very few City churches to have survived the Great Fire, it seems to have been as combustible as most,

having been swept by fire in the middle of the 16th century, at the end
of the 19th century and during the 1939–45 War. It also appears to
have had more than the usual share of rebuildings, restorations,
alterations, etc.

Records start with a church which may not have been much more
than a shrine built about 1090 by Alfune, first almoner to the Priory of
St Bartholomew and friend of Rahere who founded it. This was
erected on ground outside the gate which had become swampy from
the silting up of the Walbrook where it ran under London Wall.
Enlarged in 1333, it was rebuilt, after drainage, in 1357 and again in
1390 and once more between 1545 and 1550 after the first fire. The
tower was heightened in 1682–4 by John Bridges. Restorations took
place in 1704–5, repairs in 1764 and, in 1790–1, the pitch of the roof
was raised. In the 19th century, alterations including renewal of roof
and clerestory were made between 1858 and 1869 (see tablet on
exterior of south wall), the south side refaced and castellated in
1885–6, chancel raised and pews lowered in 1888 and there was more
restoration after a fire in 1897. In 1903–4 the north side was refaced
and castellated to match the south.

Finally, in the 1939–45 War, St Giles' was hit by an early bomb in
August 1940 but not made unusable. However, four months later it
was completely burned out.

For some years, it remained a desolate ruin in wasteland subject to
vandalism and desecration until taken in hand and restored by
Godfrey Allen, and re-opened in 1960.

Exterior

St Giles' today is cut off from the busy world outside and lies open on
all sides in a cloistered position surrounded by the dull plum-coloured
Barbican development. Most of what is seen is Victorian refacing and
castellation but the tower retains the stonework built of material
obtained from an earlier church together with the brick of the 1682–4
heightening. It is crowned with a charming open cupola of wood and
there is a prominent north-west stair turret.

Interior

A large, open and airy interior in the Perpendicular style with nave
and aisles of seven bays, formed of slender clustered columns and
moulded arches. It is typical of pre-Reformation Tudor interiors which
have survived in London like St Margaret's, Westminster, St Helen's,
Bishopsgate and St Dunstan's, Stepney.

The extension of the clerestory at the end of the 18th century has resulted in an abbreviated chancel with sanctuary arch built during the 1858–69 restoration. Stone arches in the sanctuary remain from an earlier period.

The sanctuary roof is panelled, with bosses, and coloured blue.

The west gallery and organ raised on a loft, costing £10,000, was installed after the War; so too was the good modern arched-brace roof of light tone. Pews and panelling are also new.

The only stained glass is at the east and west ends, and with few exceptions, the furnishings are post-war. The stone corbels are a pleasant survival from the past and the door to the rood-loft can be seen on the south wall.

Furnishings

Organ The organ came from St Luke's, Old Street and dates from the 18th century. It was made by Jordan and Bridge (Father Willis reeds) and modernised by Noel Mander in 1970. The case contains 17th century work by Renatus Harris from St Andrew's, Holborn.

Font and cover The marble font and cover also came from St Luke's. The cover is a delightful, octagonal domed structure with pilasters at the angles surmounted by an entablature, and garlands in octagonal panels below.

Sword-rest An exceptionally fine sword-rest bearing the arms of the last four Aldermen of Cripplegate to serve as Lord Mayors is placed against the pier on the south side of the nave at the entrance to the choir.

Lectern The lectern was presented to the church by the then vicar, the Revd Prebendary Albert Barff, in 1888 as a memorial to his illustrious predecessor, Bishop Lancelot Andrewes (see *Associations*). It was saved from the bombing.

Sedilia and piscina An attractive example with Roman tiles incorporated into the sedilia.

Sanctuary furniture New sanctuary furniture was provided in 1994.

Monuments

John Speed, (like the historian John Stow, a tailor) historian and map-maker, was buried here in 1629. A memorial in the south aisle shows him clasping a book in his right and skull in his left hand. This was restored by the Merchant Taylors in 1971.

Thomas Stagg, attorney-at-law, is remembered by a tablet in the south-east corner. This records that he was 'Vestry Clerk of this Parish

St Giles' without Cripplegate

March 1731 19th February 1772 on which day he died in the 76th year of his age. That is all.'

Associations
St Giles' is very rich in associations.

John Milton The poet and his father were both buried in the church, John in 1674 and his father in 1647. A bronze statue (once outside) in the south aisle commemorates the poet and a stone in the floor of the chancel marks where he was buried. There is also a bust of him in the south aisle by John Bacon. It is rumoured that the grave of John Milton was opened in 1793 and that parts of his body were sold to ghoulish viewers. A lock of hair alleged to be Milton's can be seen in Milton's Cottage at Chalfont St Giles.

Milton was reunited with his first wife Mary in St Giles'.

Oliver Cromwell was married to Elizabeth Bourchier in the church on 22nd August 1620.

Lancelot Andrewes, the great Anglican divine and one of the translators of the Authorized Version of the Bible, was vicar here from 1588 to 1605. Later, he became Dean of Westminster and held various bishoprics.

Sir Martin Frobisher, the great Elizabethan mariner and Arctic explorer, who died from wounds at Brest, was buried here in 1594. In 1888, a memorial was erected to him to commemorate the tercentenary of the defeat of the Spanish Armada. This was demolished in the bombing of the church.

Holman Hunt, painter of 'The Light of the World' (copy in St Paul's Cathedral) was baptised here in 1827.

William Shakespeare attended St Giles' for his nephew's baptism in 1607.

Plague St Giles' suffered more than most from the dreadful Plague which swept through the City in 1665. In the last week of August of that year, there were 600 deaths and, altogether, 8,000 people died in the parish; on one single day (18th August) there were 151 funerals. The very high death-rate may have been due to the parish pump being located in the churchyard. After the Fire in the following year, many refugees camped out around St Giles' in tents and this was the nucleus of the building development which followed.

General
St Giles' has a long and distinguished history. The mediaeval guilds who were the forerunners of the City Livery Companies first

established chapels in the church and it has been the place of worship of many great figures of the past. From an architectural point of view, although so much Victorianised, it is an interesting survival of a Tudor church. Now today it is taking on a new lease of life with another set of residents, already numbering 4,500, and maybe increasing to 7,000, living in the Barbican flats (the Barbican was a mediaeval watch tower). It ministers both to the City working population and, unlike most City churches, to a full resident population.

St Luke's, Old Street, which was carved out of St Giles' in 1733, was reunited with the parish in 1966. The strange steeple (see plate p. 181) remains amongst the ruins.

20 St Helen's, Bishopsgate with St Martin Outwich

Dedication
A rare dedication in London to the mother of Constantine, the first Christian Roman Emperor; St Helen is credited with having miraculously discovered in Jerusalem the true Cross upon which Christ was crucified.

History
There is no evidence to support the claim that Constantine founded a church here in memory of his mother and the first authentic mention is in 1161 in a grant of land made to the Priory at Southwark. A few years later the church is mentioned as belonging to the Dean and Chapter of St Paul's Cathedral who, in 1210, gave permission to a man named William, the son of a goldsmith, to found a Benedictine nunnery in the grounds of the church.

At that time, the parish church probably did not extend beyond the limits of the present south door but when the nuns' church was built alongside in the 13th century terminating where the west end is now, the parish nave was extended to the same point, thus producing the famous and very unusual double nave which was such a hallmark of the church. A line of arches and some kind of screen were set up between the nuns and the parish congregation but this did not prevent sly winkings and there were reproofs from the Dean and Chapter of St Paul's for the ostentatious veils worn by the nuns and the number of small dogs kept by the Prioress. Later, they were told that dancing and revelling must cease except at Christmas and at other times of recreation, and on no account must 'seculars' be present.

Text visible on the monument:

HIC SITVS EST IOANN
EQVES AVRATVS CIVI
DINENSIS. EIVSDE
OR ANNO DÑI
ALICIA BR
NICAM RELIQ
TH GVILIE
ENVPTA
SALVTI

St Helen's, Bishopsgate. Daughter of Sir John and Lady Spencer

St Helen's Church. Poor-box of bearded beggar holding out his hat *c* 1620

A south transcept was added when the parish nave was lengthened and, in 1374, two chantry chapels – the Chapels of the Holy Ghost and of Our Lady – were built to the east of the transept. About 100 years later Sir John Crosby, alderman, business man and diplomat, left money for 'renewing and reforming' the church which resulted in the nave arcade being built and the roofs reconstructed.

The nunnery, suppressed in 1538, came into the ownership of the Leathersellers' Company but the conventual buildings, other than the nuns' choir which had been preserved intact, were not finally dismantled until 1799. In the meantime, certain Livery Companies paid for repairs and alterations to the church in the 1630s from which time date the sumptuous doorcases and the exterior south door.

Numerous repairs took place in the 18th and 19th centuries culminating in a major work by J. L. Pearson, the eminent Victorian architect, in 1892–3, particularly affecting the chancel and the level of the floors. Most of the glass dates from the 19th century.

St Martin Outwich Church, which used to stand where Threadneedle Street and Bishopsgate meet, was a mediaeval place of worship which was burnt in a fire in 1765 and rebuilt in 1796; when the later building was demolished in 1874, the parish was joined to that of St Helen's.

Having survived the Great Fire and the 1939–45 War, disaster struck in most cruel form when two massive IRA bombs exploded, one on 10th April 1992 outside the Baltic Exchange and the other on 24th April 1993 in Bishopsgate. The bombs also caused severe damage to St Andrew Undershaft and virtually demolished St Ethelburga the Virgin, two other of the four City churches which survived the Great Fire and the 1939–45 War.

When the author visited St Helen's on Monday, 7 November 1994, the church was hardly recognisable. The pulpit, screens, monuments, organ, doorcases and much plaster work has been stripped out for restoration work on the fabric. However, after a certain delay due to the holding of a Consistory Court, an imaginative scheme of reordering, which will lead to the screens, organ and some monuments etc. being brought back although to new positions, has been drawn up with Quinlan Terry as the architect and, after going out to tender, James Longley & Co. as contractors (see plate opposite).

There will be changes but those concerned are confident that, when the church reopens in the spring of 1996, the parish will be provided with a building suitable to its special work among young professional people as well as for the conferences for clergy and ministers that have been held in St Helen's during recent years.

St Helen's, Bishopsgate, looking towards the west end, 1994

It is hoped to restore the monuments although the tomb of Sir Julius Caesar Adelmare was badly damaged. It will be moved into the south transept and the tomb of John de Oteswich will be transferred from the east to the west side of the transept. The memorial (illustrated) of the daughter of Sir John and Lady Spencer, which used to be on the wall beside the steps leading down into the church from the west end, will probably also be restored although its future location is not yet determined. It will be recalled that she was alleged to have eloped with the Marquess of Northampton who spirited her away in a bread basket. Her parents cut her off but when a child was born to her, she asked the great Queen Elizabeth, whom she served as a maid-in-waiting, to be one of the child's godparents. She then consulted the Queen as to who might be the godfather as she no longer had parents and the Queen chose Sir John Spencer, the father from whom she was estranged. Inevitably this led to a reconciliation.

Exterior
This will not be greatly affected and the pedimented doorway on the south side will continue to exist.

Interior
It will be premature to say more than is written above until the restoration is completed except that the floor level will be raised throughout and that there will be a floor hot air heating system. There is every hope that the building will not only be attuned to the needs of the day but also that it will be visually attractive and a joy in which to worship. A central font, permitting total immersion if required, has already been sunk into the floor. The chantry chapels to the east of the south transept will not be restored.

21 St James's, Garlickhythe

Dedication
The Apostle James, sometimes called St James the Great, became the patron saint of Spain after what was presumed to be his body was discovered in a marble coffin by a Galician peasant during the year AD 816. Around his shrine was built the famous cathedral of St James of Compostela, which during the Middle Ages became a leading centre of pilgrimage. 'Garlickhythe' recalls the sale of garlic on the bank of the Thames nearby.

History
The first mention of a place of worship on this site is 1170; whatever existed was rebuilt in 1320 and later endowed with several chantries, no doubt for the saying of prayers for the souls of some of the six Lord Mayors who were buried there. Repaired in the first half of the 17th century it fell a victim to the Great Fire in the second.

Much of the subsequent history is recorded inside the tower through which one enters: the rebuilding by Wren between 1676 and 1683, repairs to the steeple in 1854, restoration 1883–5, and finally the post-war restoration of 1954–63. There were other repairs and alterations in 1838, 1866 and 1897 when the plaster was removed from the tower. The Churchwardens' accounts contain details of the expenditure incurred at the re-opening in 1682; they included 4s 6d for 'Wax Lights to enlighten my Lord Mayor home'.

Damage was caused by a bomb from a German aeroplane which fell on 13th June 1917 and from a 500 pounder which fell in 1940 but fortunately did not explode; greater damage was caused by flames from incendiaries sweeping across the road from the other side.

Due to the sympathetic restoration after the War by Lockhart Smith and Alexander Gale when the roof (ravaged by death-watch beetle) and upper part of the walls were rebuilt, the tower refaced, and the stained glass removed, St James's has emerged as an authentic Wren church with much to enjoy both inside and out.

On 20th September 1991 at 7.30 a.m., a crane operating on Vintners Place and on the other side of Lower Thames Street collapsed across the church destroying the rose window and all the congregation pews. The east and west ends were unscathed, apart from dirt, damage and dust in the organ. All has been restored (although the organ needs much work) and the church was reopened by the Bishop of London on 7th March 1993.

Exterior

Seemly and dignified with one of Wren's delightful little spires (cf. St Michael Paternoster Royal next door and St Stephen's, Walbrook), this was added in 1714–17 some time after the tower was built.

The 125 ft high steeple consists of a plain tower which projects from the west end completed with pierced parapet and vases, above which rises the charming spire. This is in three square stages, the lowest with diagonally projecting coupled colonettes and entablature, rising by means of scrolled ramps to the second stage and the whole completed by an attractive weather-vane. This design creates strong contrasts of light and shade.

A handsome clock supported on a bracket and surmounted by a quaint figure of St James complete with staff, shell, wallet and hat projects from the tower at the junction of the first and second storeys. It was damaged during the 1939–45 War but the parts were kept in the tower and the clock was restored to full use on 3rd July 1988.

The central windows in the sides are much higher than the others. The west door is arched and adorned with a cherub's head keystone and demi-columns carrying a pediment. The handsome iron railings with grape motif were the gift of the Vintners' Company.

At the east end is the unusual feature of a projecting chancel.

St James's, Garlickhythe

Interior
This tallest of Wren's interiors with lofty columns raised on high bases encased in wood has similarities with that of St Stephen, Walbrook, in that the columns open out in the middle to create transepts. The aisles are lower than the nave, which has a deeply coved ceiling leading up to a central flat portion richly plastered and gilded to pick out the design. The coving is penetrated by the clerestory vaulting. The chancel, unusual in that it is structurally separate, has a barrel vault.

The many windows, now happily relieved of their Victorian stained glass, and the clerestory, led to St James's being called 'Wren's Lantern', but the east window has been replaced by a painting (see *Furnishings*) The centre windows in the side aisles are circular.

The walls are panelled up to a height of nine feet and the only gallery – at the west end – is carried on graceful gilded Corinthian stanchions of Sussex iron.

Furnishings
The iron (sword-rests, lion and unicorn etc) and woodwork are both notable. Some of the finest of the woodwork came from St Michael's, Queenhithe, after it was demolished in 1875.

Pulpit From St Michael's. A beautifully carved furnishing with fine tester and elegant staircase of twisted balusters and with the refinement of a peg for the wig of the preacher

Stalls The backs of the well-carved stalls also came from St Michael's.

Organ The pride of the church and one of the few Bernard Smith instruments that could be restored to its original condition although it incorporates alterations to the casing, all the front pipes are original. On the top are trumpeting cherubs, the shell of St James and the usual crown and two mitres.

Chandelier A recent and very attractive furnishing, the chandelier was a gift after the War from the Glass-Sellers' Company and is modelled on one in the Wren chapel at Emmanuel College Cambridge.

Royal Arms An excellent Stuart coat of arms which came from St Michael's, Queenhithe, is placed on the west gallery

Painting The painting above the altar-piece of the Ascension is by Andrew Geddes and was given by the curate in 1915 who later became rector.

Hatchments On the south wall are two hatchments (coat-of-arms in a lozenge-shaped frame).

Amongst other furnishings are churchwardens' pews, altar table, altar-rails with two ranges of spiral balustrades, fine doorcases (from St Michael's) in the north and south-east corners acting as screens, and a 17th century font cover. An amusing feature is the row of wig-pegs at the west end.

Associations
Ten Livery Companies hold their annual services in St James's.

General
After being out of action for nearly ten years, it is satisfying to see a church reappear, one with which Wren himself would probably not be displeased. The parish now includes St Michael Paternoster Royal next door, the transfer of which bought with it the parishes of St Martin Vintry and All Hallows the Less (not rebuilt after the Great Fire), St Michael's, Queenhithe, All Hallows the Great and Holy Trinity the Less (demolished in the 19th century).

St James's, Garlickhythe is the headquarters of the Prayer Book Society and is the venue for the Schools Thomas Cranmer Competitions, prizes for which are usually awarded by members of the Royal Family.

To this day, only the Book of Common Prayer is used at services. Every Sunday, except in August, Sung Eucharist is celebrated at St James's, although most City churches do not have Sunday services.

N.B. The church is open Monday to Friday from approximately 10.00 a.m. to 3.00 p.m.

22 St Katharine Cree

Dedication
St Katharine (Katherine or Catherine) professed her Christian faith at a sacrificial feast at Alexandria decreed by the Roman Emperor Maximilius. For this, she was subjected to torture on a toothed wheel but, upon the wheel breaking at her touch, she was executed with a sword in AD 307. The Catherine-wheel became her emblem and, being of royal blood, she was later the patron saint of the reigning Queen of England.

Cree was another word for Christ and recalls the link with the important Augustinian Priory of Holy Trinity within Aldgate, sometimes called Christchurch, in whose cemetery St Katharine's was built.

History
The first church called 'St Katharine de Christ Church at Alegate' was built about 1280 by the prior of the monastery in order that the canons 'be not disturbed by the presence of the laity at the services' (compare St Margaret's at Westminster.)

Rebuilt at the end of the 15th century this church, except for the lower part of the tower, was pulled down by Sir Thomas Audley after it had been given to him by Henry VIII. There was no further reconstruction until Charles I's reign at a time when Gothic forms were giving way to Classical. This third church, sometimes wrongly ascribed to Inigo Jones, was erected between 1628 and 1630 (the latter date can be seen on the keystone of an arch in the north-west corner) and consecrated in January 1631 by Archbishop Laud. The strange rituals, his 'Bowings and Cringings' at the consecration were later used at his trial as evidence against him.

An engraving of 1736 shows odd, wavy cresting round the outside of the building which has all but disappeared, and also a square turret which was replaced by the present Tuscan colonnade surmounted by a cupola in 1776. Repairs and 'beautification' were carried out in 1805 but, apart from new glass, some of which is no longer there, little more was done in the 19th century.

As St Katharine's had apparently escaped serious damage in the 1939–45 War, the Laudian church has come down to us relatively little changed. Repairs, however, to the damaged south wall revealed more serious structural trouble than anticipated; the church was classed as dangerous and in danger of demolition. Fortunately means were found of consolidating the walls and a new use found for the building as Headquarters of the Industrial Christian Fellowship. The able restoration by Marshall Sisson led to reconsecration on 6th July 1962.

The church of St James, Dukes Place, was demolished in 1874 and the parish added to that of St Katharine's.

Exterior
The mediaeval south-west tower, erected at the turn of the 14th/15th century (although the top was rebuilt in 1776), remains, but the rest of it (apart from the later cupola) is Carolean. The windows are a curious mixture. There is a large west window but in the tower south wall, a strange reversion to Saxon-type openings is found; on the south façade

THIS GATE WAS ... AT THE COST
AND CHARGES OF WILLIAM AVENON
CITEZEN AND GOLDSMITH OF LONDON
WHO DIED IN DECEMBER ANNO DNI 1631

Anno Dni 1965
THE FITCH GARDEN
was dedicated to all those who work in this
City & to the memory of JAMES FITCH
1762-1818 who in Mid-Summer 1784 opened
his Cheesemonger's shop East of the Church of
SAINT KATHARINE CREE
his nephew George Fitch 1780-1842 and his direct
descendants Frederick Fitch 1811-1909, Edwin
Frederick Fitch 1839-1916 Stanley Fox Fitch
1867-1931 Hugh Bernard Fitch 1883-1962
all Cheesemongers of London successors
Principals of the firm now known
as Fitch Lovell Ltd

St Katherine Cree, Gateway

facing Leadenhall Street the windows are squareheaded with Gothic
tracery and the centre light a little higher than the others; the large
east window is square, the lower half being blocked in.

A sundial on the south wall, dating from 1706 is inscribed 'Non sine
Lumine'

A quiet churchyard-cum-garden is entered through the church. It
has a large plane-tree and an arch with skeleton on top enclosing a
tablet recording its laying out by the firm of Fitch Lovell Ltd (see
Associations) who also provided the fountain. The gateway used to be
on Leadenhall Street and was built by William Avenon in 1631. The
skeleton on top is a reminder of the graves that used to lie in the
churchyard.

Interior

This most interesting hybrid provides a bright and attractive interior.
The arcades of six bays have Corinthian columns supporting arches
with Renaissance rosettes under the soffits, whilst the clerestory with
pilasters above follows late Gothic forms. There is no division between
chancel and nave which has necessarily lost much of its character by
the aisles being boxed in for offices. The view eastwards, however, to
the Catherine-wheel window in a square frame, remains less affected.

The plaster ceiling is an intricate Gothic pattern of ribs with
tiercerons made even more ornate over the chancel. Seventeen
coloured bosses represent armorial bearings of City Livery Companies.

The south-east and north-east corners have been converted into a
Laud Memorial Chapel (his portrait is on the wall) and baptistery
respectively. The Laud Chapel was furnished by the Society of King
Charles the Martyr, the sovereign who was Laud's patron but who
eventually signed his death warrant. From the baptistery a fine
doorcase of 1693 leads to the vestry and beyond to the garden.

Interior walls are panelled with wood from the old pews.

Furnishings

The *organ* was made by Father Smith in 1686 and rebuilt by Father
Willis in 1866. Some of the stops have original 'Father Smith' pipes;
the finely carved case is supported on fluted columns of oak with
carved capitals, attributed to Grinling Gibbons.

Royal Arms The Royal Arms in the north-west corner of the church
are those of Charles II.

Font The small octagonal marble font was given by Sir John Gayer (see *Associations*) who was Lord Mayor in 1646. It has an ogee cover painted blue and gold with the City's arms.

Pulpit Of cedar wood and finely carved with the usual cherubs' heads, leaves and pods. The sounding board is hexagonal and is inlaid with seven different woods.

Reredos Came from St James's, Dukes Place, after that church was pulled down. Enclosed in fluted Corinthian columns and pilasters.

Altar-rails and table Semi-circular rails enclose the sanctuary, where there is a fine Adam-type altar table with delicately carved legs, restrained swag decoration and ovals round the top rails.

Monuments

Sir Nicholas Throckmorton, died 1577. After nearly losing his life in the Marian Persecution, he became Ambassador to France and Chief Butler. He is shown recumbent under a canopy between Tuscan columns supporting an entablature and above a skeleton. There is elaborate strapwork at the back. It is in the Laud Memorial Chapel.

Samuel Thorpe, died 1791. At the west end there is a bas-relief to Samuel Thorpe by John Bacon with a standing woman bending over an urn.

Associations

Sir John Gayer, who provided the font, encountered a lion in the Syrian desert in 1643 when on a mission to the Near East. The lion, however, in answer to prayer left him alone. Out of gratitude for his escape, he endowed the Lion Sermons, preached each year in the church on October 1.

James Fitch set up his cheesemonger's shop nearby in 1784. His descendants developed it into the well-known firm of Fitch Lovell Ltd. They restored the little garden (north-east of the church) which used to be part of the Priory churchyard.

SS Lancastria A wooden tablet on the south wall commemorates 4,000 people who lost their lives in the troopship *Lancastria* when she was sunk on 17th June 1940 and lists the names of the rescue ships.

General

St Katharine's is a rare survival of a church built at a time when few churches were constructed, between the age of Inigo Jones and that of Christopher Wren. Many commercial and industrial City concerns have contributed to the furnishings and the church is exercising a valuable ministry as Guild Church for Finance, Commerce and

Industry, in promoting the study of such matters as full employment, the impact of automation and income distribution, with teach-ins, lectures, seminars, study groups etc. amongst those intimately concerned with these matters in the City.

Parish work is now looked after by St Andrew Undershaft.

23 St Lawrence Jewry

Dedication

According to tradition, St Lawrence suffered martyrdom in AD 258 under the Roman Emperor, Valerian. When told to give up the treasures of the Church he disposed of the plate secretly, assembled poor and outcast citizens and presenting them said '*these* are the treasures of the Church'. For this, he was flayed and roasted alive on a gridiron which became his symbol and is represented on the weathervane of this church.

It is generally thought that 'Jewry' refers to this part of the City where the Jews lived from the time of William I until they were expelled in 1290 by Edward I.

An alternative theory is that 'Jewry' is a corruption of '*jus, juris*' as being in the centre of the Roman city close to the ampitheatre, now rediscovered in Guildhall Yard, and on the way to the forum, which is nearer Cornhill.

History

The first mention of a church on this site was in 1136 but a Saxon building may have existed here before that. The mediaeval place of worship was consumed in the Great Fire of 1666; the foundation stone of Wren's rebuilding was laid in 1671 and it was reconsecrated in 1677 at a service attended by Charles II.

From 1294, patronage was in the hands of Balliol College, Oxford, but when the parish of St Mary Magdalene, Milk Street was united with that of St Lawrence after the Fire (St Mary's was not rebuilt), the living was shared jointly with the Dean and Chapter of St Paul's Cathedral; this lasted until 1957 when it became the Guild Church of the Corporation of London.

In 1892, the parish of St Michael Bassishaw was closed and joined to St Lawrence's, but the latter has now itself become temporarily part of the new parish of St Vedast-alias-Foster, although it may revert before long to being on its own again.

St Lawrence Jewry

The church was gutted during the air-raid of 29th December 1940; restoration was carried out by Cecil Brown and it was reopened in 1957. The Wren vestry (see plate p. 98) decorated with paintings by Sir James Thornhill and reputed to be one of the finest small rooms in Europe could not, however, be restored – a grievous loss.

Exterior

St Lawrence's is set forward in the forecourt of Guildhall with the east end facing the approach to it, and the south alongside Gresham Street. Although Wren did not normally pay a great deal of attention to the adornment of walls if they could not be seen, the importance of the east side approach led him to create a façade for it with Corinthian columns supporting a pediment. The south side is plainer with five round-headed windows flanked by two doors with circular windows above.

The building is of irregular shape. After the Fire, buildings took the external dimensions of property boundaries as a means of establishing claims. Wren consequently had to conform to the sites he was given, and he squared off interiors by varying the thickness of the walls, although here there is irregularity inside also. The tower is aligned with and projects from the west wall but the steeple – a glass-fibre copy of the old one – faces down Gresham Street; it rises to a height of 175 feet and the shaft is in the form of an incendiary bomb!

Interior

Stately, as befits the official Corporation place of worship, and handsomely restored. The interior is of the 'hall' type, designed to enable as many people to see and hear the preacher as possible. There are, however, two chapels, one on the north side called the Commonwealth Chapel in memory of the part played by the City – and which it still plays – in the development of the Commonwealth, and the other at the west end called the Tower Chapel, a replica of that used temporarily after the bombing for holding services from 1943 until St Lawrence's was re-opened.

The effect created is one of spaciousness: pilasters with Corinthian capitals, a coved ceiling, dark oak panelling round the walls, and gilded plaster work on the ceiling, which reproduced the original Wren decoration, all combine to make a dignified setting for the Corporation Church.

An interesting feature of the east windows is that, due to the

St Lawrence Jewry. Wren vestry

irregularity of the building, the reveal on the altar side is at right angles to the wall whilst the one on the other side is splayed.

The west gallery accommodates the choir and part of the large new organ. Another to the north, which is quite small, above a doorway, is called the Trumpeters' gallery, evidence of the use of the church for the ceremonial occasion.

Furnishings

The furnishings are in keeping with the high estate of the church. There are pews for the Lord Mayor (front right), the Queen's Sheriffs, the Court of Aldermen and, in the south aisle, the Esquires. The main pews came from Holy Trinity, Marylebone. Many of the other furnishings are the gifts of City Companies with whom the church has had long associations.

Organ This was built by Noel Mander in 1956 to replace the one destroyed and has three manuals. The choir organ is detached from the rest of the instrument and is placed on the west wall of the Commonwealth Chapel to enable the case to remain in appearance like the old Renatus Harris one.

*Vestry door The doorcase with Corinthian capitals leading to the vestry is especially fine. There are cherubs' heads and swags above.

Font Dates from 1620 and comes from Holy Trinity, Minories. It lies under the organ gallery. The cover incorporates wood from the roof of Guildhall.

Screen A carved oak screen separates the Commonwealth Chapel from the nave; it incorporates in the centre a section of wrought-iron made and given by the Royal Marines to mark their affiliation in 1974 to the church. Gates similar in design now complete the screen; they were donated by the Airborne Forces and the Parachute Regiment, being made in the REME workshops. The arms, apart from the Royal Arms, are those of the Province of Canterbury and the Diocese of London.

*Chandeliers A magnificent set of eight chandeliers designed by Cecil Brown adds further distinction to the interior.

Piano The Steinway Concert Grand was once the property of Sir Thomas Beecham.

Stained Glass Although a departure from Wren tradition, and one may have reservations concerning it, the stained glass, being all, except for the roundel windows in the sanctuary, by one man – Christopher Webb – imparts a harmony and illustrates much of the building's history and associations. It also provides colour without which the church might appear unduly sombre.

The east windows represent St Paul (commemorating the Dean and Chapter of St Paul's) and St Catherine (the patron saint of Balliol College, Oxford) signifying the former joint patronage. They also show the arms of the Dioceses to which the vicars of St Lawrence's later became Bishops. On the south side, the patron saints of the three united parishes appear and there are windows to Sir Thomas More, who was born in the parish and to William Grocyn, St Lawrence's most famous vicar. Sir Christopher Wren, accompanied by his Master Carver and Master Mason, are depicted in the vestibule.

Reredos The tall reredos, embellished with pediments and angels with trumpets, replaces the one lost in the bombing but the painting showing St Lawrence's martyrdom was saved and is in the vestry; the one now seen in the church is modern and depicts the incident leading up to the martyrdom.

Monument
On the north wall of the chancel, a memorial (which survived the air-raid) commemorates *John Tillotson* who was Archbishop of Canterbury from 1691 to 1694 and was lecturer (a kind of lay-reader) here for thirty years. He was married and buried in the church.

Associations
William Grocyn The most notable of the incumbents was William Grocyn, who was appointed in 1496. He was a great teacher of Greek and, as can be read on the window commemorating him, Erasmus wrote 'He is the patron and preceptor of us all'.

Sir Thomas More Lived in the parish and delivered discourses on St Augustine's 'City of God' in 1501.

Samuel Pepys Attended Divine Service here on 12th February 1664. He did not think much of the preacher but was pleased with the church which he considered 'very fine'.

City Companies The associations go back many years. The Girdlers' Company have held their annual service here since 1180 – probably a unique length of time. The Loriners, who presented the litany desk, and the Haberdashers also hold their annual services here.

New Zealand Society St Lawrence's is the church of the New Zealand Society, who actively support it and each year commemorate their National Day here.

General

Although St Lawrence's is the official civic place of worship, there are weekday services for all, as well as music recitals and talks by prominent people, and it is used by countless City workers as a centre of quiet and spiritual refreshment during the busy daily round. Despite the irreparable loss of the Wren vestry, we must be glad that it lives again and that we can enjoy what has been described by Alec Clifton-Taylor as 'the most beautiful of the restored interiors' of London.

24 St Magnus the Martyr

Dedication

The Magnus officially regarded as the patron saint of this church was the Norwegian Earl of the Orkneys. He was killed by his cousin Haakon in 1116, buried in Kirkwall Cathedral and canonized in 1135. There was, however, a stone church on the site mentioned in 1067 dedicated to St Magnus so that this must have been an earlier saint.

History

The stone church mentioned in 1067 was granted by William the Conqueror to Westminster Abbey, although patronage during the mediaeval period appears to have been shared with Bermondsey Abbey. Information is scanty. The parish received an annual levy from a chapel on London Bridge, dedicated to St Thomas of Canterbury, as compensation for loss of alms from travellers entering London from the south. William Yevele, the master mason who worked on Westminster Hall and built the nave of Canterbury Cathedral, founded a chantry in the church and was buried there; woodwork from Westminster Hall can be seen in the baptistery.

An early 16th century visitation exposed lax habits amongst the clergy who were accused of spending time fishing and in taverns when they should have been taking services.

The church escaped a fire on London Bridge in 1600 but being close to the source of the Great Fire in 1666 was one of the first to be destroyed; Wren used what was left of the walls to rebuild the church between 1671 and 1687, the steeple as usual following later (between 1703 and 1706).

The combination of another fire in 1760 which started in an 'oyl' shop next door and the widening of London Bridge in 1759–60 brought great changes to the structure. The fire destroyed the vestries

St Magnus the Martyr

at the west end and damaged most of the roof; the widening of the bridge led to the westernmost bays of the aisles, including the vestries, being removed to make space for a portico and footway for pedestrians under the tower. The north doorway was also taken away which spoilt the balance of this side.

These losses must have been largely compensated for by the commanding position which the alterations gave to the church at the City end of the bridge. This was to a great extent lost when London Bridge was moved further west in 1832, exposing the church to the ultimate indignity of having Adelaide House rammed up against it so that today it has ceased to have any contact with the bridge, and those crossing it approach the church at belfry level.

In 1782 the windows on the north side were reduced to small circular openings to reduce traffic noise. In 1924–5 the ecclesiastical decorator, Martin Travers, rearranged the interior, including the creation of the Lady Chapel and the South Chapel, giving it the strong Anglo-Catholic flavour it now has. 1939–45 War damage was slight; there was a restoration in 1951. In 1965, the church was redecorated, and again *c.* 1980.

Exterior

The obscuring of the view from London Bridge and the overpowering mass of Adelaide House has spoilt the approach from the south and west; on the north the reduction of the windows to circular openings, although decorated with swags and panels, has limited the view to a blackened wall. But the steeple, 185 ft high, closely resembling although a much plainer version of the one at St Charles Borromeo at Antwerp, remains a striking feature. Built of Portland stone, a tall octagon capped by a lead dome and spirelet surmounts the balustraded tower; this has arched windows and is enriched with coupled Corinthian pilasters at the angles. As at St Charles Borromeo, there are vases at the corners of the balustrades.

On the west side, one of the City's handsome projecting clocks remains, dated 1709. At one time, it was decorated with gilded figures. The donor was George Duncombe, the Lord Mayor of that year who, it is stated, wished to promote punctuality because of having been thrashed by his master when an apprentice for being late for work.

In the tiny churchyard is a piece of timber from a Roman wharf dated AD 75 and stones from the first arch of the original London Bridge dating from 1173.

Interior

Votive candles, statues and even an icon make one realise the wide range of Anglican churchmanship. Much of what is seen dates from the restoration in neo-Baroque style by Martin Travers in 1924–5; he reassembled the old reredos, added the side altars which are set diagonally, and placed the modern rood on the top of the reredos.

The statue of St Magnus also dates from that time.

Wren's structure is spacious, consisting of nave separated from aisles by tall slender and fluted Ionic columns with panelled walls and barrel-vaulted ceiling penetrated by openings from the oval clerestory windows. The various restorations have left unaltered the old floors and original levels – an attractive feature.

Fine double staircases with turned balusters and Corinthian columns lead to the organ which is placed above a gallery supported on wrought-iron posts as at St Mary's, Rotherhithe.

This is a fine interior and T. S. Eliot writes of St Magnus's 'inexplicable splendour of Ionian white and gold'. (plate p. 102).

Furnishings

There is much excellent iron and woodwork although some of the later additions bring a splash of colour of which Wren would hardly have approved.

Organ Another gift from Sir Charles Duncombe (see clock in *Exterior*). Made by Abraham Jordan in 1712, it was the first to operate with the swell mechanism. The case, enriched with musical instruments, comes from the Grinling Gibbons school.

Font Given by three parishioners in 1683, it is of marble with a nice oak cover looking like a house. The figure of Charity appears in a cartouche on the top.

Box-pews Two box-pews used as cupboards remain at the west end.

Bread-shelves The shelves in the vestibule were used for distributing bread to the poor.

Icon The 19th century Russian icon on the north wall depicts Our Lady of Perpetual Succour. It is said that the last Tsar used to give icons of this type to friends.

Stained glass In the westernmost window of the north side is a panel which came from the old hall of the Plumbers' Company of glass dating from 1671 with arms of the City of London and the Plumbers' Company. Other glass on this side by Alfred L. Wilkinson includes the arms of the Plumbers', Coopers' and Fishmongers' Companies. The post-war glass on the south side shows patron saints of the combined parishes, plus St Thomas of Canterbury. It is by Lawrence Lee, one of the most talented and expert of present-day stained glass artists.

Crucifix The large mother of pearl crucifix near the south altar was made in Bethlehem.

*Reredos and side altars The reredos is a splendid piece although the upper part is modern. The pelican symbolizing sacrifice can be seen above the Commandments. It is decorated with four Corinthian columns, entablature and pediment. In front are fine 17th century rails made of Sussex wrought-iron displayed to advantage.

The side altars were made up from a doorcase (from the old north doorway) and old woodwork and carvings. The south-east chapel has Wren's altar table. The altar-piece of this chapel has urns on top.

Pulpit The notable pulpit, dating from Wren's time, has a very large sounding-board and is supported on a slender stem.

Paintings Most of the paintings are copies; the picture of St John the Baptist in the baptistery is by Alfred Stevens.

Statue The 1924 statue of St Magnus on the south side shows him in horned helmet, holding an axe and a model of the church. Close by is a votive lamp in the form of a sailing ship.

Other furnishings include a 1708 sword-rest with arms of Queen Anne; the other arms are of Lord Mayors of 1764, 1792 and 1824; Lord Mayor's seat, combined bishop's throne and stall, wrought-iron candlestick with seven branches, hatchments, a marble stoup on pillar in the vestibule, and chests dating from 1614 and 1673. There is also a statue of our Lady of Walsingham by Martin Travers in the Lady Chapel.

Associations
Miles Coverdale After publishing in 1535, probably working for a time with William Tyndale, the first Bible in the English language, Miles Coverdale became rector here between 1564 and 1566. He was buried in St Bartholomew-by-the-Exchange but after that church was demolished in 1841 his body was brought here together with the tablet dating from 1837 on the east wall.

City Companies The Coopers', Plumbers' and the Fishmongers' Companies all hold their annual services here.

General
There are probably few churches in the City which have suffered visually so much from property development. Internally, the bright

colour helps to light up one of the notable but sometimes dark City interiors with fine furnishings.

St Magnus' is still a parish church, incorporating St Margaret's, New Fish Street, which lay where the Monument now stands and where lampreys used to be sold under its walls (not rebuilt after the Fire), and St Michael's, Crooked Lane (demolished in 1831 to make way for King William Street).

25 St Margaret's, Lothbury

Dedication

St Margaret, the maiden of Antioch, was martyred for refusing to give up her Christian beliefs. The origin of 'Lothbury' is unknown but it may be another name for the Walbrook stream which used to run beneath the church.

History

The history of St Margaret's follows the familiar pattern of many City churches. First mentioned in early mediaeval times (in this case in 1181 when it was recorded that a certain Reginald was priest there), rebuilt in the 15th century (about 1440 according to the historian Stow), destroyed in the Great Fire of 1666 and again rebuilt by Sir Christopher Wren. Mercifully, however, it escaped World War II bombing.

Prior to the Fire, St Margaret's was repaired by the parishioners in 1621.

Wren carried out the rebuilding between 1686 and 1690 in Portland stone. The tower, however, and spire were not built until 1698 to 1700.

At one time, small shops clung to the church wall until they were removed in 1771 .

Under the City Churches Re-organisation Measure a new parish was created in 1954, the full designation of which is St Margaret's, Lothbury and St Stephen's, Coleman Street with St Christopher-le-Stocks, St Bartholomew-by-the-Exchange, St Olave Jewry, St Martin Pomeroy, St Mildred Poultry and St Mary Colechurch. St Martin Pomeroy and St Mary Colechurch were destroyed in the Great Fire, the others, with the exception of St Stephen's, Coleman Street, which perished in the 1940 air-raids, were demolished in the 18th and 19th centuries.

Exterior

Set sideways to a quiet street, St Margaret's is of irregular shape with the tower on the south-west corner. The fine jointing of the Portland stone, the elegant doorcase balanced by a vestry window at the other end and the charming lead obelisk spire raised on a bellshaped dome all combine to give pleasure.

Interior

The interior consists of a nave and south aisle separated from the main body by two Corinthian columns; the aisle was made into a chapel in 1891 by the erection of a low screen with alternate wood and iron uprights, the lower half constructed from altar rails which were once at St Olave Jewry and the upper half designed by the Victorian architect, G. F. Bodley.

On the north wall, which is shorter than the south due to the irregular shape of the site, pilasters – taking the place of the columns on the other side – support the entablature. Panelling covers the walls up to a height of eight feet.

A small gallery on the west side contains the organ.

The ceiling is flat but coved at the sides.

Furnishings

The losses of the churches with which St Margaret's is associated were St Margaret's gain. It has been the recipient of one of the finest sets of furnishings in the City which, tastefully arranged by Bodley, are a major attraction.

*The pièce de résistance is the *Screen*. Stretching right across the interior and one of only two such Wren furnishings (the other is at St Peter's, Cornhill), this is a sumptuous piece. Presented originally by a wealthy Hanseatic merchant, Theodore Jacobsen, to All Hallows the Great, Upper Thames Street, it came to St Margaret's when All Hallows was demolished in 1894 to make way for a brewery. It has four divisions on each side of the middle entrance which is capped by a wide open segmental pediment with William & Mary Royal Arms; below is a large eagle. The divisions are separated by twisted balusters, winding round one another in spirals of exquisite delicacy.

Reredos This is another splendid furnishing with Corinthian columns carrying two segmental pediments. It has openwork foliage volutes at the sides, and above, a bas-relief of the Ascension by Bodley. Paintings of Moses and Aaron dating from about 1700 which came from the church of St Christopher-le-Stocks fill what were once windows on each side. Stone medallions of the patron saints of the associated churches are carved in the reredos.

Pulpit Yet another sumptuous furnishing with tester but not from the same hand. The tester, enriched with fruit and flowers, came from All Hallows, but the pulpit of which it originally formed part was considered too large for St Margaret's and went to St Paul's, Hammersmith. The pulpit at St Margaret's was made specially for it.

Organ Dates from 1801 and was made by G. P. England.

Candelabra The two brass candelabra in the sanctuary, dating from the beginning and end of the 18th century came also from All Hallows. Those in the nave are copies of the candelabrum on the left side of the sanctuary and were installed in 1962.

Communion rail This furnishing with delicate two-strand openwork balusters came from St Olave Jewry.

South Chapel The screening off of the south aisle to make this chapel gives it the appearance of a separate miniature church with its own individual furnishings. These include:

Font This small stone font has been attributed to Grinling Gibbons and shows fine craftmanship. Supported on a baluster stem, the round bowl is decorated with cherubs' heads between which are cut reliefs of Adam and Eve in Paradise, the Return of the Dove to Noah in the Ark, the Baptism of Christ in the Jordan by John and of the Eunuch by Philip. The wooden cover depicts the dove of peace within a cherub-headed crown.

Reredos Less elaborate than the main reredos, it is nevertheless a feature of interest with two pilasters, an open segmental pediment, two inscription boards and hanging garlands. Above is the sacred tetragrammaton (the Hebrew consonants of the Divine Name) which indicates that it may have come originally from a synagogue in Old Jewry.

Stained glass The central window on the south side of the chapel contains the arms of the Scientific Instrument Makers' Company who hold their services in St Margaret's. The window on the north side which was presented in 1969 contains the coat of arms of the Tin Plate Workers' Company.

Monuments

Mrs Simpson The beautiful bust of Mrs Simpson on the side of the door leading to the chapel, dating from 1795, is by Joseph Nollekens.

Alderman John Boydell On the other side of the door is a tablet in memory of Alderman John Boydell, who was Lord Mayor of London

in 1790. It was designed by Thomas Banks and carved by F. Smith in
1791 for St Olave Jewry.

General
This small place of worship measuring 66 by 54 feet and 36 feet high is
like a casket containing great treasures. Although less than 200 people
now reside in the parish, it serves some 10,000 City workers who
pursue their labours within the confines of the area covered by its
ministry. Music recitals are also given in the church.

26 St Margaret Pattens

Dedication
St Margaret of Antioch, according to tradition, was beheaded for her
faith after many sufferings, choosing prison rather than submit to the
will of a local ruler.

'Pattens', wooden soles mounted on large iron rings to raise the
wearer above the mud, used to be made and sold in the lane beside the
church but, although there are two pairs in a glass case on the south
wall and a notice in the vestibule asking women to take off their
pattens before entering, it is by no means certain that the name is
derived from this footwear.

History
Reference is made to a small wooden building in the year 1067 and to
'St Margaret de Patins' in 1275 but nothing is known of the mediaeval
place of worship. Whatever existed was taken down in 1530 and a rood
or cross was set up in the churchyard (hence Rood Lane) to collect
money for a new church. Reforming zeal led to the destruction of the
cross a few years later but the church was completed in 1538. Repaired
in the first half of the 17th century, it did not last beyond the Great
Fire.

The Wren rebuilding, which started in 1684 and was completed in
1687, except for the steeple, was later than most. St Gabriel's,
Fenchurch Street (not rebuilt after the Fire) was then added to the
parish. The steeple followed between 1699 and 1703.

Subsequent history was relatively uneventful. 'Beautified' in 1855,
re-seated in 1879–80 and restored in 1955–56 after bomb damage when

the north gallery was converted into lecture rooms, St Margaret's remains a basically Wren building.

Exterior
The church lies at the corner of Eastcheap and Rood Lane set back from the pavement with attractive 18th century frontages on the right, and filling the view as one looks up St Mary at Hill. The plain exterior is dominated by the north-west tower and spire rising to 200 feet, the highest in the City after St Mary-le-Bow and St Bride's. Mediaeval in spirit, the needle-shaped and lead-sheathed spire capped with ball and vane is the only Wren example of this type, and is decorated with sunk panels.

The tower terminates in a handsome balustrade and sharply-pointed stone pinnacles at the corners, echoing the somewhat severe lines of the spire.

Two lead rainwater heads on the north wall are dated 1685.

Interior
Also plain structurally, but with enjoyable furnishings. It is rectangular with one aisle on the north side separated by piers from the nave forming a Lady Chapel. The piers support the north gallery but change to columns above. A gallery on the west side supports the organ. All the clerestory windows are circular.

The Lady Chapel has a former doorcase as reredos.

The panelled vestry dates from the Wren period.

Furnishings
*Churchwardens' pews The only examples of this type in the City, with carved canopies and some crown-glass lunettes in the backs. Many feel that the inlaid 'CW' with date 1686 stands for Christopher Wren who attended service in this church but the letters could also indicate 'Churchwarden'. Initials St G. F. on the south and St M. P. on the north side stand for St Gabriel's, Fenchurch Street and St Margaret Pattens.

Beadle's pew The beadle's pew remains but the reputed punishment bench below has been stolen.

Reredos An attractive furnishing. It contains a painting by the 17th century Italian artist, Carlo Maratti, of Christ attended by ministering angels in the Garden of Gethsemane. A peapod in the wood carving possibly means that it is the work of the Grinling Gibbons school.

Choir-stalls These were made out of the original high pews of the

St Margaret Pattens. Drawing of 1881

nave and the date 1709 with initials 'PH' appears on the front panel of one of them. Those nearest the nave carry a rather mettlesome lion and unicorn.

Lectern Unusual in that the eagle has a viper gripped in its talons.

Sword-rests Notable – one of pole design and a larger one of frame design which includes the arms of Sir Peter Delmé (see *Monuments*). They are made of Sussex iron.

Hour-glass stand The stand enclosing the hour-glass beside the pulpit was specially made from 18th century wrought-iron.

Cross The copper cross in the middle of the south wall weighs ¾cwt. and is a copy of the one at St Paul's Cathedral. It was taken down for safety from the top of St Margaret's spire.

Organ The organ in its 18th century case has been extensively rebuilt since it was installed.

Font Decorated with four cherubs' heads and dating from 17th century, it has an 18th century cover.

*Royal Arms A fine example of Stuart Royal Arms dating from the reign of James II.

Wooden pegs A reminder of past fashions is the line of wooden pegs at the west end of the Lady Chapel and on the south wall for hanging wigs during hot weather.

Monuments

Charles I Below the cross is a wooden board painted with the Arms of the King and containing the words 'Touch not mine anointed'. This was brought to the church by the Rev James Fish (see *Associations*).

James Donalson A tablet on the south floor recalls James Donalson, who died in 1685. It states that he was the City Garbler whose job was selecting the best in spices.

Sir Peter Vandaput, a merchant who was Sheriff in 1684. The monument is wrapped round a pillar on the north side.

Susannah Batson, died 1727. Attractive small memorial with cherubs' heads. By vestry door.

Sir Peter Delmé, who died in 1728 – fishmonger, governor of the Bank of England, alderman and later Lord Mayor. The monument which hangs on the south wall near the chancel is by the great Flemish sculptor, Michael Rysbrack.

Associations

Thomas Wagstaffe Rector at the time William III came to the throne and deprived of the living because he refused to give his oath of allegiance to the Dutch monarch. He later became non-juring Bishop of Ipswich. A Della Robbia plaque in the middle of the Lady Chapel reredos was given by parishioners in his memory.

Dr Thomas Birch This distinguished rector wrote a history of the Royal Society of which he was secretary. He died in 1766 as a result of falling from his horse.

James Fish, rector from 1866 to 1907, was a well-known Tractarian and during his time the church became famous for its musical services. He instituted services in memory of Charles I on January 30th each year, the anniversary of the King's execution.

Crew of submarine K4 In the Lady Chapel is a shrine (made of teak from the ship '*Britannia*' in which they were trained) to the crew of the submarine K4 rammed by accident on 31st January 1918. It was presented by the wife of the commanding officer Commander David de Beauvoir Stocks.

Pattenmakers' Company and Basketmakers' Company hold their annual services here. Flemish immigrants made baskets in Rood Lane.

General

Although, apart from the spire, this is not structurally one of Wren's great churches and is not helped by the stained glass, especially the yellow cross in the east window put in after the 1939–45 War, the furnishings have much to offer to the visitor. Many are unusual and some, such as the churchwardens' pews, are unique. They are made more enjoyable by the clear descriptions.

The priest-in-charge has been entrusted with the task of co-ordinating the Busoga Trust, the purpose of which is to instal clean, piped water in the Busoga province of Uganda. Offices are provided for this purpose and an Administrator of the Trust.

27 St Martin-within-Ludgate

Dedication
St Martin, according to Sulpitius Severus, was a Roman soldier who met a beggar when riding in bitter weather to Amiens. Having no ready money, he cut his cloak with his sword and gave half to the beggar. He became a Christian and later, in AD 372, he was made Bishop of Tours and spread the Christian faith in northern Gaul.

'Ludgate', named after the mythical King Lud, was one of the six gates leading into the City. Called 'Lutgata' in the early 12th century it had become 'Ludgate' by 1235; a chapel dedicated to the Virgin Mary above the east front of the gate was linked to the church of St Martin's. Rebuilt in 1586, the gate survived the Great Fire but was pulled down in 1760. The statue of Queen Elizabeth was transferred to St Dunstan in the West. Unlike the other 'gate' churches, St Martin's was situated within and not outside the gate.

History
Tradition takes the story back to Cadwallader, King of the Britons, who – according to a 13th century chronicle – is said to have built the first church in about AD 600 and to be buried in the crypt. He was in fact buried in Rome. Recorded history does not go back beyond 1174 when there existed a church hard up against the Wall. This was rebuilt in 1437 and contained a chantry to Wm. Sevenoke who some say was another 'Dick' Whittington rising to become Lord Mayor. There were also many chapels.

Although Ludgate, which the mediaeval church touched, survived the Great Fire, St Martin's did not. Moreover, the steeple had been damaged earlier on 4th June 1561 by the same flash of lightning which brought down the spire of Old St Paul's. The Wren rebuilding was a late one (1677–87). He moved the site a little further north and incorporated part of the Wall in the western part of the new church.

Since then, St Martin's has been treated fairly gently and, as it managed thanks to a favourable wind to escape destruction in the December 1940 air-raid, we have a largely authentic Wren place of worship to enjoy.

Exterior
St Martin's is set sideways to, and can only be approached from, Ludgate Hill. The front facing it (south) has an elegant three-bay façade of Portland stone with tower in the middle slightly projecting and segment-headed windows with horizontal mouldings and pedimented niches flanking it. Above, scrolled volutes lead the eye easily towards the belfry stage of the tower and then skilfully merge via an octagonal stage to the lead-covered upper part of the steeple, consisting of ogee dome, charming balcony, lantern and obelisk steeple. This slender Continental-looking spire was designed to provide a counterpoint to the swelling lines of the dome of St Paul's and is matched on the other side of the Cathedral by the spire of St Augustine's, Watling Street; there is a point halfway down Fleet Street from which the spire can be seen to cut the dome exactly in half.

Interior
This is one of Wren's most ingenious designs. He succeeded in converting a sloping site which was wider from north to south than from west to east into a square by inserting a lofty south aisle containing vestibule and vestry between the outer wall and the body of the church. This is screened off by a partially enclosed arcade with beautifully plastered coffered arches and embellished with pilasters. By so doing, he killed another bird by insulating the interior from the noise of the outside traffic.

In the square thus created, Wren constructed another of his cross-in-square designs (cf. St Mary at Hill and St Anne and St Agnes) but here, the columns – elevated on unusually tall pedestals – are closer together and very lofty. The barrel vaults of the arms of the cross, the entablatures of which reach to pilasters on walls where they stop abruptly, meet in the centre to form a groined middle section. As at the other two churches, the spaces between the arms are lower and have flat ceilings.

Galleries which formerly existed on the north and south sides have been removed but the west organ gallery reached by stairs with twisted balusters remains. The walls are panelled.

Chancel and sanctuary were raised in the 1890s but this does not detract from the impressive, if rather dark, interior, although the cutting down of the pews accentuates their lack of height in relation to the pedestals of the columns.

Furnishings
The furnishings are good and largely original.

Organ Nothing remains of the original organ and the present instrument dates from 1848; it is the work of Bates and Lewis. Below the gallery there is a white marble pelican.

Font The font, given by one Thomas Morley in 1673, is a small elegant example in white marble with fluted bowl. Like the font at St Ethelburga's, Bishopsgate, it is inscribed on top with a Greek palindrome which, roughly translated, reads 'Wash my sin, not my face only'.

Candelabrum The fine, large brass chandelier in the centre was once in the Cathedral of the Island of St Vincent in the West Indies. How it came here is not known.

Stained glass There are three Victorian windows, representing the patrons – Westminster Abbey, The Bishop of London and St Paul's Cathedral.

Pulpit Original of standard hexagonal type. The sounding-board which has been made into a table came from St Mary Magdalene, Old Fish Street (burnt down in 1886).

Reredos The reredos is rather flat and has pilasters only. The raised centre carries a segmental arch and there are vases at the sides.

Paintings On the north side of the altar is a painting of the Ascension by R. Browne (wrongly attributed to Benjamin West) dating from 1720. On the south side are panels of St Mary Magdalene, St Gregory and St Martin copied by a Belgian artist.

*Churchwardens' Double Chair The most remarkable furnishing is the double chair for churchwardens to the south of the reredos, dating from 1690 and the only known example of its kind.

*Doorcases On the south side giving access to the vestry and vestibule are three splendid doorcases, notably the one attributed to Grinling Gibbons in the south-east corner decorated with large winged cherubs' heads in the spandrels, garlands down the sides and Corinthian pilasters. Another on the north side leads to a chapel.

Monuments

Thomas Berry A brass with figure in fur gown in the vestry records a benefaction of '12 penie loves to 12 poor foulkes every Sabathe day for aye' by Thomas Berry (Beri), a fishmonger. It is dated 1586. Fine carved bread-shelves can be seen on request.

Richard Harris Barham, author under the name of Thomas Ingoldsby of 'Ingoldsby Legends' was buried in St Mary Magdalene's in 1845 and his memorial was transferred to the wall near the entrance. There is also a memorial to his three children in the vestibule.

Bell A 1693 bell is placed on a square iron chest in the north-east corner.

Cistern A lead cistern dated 1779 is kept in the vestry.

Associations

Samuel Purchas, publisher of Richard Hakluyt's *Pilgrimes* known as 'the English Ptolemy' became rector in 1614. He was a friend of the American Indian Princess Pocahontas and her husband, John Rolfe.

Captain (later Admiral) William Penn, father of the founder of Pennsylvania, was married here on 6th June 1643.

Middlesex Yeomanry St Martin's is Regimental Chapel of the Middlesex Yeomanry.

General

St Martin's is no longer a parish church and now forms part of the parish of St Sepulchre without Newgate. The transfer carried with it the former parishes of St Gregory's by St Paul's (not rebuilt after the Fire) and St Mary Magdalene, Old Fish Street (now part of Knightrider Street). The latter was burnt down in 1886.

Its Guild activities relate to liaison with the Metropolitan Police. It is also the Chapel of the Honourable Society of the Knights of the Round Table.

28 St Mary Abchurch

Dedication

An earlier spelling – 'Abechurch' – led the historian, Stow, to think that the prefix 'Abe' might mean 'Up', referring to the slight eminence upon which the church was built; or it may be derived from the name of a founder or benefactor such as 'Abba'.

History

Earliest mention is of 'St Mary of Abechurch' at the end of the 12th century. Little is known of the building described in mediaeval times as 'a fair church' except that it had aisles, a bell tower and was decorated with murals, and that it had chantry chapels dedicated to St George and the Holy Trinity.

Being near the seat of the 1666 Fire, it was soon consumed and the parishioners had to wait some time before Wren rebuilt it between the years 1681 and 1686. In the meantime, they used on the site a temporary tabernacle from which the altar table still remains. This was housed in St Paul's Cathedral during the 1939–45 War and upon it in 1951 was laid the the American Roll of Honour presented to the Dean by General Eisenhower.

Subsequently, St Mary's has been singularly fortunate in the sensitive treatment received at the hands of restorers. 'Beautified and repaired' in 1708 when the ceiling was probably painted, Victorian 'improvements' relatively few, and skilfully restored by Godfrey Allen after the 1939–45 War, St Mary's is little altered. Although the ceiling and the organ were seriously damaged by blast and water the bombs led to the discovery of a mediaeval crypt, probably 14th century, under the courtyard and removed the Victorian glass and tiled floor, which was then lowered 18 inches to its former level.

The living originally belonged to the Priory of St Mary Overy, Southwark, from whom it passed in the 15th century to the Master and chaplains of a College of Corpus Christi attached to St Lawrence Pountney Church nearby. Later, Queen Elizabeth was persuaded by Archbishop Matthew Parker to grant it to the College of Corpus Christi and the Blessed Virgin Mary, Cambridge, of which he had been Master, in whose patronage it still remains.

St Lawrence Pountney was not rebuilt after the Fire, its parish being added to St Mary's, but in 1954 the latter became a Guild Church and its parish added to that of St Stephen's, Walbrook.

Exterior
The church is tucked away in a quiet courtyard between King William Street and Cannon Street, with a paved forecourt – once the churchyard – cobbled in geometrical designs. Externally, St Mary's is in much the same homely vein of hipped roofs and dark red brick with stone dressings as St Benet's, Paul's Wharf, and also has a similar if not quite so charming lead steeple, made up of an ogee-shaped dome supporting an open lantern and a simple spire, all in lead. Cherubs are carved above some of the windows.

The red brick was once covered with stucco.

Interior
The interior is larger than that of St Benet's, measuring 63 by 60 feet, and is without aisles. It has the unique features in a Wren City church of a painted domed ceiling and a genuine Grinling Gibbons reredos – the only authenticated Gibbons' work in the City other than the font cover at All Hallows by the Tower and furnishings in St Paul's Cathedral.

Although architecturally the dome falls short of that at St Stephen's, Walbrook it is nevertheless a masterly achievement, for Wren succeeded in supporting it on the four brick walls without creating any outward thrust and so dispensing with the need of buttresses. It rests on capitals used as corbels, except at the west end where a column and pilaster are used.

The painted ceiling depicts female figures representing the Christian virtues seated above the wide diameter modillion cornice (the dome is over 40 feet across) with shells between. In the centre the Hebrew name for God (tetragrammaton) is surrounded by rays of glory and a worshipping chorus of angels and cherubs. There are clouds too and garlands. This fine feature which was originally painted by William

Snow – 'painter-stainer' – (not Sir James Thornhill as at one time thought) was beautifully restored after the War by Walter Hoyle.

There is a fine west gallery once used by the boys of Merchant Taylors' School.

The walls are panelled.

Furnishings

Most of the original ones remain, including the superb reredos. Taking them in order as one enters, they consist of:

Doorcases Two richly carved doorcases with fluted pilasters, garlands in the segmental heads and urns on top, the north one carrying in addition a copper pelican and nest which, until it was removed in 1764 for safety reasons, used to be the weather vane.

Royal Arms The Royal Arms of James II are above the south doorcase.

Poor-boxes Original boxes to receive alms, square in form on square pedestals, remain on each side of the west vestry door – a rare feature.

Font and font-cover The marble font in a railed enclosure was made by William Kempster, one of Wren's best craftsmen (his brother Christopher carved the stonework) in 1686. The font-cover by William Emmett is a delightful piece, showing the four Evangelists in niches under shaped arches, the whole looking like a small pavilion.

Pulpit The 1685 pulpit with the uncommon feature of having its original steps was made by another of Wren's great craftsmen, William Gray. It is similar to that at St Clement's, Eastcheap, in having a very large tester, not unlike an old tricorne hat.

Pews The richly carved pews on the north, south and west sides are original and one of those on the south side once had a cupboard or kennel beneath for dogs!

Organ St Mary's had no organ before 1822 when one was built by J. C. Bishop. It was so badly damaged during the War that a new one by Noel Mander was installed. The carved oak front, however, dates from 1717 and came from All Hallows, Bread Street (demolished 1877), after a spell at All Hallows, East India Dock Road.

Candelabra The mahogany columns which support the lights come from Lockinge House, Berkshire and were given in 1957.

*Reredos The star furnishing, known to have been designed by Grinling Gibbons himself. As late as 1946, a letter signed by him addressed to the churchwardens of St Lawrence Pountney requesting their share of the cost of the 'Olter Pees' was discovered. The reredos is a magnificent furnishing and the largest to be found in a City church.

Corinthian columns support an entablature with parts of a segmental pediment above. Behind these is an attic with a raised concave centre and urns emitting flames, a reminder of the Fire. Wherever space permitted Gibbons himself carved trails of flowers and fruit of great delicacy and lightness; the pelican above the central round-headed panels is also his work but joiners made the columns, urns and the main structure of the reredos.

Monuments

Sir Patience Ward, who died in 1696. To the south of the reredos is a fine monument to this former Lord Mayor (1680) and Whig politician. It is in the form of a tablet with mourning putti and above, between urns, an allegorical figure on a concave-sided pedestal.

Edward Sherwood On the south wall of the chancel is an elaborate memorial to Edward Sherwood, who died in 1690.

Associations

St Mary's is perhaps not so rich in associations as other City churches but, as well as Sir Patience Ward, two other Lord Mayors were parishioners and gave sword-rests to commemorate their mayoralty.

General

Perhaps the least altered of Wren's City churches and containing the work of some of his best craftsmen, St Mary's is a fascinating church to visit. Lovable and homely without, beautifully furnished within, we must indeed be thankful that this church has been spared.

No longer a parish church, it is now a Guild Church. Whilst it has some associations with various Livery Companies, its closest is with the Fruiterers', whose arms are now in the great south window.

29 St Mary Aldermary

Dedication

As a church on this site was mentioned about 1080, 'Aldermary' may mean that it was older (alder) than St Mary-le-Bow, once called St Mary Newchurch; but St Mary-le-Bow argues that 'alder' could also indicate 'altera' (the other) Mary, i.e. Mary Magdalene.

History

The old church was the burial place of many Lord Mayors, for one of whom – Thomas Romeyn, Lord Mayor in 1310 (grocer) – a chantry chapel, according to the historian Stow, was endowed. Two hundred years later, the then Lord Mayor (Sir Henry Keble) provided funds for a new church. Started in 1510, it was completed after his death in 1518, except for the tower. Work on this began in 1530 and the lower part erected; the material was Caen stone (also used for the tracery of the windows on the south side). The upper part did not follow until nearly a hundred years later in 1629. What may have been the crypt of Keble's church, measuring approximately 50 by 10 feet, was discovered in 1835.

The tower partially survived the Great Fire; the upper part was rebuilt by Wren and the whole of it faced with Portland Stone. The rest of the church had to be rebuilt. Another benefactor – Henry Rogers – left money for the repair or building of a place of worship and his niece-executrix directed this to St Mary Aldermary on the condition, so it is stated, that the new church should be a faithful copy of the old, although no written evidence has been produced. This is probably the reason why Wren's rebuilding in 1691–2 follows Gothic instead of the usual Classical forms.

Repaired in 1823 it later – 1876–7 – underwent one of the most drastic Victorian restorations in the City. St Mary's was stripped of most of its furnishings (reredos, altar-rails, panelling, organ screen, gallery front and pews) and Victorian replacements were installed. A screen was put up at the west end dividing the lobby from the nave and stained glass introduced.

The glass was destroyed during the 1939–45 War and a post-war restoration was carried out by Arthur George Nisbet.

Exterior

The opening up of Queen Victoria Street has given St Mary's a conspicuous position. Ashlar stone-faced throughout and with a commanding south-west tower, it stands out amongst the routine commercial buildings.

The tower has prominent polygonal buttresses shafted at angles; these are panelled to their full height and culminate in pinnacles topped with finials renewed in fibre-glass *c*. 1955.

Interior

Slender clustered piers, slightly pointed nave arcade arches, threelight aisle and clerestory windows combine to produce a typical

Perpendicular interior, but the ceiling is another matter. Although it might have followed the pattern of contemporary work, there is no similarity to the stone fan-vaults of the 16th century. The rosettes in large saucer domes and the fan tracery are beautiful but the use of plaster instead of stone gives what Elizabeth and Wayland Young describe as 'the sweetness of confectionery'. There is more plaster decoration in the spandrels of the arcade (foliage and coats of arms).

The east wall is slanted owing to the shape of the site.

Furnishings
The furnishings left after the Victorians had gone their determined way consist of:

Font This, as the Latin inscription records, was given by someone named Dutton Seaman in 1627. It is unusual in being enclosed with twisted baluster rails probably salvaged from the old altar-rails. The material is marble and the font is scalloped underneath; the ogee font cover is plain.

Organ The organ is one of the finest in the City. It was built by George England in 1781, rebuilt by Holditch in 1876 and substantially rebuilt by Norman Beard in 1906. Some of the original Georgian pipes still remain.

Poor-box On a flat twisted barley-sugar stem.

*Doorcase A splendid piece with broken segmental pediment, now at the west end, decorated with fluted Corinthian pilasters, fruit and flowers. It came from St Antholin's (see *General*).

Sword-rest A notable example in wood with cherub's head at foot and lion's head accompanied by more cherubs and crown at top. Dating from 1682 it is fixed to the south-east pillar of the nave.

Pulpit A fine Wren-period example but minus its tester. It is hexagonal with panels and is decorated with cherubs' heads and garlands of fruit and flowers.

Of post-restoration furnishings the *lectern* is embellished with four carved figures of saints on posts and the *glass* in the north window contains the coats-of-arms of the Innholders', Vintners' and Salters' Companies. The west window by John Crawford and dating from 1952 commemorates the defence of the City during the 1939–45 War.

Monuments
John Seale who died in 1714. The monument depicts figures representing Time and Death hanging a draped curtain and is adorned

with two cherubs. It is supported on the north wall by corbel brackets carved to resemble bunches of grapes.

Margaret Bearsley who died in 1802. A simple tablet with a wreathed urn by the younger Bacon. It lies on the south wall of the chancel

Rene Baudouin who died in 1728. A cusped wall cartouche having small dark red and blue panels with shields and an oval dome. Baudouin was a Huguenot refugee. It is attached to the south wall.

Blank monument A curiosity is a completely blank monument with urn and swag on the north wall of the chancel. The story is that it was put up by a woman for her husband. But she married a second husband before she had thought what to say about the first. The sculptor was Francis Bacon.

Associations

Henry Gold Rector in Henry VIII's reign and involved in the 'Holy Maid of Kent' visions. For this he was condemned to stand in St Paul's Cathedral throughout the sermon and thence taken to the Tower, being finally executed at Tyburn.

John Milton married his third wife in the pre-Wren church in 1663.

Lord Chief Justice Jeffreys, the despicable judge, was buried here on 2nd November 1693.

Skinners' Company hold their annual services in the church.

General

It is sadly ironic, and a measure of the harm done by the Victorians, that the money for the restoration in 1875–6 from which this church has visually so much suffered came from the sale of the site and the demolition of St Antholin's Church, Budge Row. The latter was one of Wren's most original creations, being in the form of an elongated octagon with oval dome and stone spire. (St Antholin's dedication was derived from a 4th century Egyptian hermit, St Anthony, corrupted to Antholin.)

St Mary Aldermary is in the parish of St Mary-le-Bow together with St Thomas the Apostle, St John the Baptist, Walbrook (not rebuilt after the Fire) and St Antholin's; it is now an independent Guild Church to promote retreats and the devotional life.

30 St Mary at Hill

Dedication
The suffix 'at Hill', referring to the ascent from Billingsgate, helped to distinguish this church from various other St Mary dedications.

History
Earliest mention is 1177 when the Norman church, called 'Sanctee Mariae Hupenhulle', was described as adjoining the Town House of the Abbots of Waltham Abbey, Essex. It later had a chantry and four chapels.

The church was enlarged towards the end of the 15th century and aisles added on each side, the southern one being on the site of the Abbot's kitchen. It had pews (unusual at such an early date) and the number of chapels rose to nine. A piece of stone carving from the church depicting in relief the Resurrection, which probably once stood on a gateway (cf. St Giles-in-the-Fields) is placed on the wall beside the south entrance door in the vestibule. It dates from about 1600.

Not completely destroyed in the Great Fire, the tower and part of the side walls were incorporated into Wren's church, begun in 1672 and one of the first of his rebuildings to be completed (in 1677). In 1695 money was provided for a spire.

A hundred years later, the steeple had to come down and in the 1780s George Gwilt erected the present brick one. He also rebuilt the west front (moving the main doors further west), reconstructed part of the south front and renewed the vaults and ceilings.

In 1827–8 what remained of the old walls was rebuilt by the architect James Savage, at which time he repaired and refitted St Mary's. Twenty years later in 1848–9, the same architect was responsible for a thorough restoration, during which the ceiling decoration was changed to its present delicate Adam-type design and William Gibbs Rogers was engaged to provide new furnishings.

Towards the end of the 19th century, St Mary's – like St Mary Woolnoth – was under threat from railway extension but survived this and the 1939–45 War. In 1967 the architects Seely (Lord Mottistone) & Paget embarked on a two-year programme of cleaning and repairs to the plaster and wood; at the same time ugly Victorian light fittings were replaced with the present pendant ones and the church brightened by alterations to the glass, notably removing most of the Victorian glass and substituting pure white Reamy antique, a translucent glass which allows the natural light to filter through. This restoration greatly enhanced the visual pleasure of this City church.

Sadly, owing to a blow-lamp being left on the roof, a disastrous fire occurred in May 1988 which caused great damage to the furnishings.

Exterior

The west end and main approach is in Lovat Lane; the east end abuts on to St Mary at Hill Street from which one can enter via the small churchyard. The red brick battlemented tower (the rest of this front is yellow brick) has a homely appearance and is set at an angle to the Lane; the east end is slightly more circumstantial with its splendid projecting clock, Venetian window, some rustication and broken if awkward pediment. There is Portland stone facing but the plinth has been covered in stucco. In the churchyard is a lead cistern dated 1788 and, beside the south door, a tablet recording that the burial ground was closed on 21st June, 1846.

Interior

Before the 1988 fire this was one of the most enjoyable interiors in the City. Although it has been restored to use, the loss of so many superlative furnishings has robbed it of this distinction. The structural design shows one more facet of Wren's versatility in planning. It is a Greek cross in an irregular rectangle, the barrel-vaulted arms of the cross leading into a central square formed by four fluted Corinthian columns from which rises, by means of pendentives, a shallow dome. The four corners between the arms of the cross have low flat ceilings. The plan was drawn by Wren from Dutch mid-17th century interiors to which it is closely akin.

A west gallery is supported on pillars.

Savage's plasterwork on the coved ceiling has been restored. It consists of delicate rosettes and arabesques with much coffering (dome and arches) executed in a restrained manner. The corner ceilings are plain except for egg and dart cornices and the use of little rosettes. The walls with pilasters are painted in two shades of white.

Adjoining the first bay of the south wall from the east end of the church is a panelled study, dating from the 17th century but rebuilt in a building and repair programme, started in 1834.

Furnishings

With the exception of the stained glass, the chandeliers, the altar and the communion rails, all are awaiting restoration. Much was the work of a very talented Victorian carver, William Gibbs Rogers, who closely studied Grinling Gibbons.

Stained glass This consists of highly coloured (gold, blue, red) interlinked circles as a border in the north and south windows, six circular medallions, two heraldic shields and inscription in two east windows.

Chandeliers Two double-tiered eighteen-branched gilt-fired chandeliers above the choir stalls were given to mark the rehabilitation of the church in 1968–9 by the Watermen's and Lightermen's Company of the River Thames, and by the Billingsgate Ward Club respectively.

Altar table and communion rails These are original and date from Wren's time.

Monuments

John Wade, died 1658, his wife and son. A tablet with Corinthian side columns and a shield of arms. On the north wall.

Daniel Wigfall, died 1698. A fine, carved tablet which came from St George's, Botolph Lane.

John Harvey, died 1700. A tablet on the south wall also with shield of arms.

Thomas Lavall and his wife. An elegant wall monument with urns and arms.

Associations

Prebendary William Carlile, founder of the Church Army, was rector here from 1892 to 1926. He filled the church, and the trombone which was used at his services is preserved in a glass case in the vestibule.

General

Mercifully, about 50 per cent of the woodwork was saved and it is to be hoped that one day the church can be restored to its former rich glory. This, however, is dependent upon being able to find the £500,000–£750,000 which it will cost.

The parish of St Andrew Hubbard was joined to St Mary's after the Fire. St George's, Botolph Lane was demolished in 1904 and together with its attached parish, St Botolph's, Billingsgate , was also added to St Mary's, which is the parish church of Billingsgate Market. Finally, when St Margaret Pattens became a Guild Church in 1954, this, together with St Gabriel's, Fenchurch Street, was included in the parish of St Mary at Hill.

31 St Mary-le-Bow

Dedication

The most likely supposition is that 'le Bow' refers to the arches of the crypt under the church, giving rise to the name of St Mary of the Bows or Arches.

History

The Norman place of worship of which the crypt remains – the oldest parochial building in London – was called St Mary Newchurch which could mean that it replaced an earlier building or that it was not as old as St Mary Aldemary (Alde Mary) at the other end of Bow Lane.

The history of the mediaeval church is remarkably full of incident. In 1091, the roof blew off, killing several people, in 1196 a bad character called William Fitz-Osbert, who had killed an officer, barricaded himself in the tower and had to be smoked out; in 1271, the tower – no doubt weakened by the previous incident – collapsed, killing more people and in 1284, a quarrel over a woman led to a goldsmith, Lawrence Duket, being hanged inside the church; this necessitated stopping up the doors and windows with thorns until the building had been purged of this desecration. In 1331, a temporary wooden structure placed beside the church fell at a time when Queen Philippa, wife of Edward III, was viewing a tournament.

The tower took a very long time to rebuild; it was not until 1512 that the new steeple, built of Caen stone, was completed on a new site. Although perhaps not so notable as its successor, it must have been impressive for it had four lanterns at the corners and a fifth supported on flying arches, all intended to provide illumination for the street.

Much of this tower survived the Fire but it had to be taken down and, ample funds being available, Wren was given the opportunity to erect one of the greatest creations of his genius. Buildings were acquired to enable him to stand the new steeple on Cheapside and it was connected by a vestibule to the body of the church. In the rebuilding, he came across the Norman crypt and also a Roman tesselated pavement and, being impressed by the solidity of the Norman columns, he used the crypt to support the north and south sides of the new St Mary's with consequent problems when it had to be rebuilt again after the 1939–45 War. Wren's rebuilding was completed in 1673 except for the steeple which took another seven years. It was the most expensive of his City churches.

There were modifications in 1867 (galleries removed) and in 1878–9.

On 10th May, 1941 the whole building was engulfed in flames from incendiary bombs. Restoration began in 1956 under the direction of the architect Laurence King and was finished eight years later. This time it was possible to save the steeple but it had first to be taken down and the foundations strengthened; the bells, a semitone lower after being recast, rang out again on 20th December 1961. The rest of the church, including the Norman crypt of which the walls and columns survived, was rebuilt on the structural design of the old building but with modern furnishings.

St Mary-le-Bow has close links with the Province of Canterbury and the City of London. The Court of Arches, the supreme Court of the Province of Canterbury, has continued to meet in the crypt since the 12th century and, until 1847, the whole church came under the Archbishop. The legend that to be a Cockney or true Londoner you must be born within the sound of Bow Bells probably derives from the ringing of the curfew which came to define the City's limits, although the curfew was also rung at All Hallows by the Tower, St Giles', Cripplegate and St Bride's, Fleet Street.

Exterior

The exterior is dominated by the steeple. This rises majestically to the belfry stage, decorated by pairs of Ionic pilasters. Lively corner ornaments of scrolls with vases on top make an easy transition to the spire stages. These consist of a circular colonnade of 12 columns thrusting upwards by means of flying buttresses to a square stage, also with 12 columns, and completed with an obelisk spirelet of Aberdeen granite which is topped by a copper ball and the famous dragon weather-vane nearly nine feet long, all in the most harmonious proportions. The steeple is indeed a masterpiece. (Plate opposite.)

On the north face of the tower, Wren affixed to the second storey a balcony to commemorate the Crown Sild from which royalty in the Middle Ages viewed jousts and other shows. This Sild, or balcony, was built after the collapse of the wooden structure in 1331. On the north and west fronts of the lower storey, Wren introduced fine doorways with much decoration including oval windows and cherubs holding garlands of fruit all enclosed in a rusticated arch.

The west front shows clearly how the steeple is joined to the church by a vestibule. In front is a garden with a statue of Captain John Smith (1580–1631) first among the leaders of the Settlement at Jamestown, Virginia.

St Mary-le-Bow. Steeple

Interior
The interior follows Wren's structure, with arcades of three arches
divided by piers with attached Corinthian half-columns and a broad,
curved elliptical ceiling, divided into panels (mainly green in colour)
and pierced by the clerestory windows. The proportions are almost
square (65 x 63 feet) but given direction by the wrought-iron
parclose screens at the east end which enclose the Norwegian chapel
and sacrament house respectively. There is no division between nave
and chancel.

The internal space has been arranged to suit modern needs with
flexible seating, a free-standing altar and the cross raised aloft. The
impression is one of openness and adaptability with a minimum of
furnishings to enable the church to be used for various purposes as
well as liturgical worship.

The carved corbel heads at the tops of the nave arches represent
people concerned with the rebuilding (bishop, architect etc.).

Furnishings
None of the old furnishings remain. The modern ones consist of:

Organ There was no organ when Wren rebuilt the church.

Pulpits The provision of two pulpits harks back to the early days
when there were separate ambos or reading desks on each side of a
church. This arrangement is admirably suited to the lunch-time
dialogues between the rector and well-known celebrities on topics of
Christian concern which are so much a feature of St Mary-le-Bow
today.

Stained glass Designed by John Hayward and dating from 1964, the
east window shows Christ in majesty; to the north the window depicts
St Mary cradling the church in her arms with representations of the
bombed City churches around, whilst on the other side the window
shows St Paul with the sword of his martyrdom and the book of his
Epistles. Other windows depict the seals of the City in ruby with
St Paul and St Thomas à Becket, who was born in Cheapside; below
appear the arms of the twelve great Livery Companies. They provide a
vivid splash of colour with the green of the lizards in one of the coats
of arms particularly sprightly.

Monuments
Admiral Arthur Phillip In 1992, a handsome memorial to Admiral
Arthur Phillip (1738–1814) was installed on the south-west wall
consisting of a bronze bust by C. L. Hartwell and a plaque. The bust

was originally in St Mildred's Church, Bread Street. Born in Bread
Street nearby, Admiral Phillip was founder and first governor of
Australia.

In the same area are a banner and plaque for the order of Australia.

Joseph McCulloch (1908–1990) and his wife Betty (1911–1982). In
the Norwegian Chapel, a slate oval tablet commemorates Joseph
McCulloch and his wife. The inscription for him reads 'rector and
rebuilder of this church'. He was noted for his dialogues with famous
people and these continue.

Bells Although this book normally does not cover bells, Bow Bells
are so famous that it should be mentioned that there are 12 of them
with names like Katherine, Fabian, Cuthbert etc. and that the Great
Bell of Bow which ends the nursery rhyme 'Oranges and Lemons' was
recast in 1956.

Associations

SPCK The Society for Promotion of Christian Knowledge was
founded in the vestry in 1698.

Trinity Church, Wall Street, New York In 1697, Bishop Compton
obtained a charter from William III for Trinity Church, New York, in
which it was laid down that all should be ordered there 'as it is in our
church of St Mary-le-Bow in London'. This led to an association which
has continued ever since.

Sir Richard Whittington The story of Dick Whittington turning again
upon hearing the bell of Bow may be legendary but there is no doubt
that it could have been heard on Highgate Hill.

General

St Mary-le-Bow could well claim to be the most renowned of the City
parish churches. It has emerged from fires and destruction as strong as
ever with a special affection in the hearts of people all over the world
and with a distinctive place in the ministry of the Church in London.

The following parishes are now annexed to St Mary-le-Bow: St
Pancras Soper Lane, All Hallows Honey Lane, All Hallows Bread
Street, St John the Evangelist Friday Street, St Augustine's Watling
Street, St Faith under St Paul's, St Mildred's Bread Street and St
Margaret Moses.

32 St Mary Woolnoth with St Mary Woolchurch Haw

Dedication
The full mediaeval title was St Mary Woolnoth of the Nativity.
'Woolnoth' is obscure in origin. It could be a corruption of Wulfnoth
who was possibly the first church's founder or it may derive from the
wool market which stood nearby in the Middle Ages, added to the
dedication to distinguish this from other churches called St Mary. A
neighbouring church, St Mary Woolchurch Haw, not rebuilt after the
Great Fire and which used to exist where the Mansion House now
stands, was unmistakably connected with wool.

History
A timber church may have been built here in Saxon times by Wulfnoth
and replaced after the Conquest by a stone one but the first sure
ground is a reference to the 'Parish of Winodmariecherche' about
1198. 'St Mary Wolnoth' is mentioned in 1273. Whatever there was
gave way to a rebuilding about 1440 and, according to the historian
John Stow, another in 1486.

The mediaeval place of worship escaped complete destruction in the
Great Fire, the steeple and part of the walls surviving. Wren rebuilt
the north side facing Lombard Street, and put on a new roof but
otherwise used what remained. This cosmetic treatment was not a
success and the church became so insecure that the parishioners were
afraid to worship in it.

They petitioned the Commissioners under the Fifty Churches Act of
1711 for a new church and, although the Act was designed to
encourage the building of churches where none existed before, they
were successful and obtained Nicholas Hawksmoor as architect.

As usual, he built (between 1716 and 1727) something highly original
and this, although extensively altered by William Butterfield in 1875/6,
has come down to us today. Many attempts have been made to do away
with the church (in 1863,1892,1897,1900 and in the 1920s); in particular
the City and South London Tube Railway tried to acquire the site in 1897
for their station at the Bank but they had to be content with burrowing
underneath, having the bones in the vault removed to Ilford (see
inscription on south wall) and underpinning the church with huge girders.

Exterior
St Mary Woolnoth occupies a prominent position in the hub of the
City. It presents one of the most unusual façades of any church in the

area, massive, uncompromising and of almost fortress-like aspect.
Hawksmoor has concentrated his ingenuity on the west side facing the
open area and the north side facing Lombard Street. The south side
could not be seen before King William Street was cut through in the
19th century. The forecourt to the west face which provides the main
entrance is enclosed by gates dating from *c.* 1900. They were
refurbished in 1991 when new flanking railings were supplied in place
of the former walls which incorporated the now demolished entrance
to the Bank Underground station. Cherubs' head decoration remains
over the old entrances. The lower part of the projecting centre has
banded rustication running right across and curving round the Tuscan
columns at the corners; above, a stage with attached Corinthian
columns extending the full width supports a heavy entablature and
only then does the steeple divide into two low, balustraded turrets.
There are few curves and the impact made is one of mathematical
solidity.

The Lombard Street façade carries three large rusticated niches
enclosing Corinthian columns supported on concave pedestals set
diagonally and carrying an entablature which curves inwards. Above is
a heavy cornice on console brackets. A prominent feature is the
projecting clock, mentioned by T. S. Eliot in '*The Waste Land*.

Interior
The lofty well-lit interior provides a pleasing contrast to the
formidable exterior. The plan is that of a Roman atrium with a square
central area set in a larger square which forms an ambulatory around
it. The inner space is carried up above the roof to create a lantern with
large semicircular windows acting as a clerestory and giving plenty of
light. The ceiling has a gilded rose in the centre which appears to be
original; the star decoration was added by Butterfield. The lantern
rises above an entablature which is carried on groups of three large
Corinthian columns at the corners.

These columns look unduly massive for the relatively small interior,
an impression accentuated by the removal of the galleries which were
considered unsafe by Butterfield. Being too good to discard, the
curious expedient was adopted of affixing them to the walls with their
tapering supports dangling.

At the east end, an imposing black canopy with barley-sugar
columns over the altar, echoing Bernini's famous baldacchine at
St Peter's, Rome is a striking feature. It is squeezed into an arched
recess.

Butterfield raised the chancel using polychrome tiles and took away the high pews. The tiles were covered in the 1950s but, since October 1994, can now be seen again.

Furnishings
Altar-piece This is of oak and carries the Decalogue (Ten Commandments).

Pulpit A Hawksmoor furnishing, square and rather bulgy in outline with panelled sides. Butterfield lowered it and raised the sounding-board which is elevated on square piers, thus creating an absurd relationship between the two.

Organ The original organ was a Father Smith instrument and the case on the west wall is mainly of his time. There is now a second and larger instrument by W. Hill & Son of 1913.

Chandelier From the central rose in the ceiling hangs a handsome brass 16-light candelabra of 1993.

Communion rails These are of wrought-iron and a fine fitting.

Monuments
John Newton A marble tablet on the north wall commemorates John Newton whose ministry led to the abolition of slavery (see *Associations*). The words on the tablet were written by Newton himself.

W. A. Gun, who died in 1806. The monument is situated in the gallery at the west end. It shows a woman standing by an urn.

Edward Norman Butler (1907–63) A tablet on the south wall commemorates this 'Churchwarden, Banker, Goldsmith, Oarsman, Gardener, Antiquary'.

Associations
John Newton St Mary Woolnoth will always be remembered for the ministry of John Newton (1780–1807) who, in his own words on the tablet near the pulpit, was 'once an infidel and libertine' but was 'appointed to preach the faith he had long laboured to destroy'. It was his sermons which inspired William Wilberforce to have slavery abolished.

Some of our most popular hymns – 'Amazing Grace', 'How sweet the name of Jesus sounds', 'Glorious things of Thee are spoken'– – were written by John Newton.

A case contains his biography and other articles associated with him.

Lord Mayors Many Lord Mayors, going as far back as mediaeval times, have contributed generously to rebuildings, restoration and chapels. The bones of no fewer than five lay in the vaults until they were moved to Ilford in 1897 when the Tube line was built. One of the most famous was Sir Martin Bowes, ancestor of the Queen Mother, Lord Mayor in 1545.

Claudius Buchanan According to an inscription near the pulpit, Claudius Buchanan, founder of many Anglican missions in India, owed his conversion to sermons preached here.

Hannah More Hannah More, the originator of cottage meetings, received 'Spiritual inspiration' here.

William Owtram This former rector was one of the eleven clergy who stayed at their posts in the City during the terrible Plague of 1665.

General
Next door to the Mansion House, the church must owe its continued existence to the patronage of the Lord Mayors. It is Nicholas Hawksmoor's only City church and, because of its compactness, is one of the most commanding ecclesiastical buildings of this forceful architect.

It is now a parish church, the parish being known as St Edmund, King and Martyr, and St Mary Woolnoth, Lombard Street, Its work is to provide liturgical worship, opportunity for private prayer, and spiritual direction and counselling.

33 St Michael's, Cornhill

Dedication
St Michael, the leader of the angels against the forces of evil, is sometimes portrayed with the orb and sceptre, symbols of heavenly and earthly rule. In Doom paintings it is often he who weighs souls to assess whether they go up to Heaven or down to Hell. More than 600 churches in this country are dedicated to St Michael.

'Cornhill' is one of the two hills (the other 'Ludgate') which attracted the Romans to found their British capital at London; and John Stow, the historian, refers to the corn market being held there 'time out of mind'.

History
St Michael's is one of the few Saxon foundations in the City, and it is recorded that the living was given by Alnothus the Priest to the Abbot

of Evesham in AD 1055. In 1503 it came into the hands of the
Drapers' Company who have held it ever since. During the Middle
Ages the church received many bequests from distinguished residents
for the saying of masses for their souls and to relieve the poor; there
were as many as five chantries. Stow mentions that there was a cloister
on the south side where members of the choir lived and where there
was a pulpit cross similar to the one at St Paul's. His father,
grandfather and great-grandfather were all buried in the cloister garth.

It was one of the first churches in the City to have pews, dating from
as early as 1475.

It appears to have always had a tower and, before this was rebuilt in
1421, even a spire. The curfew was rung from it for 160 years after that
date. The tower survived the Great Fire and was patched up by Wren
when he rebuilt the church between 1670 and 1677. However, it
became unsafe and in 1715 work started on a new one but came to a
halt for lack of funds in 1717. It was only resumed with the aid of a
grant from the Fifty New Churches Fund, not being finally completed
until 1722, when Wren was 90. The earlier work may have been his
but, after resumption, is generally ascribed to Nicholas Hawksmoor,
who worked in Wren's office, although Gerald Cobb thinks it more
likely that the later work was carried out by another member of his
staff, William Dickenson.

The Cornhill fire of 1748 seriously threatened the steeple. Many
repairs to the fabric took place in the 18th century, especially in 1790
when the windows on the south and east sides were made circular and
various new furnishings including a pulpit installed. The character,
however, of the church today largely stems from a drastic 'restoration'
by Sir George Gilbert Scott between 1858 and 1860 and later in
1867–8.

St Michael's did not suffer in the 1939–45 War and in 1952 some of
the harm done by Scott was corrected, but the church remains
essentially Victorian.

Exterior

Even for the City, St Michael's is hemmed in more than most
churches. From Cornhill there is only an imperfect view of the church's
main feature – the fine, well proportioned 130 ft high Gothic tower –
and at pavement level, buildings obscure all but Scott's over-encrusted
doorway. On the south side, however, a small churchyard remains.

The tower has large angle turrets with panelled and crocketed
pinnacles terminating in foliaged finials with sharp spikes; these once

St Michael's, Cornhill. Pelican in Piety

had vanes. Three-quarters of the way below the top there is a string-course of carved heads, alternately old and young.

The tympanum of Scott's doorway shows St Michael trampling on devils and on the right side is a bronze statue of him by Richard R. Goulden, a memorial to those from the parish killed in the 1914–18 War.

From the south side the round-headed Lombardic aisle and circular clerestory windows give a chapel-like effect.

Interior

The redecorated interior has nave and aisles of four bays in semi-classical style with groined vaulting. The plain arches are carried on Tuscan columns with low bases. Ceiling decoration is confined to transverse bands of rosettes. The chancel slightly projects. Scott's mark is left in the Lombard-type tracery of the windows, the stained glass, the choir, the pink marble reredos of mainly Italian design, the black and white tiles on the floor and the carved wooden angels with wings below the corbels. He cast out the old Communion rails, which found their way to Great Waldingfield in Suffolk. He also covered the walls with polychrome decoration, but this has been whitewashed over and none of the polychrome decoration can now be seen from the church. The windows were lightened and he engaged W. Gibbs Rogers to work on the pews; he, as at St Mary at Hill, did excellent work.

Furnishings

The only original furnishings are the font, part of the organ and the altar-table.

Pelican On a pedestal at the west end is this magnificent bird carved in wood standing on its nest and feeding its young. (Plate p. 137). It is very large and one of the finest examples of this emblem of sacrifice, the long curved bill being particularly well executed. It was supplied through George Paterson, a painter, in 1775.

Organ Originally Renatus Harris but enlarged in 1790 and subsequently altered several times, but retaining nine of the original Harris stops. The organ was rebuilt in 1976 and again improved in 1993. The church has a fine tradition of organ playing and Purcell may have used this instrument. Amongst organists known to have played on it were Dr Harold Darke, the composer William Boyce who wrote 'Hearts of Oak', and Dr Theodore Aylward. William Boyce was Master of the King's Music and another organist's (Richard Limpus, 1824–75) 'zeal and devotion led to the foundation of the Royal College of Organists, which was established in 1864.' It is not surprising, therefore, that St Michael's is held in such high esteem in musical circles.

Bench-ends These were carved by Rogers and repay detailed examination. At the west end of the south aisle can be found the Scapegoat with the mark of the High Priest on its forehead (taken from Holman Hunt's picture) and the Return from Egypt after Herod's death; in the north aisle there is a figure of Charity feeding and protecting three children, and another Pelican.

Pulpit and Lectern These are also Rogers' work. The lectern won a prize at the great exhibition of 1851.

Altar-table The original late 17th century oak table remains.

Monuments

John Newman, died 1615. The monument is a demi-figure 'elegantly gesticulating' (Pevsner).

John Vernon, who died in 1616. This monument, high up on the north wall, is also in the form of a half-length figure and replaces one destroyed in the Great Fire. It bears the cartouche of the Merchant Taylors' Company, of which he was a Master.

Cowper family Near the south-west door in the vestibule are monuments of three of the illustrious ancestors of William Cowper, the poet.

Stained glass Early Clayton and Bell work (1858) of good quality. It depicts the life of our Lord on earth from Annunciation to Crucifixion and Glory.

Associations

Thomas Gray, the author of Gray's *Elegy*, was baptised here in 1716.

Coffee-house The first coffee-house to be opened in England was situated in St Michael's Alley and in 1657, when it was introduced, a tent was pitched in the churchyard for the sale of coffee.

City Companies The Drapers, the Merchant Taylors, the Woolmen, the Master Mariners, the Upholders and Water Conservators, and the Guild of Air Pilots and Air Navigators all attend their annual Election-day services here.

General

St Michael's shares with St Mary Aldermary the distinction of having the only purely Gothic steeple in an existing Wren church, although the tower of St Alban's, Wood Street remains. It also shares with

St Mary's the dubious distinction of being one of the most
Victorianised churches in the City and, even allowing for the
brightening of the interior since the War, the harm done by insensitive
restoration cannot be undone.

The Rector's main ministry is to people working in the vicinity,
principally the stockbroking and Lloyd's underwriting fraternities, as
the Rector is also the Chaplain to the Stock Exchange.

St Michael's musical reputation continues high and many memorial
services for the City are conducted in the church no doubt because of
its reputation for good music. Two other parishes (St Benet Fink and
St Peter le Poer) were incorporated some time ago, after demolition of
their churches in 1844 and 1907 respectively.

34 St Michael Paternoster Royal

Dedication
The archangel Michael (the name means 'who is like God') is the
leader of the forces of good against the forces of evil represented by
Lucifer, the Fallen Angel of light. He is sometimes portrayed as in the
centre light of the east window – as thrusting Lucifer down with a
lance.

'Paternoster' refers to Paternoster Lane, where rosaries used to be
made and 'Royal' comes from the town of La Reole near Bordeaux
from which merchants in the City imported wine as early as 1282. A
neighbouring church, destroyed in the Great Fire and not rebuilt –
St Martin Vintry – also recalled the wine trade.

History
St Michael's is first mentioned about 1219 when it was referred to as
'St Michael of Paternosterchierch' and was also included in a list of
churches for taxation compiled by Pope Nicholas IV in 1291. In 1361,
the church was called 'S. Michael in the Riole'.

Its mediaeval fame, however, will always rest upon its being
Sir Richard Whittington's church. In 1409, this admirable four-times
Lord Mayor (to whom however the legend of Dick Whittington and
his cat did not attach until nearly 200 years later), who lived next door,
provided funds for the building of a new church. He also founded, for
the saying of prayers for his soul and the souls of his family and
benefactors, a College of Priests adjacent, from which College Hill gets

St Michael Paternoster Royal

its name. In 1424, masters of the College became rectors of
St Michael's. It was dissolved in 1540.

Sir Richard was buried in the church when he died in 1423 but his
body has more than once been disturbed and now cannot be found.
Efforts made in 1949 to locate his tomb only produced a mummified
cat which, however, was unlikely to have been Sir Richard's, the
church with his monument having gone up in flames during the Great
Fire – it was rebuilt under Sir Christopher Wren between 1686 and
1694 except for the steeple, which was not completed until 1713.

The usual Victorian 'doing-over' was carried out in 1866 by the
ubiquitous William Butterfield, ostensibly in memory of Whittington.

St Michael's survived the early air-raids of the 1939–45 War but
unfortunately fell to a flying bomb in 1944. After some opposition
from the diocese and the Royal Fine Arts Commission which was
overcome by the City Corporation, it was restored by Elidir L. W.
Davies, designer of the Mermaid Theatre, the Whittington Hall being
added at the west end. Re-consecration took place in December 1968.
The area south of the building has been laid out as the Whittington
Garden.

No longer a parish church, nor made into a Guild church, the tower
and west end have been converted for use as the headquarters of the
Missions to Seamen, and the status of St Michael's is that of a chapel
under the Bishop of London, the parish being joined to that of
St James Garlickhythe nearby. The transfer of the parish carried with
it the parishes of St Martin Vintry and All Hallows the Less (not
rebuilt after the Great Fire), St Michael's, Queenhithe, All Hallows
the Great and Holy Trinity the Less (demolished).

Exterior

The exterior shows a simple building of stone with tall roundheaded
windows and a tower in the south-west corner. The windows have the
nice little touch of cherubs' heads as keystones. There is a strong
cornice which carries on round the tower and binds it to the body of
the church. The steeple (plate p. 141) is plain in the lower parts but as
at St James's Garlickhythe next door and St Stephen's, Walbrook,
Wren has exercised his ingenuity in the top stages, all three displaying
varying examples of his skill. At St Michael's they form an appealing
composition, consisting of a recessed octagon carried round in a circle
with eight columns at the angles, each with its own entablature, above
which is a small octagon with a domed top stage and weathervane. The

tower has square-headed windows at belfry level with a pierced parapet on top. The whole steeple is just over 128 feet high.

Interior

A simple rectangle without aisles measuring 67 x 47 feet. The walls are panelled. Some of the original furnishings remain despite war damage. There is a west gallery supporting the organ (dating from 1749) with coat of arms.

Furnishings

The woodwork is fine.

Candelabrum The single candelabrum is an exceptionally fine piece and unusually early. It is marked 'Birmingham, 1644'. This came from All Hallows the Great.

Sword-rests The gilded sword-rests are for the Lord Mayor's sword of state on the north side and, on the other side, for the hats of his attendants.

Altar-piece, Pulpit, Lectern, Door-cases These are all original, carved in wood. The pulpit has a canopy. The figure in front of the lectern represents Charity. It is a copy of one which came from All Hallows but which was stolen. The copy was made by the Master Craftsman of St Paul's Cathedral. There are altar-rails with turned balusters on three sides of the sanctuary, which is unusual.

Moses and Aaron These figures on the east wall also came from All Hallows the Great.

Stained glass The glass destroyed in the War has been replaced by interesting modern glass by John Hayward. The theme is the confrontation between good and evil.

The westernmost window on the south side depicts the young Whittington at the base, complete with cat, and above, the City with streets paved with gold and at the top in red the seal of the Mayor with heraldry on either side.

Monument

Sir Samuel Pennant died whilst Lord Mayor in 1750 from jail-fever contracted from prisoners in the dock. Such hazards led to sweetsmelling herbs being placed in docks to guard against infection.

Associations

The chief associations with Sir Richard Whittington are recorded under 'History'.

Peter Blundell, founder of the famous school near Tiverton, Devon, familiar to readers of *Lorna Doone*, was buried here in 1601.

General
The uninterrupted view from the south due to the layout of the Whittington Garden and the careful restoration of the building adds to the pleasure of visiting this church.

35 St Nicholas Cole Abbey

Dedication
The popular but little-documented St Nicholas, beloved of children as Santa Claus, was Bishop of Myra in Asia Minor during the first half of the 4th century. The patron saint of travellers and seamen, nearly four hundred churches are dedicated to him in this country, mainly round the coast.

The origin of 'Cole Abbey' is obscure. The most widely accepted theory is that it is a corruption of 'Cold Harbour', a mediaeval type of lodging house, and that such an establishment existed nearby.

History
The church is mentioned in a letter of Pope Lucius II in 1144 and in 1272–3 it is called 'Sci Nichi retro fihstrate' (St Nicholas behind Fish Street), a reminder of the pre-Billingsgate fish market which used to exist here. The historian Stow records that, in Elizabeth's reign, a lead and stone cistern fed by lead pipes from the Thames and donated by a rich fishmonger was set up against the north wall of the church 'for the care and commodity of the Fishmongers in and about Old Fish Street'. Many of them were buried at St Nicholas'.

The steeple and south aisle were rebuilt in 1377 and, at the time of the Reformation, there were three chantries served by chantry priests. A carved stone head from the mediaeval church found during the 1962 restoration lies behind panelling near the south-west door.

More than once renovated in the early part of the 17th century when new battlements were added to the steeple, it was one of the first churches to be rebuilt by Wren after the Fire, the work being started in 1671 and completed in 1677. During the 19th century, rearrangements were carried out in 1874.

In more recent times the fabric was so blackened by smoke issuing through a vent from steam trains of the underground railway which

St Nicholas Cole Abbey. Trumpet-shaped spire with ship vane

passed beneath, that the church came to be called 'St Nicholas Cole Hole Abbey'.

Gutted by fire-bombs in May 1941, restoration in the Wren style was completed by Arthur Bailey in 1962.

Patronage during the 16th century passed from St Martin-le-Grand through various hands and, in the following century, was for a time with a Puritan Colonel Hacker, one of the Charles I regicides who was beheaded at the Restoration.

Exterior

Before Queen Victoria Street was built between 1861 and 1871, St Nicholas' lay in a narrow street and entrance was from the north side, but now the church stands out prominently at the top of the road which runs beside the podium, now tidied up and planted, on the south side after the bomb devastation. There is no clerestory but a handsome balustrade encircles the top and the round-headed windows have a refinement of straight hoods supported on console brackets. Those on the south side, built of Portland stone, used to have shops hard up against them.

The north-west steeple consists of a low tower with good belfry windows but under skimpy pediments rising above the cornice, and a rather endearing inverted trumpet-shaped spire (see plate p. 145).

This, with many round and oval lunettes, was destroyed in 1941 but has been rebuilt; the slightly concave sides are surmounted by a balcony similar to the one at St Martin's, Ludgate, and is crowned by a delightful vane in the form of a ship which was once at St Michael's Queenhithe (demolished in 1876). The spire has also been likened to a lighthouse – perhaps in deference to St Nicholas.

Interior

An open, rectangular box without divisions of any kind. The walls, apart from gilt Corinthian pilasters and panelling, are perfectly plain and without colour; but the light woodwork of the furnishings, which include some which were rescued, and the decorative treatment provide plenty of life.

A screen at the west end containing some of the original panels and richly carved with fruit and flowers shuts off the stairs to the organ gallery, vestry and base of the tower. The east end is made striking by the rather dark glass of Keith New and the elaborate gilt adornment of swags, fruit, flowers and cherubs' heads with a chalice over the altar.

Furnishings

Doorcases The three west doorways and the main entrance on the south are liberally supplied with cherubs' heads, which abound in this church. Carvings from the former reredos are to be seen above the south doorway.

Font The richly and beautifully carved font cover with ogee supports carrying a crown is original.

Royal Arms These are the Arms of Charles II.

*Chandelier A splendid example and also original.

Pulpit Another Wren furnishing, elaborately carved but without tester.

Stained glass The three east windows by Keith New, dating from 1962, depict in the form of rivers the rôle of the church (shown as an Ark) in spreading the Gospel throughout the world with the help of the Seven Gifts of the Holy Spirit.

Organ The original instrument dated 1779 was disposed of and replaced by the present new one.

Associations

Plague Ninety-one out of the 125 parishioners died in the 1665 Plague – an appalling proportion.

George Whitefield, the great Methodist preacher, delivered his sermon on Profane Swearing here in 1737.

Bowyers' Company In the north-east corner, a brass plaque commemorates a famous Bowyer, James Wood, who was buried here in 1629.

Thomas Sowdley, who was vicar here during the reign of Edward VI, obtained a licence to marry. For this he was probably deprived during the reign of Queen Mary but came back again as soon as Queen Elizabeth ascended the throne, thus becoming the church's first married incumbent.

He hawked his wife round the streets during Mary's reign to try and rid himself of what had then become an embarrassment.

General

This is an interesting little church, now leased to the Free Church of Scotland although ownership remains Anglican.

The former parish which used to include St Mary Mounthaw, St Mary Somerset and St Peter's, Paul's Wharf (all disappeared except the tower of St Mary Somerset) has been transferred to St Andrew by the Wardrobe.

36 St Olave's, Hart Street and All Hallows Staining
with St Katherine Coleman

Dedication

Olave Haraldson was a popular figure in early 11th century London because he helped the English king, Ethelred the Unrede, to throw back the Danes. At the Battle of London Bridge in 1014, he fastened cables round the supporting piles and pulled the bridge from under the invaders. Later he became king of Norway, where he was killed in battle in 1030 by nobles opposed to his forceful propagation of Christianity.

'Staining' may indicate an early use of stone instead of timber for building churches, or refer to a holding belonging to the manor of Staines. 'Coleman' was possibly the name of the builder of St Katherine's (pulled down in 1925 after being rebuilt in 1734).

History

The dedication to St Olave would argue that there was a place of worship here in Saxon times but first mention is not until 1222, when the church was called 'St Olave towards the Tower'. A ribbed- and groin-vaulted crypt of about 1250 with the unusual accompaniment of a well remains; it is used as a chapel.

Most, however, of what we see today is basically mid-15th century, when two fellmongers (skinners), Richard and Robert Cely, contributed generously to the rebuilding of the church, following the current plan of nave, aisles, clerestory and large east window.

Pews with their own outside staircase for the Navy Office, then in Seething Lane, were installed in 1661 on the south side and, in the following year, the present vestry was added.

Admiral Sir William Penn (father of the founder of Pennsylvania) and Samuel Pepys used their influence to save St Olave's in the Great Fire of 1666 by having houses in the path of destruction blown up so that this church was one of the few to escape destruction.

In 1731–2, a brick top was placed on the tower by John Widdows and a new east window was installed in 1822 but, apart from the attentions of Sir Gilbert Scott in 1863 and Sir Arthur Blomfield in 1873 (the Navy Office pews had been removed in 1853), St Olave's remained relatively intact until April/May 1941 when it was hit by four bombs.

Work on restoration started in 1951 when King Haakon VI of

St Olave's, Hart St. Entrance gates to former burial ground – 'St Ghastly Grim'

Norway laid a dedication stone, next to which is a fragment of Nidaros Cathedral, Trondheim, and the church was re-hallowed for use in April 1954. The architect was Ernest Glanfield.

Exterior
A typical, low-roofed, 15th century church of ragstone with a southwest tower. The bell-turret was enlarged after the War and a south porch added.

The clock came in 1891 from All Hallows Staining (demolished 1870). The 15th century tower of All Hallows still stands in Mark Lane.

One of the most striking features is the churchyard gate of 1658 in Seething Lane (see plate, p. 149) with its skulls, crossbones and spikes called by Charles Dickens (see *Associations*) 'St Ghastly Grim'. It has a large segmental pediment.

The entrance to the old South Gallery and Navy Office Pew is marked with an inscription.

Interior
The walls and most of the arcades survived the bombing and the structure has been carefully restored to its original state. The wide arcade is of three bays with columns of Purbeck limestone (not the more familiar so-called marble) separating nave from aisles. There is no division between the nave and chancel. The rebuilt low-pitched roof, unchanged by the Victorian restorers, was constructed in 1632; it is panelled and has bosses at the intersections.

Aisle windows consist of three pointed lights under depressed arches and the large unorthodox 1822 window remains at the east end with new glass.

A fortunate survival from the bombing was the 1662 vestry which has a 15th century doorcase and a delightful stucco ceiling with fine panelling (it came from St Katherine Coleman) and adorned in the centre with an angel in an oval.

Furnishings
Organ A new instrument hides behind the western screen.

Font The attractive and well-designed font replaces a Victorian one. It is moveable and made out of Canadian hardwoods. It was a gift for the post-War restoration from St Olave's Church, Toronto in gratitude for receiving a font from St Olave, Hart Street when their church was being built between the Wars.

St Katherine Coleman

Pulpit This late 17th century furnishing stands on a wooden base and was saved by being stored in the crypt of St Paul's Cathedral during the war. It was once in St Benet's, Gracechurch Street.

Communion rails These are contemporary with the pulpit; they have twisted balusters and are decorated with three little lions.

Stained glass With the exception of the Churchwardens' window in the north aisle, all the stained glass is post-war dating from 1953 by A. E. Buss. St Olave can be seen in the left light of the east window.

Monuments

There is much of interest; some are brightly coloured.

Sir John Radcliffe, died 1568 and wife. Fragments of him recumbent and his wife kneeling remain in the north aisle.

Peter Cappone, died 1582. A kneeling figure.

James Deane, died 1608 and wife. They are shown kneeling under an arch and between columns with gilt Corinthian capitals. Attractive designs in the corners.

Two children in chrysoms lying on a skull (indicating that they died soon after birth) and looking like small mummies are placed pathetically below. This monument is perched above the vestry door.

Andrew, died 1610 and *Paul Bayninge*, died 1616. To the left of the sanctuary and against the wall there is this interesting but somewhat comical monument to the two Bayninge brothers, both Aldermen of the City. Their hands are raised beseechingly and, being set on a circle, they look like figures on a clock.

Elizabeth Pepys, died 1669. Next to the brothers and in the northeast corner is a frontal bust erected by Samuel Pepys to his long-suffering wife with the inscription that says she bore no children because she could bear none worthy of herself. By John Bushnell, it was stored in St Paul's crypt during the War.

Samuel Pepys He outlived his wife by over 30 years and died in 1703. There was no memorial until Sir Arthur Blomfield designed one based on Pepys' portrait in the National Portrait Gallery. It was placed on the south wall in 1884 where the old Navy Office pew used to be. A pew end on this side has been carved with a replica of the Navy Office Verge (wand or staff of office).

Pepys was buried beside the Communion Table, alongside his wife.

Sir Andrew Riccard, died 1672. Kneeling being no longer fashionable by this date for memorials, Sir Andrew is shown in a standing posture in the north aisle.

Brasses There are several 17th century brasses.

Associations
Rev John Letts' daughter A tablet on the tower records the remarkable
escape from death of the daughter of a rector, who fell from the top
floor of the rectory to the basement stones below.

  Charles Dickens, in his *Uncommercial Traveller* writes of the
churchyard of St Ghastly Grim with affection, despite his name for it.
He refers to its 'ferocious strong spiked iron gate, like a jail'.

  Clothworkers' Company St Olave's has close associations with this
Company which holds its annual service here and whose arms appear
in a south aisle window. They transferred the old Norman crypt, now
at All Hallows Staining, from Islington, where it lay under Lamb's
Chapel, and also provided the present church hall.

General
This small church is a precious survival of a typical City mediaeval
place of worship, one of only the very few remaining. Still an active
parish church, it will long be remembered for that lovable diarist with
a roving eye who told us so much about the London of his day and
carried out so efficiently and honestly his important duties as Secretary
to the Admiralty. Pepys referred to St Olave's as 'our own church'.

37 St Peter upon Cornhill

Cornhill
'Cornhill' was one of the two hills upon which the Romans founded
London. The corn market, according to John Stow the historian, was
held here 'time out of mind'.

History
A brass tablet in the north-east vestry which is probably an early 18th
century copy of a 14th century plate states that St Peter's was founded
by King Lucius in AD 179 and that it was 'the Metropolitan and chief
church of this kingdom' for 400 years until St Augustine moved it to
Canterbury. Whatever may be the truth of this – there was certainly a
Bishop Restitutus of London who attended the Council of Arles in
AD 314 and may have come from St Peter's. In any case, it has stood
the church in good stead for, despite rival claims, the rector of St
Peter's had precedence in the mediaeval Whit Monday procession to
St Paul's Cathedral which actually used to start at St Peter's. In more
recent times St Peter's, because of its importance, was specifically

excluded from the operation of the Union of Benefices Act of 1860 and therefore saved from demolition and had no other parishes joined to it. The church, with what William Kent called 'holy boldness', celebrated its 1700th anniversary in 1879 and 1800th in 1979.

First mention goes back to pre-Conquest times when, about 1040, it was called 'St Peter binnon London'. As with its neighbour, St Michael's, there were many chantries and St Peter's had its quota of Lord Mayors' burials; altogether seven altars existed. It was a sanctuary for fugitives from justice.

Another indication of its importance was that one of the four grammar schools in the City, founded in 1425 (refounded by Henry VI in 1447), was established at St Peter's and there was also an important library attached to this church. The school continued until the 18th century.

There was a Brotherhood and Guild of St Peter's connected with the Fishmongers' Company founded for religious observances.

In addition to a main square tower there was a battlemented turret at the south-east corner.

All but the base of the tower was destroyed in the Great Fire. Wren turned his attention to the rebuilding of St Peter's between 1677 and 1681 and it was reopened the following year. A curious vestry minute of St Michael's, 24th April 1679, resolves: 'That leave be given to the Parson of St Peter's to walk in the churchyard'. Presumably his own was out of use at this time.

The Victorians did not interfere greatly. In 1872, J. D. Wyatt repaved and provided reseating in the church and some highly coloured glass in the east window.

Exterior

St Peter's is best viewed from the south and east. On the north side, as at St Michael's, nothing can be seen except the entrance. St Peter's also has a little churchyard in the south from which one can see that the exterior materials are painted stone, dark red brick and copper.

The principal façade, which has no doors, is the eastern one facing Gracechurch Street. Wren had to give up 10 feet on this side for road-widening but, in view of its importance, made it more ornamental than usual. Five uniform arched windows on the ground floor, separated by pilasters, are surmounted by an upper floor with one arched and two circular windows, and the whole is capped by a pediment. Carved pieces join the upper to the lower floor in Italian fashion.

The 140-ft high steeple retains its pre-Fire lower stage of brick. The upper part of the tower has three round-headed louvre windows on each side, above which rises the harmonious group of small dome, lantern and obelisk spire all covered in copper. There are many string-courses on the tower giving horizontal emphasis.

A carved, gilded figure of St Peter with keys can be seen on the churchyard gate.

Interior

The south door gives access to the vestibule under the organ gallery, with the main body of the church, of which the east and west walls are not parallel, on the right. The atmosphere is one of homely comfort and warmth enhanced by some excellent furnishings. Five bays separate the tunnel-vaulted nave from the narrow aisles, which have transverse tunnel vaults opening out into the nave and their own arches. The panelled ceiling is attractively decorated with plaster designs.

Pillars with Corinthian capitals become pilasters further up, showing where the former galleries existed. Their high panelled bases are on a level with the wall panelling which extends to the height of the windowsills.

Furnishings

The following are the main furnishings of interest:

Doorcases Four fine doorcases in the vestibule are contemporary with Wren's rebuilding. They have Corinthian pilasters.

Table A notable 17th century long wooden table, now in the vestibule, was once used for Holy Communion by Puritans.

Chest An ornate Hanoverian chest is placed against the wall behind the font.

Bread-shelves Affixed to the wall above the table in the vestibule are capacious bread-shelves once used for storage and distribution of bread to the poor.

Organ Originally 'Father Smith' (1681) but much altered. The gallery and case date from the same time. The original keyboard upon which Mendelssohn played in 1840, leading him to pronounce the organ as 'the finest in London' and on which he has left his autograph dated 1st September 1840, is in the organ loft.

Pews Two high pews of the old Wren seating remain, forming a break between the vestibule and the nave, but the rest of the pews were removed in a reordering executed in 1990. A new tiled floor was laid skilfully matching the Victorian flooring in the side aisles and seating is provided by chairs.

Pulpit A fine large furnishing with stairs and a big tester. It was as usual lowered by the Victorians.

*Chancel-screen The pièce de résistance; it is one of only two from Wren's time in the City and the only one in its original setting. (St Margaret's Lothbury has the other but this was originally in All Hallows the Great.) Wren was not in favour of screens and we owe its presence to the insistence of the rector at the time of the reopening, William Beveridge (later Bishop of St Asaph). He emphasised the special sanctity of the chancel and the desirability of privacy for communicants. The design is said to be by Wren and his sixteen-year-old daughter. The sections are divided by very thin shafts whilst the centre curves up and is flanked by broad, fluted pilasters. There is a Royal Arms of Charles II in front.

Reredos Also contemporary with the Wren rebuilding but less ornamental than usual. It has the uncommon decoration of the Lamb of Sacrifice with the sun or morning star shining forth from it and burning in its rays the sacred name of Jehovah.

Communion rails Date uncertain. They have balusters in the shape of Doric pillars.

Font Made of marble, octagonal and with leaf decoration growing up the upper part of the stem. It also dates from 1681 but the cover is said to have escaped the Great Fire and therefore to be earlier. The font and its cover were both restored by the St Paul's Cathedral workshop in 1988 and have been placed under the bracket in the south-east corner where the font may previously have stood. The bracket may now be used to raise and lower the cover.

Monument

Appropriately on the south wall of the baptistry is a poignant circular memorial with seven cherubs' heads to seven children of James Woodmanson, who all died in 1782 in a fire at their home whilst their father was at a ball in St James's Palace.

Associations

George Borrow, traveller, linguist and author, was married here in 1840.

Charles Dickens The churchyard of St Peter's has been identified as the churchyard where Lizzie Hexham received the unwelcome attentions of Bradley Headstone in the novel *Our Mutual Friend*.

The Poulters Company and the *Lime Street Ward Club* hold annual services here.

British Sailors Society The church is associated with the British Sailors Society.

General

St Peter's has an attractive interior with outstanding woodwork. Extensive conservation was carried out in 1988 under the direction of Geoffrey Claridge RIBA of Chichester who also directed the subsequent reordering. Although in law remaining at present a parish church it is used extensively by the Proclamation Trust, which organises an annual course of Bible Study specifically designed for future preachers. No regular services are held and the church can only be visited by prior arrangement. It is the Regimental Church of the Royal Tank Regiment whose arms may be seen in the memorial windows to the fallen of that regiment on the north side while, on the south side, there are windows and memorials to the fallen of Gough's Fifth Army, the Bedfordshire and Hertfordshire Regiment and the Devonshire Regiment.

38 St Sepulchre without Newgate

Dedication

This place of worship was dedicated to St Edmund until the Crusades. The name 'Sepulchre' then began to appear. The church served an order of crusading knights who kept the Augustinian Rule and it may be that its position just outside the north-west gate of the City corresponding almost exactly with the position of the Jerusalem Church, built over the site of the Sepulchre and Calvary, may have had an influence. In any case, there was an inn called the Saracen's Head next to the church which could have served any crusading knights who may have started their journey from the church. It is now generally called St Sepulchre or St Sepulchre without Newgate.

'Inside there is a model of the Church of the Holy Sepulchre in Jerusalem.

History

First mention was in AD 1137 when Rahere, the Prior of St Bartholomew's, Smithfield granted the living to Hagno the Clerk. Whatever then existed was rebuilt in the middle of the 15th century at the expense of Sir John Popham, Chancellor of Normandy and Treasurer to the Household of King Henry VI. The historian, Stow, states that this magnificent patron also added a handsome chapel on the south side. There were a number of fraternities linked to the church and many chantry chapels.

Although a gilt cherub high up on a wall at Pye Corner where the adjacent Giltspur Street and Cock Lane meet is supposed to mark the spot where the Great Fire burned itself out (started in Pudding Lane and ended in Pye Corner), this did not save Holy Sepulchre, as the church was then called, from being all but destroyed. It had to be rebuilt and this was completed in 1670, although the money (£4,993. 4s. 0d) was not handed over until 1677; Sir Christopher Wren had delayed granting the certificate which enabled the vestry to claim the rebuilding money from the Commissioners.

Subsequently, the building was subject to changing tastes and fashions. In 1790, the exterior including the porch was remodelled with round-headed windows to conform with the interior and the fifteenth century battlements were taken down, but, less than a hundred years later in the restoration of 1873–79 the Gothic windows and the battlements were put back again. So far as the tower was concerned, the original intention was to reface the whole tower, which would not have resulted in the rebuilt pinnacles looking top-heavy as they in fact do. This was due to a change of architects with unfortunate results. Internally, the round-headed arches were taken out from under the tower and the 15th century arches were restored. Galleries and pews were removed. The ceiling, however, is of 1834.

As presently ordered, the interior owes a great deal of its appearance to the work of Sir Charles Nicholson. Much of the stained glass is the work of his brother, Archibald Nicholson.

St Sepulchre's survived the 1939–45 War intact except for minor damage. It was redecorated in 1967.

Exterior

St Sepulchre's presents a Perpendicular exterior in Victorian dress, complete with battlements, tall sturdy tower of ragstone and three-storeyed porch. The oversize pinnacles are crocketed.

The tower is in four stages with angle buttresses terminating at the third stage and windows (paired at the top) with ogee crocketed hood-moulds. There is a balustrade and the pinnacles are panelled. The aisles, faced externally in Portland stone, are continued alongside the tower and there is an attractive 17th century sundial on the south aisle parapet.

A watch-house used for deterring body-snatchers (destroyed in the War) was rebuilt in 1962.

Interior
The interior of the porch is the most impressive mediaeval feature as its fan groined vaulting with cusps and liernes reaches right down to the floor. Seventeen carved bosses are placed at the intersection of ribs.

The main body of this largest of City parish churches, measuring 150 by 162 feet, has an air of dignified spaciousness. Being outside the walls and serving a large parish, there was more available land than inside the crowded city. Tall classical round-headed arcades of seven bays supported on Tuscan columns with high plinths exposed by removal of box-pews separate the nave from the north and south aisles. The 1834 nave ceiling is flat and deeply coffered with gilt domes; the aisle ceilings are groined and there is no division between nave and chancel.

The north chapel was originally dedicated to St Stephen but, after 1939–45 War, was made over to the Musicians and is now known as the Musicians' Chapel.

At the west end of the north aisle in front of the City of London Rifles memorial are a few small tiles which Wren used in the rebuilt Christ Church, Newgate after the Fire but when Christ Church was itself gutted by incendiaries in the 1939–45 War, the tiles were moved to St Sepulchre and relaid in the church in 1967.

On the south side is the Regimental Chapel of the Royal Fusiliers, the City of London Regiment, and, just in front of this, the calcined remains of a piscina with parts of a shelf for cruets and a drain. Being almost opposite the door to the rood-loft high up on the north wall, it is clear that the piscina would have been next to the former rood-screen.

Furnishings
Starting with the vestibule, the main furnishings of interest are:

Font and font-cover At the north end of the vestibule is a finely carved cover of 1690 on a white pedestal which at one time was in Christ Church, Newgate but which was rescued from the burning building by an unknown postman on the night of the 30th/31st December 1940 raid.

St Sepulchre's own font, at the West end of the south aisle, is an

attractive marble furnishing with baluster stem and fluted bowl
adorned with cherubs' heads which was given by a parishioner in 1670.
The cover is octagonal.

Pews Fragments of 17th century pews incorporated in the
churchwardens' pews remain at the west end.

Pulpit and Reading desk These were designed in 1854 and cost £241
for the pair. They replaced a huge 1830 3-decker pulpit with a
parabolic sounding board.

Organ After the Great Fire, Renatus Harris built an organ in the
west gallery; the rather spectacular case is virtually all that is left of it.
The organ was altered and enlarged many times over the years and, in
1879, it was moved to the north chapel. Later it fell into decay but part
of it was rebuilt in its present position by Harrison and Harrison in
1932.

Altar-rails and sword-rest These are fine early 18th century wrought-
iron examples.

Reredos This is a plain example with fluted gilt pilasters and
embroidered panels of Wren period; it has a segmental head.

Royal Arms There is a Hanoverian Royal Arms at the west end of
the south aisle.

Painting East of the rood-loft door is a copy of Raphael's 'The
Marriage of the Virgin'. The original, painted in 1504, is in Milan.

Stone Built into the north-east pillar is a stone presented in 1963 by
the Church of the Holy Sepulchre, Jerusalem.

Bells Although these are only occasionally covered in this book, the
famous bells of Old Bailey are within the tower. The oldest extant
ones date from 1739 but there were bells in the tower long before the
Great Fire for, after the Dissolution of the Monasteries, five bells came
from the Priory Church of St Bartholomew the Great in Smithfield.
The present ring of twelve was restored and rehung in 1985 after
having been silent since 1939.

Monuments

Many attractive memorials are draped around pillars and set on walls.
Worthy of especial note is the one to *Edward Arris* (d. 1676) and wife.
This memorial is in the form of two frontal busts in circular niches and
is on the south wall near the font.

Associations

Newgate Prison Where the Central Criminal Court of the Old Bailey
now stands was once Newgate Gaol. The greatest bell of St Sepulchre

continued to be rung at public executions outside Newgate until 1868 and thereafter (when executions were inside) until 1897. The sexton would also ring his handbell (in a glass case by the south-east pillar) outside the victim's cell at midnight on the day of his execution and recite admonitory lines. These 'services' were paid from a sum of £50 given in 1605 by Robert Dowe for this purpose.

Smithfield Martyrs John Rogers who was rector from 1550 to 1555 was the first Protestant martyr to be burned at Smithfield in 1555.

Robert Ascham, the beloved tutor of Lady Jane Grey and Queen Elizabeth, was buried here in 1677.

Resurrection Men During the 18th century, the burial ground of St Sepulchre's was a convenient place for the resurrection men to ply their macabre trade. It was the source for specimens for hospital anatomy lectures at St Bartholomew's; these were left at the inn opposite, labelled with the dealer's name, to be collected the following morning. The Watch House erected to defeat their ends was built in 1791.

Musicians' Chapel As a boy, Sir Henry Wood learned to play the organ in this church and became Assistant Organist at the age of 14. His ashes were brought here in 1944 and lie under the central window to St Cecilia, the patron saint of music.

Kneelers and furnishings are practically all connected with musicians. The windows are in memory of St Stephen Harding (there is a St Bernard dog to remind one that he introduced St Bernard to the Cistercian Order): of John Ireland showing scenes from his life and of Dame Nellie Melba with peaches at the bottom right-hand corner to remind us that she gave her name to her favourite dish – Pèche Melba. The east Magnificat window above the altar commemorates Walter Carrel.

Sir Malcolm Sargent The blue carpeting, some kneelers and one of the altar frontals in the sanctuary were given in 1969 in memory of Sir Malcolm Sargent.

Captain John Smith The brass plate on the south wall of the choir is a copy of the one (no longer identifiable) which originally marked the spot where he was buried. It records his adventures when he was reputed to have cut off the heads of three Turkish champions in individual combat as a soldier in Hungary and his rescue from death by the Princess Pocahontas. He later became the first effective Governor of Virginia and Admiral of New England. A window on the south side is also in memory of him.

Regiments At the west end of the north aisle is a War Memorial and

Book of Remembrance to the 6th City of London Fusiliers ('The Cast-Iron Sixth') and on the other side the Regimental Chapel and Book of Remembrance of the Royal Fusiliers who are also commemorated by the Memorial Garden of Remembrance outside.

General

Although only just mediaeval, St Sepulchre's will always attract visitors because of its musical traditions and its rich associations. The present Royal School of Music owes a large part of its origin to St Sepulchre's when Sir Sidney Nicholson was organist in the early '70s. For many years until 1989 the Annual Festival of St Cecilia was held in St Sepulchre's.

The ancient parish lay outside the City wall ('without-Newgate') although it was mostly within the City boundary, part of it extending into the County of Middlesex. In 1954, the parish boundaries were altered to include the former parish of Christ Church with St Leonard, Foster Lane.

39 St Stephen's, Walbrook

Walbrook

Walbrook refers to the small stream which, like the Fleet, used to flow through the City into the Thames. In Roman times it was wide enough for barges but it is now barely a trickle.

History

The first church – Saxon, built *c.* AD 700 but earliest reference about 1096 – was built on the bank of the brook. The second church, erected 1439 and destroyed in the Great Fire, was put higher up on the east bank, and Wren's building was constructed in 1672–9 on almost exactly the same site. The dome (the first built in England) was badly damaged by incendiary bombs in May 1941; the church was restored by the architects, Godfrey Allen and Gilbert Meadow, including reconstruction of the wood and plaster dome in 1951–2 and reopened in 1954.

The parish includes the former parishes of St Swithun's, London Stone, St Benet Sherehog, St Mary Bowhaw and St Laurence Pountney.

St Stephen's, Walbrook

St Stephen's, Walbrook. Roof of dome

Exterior

Except for the steeple, which was not begun until 1713, the exterior is fairly plain. The steeple, which has been described as 'playful', consists of a square stage at the base with three projecting columns at each angle, deeply recessed behind the balustrade and with the entablature carried outwards round the columns. Above this there is a smaller square stage without columns crowned by a dimunitive lantern. The steeple is some inches out of the perpendicular.

Interior

Entrance is by the unusual route of climbing 13 steps which follow the old line of the east bank of the Walbrook to a lobby which is the western apse of the church. One is greeted by what many call Wren's masterpiece in parish church architecture – a most ingenious and intricate design in what is virtually a plain rectangle. A forest of 16 beautifully proportioned Corinthian columns sort themselves out into a pattern which gives both a longitudinal effect with nave stretching towards the altar and that of a centrally planned church with arms radiating from the middle like a Greek cross and the whole surmounted by a most impressive dome. This unique double effect is achieved by omitting some of the columns in the middle to form a circular space but without interfering with the straight line of nave and chancel. The dome, weighing over fifty tons, is carried on eight arches. This design has been much admired over the years and is generally regarded as Wren's smaller masterpiece.

In 1888, the box-pews were removed and a mosaic pavement was laid in the centre. This was replaced in the restoration of 1978–87 by marble and a central altar by Henry Moore placed under the dome.

Furnishings

Most of the furnishings were saved from war damage and are of interest The woodwork is by William Newman.

West lobby with splendid organ gallery and case above All woodwork of the Wren period except the beechwood pews round the Moore altar which are by Andrew Varah.

Font Of stone, with an exceptionally beautiful octagonal font-cover, each panel decorated in high relief with garlands above and small figures on top (Christ and 3 Christian plus 4 Classical virtues).

Pulpit The staircase has twisted balusters and the tester is decorated with putti standing on it – the work of Wm Newman.

Baptistery screen The front of one of the Victorian choir stalls carved by Thomas Colley has been made into a baptistery screen.

Monuments
John Dunstable On the south wall is a monument to John Dunstable, father of English music.

Dr Nathaniel Hodges On the north wall is a tablet to the hero of the Great Plague in 1665 who died in a debtors' prison.

Associations
Sir John Vanbrugh was buried in the north aisle.

Grocers' Company The arms of the Grocers' Company are displayed in the church and on the wainscot.

Charlotte Brontë visited St Stephen's with her sister Anne in 1848.

Henry Pendleton, rector in the 16th century, was the famous 'Vicar of Bray'.

General
This is a church which perhaps fires the intellect more than the emotions and displays the scientific brain of Wren at its most brilliant, known as his masterpiece because he personally supervised the work. But St Stephen's today is far more than a building and through The Samaritans, the society founded here in 1953, is bringing solace and help to some of those most in need of it.

A noticeboard outside announces that 'the most perfectly proportioned interior in the world is not only a thing of beauty to delight the eye but a house of God to refresh the soul'.

40 Temple Church

Dedication
Dedicated to the Virgin Mary, the Temple Church takes its name from the Crusading Order of Knights Templar, founded in 1118 to protect pilgrims on their way to the Holy City of Jerusalem.

History
The Templars moved from Holborn to the Temple area in 1161. Here they built a church which was consecrated on 10th February 1185, probably in the presence of Henry II, by Heraclius, Patriarch of the Church of the Holy Sepulchre in Jerusalem (an inscription above the

inside of the entrance door records this). Like other Templar churches (Little Maplestead in Essex and Northampton), the nave was round, modelled on the Holy Sepulchre Church itself.

The original chancel was replaced in 1220 by the enlarged chancel consecrated in 1240 in the presence of Henry III.

When the Knights Templars Order was dissolved by Pope Clement IV in 1312, the property went to their rivals, the Knights Hospitaller, and it remained in their hands until they in their turn were suppressed at the Reformation. The church then passed to the Crown, but the lawyers, who had settled in the Temple as tenants of the Hospitallers, were allowed to remain, and in 1608, were granted the freehold by James I. It thus became the lawyers' private chapel, not subject to the jurisdiction of the Bishop of London.

The church escaped the Great Fire but, in 1682, it was refurnished by Sir Christopher Wren with box pews, pulpit and screen; he also designed the reredos.

Further restoration by Robert Smirke took place in 1828 and, in 1842, the building fell into the hands of the Gothic Revivalists who, under the architect Blore, made their presence felt throughout the church. The pavement of the chancel was then lowered about 16 inches.

During the air-raid of 10th May 1941 the nave roof fell in flames on the effigies of the knights below and caused considerable destruction elsewhere.

Carefully restored by the architect Walter Hindes Godfrey and his son, Walter Emil, it was re-dedicated in 1954 and is once more in full use by the lawyers of the Middle and Inner Temple.

Exterior

On the south side, where it lies back from an open courtyard, the church now presents a smooth ashlar-faced front with the drum of the round nave on the left and the triple lancets and buttresses of the rectangular chancel on the right.

A gabled rib-vaulted west porch provides protection for the sumptuously decorated, if somewhat weathered, Norman doorway of three orders with colonettes between; the decoration consists of lozenge, bobbin and ribbed leaf motifs. The half-length statues on the north side may represent Henry II presenting their foundation charter to three Templars.

Above the west door is an unusual circular window with tracery resembling a chariot wheel.

The north is a muddled composition with walls of coursed rubble. The organ chamber, rebuilt in 1953, has a rather formidable aspect.

On the ground, a gravestone inscribed 'Here lies Oliver Goldsmith, 1728–1774', marks the poet's supposed burial-place.

Interior
The interior is of outstanding interest, being one of the earliest examples – and a very fine one – of Gothic architecture in the whole country and using Purbeck marble on a large scale.

Despite being a victim of the Blitz, the round nave – or the 'round' as it is called – probably looks much the same today as when it was built 800 years ago. It consists of a circular Transitional Norman arcade with twisted arches supported by Purbeck marble shafted piers having prominent shaft-rings; above this is a triforium of interlaced arches and a clerestory of simple round arches. Beyond the nave runs an ambulatory with blind arcading along the wall, and a continuous stone bench underneath. The central portion of the nave is roofed in wood but the ambulatory is stone-vaulted.

In the spandrels of the blind arcading is a series of grotesque heads, some restored, said to represent souls in heaven and souls in hell Charles Lamb's heads that 'gape and grin'. Most of their owners appear to be in hell, suffering in many cases the most appalling toothache or having their ears tugged by fearsome monsters. They are worthy of detailed examination. A more serene face is the beautiful seraph's head corbel beside the entrance arch to the south aisle.

*The five-bay chancel is a superb piece of architecture, described by Pevsner as 'one of the most perfectly and classically proportioned buildings of the 13th century in England'. The aisles, entered by skilfully designed side arches, are the same height as the nave passage and the whole – vaulted throughout – is carried on slender shafted Purbeck marble piers and wall-shafts of the same material, both with moulded caps and bases. The piers have had to be renewed, and some of the shafts which were previously made from one block are now assembled in smaller sections (canisters), but the vaulting is original.

Stepped groups of three lancets have rere-arches with Purbeck marble shafts; they are slightly elaborated at the east end.

In the south aisle there is a double piscina, a type which was only used for a short time; later, by Papal decree, celebrants of Holy Communion were forbidden to throw away rinsings of the chalice but had to consume them, so that single basins then became customary.

A grim reminder of the past is the 'Penitential Cell' to which a door in the north-west corner of the choir gives access and which has slit windows looking into the church. Knights who disobeyed the Master or broke the Rule of the Temple were confined here and it is said that Walter le Bacheler, Grand Preceptor of Ireland, starved to death there.

A basement chamber, discovered and cleared of many bones and coffins in 1950, is reached by a stairway in the south porch. This is thought to have been the Treasury of the Knights Templar. One of several wall shafts has a finely carved Transitional capital. A grille on the stairway gives access to all that remains of St Anne's Chapel, which stood against the Round Church and in which the secret initiation of the Knights is said to have taken place.

Furnishings
Effigies of knights The effigies, dating from the 13th century – two may be even earlier – lying on the floor of the round part suffered much from the bombing with the exception of the one in the south aisle to de Ros; they have been repaired as far as possible. It is generally thought that they are memorials to illustrious supporters of the Order rather than Templars themselves, although 'illustrious' hardly applies to Geoffrey de Mandeville in the cylindrical helmet who was 'a ruffian of the worst order'.

The effigies have been many times moved and the burial places of the actual people are unknown.

Effigy of bishop The monument to the fully robed bishop with feet resting upon a dragon, in a recess in the south aisle wall is one of the finest 13th century monuments in the country. There is speculation whether it represents the Patriarch Heraclius, Bishop Hugh of Lincoln, who had a house nearby and whose heart is supposed to have been returned to that city, or Sylvester de Everdon, Bishop of Carlisle, who was killed by a fall from his horse in 1255 and buried in the Temple.

Other monuments
Edmund Plowden In the north aisle is the richly decorated alabaster altar tomb, 'repaired and beautified in 1687', to Edmund Plowden (died 1584), Treasurer of Middle Temple, showing him recumbent in a long, black close-fitting gown. The effigy lies below a thin coffered arch with obelisks at the sides and heads below; there is a big strapwork cartouche at the back. The monument was saved by being bricked up during the war.

Richard Martin On the other side is a monument to Richard Martin,

Recorder of London, who died in 1615. He wears a flowing scarlet robe and splendid ruff, and is shown kneeling on an embroidered and tasselled cushion before a prie-dieu.

Richard Hooker, famous divine (died 1600), *John Selden*, great lawyer (died 1651) and *Oliver Goldsmith*, poet (died 1774). Their monuments all perished in the air-raid but John Selden's gravestone can be seen below a glass panel in the floor near the entrance.

Brass In front of the choirstalls is a late heraldic brass to Edward Littleton, who died in 1664. It has 29 shields and a Latin inscription on a winding scroll.

Organ The Temple Church was the scene of an undignified confrontation referred to as the 'Battle of the Organs' between the two most famous organ-builders of the 17th century – Father Smith and Renatus Harris. They had been invited in 1683 to erect instruments and competition was so fierce that 'tempers were roused and there was even a clandestine slitting of bellows'. The contest dragged on for five years and eventually was decided by the notorious Judge Jeffreys, the Lord Chancellor, finding in favour of Smith.

The Smith organ was destroyed in the air-raid and the present four-manual instrument, originally built for Lord Glentanar's ballroom at Aboyne, was presented by him to the Temple in 1953. It bears the Royal Arms of Queen Elizabeth II.

Reredos The wide and low Wren-designed reredos, which was carved by William Emmet – joiner and wood-carver – for £45, was banished by the Victorians to the Bowes Museum at Castle Barnard in County Durham but was brought back after the war. It is inscribed with the Creed, Ten Commandments and Lord's Prayer.

Stained glass The painted glass in the three eastern windows by Carl Edwards represents subjects and heraldry connected with the Templars, including in the north window the Middle Temple lamb and flag device, together with the figures of Henry I and Stephen, and in the south window, the winged horse Pegasus device of the Inner Temple with the figures of Henry II and III. They were the gift of the Company of Glaziers and Glass Painters.

The 19th century glass in the 'Round' was partially lost in the bombing.

Pews Victorian pews have been replaced with college-type pews facing inwards. A curious feature is the hat-pegs.

Pulpit The pulpit with staircase is raised on a slender foot which, like the pews, is of lighter-coloured oak than the reredos; another post-war furnishing.

Font The 1842 font is a replica of the one at Alphington Church, near Exeter.

Sanctuary Chairs The two sanctuary chairs are the gift of the South African Bar.

Associations

Sir Christopher Wren was married here to his first wife in 1669.

General

The Temple Church is the most important survivor of Knights Templar churches in Europe and a remarkable example of the transition from the round Norman arch to the upward-pointing Gothic style where pure Norman and pure Gothic can be seen side by side. It might even claim to be the most interesting church (not a cathedral) in London.

It has brought incalculable pleasure to music-lovers because of its tradition of fine music. Under a succession of notable organists, including the late George Thalben-Ball, who had been playing here since 1919 and who regarded the present instrument as the finest in London, the choir has achieved world-wide fame with the recording of Mendelssohn's *Hear my Prayer* in which Master Ernest Lough as treble soloist sang 'Oh for the wings of a dove'.

41 St Vedast-alias-Foster

Dedication

St Vedast-alias-Foster is a combination of the name of a Gallo-Roman saint and the English equivalent (by way of Vaast, Vastes, Fastre and ultimately Foster). St Vedast prepared Clovis, King of the Franks for baptism (this was carried out by St Remigius of Rheims) and later became Bishop of Arras. He died in AD 540.

Only one other English church (at Tathwell, Lincolnshire) is dedicated to him.

History

Early history is confined to isolated references. Variously designated as 'St Faster' (1315–16) and SS Vedast and Amandus (1352), a church has existed on this site since the 12th century; the list of rectors begins with John de Rubege in 1291. In his Survey of London, published in 1595, John Stow refers to 'St Fauster's, a fair church lately newly built'. An eastward extension was added in 1614.

The Great Fire of 1666 did not completely destroy this building. Efforts were made to patch it up but eventually Wren had to be called in and it was rebuilt using what remained of the walls between 1695 and 1701, rather later than most. As in many cases, the steeple did not follow until funds permitted and, at St Vedast, it was erected between 1709 and 1712 with stone that was cut at Greenwich and brought up by river.

The church was a casualty during World War II bombing but, fortunately, the tower and spire survived. Sensitive restoration was completed in 1962. St Vedast's being reconsecrated on 25th April of that year.

Exterior

The curve of the mediaeval stone and brick wall can be seen at the south-west corner and the old structure is now exposed at the east end. The south-west steeple is built entirely of stone, with the upper stages first concave and then convex, each being knit together with clusters of diagonal pilasters and a short obelisk spire on top. It was ascribed to Wren until recently, but versatile as he was in designing new forms to meet new needs, it seems unlikely that he would have constructed a steeple so original as that at St Vedast. It is now thought that it may be the work of Nicholas Hawksmoore who was involved in the rebuilding at St Vedast as well as Wren. To quote Paul Jeffrey in his excellent booklet written for the Ecclesiological Society: 'The massive elegance, imaginative style and emotional force of St Vedast's steeple are inevitable reminders of the steeple of Christ Church, Spitalfields and the north front of St Mary Woolnoth. The setting of concave surfaces against convex was a recurrent theme in Hawksmoor's experimental designs.' The composition acts as a charming foil to the grandeur of St Paul's dome (plate p. 174) and the elaboration of St Mary-le-Bow's steeple.

On the north side, reached through a side-door in the narthex, is a small secluded garden called Fountain Court with a covered colonnade on two sides of it. A portion of Roman tesserae forming part of a pavement found in 1886 under the site of St Matthew's, Friday Street, is mounted on the south wall.

The 17th century west doors date from before the Great Fire.

Interior

The interior is a plain rectangle with clerestory, divided into nave/sanctuary and south aisle by an arcade of Tuscan columns. Modern collegiate-type seating replaces the former pews; furnishings from other churches take the place of those lost in the bombing.

Screening above the seating completely cuts off the south side from the rest of the church and makes it a separate chapel (St Mary and St Dunstan) entered from the east end. A new aumbry by Bernard Merry was placed there in 1992; on the door is depicted the Risen Christ (Anima Christi),

The flat plaster ceiling is richly decorated with gold and silver paint which extends to the cornices; the design consists of wreaths and rectangles in a larger rectangle.

Much of the glass is clear so that the church is well lit; artificial lighting comes from shaded lights on the seating in addition to lighting in the ceiling of the nave and sanctuary.

Furnishings
Organ Originally made by Harris & Byfield in 1731, the organ was restored by Noel Mander in 1960. The fine casing is 18th century work; it was once in St Bartholomew-by-the-Exchange (demolished in 1841).

Pulpit The octagonal pulpit, decorated with fruit, flowers, lions and skulls, was originally in All Hallows, Bread Street (demolished in 1875).

Font and cover The carved wooden font and cover were once in St Anne and St Agnes at the far end of Foster Lane in Gresham Street. This is now leased to the Lutheran Church.

Altar-piece This used to be in St Christopher-le-Stocks (demolished 1781). It went to Great Burstead Church in Essex before coming to St Vedast. The altar-table was in St Matthew, Friday Street (demolished in 1884).

East windows These modern windows depict scenes and legends associated with the life of St Vedast. The designer was Brian Thomas who paid careful attention to the colour and style of a surviving Clayton & Bell window adjoining.

Associations
Robert Herrick, the nature poet, was baptised in the church in 1591. Both Herrick's father and uncle were goldsmiths whose Livery Hall is situated in the parish.

Thomas Rotherham Rector in 1465–7, Thomas Rotherham became Lord Chancellor in 1471 and held the Archbishopic of York for 20 years from 1480 to 1500.

Vladimir Vassilievitch Petropavlovsky A tablet on the south wall of

St Vedast-alias-Foster. Steeple with St Paul's dome from roof of Saddler's Hall

Fountain Court commemorates 'Petro', Major Vladimir Vassilievitch
Petropavlovsky (1888–1971), 'Soldier of the Tsar, of France, of
England' with the commendably short but expressive tribute – 'This
was a Man' (Shakespeare).

General
It is easy to overlook St Vedast with St Paul's Cathedral and St Mary-
le-Bow so near but its steeple and the careful restoration, skilfully
blending old and new, make a visit well worth while. This little church
is the sole survivor in the area of no fewer than twelve separate parish
churches, demolished or destroyed, and in one case moved. The other
eleven were St Michael le Querne, St Matthew, Friday Street, St Peter
Cheap, St Alban, Wood Street (tower remains), St Michael Olave,
Silver Street, St Michael, Wood Street, St Mary Staining, St Mary
Magdalene, Milk Street, St Michael Bassishaw, St John Zachary and
St Mary Aldermanbury (now in Fulton, Missouri, USA and described
separately on p. 187 *et seq.*) Two more, St Anne and St Agnes and
St Lawrence Jewry, are not at present parish churches.

42 The Dutch Church of Austin Friars

History
Amongst the many mediaeval monasteries that lay within or just
outside the City boundaries was the religious establishment of the
Friar Hermits of the Order of St Augustine of Hippo. Their church,
originally built in 1253 and much enlarged in 1354, was a beautiful
building with a very fine steeple (Stow wrote 'I have not seen the
like'). It contained a number of splendid monuments, including one to
the Black Prince's elder son and one to Richard II's half-brother, so
that the church came to be called the Westminster Abbey of the City.

   For a time after the Dissolution, this place of worship was used as a
warehouse for wine and later a naval store. When, however, Henry
VIII was succeeded by his son – the boy king, Edward VI –
Archbishop Cranmer invited to England a number of continental
divines to assist in working out new forms of Protestant worship which
had been greatly stimulated by the English edition of the Bible; at the
same time, there were in the country some 5,000 Dutch and German
refugees from religious persecution. As a sign of gratitude for the help
of the theologians and to provide a place of worship where the
refugees were allowed to hold their own services, the disued nave and

aisles of the church of the Augustian or Austin Friars were made over to them under a charter dated 24th July 1550 and sealed by Edward VI.

With the accession of the Catholic Queen Mary the refugees were once more on the move and after many privations settled at Emden in Germany until they were able to come back to England when Elizabeth became Queen.

During the night of October 15/16th 1940, the building was completely destroyed by bombs and services had to be held elsewhere in London, although once a year a service took place in the ruins. The foundation stone of a new church was laid by Princess Irene, the second daughter of Queen Juliana, on 23rd July 1950, the 400th anniversary of the original foundation. This was consecrated on 11th July 1954.

Exterior

The exterior shows a massing of rectangular spaces at different levels with a small flèche crowning the highest block where the church itself is sited. The flèche has open columns surmounted by a dome on which is perched a spirelet and weather vane. On the south side there is a well-tended and grass-covered area above the place where the ashes of those previously buried in the church are interred.

Interior

The interior is unusual in that the various rooms are built at different levels. On the ground floor is a spacious social hall; the church, approached by a wide flight of steps, is on the first floor.

This is an open hall without aisles and has a shallow tunnel vault. The east end is taken up by what is known in Protestant churches in the Netherlands as the Liturgical Centre. The large pulpit with canopy and the sign of the Trinity above dominates the scene, emphasizing the importance placed on the Word; there is no altar but in front there is an extendable Communion table, around which those partaking of the Lord's Supper sit for passing round the bread and wine. Instead of using a font, the sacrament of baptism is administered from a silver basin.

Underneath the table is the altar stone of the original church built in 1253.

These decorous fittings for Protestant worship are supplemented by much stained glass and a striking tapestry based on the theme of Man and Creation.

Furnishings

Organ The organ is placed above the entrance. It has approximately 2,000 pipes divided over 26 stops and was built in the Netherlands.

Tapestry The unusual tapestry is by Hans van Norden and shows the river of life flowing upwards from the tree of life and carrying multi-coloured fish which change further up into white birds, symbolising the rise of humanity. Man's participation is indicated by the representation of fire, wheel, sword, hammer and the city built by him as a mark of his almost unlimited abilities. Nakedness shows man's limitations and the uplifted head, dependence upon his Creator.

Font Given by the South African community.

Stained glass The most interesting glass, especially the west window, in which the colour green predominates, is by Max Nauta; the other glass is by Hugh Easton.

Windows to the north and south of the Liturgical Centre depict the young Christ in the carpenter's shop, appropriately given by the Carpenters' Company; and, on the other side, the meeting on Easter morning of the risen Christ with Mary Magdalene; this was given by the Corporation of London. Other windows on the south and north walls contain the coats of arms of those towns where there have in the past been Dutch Church Communities.

The west window depicts the history of this church; at the foot appears on the left the boy king, Edward VI, and on the right, Princess Irene with the trowel and mallet which she used when laying the foundation stone of the new church. The two centre lights show St Augustine who founded the order of the Friar Hermits of Hippo and Johannes a Lasco, the first Superintendent of the Dutch Church Community; the latter is seen holding the original charter.

Seal At the top of the staircase is a photograph of the original charter still in the possession of the church, granting the building to the refugees and carrying the king's seal.

General

This country owes a debt to the Dutch Church of Austin Friars for the part it played in influencing our new forms of Protestant worship and for leading us away from the more repressive dogmas of extreme sects like the Anabaptists to the more tolerant practices and beautiful liturgy which the Anglican Church knows today. The Dutch Church was a bridge between pre-Reformation Mass and post-Reformation Matins.

Towers

Sometimes alone, sometimes amidst the bomb-damaged ruins of a former church, the tower, being the most durable part of the structure, remains; or it may have been spared from earlier demolition.

City of London
Especially noteworthy are:

Christ Church, Newgate Street
This was a fine church and one of Wren's most expensive. Built between 1677 and 1691 on the site of the chancel of the Franciscan Greyfriars church, the steeple was erected between 1701 and 1704. The Friary buildings were used as a foundling school (Christ's Hospital) for the Bluecoat boys who remained there until the school was moved to Horsham in 1902. Large steep galleries were provided for them which added considerable fuel to the fire when incendiaries fell on the church in 1940. It was not rebuilt, leaving the ruined walls and the burial ground now laid out as a garden.

The steeple, however – 'one of the most splendid in London' according to Pevsner – survived and was restored by Lord Mottistone in 1960. Standing forward from the west front, the three main stages are all square, the lower belfry storey being rounded off by a curved pediment and carrying a recessed middle stage encircled by an open Ionic colonnade, above which rises a tall open spire capped by a vase. Great use is made of urns, many of which were removed early in the 19th century, being replaced during the restoration.

St Mary Somerset, Upper Thames Street (see plate opposite)
Four Portland stone plain stages of varying height with alternate circular and round-headed windows are succeeded by an exciting crown on which Wren set eight pinnacles with panelled bases and scrolls, four at the corners having vases on top and four in the middle 20 foot high obelisks, capped with balls, which overtop the vases. These pinnacles were blown off during the War but have been restored to their former state, easily visible as the tower is on a very open site. The church itself was demolished in 1871.

St Augustine's with St Faith's, Watling Street
East of St Paul's Cathedral, this is another Wren steeple built in 1695

St Mary Somerset

and deliberately designed by him, with its slender proportions,as a foil
to the swelling dome of St Paul's (cf. also St Martin-within-Ludgate). It
has a pierced parapet and obelisk pinnacles, whilst the lead spire,
blown off by bombs during the War, has been restored in glass-fibre to
its original Wren inverted trumpet shape. The church was destroyed by
bombing in 1941 and St Paul's Choir School has now been built round
the tower.

Other towers have already been mentioned: All Hallows, Staining
Street in the description of St Olave's, Hart Street, St Alban's Wood
Street, (a late Wren Gothic tower, with Victorian top stage, standing in
the middle of the road) in the description of St Michael's, Cornhill;
St Dunstan in the East has been separately covered.

There are two Victorian towers: All Hallows the Great in Upper
Thames Street and St Martin Orgar in Martin Lane off Cannon Street.
Another Wren tower, St Olave Jewry in Ironmonger Lane, remains
from a church demolished in 1872, but this has now been incorporated
into offices.

Amongst towers in other parts of London are:

Islington
St Luke's, Old Street (see plate opposite)
St Luke's was one of the Fifty New Churches under the 1711 Act and
was probably designed either by George Dance the Elder or John
James. It was built of Portland stone between 1727 and 1733. The
building became dangerous and in 1959 was closed, dismantled and
unroofed, leaving the walls and the unusual steeple.

Much criticised because of its unorthodoxy, the architect may have
been influenced by Hawksmoor; it rises straight from the ground
instead of riding awkwardly on the roof. It is strongly built of finely-
jointed masonry in three stages chamfered at the base and rebated
further up, terminating in a very tall tapering fluted obelisk spire.

Tower Hamlets
St John at Wapping, Schandrett (see plate p. 182) This church was built
in the mid-18th century to take the place of a rather curious structure
with huge dormers and a low tower.

This not particularly noteworthy building was gutted by incendiaries
in 1940 and later the nave walls had to be taken down for safety
reasons.

St Luke's, Old Street

St John at Wapping

The tower, however, was not badly damaged and was considered worth restoring. Of dark brick with stone dressings, the plain lower stages are succeeded by a more attractive clock storey and then by a most original top consisting of a concave lower part carrying a charming convex cupola, both lead-covered. This top has a somewhat continental appearance.

OTHER CHURCHES

All Hallows', North Twickenham

History

Originally in the City of London before the tower and furnishings were transferred to Twickenham, this is one of the few City churches whose recorded history is pre-Conquest; in 1053 Brightmer, a citizen of London, gave the original place of worship to the Dean and Brotherhood of Christchurch, Canterbury.

This Saxon church was succeeded by three others, the first rebuilding being in 1294 and the second between 1494 and 1516; the third was erected by Sir Christopher Wren after the Great Fire.

John Stow in his *Survey of London* dated 1603 believed that All Hallows, being then near the 'Grasse Market', was the Grass church which gave Gracechurch Street its name. Earlier records, however suggest that St Benet's, Gracechurch, may have had a better claim to the title.

Although being in the middle of the blaze, the tower still stood after the Fire. It was some time before it was decided to re-build, and the new All Hallows was not completed until 1694 (one of the last of the City churches to be re-erected).

With lavish gifts from wealthy bankers, the furnishings were of the finest and, during a re-organisation of the Lombard Street parishes shortly before the 1939–45 War, a problem arose as to what should be done about them. The fabric of All Hallows was in a dangerous state owing to soil subsidence and the building was so hemmed in by office buildings that it had become known as the 'Church Invisible'. A most imaginative solution was found. It was decided to move the furnishings together with the 104 feet high campanile and the porch – which came from the dissolved Priory of St John, Clerkenwell – to Twickenham, south-west of London, where new churches were needed, a rare example of a place of worship moving to the parishioners. A simple unobtrusive brick structure was erected by Robert Atkinson to house the furnishings. The parish in the City, which embraced St Leonard's, Eastcheap, St Dionis Backchurch and St Benet's, Gracechurch, was absorbed by St Edmund, King and Martyr, Lombard Street.

In 1946 the living of All Hallows which had remained a 'Peculiar' i.e. outside the jurisdiction of the Bishop of London, for nearly 900 years, was exchanged for that of Charing in Kent and came under the Dean and Chapter of St Paul's Cathedral.

Exterior
The austere, balustraded and starkly white tower of finely-jointed
Portland stone stands out as a conspicuous stranger in its new
surroundings in Twickenham and, although joined to the church by a
long corridor, appears separate. Tower, church and linking vestibule
form an L shape round a small courtyard, the other sides being filled
with the rectory and the busy highway. The porch is elaborately
decorated and has an open scroll pediment.

Interior
Immediately inside the tower is a gate, which used formerly to stand
where one turned in to the alley leading from Lombard Street to the
church. It was moved inside the building in 1865 when still in the City.
This somewhat forbidding structure with bars and spikes is decorated
with emblems of death (skulls, hour-glass, skeleton and Father Time).

Furnishings
Amongst the exceptionally fine furnishings are:
   Doorcases The notable doorcases under the organ are part of the
original furnishings.
   Organ Originally built in 1708, it has been modified more than once
but retains much of its low Renatus Harris tone. The supporting
gallery is new.
   Font The white marble font is a feature of much charm with a circlet
of cherubs' heads and foliage round the rim. The cover, rather large by
comparison, is richly decorated and capped with an endearing group of
Charity with her children.
   Pews The pews date from the 18th century and are appropriate to
their surroundings.
   Chandeliers The chandelier under the tower, designed by Sir Ninian
Comper, came from the bombed church of St John's, Red Lion Square
in London; the smaller and finer example, made in 1784 by the Master
of the Pewterers' Company, has been restored and placed in the
chancel where it was originally situated in Lombard Street.
   Bread-shelves Bread was dispensed to the poor from the shelves,
which are now placed on the wall beside the lectern. Before the
Dissolution, such charity used to be given by the monasteries.
   Pulpit This furnishing was actually copied from the Grinling
Gibbons pulpit at St Mary Abchurch. Cherubs' heads and foliage
decoration abound. It has a large tester and attractive curving staircase
with delicate twisted balusters.

Reredos A notable example of 17th century woodwork. Richly ornamented, much pedimented, bearing in the centre the symbols of sacrifice (the lamb, and the pelican drawing blood from its breast), and culminating in seven candlesticks representing the Seven Churches of Asia, it is a harmonious and balanced composition. Although there is no proof that Grinling Gibbons carved it, the pelican motif is also found – and there are other similarities – in the reredos of All Hallows' City neighbour – St Mary Abchurch – which is known to have been carved by him.

Royal Arms A fine Charles II Royal Arms of oak – one of only 22 known examples – is kept in the ringing chamber of the tower for lack of space in the church.

Monument
The incidence of infant mortality in the 18th century is strikingly illustrated on the tablet in the vestibule to the six children of Thomas Vardon, five of whom died before they were one year old. Thomas Vardon was the first librarian of the House of Commons library.

Associations
John Wesley John Wesley preached his first extempore sermon at All Hallows. Fifty years later in 1788, when he was in his 86th year he recalled his dismay at finding that he had left his notes behind on the first occasion and how a kindly woman, upon hearing his trouble, put her hand on his shoulder and said, 'Is that all? Cannot you trust God for a sermon?' He never took notes with him into the pulpit again.

Peter Symondes In a will dated 1586, Peter Symondes left a sum to provide a new penny and a bag of raisins for sixty Bluecoat Hospital Boys on the morning of every Good Friday.

General
Although some feel that the new church is unworthy of the furnishings, we cannot but be thankful that these were moved out of London to safer ground shortly before so many other examples were destroyed by bombing, and that we can now enjoy them in a good light instead of their being but dimly discernible in the old 'Invisible Church'.

St Mary the Virgin, Aldermanbury

Aldermanbury
The court or bury of the Saxon 'Ealdormen' (Aldermen).

History
First mentioned in 1181, St Mary Aldermanbury was situated near London Wall. The mediaeval building – one of the few London parish churches to possess a cloister – was gutted in the Great Fire and rebuilt by Wren at dates variously stated as between 1667 and 1687. He used old materials for the walls, facing them with Portland stone.

The church suffered a particularly harsh restoration at the hands of Edmund Woodthorpe – 'the prince of philistine restorers' – in 1864, when he inserted Venetian tracery in the windows and installed inappropriate furnishings. It was damaged by a zeppelin bomb in the 1914–18 War and burnt out by an incendiary bomb on 29th December 1940.

For some years it seemed that St Mary's would remain a ruin but a totally unexpected future emerged for it when the President of Westminster College, Fulton, Missouri, USA, together with three colleagues, conceived the idea of removing a ruined Wren church from London and re-erecting it on the campus to commemorate Sir Winston Churchill's 'Sinews of Peace' or 'Iron Curtain' Speech at Fulton on 5th March 1946. It would become 'The Winston Churchill Memorial and Library in the United States'.

St Mary Aldermanbury was selected, approved by the British Council for Care of Churches, and the British architect, Marshall Sisson, appointed to co-ordinate the transfer to the USA in conjunction with the St Louis architect, Frederick Sternberg.

Dismantling began in 1965. Twelve columns and 7,000 stones, each separately numbered, were salvaged, and new Portland limestone was obtained from the same quarries used by Wren to replace missing or crushed stones. The first consignment arrived in Fulton during the Spring of 1966, enabling the Bishop of London to lay the foundation stone in October of the same year and the Bishop of Dover to re-hallow St Mary's in Fulton on the 7th May 1969.

The parish in the City of London is now linked with St Vedast-alias-Foster, whilst St Alphage's, London Wall, included with St Mary's after it was demolished in 1923, is now with St Giles', Cripplegate.

Exterior

The rebuilt church is raised on a platform and the cost of restoration and redevelopment of the undercroft in which the museum and library are housed exceeded $2 millions. The Winston Churchill Memorial and Library form part of the Churchill Quadrangle on the Westminster campus.

Great efforts have been made to reproduce the pre-war church and there are many improvements. The original pineapples, symbolising hospitality, friendship and fertility, are still on the corners and remain linked to the tower by concave Italian sidepieces. Victorian interference and especially the Venetian tracery have been corrected; instead, plain Wren-type windows without tracery have been substituted. The pierced parapet is no longer there but the large central lunettes at the sides are retained from the old design.

Fortunately, the east wall and gable, minus windows, survived the incendiaries so that 'the grossly oversized, very proud and jolly volute scrolls' (Pevsner) (the scrolls are called lyres in the USA) at the side of the east window escaped and can still be seen, also the small pediments above the vestry doors from St Dionis Backchurch (a City of London church demolished in 1878.).

The 106 ft high belfry is much as before except that the small pinnacles and pierced parapet are no longer there (perhaps leaving the tower top now a little stark) and simple Y-tracery has replaced the Venetian tracery (an undoubted improvement). Twenty-four circular belfry steps from the mediaeval church survive. The distinctive bell-turret with clock and open balcony terminating in ogee cap and vane has been carefully copied.

Roof material is copper coated with lead.

To the west of the church is a small section of the Berlin Wall.

Interior

The interior is equally satisfying. The clear glass, suitably leaded, the simple furnishings in oak instead of Victorian stone, specially designed in the Wren manner for which the identical original stain has been used, and the faithful reproduction of the plasterwork (modillions, flowers and other designs) cast from original moulds, all combine to restore the Wren atmosphere which it did not have after the 1864 alterations.

The sandstone base of the columns could not be moved and five capitals had also to be replaced, but otherwise the columns are the original ones.

St Mary the Virgin, Aldermanbury, now at Foulton, Missouri

Amongst the furnishings, it is of interest to note that the case for the organ was made in 1741 for Woolwich parish church.

Associations (from City church)
William Shakespeare lived near and almost certainly worshipped at St Mary's. In the churchyard in the City, which has been attractively laid out as a public garden, there is a late Victorian memorial to two personal actor friends of Shakespeare, John Hemminge and Henry Condell, who were parishioners and to whom we owe the collection of Shakespeare's works after his death for publication, thus preserving them for posterity.

John Milton married Katherine Woodcocke at St Mary's in 1656.

Lord Justice Jeffreys An association which is probably best forgotten in the church's new home is that the notorious Judge Jeffreys, after spending four years in the Tower of London, was stated to have been buried in the family vault at St Mary Aldermanbury on 2nd November 1693. A post-war inspection, however, revealed no trace of his body.

General
St Mary Aldermanbury is now ecumenical and is the College Chapel. Services are held each Sunday during the school year and there are many concerts. The Museum in the undercroft contains Churchilliana (letters written by him to his daughter, Lady Soames, paintings relating to Sir Winston, the lectern, chair and water glass used when he delivered the 'Iron Curtain' address) and exhibits related to St Mary's when the church was in the City. The Research Library is devoted to the life and era of this great leader. To the east of the Memorial is the Isabella R. Witmarsh Memorial Garden with plants of English origin and a sundial brought from England dated 1650.

The Winston Churchill Memorial and Library is a most imaginative project and a standing tribute to the links between two of the great English-speaking nations of the Western world.

City of Westminster

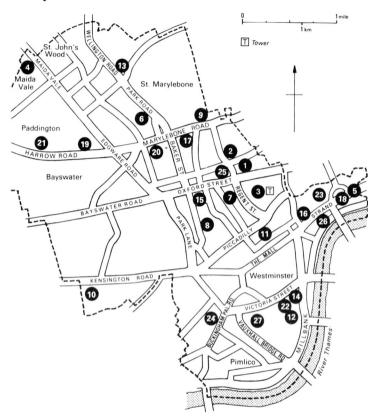

1 All Saints', Margaret Street
2 All Souls', Langham Place, with
  St Peter's, Vere Street
3 St Anne's, Soho
4 St Augustine's, Kilburn
5 St Clement Danes
6 St Cyprian's, Clarence Gate
7 St George's, Hanover Square
8 Grosvenor Chapel
9 Holy Trinity, Marylebone Road
10 Holy Trinity, Prince Consort
   Road
11 St James's, Piccadilly
12 St John's, Smith Square
13 St John's Wood Chapel

14 St Margaret's, Westminster
15 St Mark's, North Audley Street
16 St Martin-in-the-Fields
17 St Marylebone Parish Church
18 St Mary-le-Strand
19 St Mary Magdalene, Paddington
20 St Mary on Paddington Green
21 St Mary's, Bryanston Square
22 St Matthew's, Great Peter
   Street, Westminster
23 St Paul's, Covent Garden
24 St Peter's, Eaton Square
25 St Peter's, Vere Street
26 Savoy Chapel
27 St Stephen's, Rochester Row

City of Westminster

1 All Saints', Margaret Street

History
The church was erected on the site of the Margaret Chapel where, in the 1830s, Frederick Oakeley began to put into practice the teaching of the Oxford Movement. Built between 1849 and 1859 by the architect William Butterfield as a model church under the auspices of the Cambridge Camden Society, it cost about £70,000.

Exterior
The building, which is flanked by houses associated with All Saints and in similar architectural style, built at the same time as the church and its vicarage, presents a varied façade of dark red brick embellished with vitrified blackish-blue material. The dominating feature is the spire which rises over the south-west corner; it soars to 230 feet, slender and sheathed in slate, a rare form of covering in England; the steeple has a rather awkward appearance not relieved by the ring of small lunettes at the top. The tower is of the prevailing brick, a material which was not fashionable at the time and the use of which led to some criticism.

The church is approached across a little courtyard and entered by a door set asymmetrically at the opposite corner.

Interior
One is greeted by an interior of great lavishness where frescoes, marbles, carving, stained glass, mosaics and gilding all combine to enhance the effect of sumptuousness; to quote Pevsner – 'The interior is indeed dazzling . . . No part of the walls is left untouched. From everywhere the praise of the Lord is drummed into you'.

The visitor may have reservations about the taste and quality of all this but there is no doubt that All Saints' imparts a sense of vitality very welcome today and, although time has not softened the hard lines of Butterfield's work, the sense of splendour is not without attraction. There is much too to enjoy in the stained glass with its rich reds, blues, greens and browns, particularly the west window, depicting the tree of Jesse, by Alexander Gibbs, which replaced in 1877 the original one by Alfrede Gerente.

The nave of three bays is separated from the north and south aisles by richly-shafted piers of Aberdeen granite with luxuriant stiff leaf and naturalistic leaf capitals, and there are reredoses at the east end of the chancel (very large and ornate) and of the north aisle, the latter surmounted by a disproportionately large canopy. The clerestory has three small windows for each bay of the nave.

A steeply-pointed arch leads into the vaulted chancel, which is lower than the nave. Large tripartite openings with elaborate geometrical tracery and rising from dark red serpentine columns divide the chancel from the aisles. The altar is raised high.

The south aisle is completed at the west end with a baptistery under the tower, the original decoration of which has just been uncovered under seven coats of paint.

Furnishings
Font The fine marble font was a gift from the Marquess of Sligo.

Pulpit Of multi-coloured inlaid marble, the pulpit is heavy and ornate; it is mounted on granite columns with frilly capitals.

Chancel Reredos The large chancel reredos was originally by William Dyce but was repaired by Armitage in 1864 and, in 1900, new panels painted by Sir Ninian Comper were fixed over the originals. These were restored by Peter Larkworthy in 1979/80.

Screen A low inlaid alabaster and marble screen with handsome gates separates the chancel from the nave.

Tile paintings These were erected under Butterfield's direction in three phases. The largest, on the north wall, is a memorial to Upton Richards, the first vicar. Others are to be found under the west window and on the north wall of the tower. They date from 1873 to 1891.

Statue Opposite the pulpit on the other side of the chancel arch is a statue of the Virgin and Child which is covered by a triangular canopy with a curious blunted spire, designed by Laurence King and dating from 1962.

South-east aisle doors These attractive coloured doors, also designed by Laurence King, have panels showing representations of Edward Pusey (one of the founders of the Oxford Movement) who laid the foundation stone, W. Upton Richards (the first vicar – see also tile paintings), Harriet Brownlow Byron, Richard Benson and Edward King, the saintly Bishop of Lincoln.

South-east aisle stained glass The glass is of similar richness to the west window with reds, greens and blues predominating; the designer was Michael O'Connor. Two of the lights depict St Edward and St Augustine.

Organ The organ is fine four-manuel instrument, built by Harrison and Harrison in 1910. It has remained virtually unchanged.

General

High Victorian Gothic at its most assured, most ornate and most
powerful. In the forefront of the Catholic Revival in the Church of
England in the 19th century, All Saints today remains true to the aim of
its founders 'to consecrate art of the highest character to the glory of
God and the edification of his people', making the church a major centre
of Anglican Catholicism in this country and giving it the name of
'Cathedral of Oxford Circus'.

2 All Souls', Langham Place with St Peter's, Vere Street

History

All Souls' was one of four churches built at the beginning of the 19th
century in the borough of St Marylebone to meet the needs of a growing
population. They were all Commissioners' places of worship. In the case
of All Souls', the Commissioners contributed a little under two-thirds of
the total cost of £18,323. The architect was John Nash and the church
was designed to fit in with his grand piece of West End town planning
embracing a through-way from Piccadilly Circus to the Regent's Park
terraces. This had had to take a side-step at Langham Place, but Nash
ingeniously overcame the problem by placing his church where it could
be seen both from Portland Place and Regent Street and orientating the
building north-eastwards diagonal to the bend in the road.

His contemporaries were not so impressed and cried out at the lack of
architectural orthodoxy in mixing a classical portico with a Gothic spire;
a cartoon shows him impaled upon the sharp point. (See plate p. 197).

The construction of the church took just over two years between
November 1822 and November 1824, when it was consecrated. The site
was swampy and it is to this we owe the depth and strength of the
foundations, which have proved such an asset in the recent extensions.

Low mahogany pews, of which one third were free (i.e. not rented),
were substituted for the previous high-backed ones in 1876 but the
doors and dividers which separated them were not entirely discarded
until some years later. H. S. Goodhart-Rendel, the architect, carried
out repairs in 1928 and again after the 1939–45 War: on 8th December
1940 a landmine had caused considerable damage to the roof and
necessitated taking down half the steeple.

During recent years, the need for a hall for social activities
developed into one of the most imaginative schemes for post-war
alterations which have been undertaken in a London church. At a cost

of £655,000, the entire sum met before completion, the floor of the
church was removed, a new hall dug below, exposing in the process
Nash's inverted foundation brick arches (plate p. 198 and 199) and the
floor reinstated 18 inches higher. Reconsecration took place
appropriately on All Souls' Day (2nd November) 1976.

St Peter's, Vere Street (see separate description) is now a daughter
church.

Exterior
Admirably sited at the bend of Langham Place, the main feature is the
circular portico of giant Ionic columns with the unusual decoration of
Coade stone winged angels between the capitals. Before Broadcasting
House was erected, the famous and beloved candle-snuffer steeple was
more conspicuous than now, but even so the portico and steeple still
effectively close the view to the north of Regent Street.

A ring of free-standing Corinthian columns rises above the solid
circular clock base from which the exceedingly sharp fluted spire juts
upwards to end in the three foot bronze cone.

The rectangular body of the church is plain with two tiers of
windows.

Interior
All is contemporary and pristine with the circular vestibule and its
information desk slightly resembling a hotel foyer. Inside opens a
Corinthian hall with galleries on all four sides except where they open
at the east end for the sanctuary. The raising of the floor has brought
the shallow but deep galleries, the rake of which has been remodelled,
more into the body of the church. They are supported on chamfered
piers which at gallery level change to marbled Corinthian columns
supporting the coved flat ceiling, divided into large rectangular gilt
panels. The general colour tone is gold and grey and all is
resplendently fresh and bright.

At the east end the Westall painting (see *Furnishings*) with sunburst
above under a shallow arch is a valuable focal point in a sanctuary
which is completely open.

Furnishings
With the exception of the organ, which was safely stored during the
War, all the furnishings are modern and all, including the organ
console which can be brought forward into the centre of the chancel
area, are movable. This gives great functional flexibility.

All Souls', Langham Place, Nash cartoon

All Souls', Langham Place. Floor removed Aug 1975

Organ Built in 1913 and rebuilt by Willis in 1951 after the War. It has been rebuilt by Harrison & Harrison of Durham using the old casing – Spanish mahogany designed by John Nash.

Pulpit On a hydraulic jacking system because of its weight. Of bronzed aluminium.

Lectern and Font Also of bronzed aluminium. This is a single unit, which like the pulpit is on castors. The reading desk is removable to reveal a font beneath.

Altar table Of the same material as the pulpit and lectern/font.

Painting The painting by Westall depicting Christ being mocked was given by George IV, Nash's friend and patron.

General

This is the only Nash church left in the country other than East Cowes (Isle of Wight), although the tower of West Cowes is also by him.

All Souls', Langham Place. Inverted arches

The openness of the architecture is reminiscent of the post-war rebuilding at Islington, the source of the evangelical tradition which plays such a big part in the life of All Souls' today. Excellent music and vigorous Bible teaching feature at this live centre of Christian evangelism, where students and overseas visitors flock to participate in the church's activities, and where congregations of over a thousand are normal.

3 St Anne's, Soho

Dedication
Probably named after Anne, then Princess of Denmark, who later became Queen. Soho may be derived from 'so-ho' – a hunting cry used to draw off hounds when the area was in open country.

History

Nothing remains of the church consecrated on 21st March 1685.

It was bombed in 1940, the body of the church pulled down in 1953, and the area once occupied by the church turned into a shady green garden in a part of London near theatreland not well endowed with open spaces.

The very odd steeple which took the place of one erected in 1714 was the work of Samuel Pepys Cockerell and went up in 1803. It has a creeper-clad stone bell stage with chamfered corners, louvres and Doric columns squeezed into the angles. Above is the strange lead-covered stage terminating in two intersecting beer-barrels with a clock face on each side. The bell-stage has a pronounced batter (inward slope from the perpendicular).

Associations

Theodore, King of Corsica After accepting the crown of Corsica in 1736, he was driven out within a month and later settled in England in 1749. Arrested and imprisoned for debt, he mortgaged his claims to Corsica and died shortly after being released from prison. An inscription on the tower records this and concludes with the following aphorism by Horace Walpole:

> 'The Grave, Great Teacher, to a level brings
> Heroes and Beggars, Galley-slaves and Kings
> But Theodore this Moral learn'd ere Death
> Fate poured its Lessons on his living head
> Bestow'd a Kingdom and denied him Bread.'

William Hazlitt, printer, critic, essayist was buried here. He was born in Maidstone, April 1778, and died in Soho 18th September 1830. The tablet was restored by his grandson in 1901.

Dorothy Sayers, The ashes of this well known novelist and Christian theologian, who was churchwarden here until her death in 1957, are buried beneath the tower and a plaque to commemorate her was unveiled in June 1978.

General

There have been plans for rebuilding St Anne's but, so far, activities – mainly concerned with social work in this seamy area of London – have to continue from a little chapel in 57 Dean Street (Little Chapel of the Upper Room).

St Anne's, Soho

4 4 St Augustine's with St John's, Kilburn

Dedication

St Augustine was sent to England by Pope Gregory the Great to envangelize the Saxons. Landing in Kent in AD 597, his task proved to be easier than expected as, according to Bede, Bertha, the Queen of Kent, was already a Christian and the way was thus prepared for the conversion of her husband, King Ethelbert.

History

Built originally to serve a deprived area of north-west London, St Augustine's, Kilburn, stands out boldly from its surroundings. It took ten years to build from 1871 to 1880 and the tower and spire were not completed until 1898. The elaborate decoration took several more years.

The architect chosen was John Loughborough Pearson, one of the most famous of Victorian church builders, who has to his credit St Michael's, Croydon, St John's, Upper Norwood and the Cathedrals of Truro, Cornwall, and Brisbane, Australia. His work is uneven in quality but St Augustine's is generally regarded as amongst his best churches. French influence is apparent in the spire and conical-capped turrets which come direct from Normandy (St Etienne, Caen), and in the internal buttresses with their pierced openings, which recall Albi in the Tarn country of Southern France. St John's church was pulled down in 1972.

Exterior

The exterior is dominated by the spire, which rises to a height of over 250 feet and is one of the highest in London. The openness of the site enables one to appreciate the building as a whole with its long narrow and lofty lines, its acute angles and its soaring spire. Middle Pointed or Decorated style was no longer *de rigueur*, as it had been earlier in the century, and narrow lancets predominate. There are two tiers at the east end but at the west five smaller ones are surmounted by a notable rose window, in each case conical-capped turrets providing a frame. The building material is a dark and rather sombre red brick.

A lead-sheathed fleche with bell adorns the middle of the nave roof; the south-east chapel ends in an apse.

Interior

Entrance is through a porch on the north-west side under the tower, the stone vaulting being supported on a central pillar. The effect of the

St Augustine's, Kilburn

interior is dramatic. The triforium on first floor level has wide, cavernous openings and arches even taller than those of the nave, thus producing the unusual feature of twin arcades. Pearson has succeeded in accentuating the effect of height in a relatively modest-sized building by concealing the comparatively low vaulting of the aisles and by making the nave arcade appear to be that of the upper gallery. He has made the church look wider by the recession created by the double aisles and has increased the effect of length by the transept bridges, which make the chancel arcades look like extensions of the five bays of the nave.

St Michael's and All Angels Chapel on the south-east side, and the Lady Chapel on the north-east side open out from the transepts. Fine wrought-iron screens separate nave from chancel and sanctuary from ambulatory.

The chancel floor is paved with inlaid marble.

This original design affords constantly changing vistas across the nave and there is a fine view eastwards on gallery level from the west end.

Furnishings and decoration

Both furnishings and decoration are in High Victorian style, reflecting the views of the Catholic Revival in the Church of England, with much ornate carving, inlaid marble and wall-painting, all combining to illustrate the major themes of the Christian faith – Creation, Fall, Miracles, Redemption, Crucifixion and Resurrection. The decorations, starting at the west end with attractive subtly-shaded glass made by Clayton and Bell in the great rose window and lancets, continue to the east end. The murals and carved reliefs all provide colour, varying in merit, but telling a consecutive story.

Pulpit and Font Lavishly carved amber alabaster and typical of the period. The marble has a pleasing, moist-looking plastic quality.

Rood screen This is surmounted by an impressive dark figure of the Crucifixion flanked by six statues of Passion personalities.

Bishop's Chair The bishop's chair in the sanctuary has French 16th century carving.

Altar in Lady Chapel This stone altar with carved wooden reredos was designed by Sir Giles Gilbert Scott, who also provided the wooden statue of the Virgin Mary in the nave and the Stations of the Cross.

Icon The icon of St Nicholas near the font comes from Russia.

Treasures The Victorian exuberance extends to the textiles of vestments and altar hangings, silver-ware and plate, all still in use and of outstanding quality.

General
St Augustine's is a church which perhaps inspires respect rather than joy but it is one of which the Victorians can be proud and might claim to be the finest and largest 19th century place of worship in London. The acoustics are superlative and, with its fine organ and choir, nave and ambulatories so admirably suited for processional purposes, worship in this church must be an inspiration.

5 St Clement Danes

Dedication
The most likely supposition is that Danes who had married English wives were allowed by Alfred the Great to settle in AD 886 in the no-man's land between Ludgate and Westminster. It would be natural for this seafaring people to adopt St Clement for their dedication.

History
An old timber-framed church was replaced about the year 1022 by a stone building, remains of which are still to be seen in the base of the tower. The living was in the hands of the Order of Knights Templar from 1189 until the order was dissolved, shortly after which (about 1324) it passed together with some land in the parish into the hands of the Bishop of Exeter; the Bishop was soon afterwards murdered in his palace across the road.

   Although partly rebuilt in 1640 and a survivor of the Great Fire – Sir Christopher Wren felt it necessary to pull down the church and have it completely re-erected to his designs by Edward Pierce – one of his best masons – thus becoming the only place of worship outside the City to be reconstructed by Wren. (St James's, Piccadilly, was a new church built on a site where none had existed before.)

   In 1719, James Gibbs – the architect of St Mary-le-Strand next door – added the beautiful upper stage to Wren's tower, both of which survived the German bombs in the Second World War.'

   Gutted in 1941 by German Air Force incendiary bombs, the main building was left a ruin until 1955 when the RAF had it raised again to become their church. The parish was then joined to St Mary-le-Strand.

Exterior

The island site which so greatly enhances the exterior view has only existed since 1910 when a number of houses on the north side were removed. St Clement's is unique amongst Wren churches in being designed with an apse. Unlike St Mary-le-Strand, there are two tiers of windows. The heavy porch probably dates from an earlier church.

Interior

The rebuilding, so ably executed by the architect W. A. S. Lloyd, has provided the church with an interior of great richness, lighter and more spacious than before and with a striking contrast of dark oak up to the height of the gallery and white columns with richly decorated arches supporting a panelled ceiling in white, grey and gold above. The spaciousness is enhanced by the wide floor, into which have been let over 700 badges of RAF squadrons and units cut from Welsh slate, and made possible by the pews having telescopic extensions, which can be pushed back when not required.

The eye is led to the apse of double columns at the east end with encircling ambulatory. To the west, the dominating feature is the organ.

The ancient crypt – once a burial place – has been converted into a beautiful chapel. Plates from the old coffins are fixed to the wall. The Belgians, Dutch and Norwegians have given respectively the paschal candelabrum, the stone altar and the black granite font.

Furnishings

Organ This splendid instrument, designed by Ralph Downes and made by Harrison and Harrison of Durham, replaces the 'Father Smith' one which was destroyed. It was the gift of United States Air Force personnel and families.

Stalls Behind the pews at the west end are finely carved stalls for members of the Air Force Board.

Pulpit The wooden hexagonal pulpit was mercifully saved from destruction by being stored in the crypt of St Paul's Cathedral. Even there, bombs badly damaged it but restoration has removed all traces of this. Carving, which includes undercut festoons of hanging flowers, is attributed to Grinling Gibbons (*c.* 1685).

Lectern Of wrought-iron and brass, donated by the Royal Australian Air Force.

Bishop's chairs and tapestries In the sanctuary are two bishop's chairs set off by antique Florentine tapestry which was given by

Viscount Trenchard, the 'Father' of the Royal Air Force, and Lady Trenchard.

Processional Cross Made of Cornish white tin, it was carried in procession at the service of reconsecration by the young Air Training Corps cadet who designed it.

Reredos The wooden reredos is by Ruskin Spear and depicts the Annunciation. Painted in gold, it is a highly-praised work.

East windows The three windows are by Carl Edwards and depict Christ in Glory (centre), Madonna and Child (north) and Pieta (south).

Associations

Mrs Donne The tomb to Ann – wife of Dr John Donne, poet and Dean of St Paul's – who died bearing her 12th child and was buried on 16th August, 1617, was destroyed in an air-raid.

Cecil baptisms Two sons of Lord Burleigh, Queen Elizabeth's famous statesman, were baptised here in 1561. One died young but the other rose to occupy his father's place as Lord High Treasurer and to become the first Earl of Salisbury.

Dr Samuel Johnson Although St Dunstan in the West and St Bride's were his nearest churches, the celebrated lexicographer was persuaded by a lady friend to come and hear her nephew preach at St Clement's. He seems to have continued to worship here, as commemorated by the brass plate in the north gallery and, more strikingly, by the statue outside showing Dr Johnson in characteristic pose and describing him as 'Critic, Essayist, Philologist, Biographer, Wit, Poet, Moralist, Dramatist, Political Writer, Talker'.

Oranges and Lemons There is a tradition that oranges and lemons were unloaded at a nearby wharf (there was no embankment) and carried through the churchyard to Clare Market against payment of a toll to the churchwardens. The ancient rhyme is rung daily on the bells at 9.00 am, 12 noon, 3.00 and 6.00 pm. There was also a custom whereby – on New Year's Day – the head porter at Clement's Inn opposite presented an orange and a lemon to each tenant, who was expected to pay half-a-crown for the privilege.

It may be, however, that the association merely arose from the fact that Clement rhymed with lemons and this is supported by the fact that St Clement, Eastcheap, is also associated with the rhyme.

William Webb-Ellis The Rugby schoolboy who made himself famous by picking up the ball in a game of football and so initiating the game of rugby was rector here.

General

This church is now firmly enshrined in the hearts of countless flying
men and women, bearing the memory of more than 125,000 who died
in defence of their country. Beneath the north gallery is the American
Shrine which commemorates the names of 19,000 members of the
United States Air Force, who laid down their lives in the Second
World War while serving in this country. One must marvel at the way
in which this place of worship, destroyed by an enemy Air Force, has
risen again and been made even more beautiful by the Royal Air
Force, Commonwealth and Allied Air Forces.

6 St Cyprian's, Clarence Gate

Dedication

St Cyprian was a Carthaginian lawyer who, in his middle years, was
converted to Christianity and, much against his will, appointed Bishop
of Carthage. He was martyred in AD 258, accepting his fate with
forbearance and even bequeathing fifty gold pieces to his executioner.
The dedication was chosen by the founder, who had to overcome the
objections of the Bishop of London, because he was especially struck
by St Cyprian's tender loving care for people and the consideration
with which he treated them.

History

If ever a church was the creation of one man, St Cyprian's was.
Charles Gutch was the son of a clergyman and had held various
curacies, including three in London from one of which he was
dismissed for preaching against the sins which he considered were
sapping the life of young men. Although Gutch had no special
connections with the district, he felt the call to exercise a ministry in
the north-east part of the borough of St Marylebone which, at the
time, although middle-class, was poor. Many London parishes were
then being divided in order to make them easier to work and he was
able to obtain the agreement of the rector of Christ Church to hive
St Cyprian's off from his parish.

   The granting of parish status was officially confirmed in May, 1866
but it was to be a long time before a church could be built. Without
any assurance of residence or stipend, Gutch had to conduct his
various missions and to operate generally from a temporary place of
worship, consisting of two houses with a coal-shed between, which

G. E. Street, the architect and one of the trustees of St Cyprian's, had converted. Eventually, not long after Gutch's death in 1896, a site for a permanent building was obtained and St Cyprian's, although at the time consisting of little more than walls and pillars, was dedicated on 30th June 1903.

The architects were Bucknall and Comper, the latter being Sir Ninian Comper, and no church in London reflects to a greater degree his love of the mediaeval. Damage was caused by bombs during the 1939–45 War and that suffered on the south aisle floor has been left as a memorial.

Exterior

The exterior is completely plain and unpretentious without tower or steeple of any sort and consisting of a simple roofed rectangle of wall, bottle-glass windows and buttresses.

Interior

Gutch, in his earlier years, had been much influenced by the Oxford Movement and was anxious to bring back Catholic traditions to Protestant worship. Comper was, therefore, free to exercise his highly individual mediaeval style to the full. Screen, altar, frontal and dorsal, font cover, stained glass are all his and the furnishings are the most complete expression of his tastes in London.

The interior, assisted by the absence of pews, is open and spacious. The nave is separated from the aisles by seven bays with tall and slender columns; above is a low clerestory with segmental-headed windows. There are chapels on each side, a Lady Chapel on the south and the Chapel of the Holy-Name, not completed until 1938, on the north. The latter contains the original altar used by Gutch in his temporary church.

The roof is a form of queen-post truss with tracery in the spandrels of the braces and fibrous plaster panels.

Furnishings

The furnishings are the main feature. Everywhere, Comper's hand is apparent, giving light and gaiety to this 20th century mediaeval interior.

Organ The fine organ is housed in the west gallery above the narthex.

Font This was given in 1930 and has a most intricate and imposing tall, gilded, spire-like cover. Apart from the Spanish-style posts in the

Chapel of the Holy Name, this is the only item in the church which is not entirely Gothic, the lowest stage being of classical design.

Pulpit The pulpit was given anonymously in 1914 and is made of oak.

Rood-screen A reversion to the old rood-screen, stretching right across nave and aisles, with rood and loft above, elaborately carved and with painted figures representing saints on the panels. The tracery is of lace-like delicacy, providing a rare example of an open loft. It was completed in 1924.

Lady Chapel screen The figures depicted on the screen are, most appropriately, all of women saints.

Altar The stone altar in the sanctuary is one of the largest in the country. The elaborate canopy was completed in 1948.

Stained glass The symbolism of the glass is explained in detail in the excellent guide. Suffice it here to draw attention to the two quatrefoils at the top of the Lady Chapel window, showing the coat of arms of the Borough of St Marylebone; on the left the Virgin Mary and Child stand on the river 'le Bone' and on the right the river is shown with her lily and rose.

General
St Cyprian's is a highly-praised work of the Catholic Revival and has been described by Comper himself as 'the last development of a purely English parish church with lofty aisles and clerestory'. It is a period piece and unique amongst London churches as showing what Anglo-Catholic liturgy of the beginning of the century demanded. Aesthetically, it can give much pleasure, but one is inclined to overpraise because of the exuberance and colour of the furnishings.

7 St George's, Hanover Square

Dedication
St George, the patron saint of England, was born of Christian parents in Cappadocia. He was martyred during the Diocletian persecution in AD 303.

History
The memory of the 1715 uprising is underlined by the desire in the dedication to consign the Jacobites to oblivion. The spirit and, to some extent, the style of this building is Hanoverian. At one time, it was

even intended to mount a statue of George I on the pediment of the portico – but this did not materialise.

The church was erected as one of the Fifty Churches under the 1711 Act to provide a suitable place of worship for the new estate that was being developed north of Piccadilly and south of Oxford Street, an area where it was still possible at the time of building to shoot woodcock and snipe. The parish was carved out of the much larger one of St Martin-in-the-Fields.

John James, the chosen architect, had been Assistant Surveyor to Wren at St Paul's Cathedral and had succeeded James Gibbs as Surveyor to the Commissioners of the Fifty. The first stone was laid on June 20th. 1721 and the new place of worship was consecrated on 23rd March, 1725.

Fairly extensive alterations were made at the end of the 19th century, which included the provision of the chancel to accommodate a choir.

Exterior

The most striking feature is the handsome portico which projects on to the pavement in front of the church proper. It was by way of being a trend-setter to be followed almost immediately in the rebuilding of St Martin-in-the-Fields and, a little later, at St George's, Bloomsbury. However, the placing of the tower over the west end of the church proper and behind the portico resulted in an awkward composition which was not satisfactorily resolved until Thomas Archer built St Paul's, Deptford where he made the tower circular and enclosed the western projection with an embracing semicircular portico, thus integrating the two. The 'happily incongruous' (Pevsner) cast-iron hounds which were formerly within the portico at St George's came from a bombed-out shop nearby. They are now at the Queen Mother Small Animal Hospital, North Mymms, Hertfordshire.

The tower, with diagonally projecting coupled colonettes carrying a prominent entablature, is modelled on St James's, Garlickhythe, a Wren motif, emanating from the Netherlands, also found in the form of single colonettes at Chelsea Royal Hospital. The small dome above is rather an anticlimax.

At the east end, a broad flight of steps gives independent access to the vestry.

Interior

The architect had to operate on a cramped site but nevertheless John James has succeeded in providing space for a substantial congregation in a building not noticeably large. The general effect of the rather square proportions is perhaps not particularly inspiring but the ceiling of square panels is nicely gilded. Galleries on the north and south sides are supported by the square pillars of the nave, from which spring Corinthian columns. At the west end, the galleries are canted round to enclose the organ. At one time, there was an upper circle gallery on each side of the organ for charity children.

The Venetian window at the east end has a segmental head and is enclosed with coupled columns. The shallow chancel is enhanced with attractive columns gilded in the flutings.

Furnishings
Reredos This still retains the original painting of the Last Supper, by William Kent. The colours are dark and, in consequence, the painting does not draw the eye.

Pulpit Lowered during the Victorian restoration and placed on the present six columns. Rather squat with rich but shallow decoration and a wrought-iron staircase.

*Font A beautiful furnishing, oblong in shape with a fluted bowl and made of an attractive veined marble. It is decorated beneath the rim with a pleasing pattern of sheaves, oak-apples and leaves.

*Organ A splendid feature. Originally built by Gerard Smith, the nephew of the famous Father Smith, it has suffered many vicissitudes including a serious fire in 1896. Fortunately some of the old work survived and it was rebuilt by Harrison and Harrison in 1972.

Stained glass Although a muddled composition, the bright colours provide the focal interest at the east end which the reredos lacks. The glass is Flemish, dating from about 1525, and was originally made for a convent at Antwerp. It was brought to St George's in 1840. The theme is the tree of Jesse; Christ seated on an elaborate throne is shown in the centre light, at the top of which appear set in medallions the somewhat incongruous trio of St George, Victory and Minerva. Part of the original window featuring God the Father could not be fitted into the space available and is at Wilton, near Salisbury.

Candelabra A nice feature.

Associations
George Frederick Handel, the great composer, was closely associated with St George's from the time he came to live in Brook Street nearby in 1724 until his death in 1759 – a span of 34 years. It was at Brook Street that he wrote some of his greatest works – 'Saul', 'Israel in

Egypt', 'Messiah' and many other oratorios. He had his own pew and worshipped regularly in the church.

General
St George's is a dignified church, well suited to its setting in a smart area of London.

8 Grosvenor Chapel

History
Like St Peter's, Vere Street, but built a few years later, the Grosvenor Chapel was an estate chapel to serve a residential development on privately-owned land. It was completed about 1730 as part of the Grosvenor Square scheme. The builder, Benjamin Timbell, may also have been the designer.

In 1831 it became a chapel of ease to St George's, Hanover Square.

At the turn of the century Sir Ninian Comper made considerable alterations to the east end which changed the chapel's character.

Exterior
A plain and somewhat Colonial-looking structure, the chapel, built of yellow brick, has round-headed windows in front and also at the sides. The portico with four Tuscan columns is surmounted by a slightly projecting bell-turret with a short copper spire.

Interior
Sir Ninian's alterations have complicated the simple chapel interior; he installed a screen with large Ionic columns between the chancel and Lady Chapel. The east end has blue and gold decoration.

The original galleries on three sides with square pillars below and short Ionic columns above remain.

The nave ceiling is coved and the aisles groin-vaulted.

Furnishings
Pulpit The pulpit, which has an attractive carved staircase, is contemporary with the building of the chapel.

Communion rails Also contemporary. Of wrought-iron.

Reredos Divided into three parts by pilasters, a Comper fitting.

Grosvenor Chapel

General.

This is an appealing survival of an estate chapel, the only one of Mayfair, and still playing a useful part by providing a centre of spirituality and pastoral care for the people of Mayfair and beyond.

The chapel is under the care of a priest-in-charge assisted by a committee which includes the rector of St George's, Hanover Square.

9 Holy Trinity, Marylebone Road

History

Although St Marylebone Parish Church had been rebuilt only a few years before, the development of fashionable residential suburbs northwards from Oxford Street during the late 18th and early 19th centuries when the Nash terraces were growing up around Regent's Park, had, by the 1820s, already made it too small for the greatly increased population. The Commissioners, therefore, entrusted Sir John Soane with the building of a new church at the east end of Marylebone Road. Begun in 1824 and consecrated on 31st May 1828 it was one of the most expensive of all the so-called 'Waterloo' churches built after the Napoleonic Wars with the £1 million thanksgiving fund voted by Parliament in 1821. The parishioners, however, paid for the extra cost of the columns and urns on the lower stage of the tower.

In 1878, G. Somers Clarke substituted a round apse for the previously flat east end.

After the 1939–45 War the shifting of the population and the change in character of the area from studios and drawing rooms to large embassies and medical consulting rooms made the church redundant and, in 1955–6, it was adapted to become the headquarters of the Society for Promoting Christian Knowledge (SPCK).

Exterior

As at St Marylebone Parish Church, although on the opposite side of the road, the orientation is north and south. The materials used were Bath stone and brick. The west end has a handsome if shallow portico of four Ionic columns below a balcony; the tower above consists of a square main stage with free-standing Corinthian columns, each with its own entablature projecting at the angles, and urns of typical 'Soane' design. The top stage is circular with columns and the summit is a round stone cupola. The outside pulpit forms part of a memorial to

Canon William Cadman, rector from 1859 to 1891, a gifted preacher who attracted large crowds.

The long sides are straight but with Ionic demi-columns half sunk into the walls.

Interior

The western half of the nave, including side aisles and galleries, has been converted for SPCK needs, the seating going to St Lawrence Jewry in the City. Small vestry chambers have been installed in the north-west and south-west corners of the shortened eastern part. The apse remains as remodelled by Somers Clarke, with mosaic decoration, but panels of the Evangelists, the Nativity, the Last Supper and a group of angels were added at the end of the century. Seating is restored in the remaining part of the nave for occasions such as the SPCK Founders' Day, and the chancel is still fitted for worship, including a weekly celebration.

Below is a vast crypt. It was used to provide burial vaults until 1843 when an Act of Parliament forbade burials taking place in populous areas. In the 1930s, its future association with publishing was foreshadowed when Allen Lane rented storage space in the crypt for Penguin Books, the pioneers of paperback publishing.

Monument

The charming Smith monument by Sievior dating from 1834, is now in the north-west wall of the sanctuary.

Associations

Many famous people lived in the district and amongst those who attended Holy Trinity were *Lord Roberts* of Afghan War fame and *Florence Nightingale*.

General

Although there may be regrets that this 'Soane' church has been so much changed there is cause for thanks that such a good use has been found for it to ensure its continued existence.

10 Holy Trinity, Prince Consort Road

History

A successor to earlier places of worship in the neighbourhood, Holy Trinity was one of the last works of the eminent Victorian architect,

Holy Trinity, Marylebone Road

G. F. Bodley, being built in 1902–3. There was restoration in the 1950s. New lighting was provided and the church redecorated in the early 1990s, and the street façade cleaned in 1994.

Exterior

The church, faced with Bath stone, lies endwise to the street and displays an elegant west window with beautiful 14th century tracery. There are two aisle windows in the same style and a projection to the left for the extra aisle on the north; decorative niches are placed either side of the central window. A small and rather rustic gable houses the bells. The orientation is north and south.

Interior

The five-bay nave with lean-to aisles is lofty, spacious and admirably proportioned, uncluttered by pews and well lit. Clustered tall and slender shafted columns give an air of lightness and grace. The wooden roof is of the wagon type.

The Lady Chapel, dating from 1906, lies on the north side and there is an organ loft to the south.

Furnishings

Font Plain with attractive ogee cover.

Pulpit Painted in 1964.

Altar-piece Gilded and carved altar-piece dates from 1912, to Bodley's own design.

Associations

Dr Hannay (George Birmingham, the author) was rector here.

General

The excellent proportions, the beautiful window tracery and the discreet colouring add sparkle to this unexpectedly attractive church.

11 St James's, Piccadilly

Dedication

The Apostle James was beheaded by order of Herod Agrippa I in AD 42. Tradition later relates that disciples took his body to Spain and that it was discovered in a marble coffin by a Galician peasant during the year 816. St James became the patron saint of Spain and his shrine at Santiago de Compostela was a leading centre of mediaeval pilgrimage.

History
The church was erected to serve the estate being developed by Henry Jermyn, Earl of St Albans, on land originally leased and then purchased by him. Sir Christopher Wren, the chosen architect, started building in 1676 and the new place of worship was consecrated on 13th July 1684; a spire was added in 1699. St James's was the only church built by him on a completely new site. This was before Piccadilly was constructed and entrance was from Jermyn Street.

Over the years alterations and additions were made but a major renovation carried out in 1937 was erased during a German air-raid on 14th October 1940 when St James's was severely damaged by high explosives and incendiaries. For thirteen years services were conducted in the south aisle until the church was rededicated on 19th June 1954 after restoration by Sir Albert Richardson.

Exterior
A plain brick building with Portland stone dressings. On the north and south sides are two tiers of windows, round-headed above and segmental below; at the east end, a tall Venetian window is placed above a tripartite rectangular window. Projecting from the west end is a balustraded tower, now once more completed with a steeple – built in fibre-glass.

An unusual feature is the outside pulpit with sounding-board on the north wall; installed in 1902 it was used for conducting open-air services before the advent of mechanised transport in Piccadilly.

The approach from Piccadilly is made agreeable by the Garden of Remembrance which, due to the generosity of Lord Southwood, newspaper proprietor, was created out of the damaged churchyard. Lord Southwood's memorial adorned with putti is a pleasing addition.

Interior
Wren wrote in 1708 that churches should be large but not too large – 'The Romanists, indeed may build larger Churches, it is enough if they hear the Murmur of the Mass, and see the Elevation of the Host, but ours are to be fitted for Auditories. I can hardly think it practicable to make a single Room so capacious, with Pews and Galleries, as to hold above 2,000 Persons, and all to hear the Service, and both to hear distinctly, and see the Preacher. I endeavoured to effect this, in

St James's, Piccadilly. East end

St James's, Piccadilly. Grinling Gibbons font

building the Parish Church of St James's, Westminster, which, I presume, is the most capacious, with these Qualifications, that hath yet been built . . .'

The interior with north and south aisles is indeed wide and spacious. Galleries on three sides which curve round the west end as in a theatre are supported by square piers encased in oak, above which rise Corinthian columns with entablatures to carry the tunnel vault of the nave into which the transverse tunnel vaults of the aisles open; the galleries are ornamented with egg and dart and other decoration.

The elegance of the proportions and the refinement of the decoration impart an air of much distinction. The rising ceiling is divided by transverse ribs enclosing large panels; plaster-cast mouldings from surviving fragments, supplemented with drawings and photographs, enabled the restorers to reproduce the original plaster-work.

Furnishings
St James's is fortunate in having three furnishings – the font, the organ-casing and the reredos – containing work known to have come from the hands of Grinling Gibbons, saved from destruction by being stored at Hardwick Hall in Derbyshire during the 1939–45 War.

Royal Coat of Arms A fine William and Mary coat of arms is placed above the new staircase in the north vestibule.

Organ An exceptionally fine instrument, originally built in 1684 by Renatus Harris for King James II to be used in his Roman Catholic chapel at Whitehall Palace; after he fled to France it was given by Queen Mary to St James's where it was installed by Father Smith. Bomb damage necessitated its reconstruction but the Gibbons case with its six figures on top was brought back.

Font This Grinling Gibbons feature is sculptured in white marble. The shaft represents the Tree of Life with a serpent coiled round it. Figures of Adam and Eve stand on either side. Round the bowl are three bas-reliefs – the Ark of Noah with the dove bearing an olive-branch, the Baptism of Christ and St Philip's Baptism of the Eunuch.

Pulpit The hexagonal pulpit dates from 1862.

Communion rails Bronze and white marble. Very lavish.

Reredos The Gibbons work on the altar caused John Evelyn to write in his diary that: 'There was no altar anywhere in England, nor has there been any abroad, more handsomely adorned'. The reredos, carved in limewood, is crowned by a large segmental arch.

East Window Dating from 1954 and by Christopher Webb, it

contains scenes from our Lord's life and Passion, also the coming of
the Holy Ghost at Pentecost. In the upper light, Christ appears in
Glory, surrounded by Angels and seated on a rainbow. The symbolism
of the Pelican feeding its young with its own blood is depicted in the
head of the light.

Monuments
Earl of Romney, died 1704. The memorial by W. Woodman in the north
gallery has putti between twisted columns and inscription with trophies.
   Lord Huntingdon, also died 1704. This, stated to be by Francis Bird, is
nevertheless similar in style but the putti are outside the columns, which
are only twisted in the lower parts. The memorial is in the south gallery.
   James Dodsley, died 1797. In the north-west vestibule and by the
famous sculptor, John Flaxman, it is in the form of an open book.

Associations
Van der Velde Amongst the celebrities commemorated are father and
son Van der Velde, the famous Dutch marine painters, who continued
to work in this country even when England was at war with the
Netherlands.
   Baptisms These include *William Pitt, Earl of Chatham*, the great
Prime Minister; and *William Blake*, poet, artist and mystic.
   Incumbents The holding of this living seems in the past to have been
a passport to preferment. Four rectors, namely the great William
Temple who was here during the 1914–18 War, Dr Thomas Tenison
who was the first rector (1685–92). Dr William Wake (rector
1695–1706) and Thomas Secker (rector 1733 to 1750) all became
Archbishops of Canterbury. Many others were later deans or bishops.

General
The homely brick exterior set in its peaceful garden and the stately
interior make a striking contrast to the bustle outside and there is
much cause for gratitude that this outstanding Wren church, the parish
church of the Royal Academy, has come back to life.

12 St John's, Smith Square

History
St John's church was built under the 1711 Act to meet the needs of
new residential areas in Westminster, the parish – like St Martin-in-
the-Fields – being carved out of the older one of St Margaret's.

The story of Queen Anne, when asked by Thomas Archer the architect what design she would like, kicking over a footstool and telling him to build a church like that, is certainly fictitious but the name of 'Queen Anne's footstool' has stuck, the four towers being supposed to represent the upturned legs.

In fact, the positioning of massive towers at the corners was due to a tendency for the building to sink during construction and the towers were conceived by the architect to ensure that the sinking would be uniform. Alterations, however, to the pinnacles and the steps were made at the same time without his knowledge or consent.

The site in the middle of a square was purchased in 1713 but building took a long time; St John's was not consecrated until June and not opened until November 1728. Costing over £40,000, it was the most expensive of the churches built under the 1711 Act.

In 1742, not long after completion, it was gutted by fire and, in the subsequent reconstruction, 12 Corinthian columns supporting the ceiling were omitted.

Further alterations were made in 1824.

In 1941, during the air-raids, the church was once again gutted by fire and remained a burnt-out shell until it was sold for £50,000 to a Trust who have carried out a restoration enabling St John's to be used for various cultural activities, mainly concerts; the parish was united with that of St Stephen's, Rochester Row. The new church was re-consecrated in 1968.

Exterior

The outsize towers and the huge pediments give one a jolt from whichever of the four streets leading into Smith Square one first sees the church. The north and south sides, where the main entrances are situated, have large porticoes with giant Tuscan columns and pilasters supporting the pediments which are broken to allow for the introduction of deeply-recessed smaller pediments. Grand flights of steps lead up to the entrance doors.

On the other two sides are very big Venetian windows divided by pilasters. The pediments are also broken, in this case to provide space for niches.

The tall towers are decorated with pediments and enclosed with free standing columns at the corners. Both columns and pediments have Corinthian capitals. The towers are rounded off with curved entablatures with modillion cornices and crowned with lead cupolas and pineapples.

Interior

The entrance doors lead into lobbies which break up the cruciform
shape of the church. These give access into what is now the concert
hall, which is oblong with curved corners and projections at east and
west ends. The huge Corinthian columns remain and follow the curve
of what used to be the nave.

General

One of London's most controversial church designs. According to
whether Baroque was in fashion or not, opinion has varied from calling
it outstandingly ugly to considering it rather fine.

   Thomas Archer was a man of independent means who held the not
very exacting but well-paid and curiously-named post of Groom
Porter; he was the most Baroque of all our architects and St John's
which is generally regarded as his best-known work, has been
described as 'the finest example of Baroque architecture in the
country'.

   Whether or not one likes this intrusion into a quiet Queen Anne
square, it would have been a great pity if this twice-gutted and
therefore rather unlucky church had been allowed to moulder and we
can be thankful that new use has been found for it and that it still
remains to enliven the London skyline.

13 St John's Wood Chapel

St John's Wood

This was once the property of the Knights Hospitaller of St John of
Jerusalem attached to their Priory at Clerkenwell. In this wood, the
conspirators under Anthony Babington against Queen Elizabeth were
arrested.

History

The Chapel was built as a chapel of ease to St Marylebone Parish
Church to serve a new suburb, the architect of both being Thomas
Hardwick. Started in 1813, it was consecrated on 9th April 1814. It
suffered under the Victorians, the pews being reduced in 1867, but was
restored after war damage to its former Georgian state, being
redecorated in white and gold.

Exterior

Well set on an eminence at the end of Park Road and lying in a pleasant
churchyard, this church offers its most attractive face to the road with
pedimented Ionic portico and turret above, all faced in stone. The sides
are of brick. There was reordering and restoration in 1991.

Interior

The interior echoes the charm of the exterior. Doric columns support
galleries which have their own Tuscan columns bearing the slightly
curved ceiling. The chancel is narrower and projects. The nave
galleries have been glazed and are used as rooms. Box-pews painted
white complete the picture.

Monuments

There are a number of memorials of which the following are of main
interest:

Sarah Capel, who died in 1825, commemorated by a Greek seated
figure by Sir Francis Chantrey.

Gillespie children, who died in 1832–3. An appealing group by
S. Nixon.

John Farquhar, who died in 1826. Farquhar who made a fortune from
munitions bought Fonthill Abbey with its enormous tower from the
eccentric William Beckford. Three years later, the tower fell down. The
monument is an attractive profile medallion by Peter Rouw, the younger.

Associations

Elizabeth West, the wife of Benjamin West, the American-born
president of the Royal Academy, is buried in a vault below the church.

Joanna Southcott, the religious fanatic, was buried here in 1814.

General

St John's Chapel is an appealing early 19th century church, 'the
ensemble remarkably reminiscent of New England' (Pevsner). It must
be familiar to thousands of cricket-lovers wending their way to and
from Lord's Cricket Ground.

14 St Margaret's, Westminster

Dedication

St Margaret, of royal descent, became a Christian at Antioch. She was
pursued by a vicious local ruler and endured many sufferings in prison

rather than submit. Amongst these, tradition relates that she was swallowed by a repulsive dragon; with the aid of prayer and the sign of the Cross, she emerged unscathed, but she was eventually beheaded.

History

Three churches are known to have been built upon the site but there is no record of the original foundation. It seems reasonable to guess that the first place of worship was built not long after 1065, the year of the consecration of Westminster Abbey, as a church for the tradesmen, craftsmen and peasants who gathered in the village around the new Abbey.

The earliest written record dates from the first half of the 12th century when the Papal judges confirmed that the parish was exempt from any jurisdiction claimed by the Bishop of London. In fact, the Abbey exercised control right up until 1840 when it, at last, came under the episcopal hierarchy.

Although the parish was thinly populated, it stretched from Lambeth Bridge to the far end of Hyde Park, covering all that we now call the City of Westminster (except parts of the Strand), an area of 44 square miles.

By Edward III's reign (1327–77), the original church was found to be too small. The headquarters or 'staple' of the wool industry had been set up beside the site where Big Ben now stands and, the church having also become dilapidated, the parishioners and merchants decided on something better. This was the building in which Geoffry Chaucer and William Caxton worshipped.

At the end of the 15th century, it gave way to what basically is the present church, built by Westminster Abbey masons. So devoted was one of them that he regularly returned his wages, and even ordinary workmen made gifts. Started in 1486, it took 35 years to build and was not consecrated until 9th April 1523.

Seventeen years later, the parishioners had to put up armed resistance to save it from being dismantled by Protector Somerset to provide building materials for his new Thames-side palace.

In 1614, the long connection with the House of Commons began. As the Puritan movement gathered momentum, members wished to dissociate themselves from any High Church practices and 'for feare of copes and wafer-cakes' decided to worship separately at St Margaret's rather than in the Abbey. On Palm Sunday, 17th April that year, the whole House assembled in the church for corporate Communion, no doubt to test the churchmanship of each member, but all turned up.

Ever since, it has been the parish church of the House of Commons. The House adjourned here to give thanks for victory and peace in 1918 and again in 1945.

St Margaret's has been frequently in the hands of restorers. Galleries and box-pews have been installed and taken out again; it has been re-roofed twice, an elaborate apse introduced at the east end and later removed, the tower heightened and otherwise altered, porches attached, exterior refaced in Portland stone, internal walls stripped, all window tracery renewed, and, finally, the east end extended by one bay.

Much changed as it is, however, St Margaret's survives as a mediaeval church of the Perpendicular period, similar to St Andrew Undershaft, St Giles', Cripplegate and St Dunstan's, Stepney.

In 1973 the church was placed by a special Act of Parliament under the control and care of the Dean and Chapter of the Abbey. One of the canons of the Abbey serves as rector.

Exterior

St Margaret's is overshadowed by its powerful neighbours but, as such, gives them scale. It lies well back from the west front of the Abbey and the level lawn, once full of puddles, provides a charming frame. The low roof-line is typical of the 15th century but the positioning of the tower to the north-west of the building gives width when viewed from the west. In the middle of the 18th century the tower was raised 20 feet but, unless misrepresented, the tower when Canaletto painted the procession of the Knights of the Garter in 1749 looked very different even then from its appearance today with its large rectangular belfry window. Clasping polygonal buttresses extend its full length and it is capped by a small wooden octagonal cupola with ogee open top.

The renewed window tracery is in the Tudor style and gives a uniform appearance. At the east end, there are stone turrets at the angles.

Interior

The internal proportions are surprisingly large and there is seating for 650.

The spacious and graceful arcades and the tower arch are the only genuine old parts; angels with shields are placed at the springing points of the arches. The view to the large east window is uninterrupted by any chancel arch and the arcades with standard slender shafted columns stretch for eight bays. Aisles on both sides house a number of interesting monuments; the roofs are of low pitch but the interior is lightened by a tall clerestory. The 19th century chancel roof has gilded and elaborate bosses.

The south east vestry was added in 1778.

Furnishings
Font The font, by Nicholas Stone, dates from 1641. It has a supporting stem of square section and a circular bowl of granite. The octagonal base is of red granite.

Organ A fine Walker instrument installed in 1897.

Pulpit This is a heavily encrusted and crudely coloured Victorian piece. It is decorated with crocketed finials, many cusps and abounds with barber pole shafts.

Reredos The centre-piece of the triptych is the original carving in limewood of 1753, by Siffrin Alken, based on Titian's 'Supper at Emmaus'.

*Stained glass The central feature is the huge east window which contains some of the finest glass in London. It was made in the Netherlands in 1509 upon the occasion of the marriage of Henry VIII to Catherine of Aragon, both of whom are shown kneeling at the foot. It is probable that, with the Reformation troubles, Henry did not want to have the glass around and it went to Waltham Abbey. After several further moves it was purchased and presented to St Margaret's by the House of Commons in 1758.

The scene of the Crucifixion is dealt with pictorially in the Renaissance manner with a strikingly blue sky.

The west window, which contains full-length figures of Elizabeth I, Henry Prince of Wales, Sir Walter Raleigh (spreading his cloak) and his half-brother, Sir Humphrey Gilbert, is by Clayton & Bell, who also made the window alongside, commemorating John Milton. It shows him dictating after his blindness. The window includes lines from the American poet, John Greenleaf Whittier: 'The New World – – honours him whose lofty plan for England's freedom made her own more sure . . .'

The south aisle windows, by John Piper (their theme is said to be 'Spring in London') show geometrical forms in green, yellow, orange and grey against clear glass.

Monuments
The memorials are too numerous to list. Of particular interest are those to *Cornelius Vandun* (died 1577 – north aisle), *Mary Lady*

Dudley (died 1600 – south aisle), *Sir Francis Egioke* (died 1622 – north aisle), *Mrs Brocas* (died 1654 – west aisle), *Sir Peter Parker* (died 1914 – west wall). A memorial to *James Palmer*, who died in 1660, which was badly damaged by an oil bomb during World War II, has the comment that 'once a week' he 'gave a comfortable sermon in chapel of Fayer Alms Houses, which he built'.

Richard Montpasson, a contemporary of Shakespeare, kneels by the altar steps. The brass to *Thomas Cole* (died 1597) and family in the east wall of the north aisle has interesting wording.

Associations

St Margaret's is too historical a building to recount all its many associations. Amongst these may be mentioned:

Sir Walter Raleigh His decapitated body lies buried before the altar.

James Rumsey In the middle of the south aisle, it is recorded that the epitaph by Robert Herrick 'in memory of the late deceased Virgin Mistris Elizabeth Hereicke' formerly on a mural tablet in the middle of the north aisle was restored in memory of James Rumsey whom the State of West Virginia honours as the inventor of the Steamboat, which he demonstrated privately to George Washington in 1784 and publicly in the Potomac River at Shepherdstown West Virginia 3rd December, 1787'. He was buried in the churchyard on 24th December, 1792.

Cromwell Association A tablet on the exterior of the west wall was erected by the Cromwell Association in memory of those whose remains were disinterred from Westminster Abbey at the time of the restoration of Charles II and were in September 1661 summarily thrown into the churchyard. The 21 names included Oliver Cromwell's mother, John Pym, and Admiral Robert Blake.

Samuel Pepys In May 1667, Pepys entertained himself 'with my perspective glass up and down the church, by which I had the pleasure of seeing and gazing at a great many fine women, and what with that, and sleeping, I passed away the time till sermon was done'.

General

In many ways one of the best known of London's churches, it is perhaps chiefly remembered for its associations, which range from the wedding of Samuel Pepys to that of Winston Churchill, rather than its architecture. As the parish church of the House of Commons, it must always occupy an honoured place in the ecclesiastical heritage of the capital and there must be many whose memories are stirred each year by the Field of Remembrance in the churchyard. Starting life closely linked to the Abbey, St Margaret's is now once more intimately associated with its great neighbour. But it retains its own congregation on Sunday mornings, and it is one of the few churches in central London to keep a boys' choir, the choristers being drawn from Westminster Under School.

15 St Mark's, North Audley Street

History

St Mark's was built as a chapel of ease to St George's, Hanover Square between September 1825 (laying of foundation stone) and April 1828 (consecration) by J. P. Gandy-Deering, a little-known architect who had worked for Sir John Soane as draughtsman and in other capacities. The Church Commissioners contributed £5,500 towards the total cost of £13,300.

The church suffered drastic disfigurement at the hands of Sir Arthur Blomfield in 1878 when, as he had done a few years earlier at St Peter's, Eaton Square, he introduced a Byzantine remodelling totally unsuited to the original style of the building. He kept the three galleries, although Jacobean-type fronts were added later. New choir stalls were fitted in 1914.

In recent years, St Mark's – being near Grosvenor Square – was used by the American community in London, but they have now gone elsewhere.

Exterior

A striking and original neo-Greek façade with sturdy corner piers and two tall Ionic columns carrying a heavy entablature without pediment. Behind is a square lantern pierced with Somerset-type tracery (small circular apertures). This front is completely hemmed in by adjoining buildings and the body of the church lies well back.

Interior

The interior is reached through a dark and gloomy three-bay passage with classical Ionic pillars. From this opens out quite a large church with its architecture confused by the Blomfield alterations which included round-headed windows in the straight east wall of the chancel.

In the north-east corner is an attractive chapel with interesting fittings.

St Mark's, North Audley Street

Furnishings
Font Plain white marble with brown fluted bowl.
   Pulpit A fine furnishing.
   Stained glass The east window designed by N. H. J. Eastlake was
made by Lavers and Barraud. They also painted the reredos.

General
There must be serious doubts as to the future of this church, which is
now classed as redundant, but it is to be hoped that, whatever
happens, the façade which makes such an attractive accent in the
architecture of North Audley Street can be preserved. There appears
to be no change since 1976 when the author wrote the above!

N.B. Interior cannot at present be visited.

16 St Martin-in-the-Fields

Dedication
At one time known as St Martin-near-the-Cross (Charing Cross) the
saint chosen could hardly be more appropriate today in view of the
church's particular concern with the less fortunate members of society.
St Martin, according to the legend, met a beggar when, as a soldier, he
was riding in bitter weather towards Amiens. Martin had no money
but instead cut his cloak into two with his sword and gave half to the
beggar. The emblem of St Martin showing him dividing his cloak
appears on lamp-posts and door-handles in the parish.
   Open country surrounded the mediaeval church on this site so it
became known as St Martin-in-the-Fields to distinguish it from other
churches dedicated to this saint.

History
The first of the three churches erected was mentioned in a document
of 1222 but, apart from that, little is known about it. The only pictorial
record shows it as a small cruciform building and it may have been a
chapel belonging to the monks who came from Westminster Abbey to
work in the Convent Garden, or possibly an annexe to the great
religious house of St Martin-le-Grand.
   This original place of worship was replaced by a second in 1544 towards
the end of Henry VIII's reign. Because of the fear of plague, the King had
been concerned with the carriage of corpses through the Westminster

St Martin-in-the-Fields

Palace precincts for burial in the adjacent churchyard of St Margaret's. He had, therefore, caused parish status to be granted two years earlier to St Martin's so that burials could take place further away in the new parish, which stretched from Tottenham Court Road to Chelsea.

The Tudor church lasted until 1721, by which time its capacity of 400 people was totally inadequate for a parish which now numbered 40,000 people; the building was also considered unsafe. James Gibbs, who was in competition with John James for the post of architect, took the adjudication committee along the Strand to see his new church of St Mary; they were so impressed that he was duly elected by a large majority.

Exterior

The superlative siting only dates from the 1820s when Trafalgar Square was laid out – before that the church faced on to the lower end of St Martin's Lane with 'vile houses' in front of it. The improvement in the site, however, had one disadvantage in that it drew attention to the awkward placing of the steeple behind the pedimented portico on the west end of the church proper. The steeple (rebuilt in 1842) is a striking design consisting of a bell-stage with round-headed windows and coupled pilasters at the angles, above this is a recessed octagonal open lantern with attached colonettes and the whole is topped with a pierced concave-sided spire.

An imposing flight of steps leads one up to the portico, combining to make a grand entrance. The sides are impressive with giant columns and pilasters; at the east end there is a large Venetian window.

Interior

There is an almost theatrical gaiety about the interior, due in the main to the graceful plasterwork executed by the renowned Artari and Bagutti which provides sparkle and much visual pleasure. The effect is heightened by the way the nave curves round to embrace the small, narrow chancel and by the royal 'boxes' at the east end, two of which look out both into the chancel and into the nave. One old account, in fact, describes the interior as 'a little too gay and theatrical for Protestant worship'.

The lack of clerestory tends to emphasise width at the expense of height; the aisles have shallow dome vaults and there are high metal balconies at the east end.

The crypt, famed for the hospitality it gives to social outcasts, has groined vaults resting on short sturdy pillars.

Furnishings

Painting A fine copy of the painting of St Martin and the beggar by Francesco Solimena can be seen at the west end. The original, which for many years hung here, has been removed to the Italian section of the National Gallery where it is on display.

Font Oval in shape and notable for its cover. Dates from 1689. Attractive rails.

Prie-dieu The prie-dieu in the nave originally belonged to King Edward VII and Queen Alexandra.

Pews The box-pews in the aisles dated from 1799 but were lowered in 1858. Initially James Gibbs' plans only provided for pews in the galleries and permanent seating was not introduced into the body of the church until 1799.

Pulpit Although replacing an earlier one the pulpit seems in keeping with the styles prevailing at the time St Martin's was built. It has a charming staircase with twisted balusters and is decorated with inlay work.

Coat of arms A fine coat of arms is placed above the chancel step.

Communion rails Of cast-iron and they may be the earliest communion rails made of this material anywhere in England.

Chest and whipping-post A chest of 1597 and a whipping-post of 1751 can be seen in the crypt.

Monuments

Far East prisoners of war Sleepers from the Burma-Siam railway are included in a memorial to Far East prisoners of war in the crypt.

James Gibbs There is a bust of James Gibbs – the architect of St Martin's – in the vestry hall.

Associations

Royalty Buckingham Palace lies in the parish of St Martin's and the links with Royalty are very close. The 'boxes' at the chancel end are witness to this. Even before the Palace became a royal home, Charles II (born June 1630) was baptised here and George I was the first churchwarden of the present church – the only monarch ever to occupy this post.

Nell Gwynne, who died in November 1687 aged 38, was interred in the burying ground of the parish.

John Constable was married here on 2nd October 1816.

Dr Thomas Tenison, who was appointed Vicar of St Martin's and King's Chaplain by Charles II in 1680 later became Archbishop of Canterbury. He is associated with the establishment of St Martin's

Public Library which, according to John Evelyn, was the first Public
Library in London.

Registers Early registers include:

Births Francis Bacon (January 1560)

Marriages Daughter of Oliver Cromwell (November 1657)

Deaths Sir Winston Churchill, father of the great Duke of Marlborough
(1688):Richard Baxter, the Puritan divine (1691): Lord Fairfax, the
Commander of the Parliamentary army (1709): John Sheppard, the
highwayman (1742) and Louis-Francois Roubiliac, the sculptor (1762).

Link with Connecticut, USA The original design for a round church
which James Gibbs had submitted was later adopted for a church in
Connecticut, USA, owing to the close association of St Martin's with
the early history of the American Episcopal Church.

General

This church will always be remembered for the ministry of H. R. L.
(Dick) Sheppard who came here at the beginning of the 1914–18 War
after horrifying experiences as chaplain on the Western front. He kept
the church open for young soldiers as they arrived at Charing Cross
Station from France and ever since it has become known as 'the
Church of the ever-open Door', offering welcome to the homeless and
stranded. It is a beacon for those who need help or consolation,
providing what Ian Nairn describes as 'charity without strings'.

Vera Brittain, who wrote the admirable *Story of St Martin's*, has
described Dick Sheppard as 'that unusual phenomenon, a saint with a
sense of humour' and his successors, who included the great Pat
McCormick, have continued to draw huge crowds to St Martin's, so
that it has been well called 'the parish church of London'.

Over the past ten years the Social Care Unit has been expanded; a
Chinese community centre opened; a café, gallery and bookshop have
been opened in the crypt to the general public; and, building on its
long musical tradition, there are now four lunchtime and three evening
concerts a week. St Martin's is an international church where people
gather from every corner of the world.

17 St Marylebone Parish Church

Dedication

The original dedication of St John was changed to St Mary when the
second church was built and Tyburn, the name of the brook that ran

through the area altered to Bourne. The latter was no doubt due to the association of Tyburn with the place of execution at Marble Arch. So the church became known at St Mary at Bourne or St Mary-le-Bone.

History

No fewer than four churches have been built on or near the site which has been edged further north as the area developed. They have ranged from small village churches to the stately church one sees today. The first church built in about 1200, probably near the site of the former Marshal & Snelgrove's store in Oxford Street, gave way in 1400 to a place of worship built a quarter of a mile north in the High Street. The third church, on the same site, was erected in 1740; this very soon became inadequate but it was many years before a vacillating vestry commissioned Thomas Hardwick to build the present church a little further north on the Marylebone High Road, the earlier church being demoted to become known as the Parish Chapel and finally demolished in 1949. The foundation stone was laid on 5th July 1813 and consecration took place on 4th February 1817. It cost over £70,000.

In 1884/5, the architect and churchwarden Thomas Harris carried out a major remodelling in a neo-Classical style, choir stalls were put in and an apse built. The apse was restored in 1993 including replacement of war-damaged windows.

Exterior

When John Nash was laying out Regent's Park, he made the York gate entrance axial with the portico of the church. This is a magnificent hexastyle Corinthian example with a broad staircase, flanked by additional Corinthian columns. Above rises the imposing circular tower, which has free-standing columns round the main stage, a circle of caryatids round the smaller upper stage with entablature above their heads and is completed with a beehive stone cupola. A balcony runs along the top of the sides.

Flanking the window at the south end, diagonal projecting porches were built to provide a broad staircase entrance from the High Street.

The alignment of the church is north and south.

Interior

Stately but Victorianised. Originally, double galleries went right round the church, with the organ, split into two sections, framing a transparency in the east window by Benjamin West and in the strange

position of being over the altar. When the apse was built, the north
and south galleries were curved round to embrace the choir and the
upper galleries removed. Only the west end now has both upper and
lower ones. Thin columns are used for support Above the projecting
porches there were private pews, set one above the other, complete
with curtains and fireplaces and looking like theatre boxes; these have
been removed. The former coved ceiling is now flat and rather dull.
There are alcoves with ironwork screens at the east end, which has a
coffered apse decorated with Corinthian pilasters. Large free-standing
Corinthian marble columns frame the approach to the choir.

A small Browning Chapel was provided at the west end of the
church in 1946 to mark the centenary of Robert Browning's marriage
to Elizabeth Barrett, now converted to the Browning Room. Since
1976, the whole of the interior has been redecorated with restrained
colour and gold leaf; this has a pleasing effect.

Furnishings
The main furnishings of interest are:
Choir-stalls of mahogany carved with angels, harps and trumpets.
Font, circular and made of marble.
Altar and rails The Aisle Chapel contains altar and rails etc. of the
Browning Chapel and a painting of the Holy Family by Benjamin
West, American President of the Royal Academy, which was originally
the reredos of the high altar.
Organ The organ is a magnificent Reiger dating from 1987.
Stained glass Fragments of stained glass from the bomb-blasted
windows have been used as borders for the present windows.
Browning Room The contents consist of a window given by the
Browning Study Groups of Winnipeg, and a medallion portrait of
Robert.

Monuments
The monuments are minor.

Associations
One or other of the three St Mary's churches has been the scene of
many famous marriages, including the fictitious one of the Rake in
Hogarth's well-known cycle of paintings (in the Sir John Soane's
Museum, Lincoln's Inn Fields). The pew inscription in the painting can
still be seen on the wall of the west aisle. This scene was set in the
second church, where also Francis Bacon married Alice Barnham in

1606. In the third church, Richard Brinsley Sheridan married Elizabeth Linley in 1773. The most famous, however, was the secret marriage of Robert Browning to Elizabeth Barrett in the present church in 1846.

Amongst those baptised were Lord Byron (1788), Lord Nelson's daughter Horatia (1803) and Charles Dickens' son (date not available). The church is described in *Dombey and Son* and was probably the setting for Mr Dombey's second marriage to Edith Granger.

The site of the earlier church and its churchyard is now marked by the Garden of Rest in Marylebone High Street. A tablet commemorates some of the notable people buried there, including James Gibbs, the famous 18th century architect of many of London's best churches (1754) and John Michael Rysbrack, the great Flemish sculptor (1770). Charles, the brother of John Wesley and writer of many famous hymns, was also buried there and an obelisk has been erected to his memory.

Sir John Stainer's oratorio 'The Crucifixion' was written for the choir of the Church in 1886. It is performed every Good Friday evening at 6.30 p.m.

General
This church is a fine accent point in the Marylebone Road and has a long and interesting history.

18 St Mary-le-Strand

Dedication
With such a concentration of churches, it was often necessary to distinguish one London church from another similarly dedicated – in this case by adding the location.

History
Early history is conjectural. It is probable that, as this area is now seen as the centre of early Saxon London, there has been a church here since Saxon times. The earliest reference so far discovered dates from the end of the 11th century.

St Thomas à Becket was made rector here – it is thought around 1151 – while still a layman.

In 1549, the king's uncle, the Duke of Somerset, had the then existing church demolished to make way for his new mansion between the river and the Strand. The dispossessed congregation had to go to the Savoy Chapel nearby.

This continued until the reign of Queen Anne (1702–14) when the first of the Fifty Churches was erected to take the place of the pre-Somerset House Church The architect chosen was James Gibbs, a young Scot and a Roman Catholic, who later was to build St Martin-in-the-Fields. Work proceeded between 1714 and 1717 but the new place of worship was not consecrated until Ist January 1724.

Exterior

Splendid use has been made by Gibbs of the island site, which is a little to the north of where the earlier building was located, to provide London with one of its most beautiful churches. Originally the intention was to complete it with a campanile for a bell at the west end and, 80 feet in front of this, a 250 foot high column to be crowned with a statue of Queen Anne. But the last of the Stuart monarchs died in 1714 and presumably with the Hanoverian accession this was no longer considered appropriate. The idea was happily abandoned, therefore, in favour of a steeple and rounded west porch, a most felicitous combination which adds greatly to the visual enjoyment of this building. The steeple consists of a rectangular stage with detached columns at the angles and pairs of coupled pilasters on the west and east faces, carrying a narrower stage with similar embellishment but with single pilasters, the whole being surmounted with a concave-sided top stage capped with a little lantern.

The flanking façades on the north and south are adorned on the upper floor with alternating round arches and pediments which effectively break the line of the balustrade whilst the apsed east end is decorated with delicate vine trails between the windows. The absence of windows on the ground floor served to prevent the worshippers from being distracted by passing traffic.

St Mary's is built of Portland stone.

Interior

A rather narrow interior of which the most arresting features as one enters are the coved ceiling, coffered with alternate lines of lozenges and squares, and – less agreeably – by the windows of madonna blue in the apse. The walls are panelled and prints glued to the wood and varnished over are placed round the altar. There are no aisles but the apse is framed by coupled columns and is charmingly decorated with cherubs' heads, clouds, etc.

During a visit to Rome between 1703 and 1708, Gibbs came under the influence of Carlo Fontana, Surveyor to Pope Clement XI, and St Mary's is the most Italian in feeling of Gibbs' churches – so much so that it has been called an 'expatriate Roman'. The ceiling is similar to two of Fontana's churches in Rome.

Furnishings
Font The font is of marble on a baluster stem.

*Pulpit The ample double-curved pulpit had at one time a sounding-board in the shape of a shell supported by two pillars. The short thick foot is original but had two feet cut from it to lower the pulpit. It was carved, as was all the rest of the woodwork, by John Simmonds. A fine furnishing. It is at the east end.

Doorcases Attractive pedimented doorcases lead to vestries.

Altar-rails The fluted rails have turned balusters of slender proportions typical of the early 18th century.

Monuments
A brass plate on the south wall of the chancel commemorates a former rector, Alfred Bowen Evans DD, 'who with quaint sallies of native genius adorned the graver studies of the divine and the fervid eloquence of a thoughtful preacher . . . '

James Bindley On the gallery is Kendrick's monument to James Bindley, Commissioner for Stamps (d. 1818). The inscription states: 'His knowledge, of which his modest simplicity of character forbad everything like ostenatatious display, while his unaffected urbanity made him at all times ready to impart it, was various, extensive and accurate.'

Associations
Charles Edward Stuart It seems likely that St Mary-le-Strand was the church where Charles Edward Stuart, the Young Pretender, who was on a secret visit to London (there is a plaque on the house in Essex Street nearby where he stayed), was received in 1750 into the Church of England – no doubt with a view to furthering the Jacobite cause.

Charles Dickens' father, who was clerk in the Navy Pay Office of Somerset House, was married in St Mary-le-Strand on 13th June 1809.

Hackney Cabs The first rank was established in 1634 in front of St Mary-le-Strand.

Wrens St Mary's is the official church of the Association of Wrens.

General

St Mary's commandingly closes the vista east of the Strand. With
St Clement Danes behind, the churches look like two great galleons
sailing down the highway. The diminutive island site is attractively
planted with magnolia trees.

   A £400,000 restoration fund was launched in September 1977 to
make urgent structural repairs, to clean and to provide new glass; over
the past 15 years, about £750,000 has been spent on the restoration of
the church.

19 St Mary Magdalene, Paddington

History

The church of St Mary Magdalene is an offshoot of All Saints',
Margaret Street. The moving spirit behind its building was R. T. West
who was curate at All Saints'; the architect was G. E. Street who was a
member of the congregation and the church was erected to
accommodate those people wanting a similar High Church form of
service who lived in Paddington.

   Built in stages between 1868 and 1878, during which period the roof
caught fire and had to be re-erected, St Mary Magdalene was
consecrated in 1878.

Exterior

The lay-out of St Mary's was largely determined by the difficult site
upon which it was built. It had been a dumping ground of the spoil dug
out of the Regent's Canal which runs alongside and the plot of ground
was neither level nor were any of the sides parallel. There was room
for a south but not a north transept and the polygonal apsed east end
(actually south) followed the boundary line of the land, the thin tower
with its banded horizontal belfry stage and tall spire being fitted in
between the transept and the apse. The tower and spire, as at All
Saints', look German in their proportions.

Interior

The same site limitations made themselves felt inside for there was no
room for more than a small passage aisle on the north side and this
provides a disturbing contrast with the broader south aisle. Some,
however, consider this an ingenious solution to the problem. The sexes
in High Churches of this type were separated at the time it was built

and, as it was thought that there would be more women than men attending services, they were given the benefit of the south aisle; in fact, men outnumbered women and they must have been pushed for room in the north aisle.

The lack of balance between the two sides is further accentuated by different arcades, the south consisting of clustered columns with 13th century foliage decoration, the north, adorned with statues and medallions, of plain octagonal pillars with the bays divided by two sub-arches; the clerestories, however, which are similar, help to pull the design together.

The painted roof is of the ceiled wagon type.

Again because of the difficulties of the site, the architect put the vestries below, where there is also a charming chapel – the Chapel of St Sepulchre – with gay and colourful fittings by Sir Ninian Comper completed in 1895. These include screens, altar with tester, wall-painting, glass and a small organ with an attractively painted case.

General
The open site and low-rise surrounding buildings make this church a prominent feature in a largely residential area.

N.B. Not normally open except during services.

20 St Mary on Paddington Green

History
The history of worship on this site goes back to a small chapel which existed prior to the founding of the parish by Westminster Abbey in the early part of the 13th century. The Abbey administered and maintained the church they built until the Reformation, after which it continued to serve the parish until it was demolished in 1678.

The second church, which had a much shorter life, had a bell-turret at the west end surmounted by a small spire. From this steeple bread used to be thrown – according to a strange annual custom – to be scrambled for by the people below.

The present place of worship was built between the years 1788 and 1791, being consecrated on the 27th April of the latter year. The architect was John Plaw and St Mary's is the only ecclesiastical building put up by him. It remained the parish church until 1845 when this status passed to St James's, Sussex Gardens.

St Mary Magdalene, Paddington. View from south-east

Alterations in the 19th century considerably changed the character of the building but a quite outstanding restoration begun in June 1972 by the architect Raymond Erith has brought back the original 18th century atmosphere and made St Mary's into a place of exceptional charm and one admirably suited to its present needs.

Exterior

The yellow brick church is situated on slightly raised ground on a Green now hemmed in by the motorway which runs alongside. The building is in the form of a Greek cross, the centre square with a white cupola above – and the arms lower and narrower. There are porticoes on the south and west sides, the former being the main entrance.

Interior

The work so splendidly conceived by Raymond Erith was completed in 1973. Box-pews have been brought back, the floor has been re-paved with Portland and York stone slabs, with marble in the central aisle and sanctuary, and new lighting, including an attractive chandelier designed by Erith, has been provided. The original font, pulpit, altar and altar-rails of very thin iron have been made good whilst a new organ, designed by Quinlan Terry and built by Peter Collins, was installed in Erith's nemory.

Galleries on three sides recede into the arms of the cross, making with the angles five sides of an octagon. The galleries are supported by columns, those at the angles being especially robust to carry the four upper columns, on which the shallow dome rests. Considerable play is made with segmental vaults and arches, helping to give this enchanting interior its special appeal.

Furnishings (see *Interior*)

Monuments Amongst many fine monuments there are two by Peter Scheemakers and one by John Bacon.

The two Scheemakers memorials are in the south-east corner of the gallery commemorating:

Eleanor Boucher, 'of respectable family of the Addisons in Maryland' USA, born 1740 died 1784. She was the wife of Revd Jonathan Boucher.

John James The inscription states that 'in a monument in this churchyard belonging to Rev Jona^n Boucher are laid the remains of Rev John James sometime curate and afterwards rector of Arthuret

St Mary on Paddington Green. From south-east

and Kirkandrews upon Esk, County of Cumberland'. He died in 1786 in the 27th year of his life.

Frances E. Aust Only the lower part with a relief medallion remains but it is a fine example of John Bacon's work, dating from 1796.

Charlotte Cumberbatch, who died in 1818. Two ornate figures.

Thomas Combe A tablet on the south side below the gallery commemorates Thomas Combe, Prebendary of Canterbury Cathedral, born in Philadelphia, Pennsylvania, who died in 1822.

Joseph Nollekens, the sculptor, by W. Behnes on the south wall of the chancel, dating from 1823.

Sarah Siddons, the famous actress who died in 1831 is commemorated by a tablet, but outside on the Green there is a statue to her and her tomb is in the churchyard.

Burials include Mary Cadogan, Emma Hamilton's mother and William, the father of Wilkie Collins, the author of *The Woman in White*.

Associations
John Donne, the famous Dean of St Paul's Cathedral, preached his first sermon in the original parish church.

William Hogarth was married to Jane Thornhill in the old church in 1730.

General
This is one of London's most delightful church surprises. Motorists hurtling along the Westway probably have little idea that just below them is an exquisite little 18th century church, beautifully restored and with a vigorous life. Its excellent acoustics make it particularly suited for the concerts which take place at St Mary's in addition to the regular worship.

The recent restoration has removed 19th century excrescences, brought back the 18th century beauty and adapted the church to 20th century needs.

21 St Mary's, Bryanston Square

History
St Mary's was one of four Commissioner churches built to serve the needs of the St Marylebone area, in this case the Portman estate west of Baker Street. The Commissioners contributed just under two-thirds of the cost. The architect, Sir Robert Smirke, who was one of three

official members of the profession attached to the Board of Works, was about to begin work on one of his famous London creations, the British Museum. His churches, however, show an extraordinary lack of versatility and the characteristic, not very well-proportioned elongated, pepper-box was to appear at churches going up simultaneously at Wandsworth, West Hackney and Bristol, whilst his St Philip's Church, Salford, near Manchester (built 1825) is almost a carbon copy of St Mary's, upon which work began in 1821, consecration taking place on 7th January 1824.

In 1875 Sir Arthur Blomfield made various alterations, including provision of space for a choir, and we owe to him the separation of the font, pulpit and altar which previously lay one in front of the other – a 'low' Church arrangement not uncommon at the beginning of the 19th century.

An expert redecoration was carried out by Sir Albert Richardson after the 1939–45 War.

Exterior

The tower is finely sited in Wyndham Place and the hope that one day the forecourt might be turned into a precinct has now been realised, but the opportunity of a through vista from Marble Arch was lost when Bryanston Square was laid out.

Differences in detail of the tower from that at St Anne's Wandsworth are that the lower stage has attached fluted half columns instead of pilasters and the openings in the top stage are longer, whilst it retains its original clock made in 1823 by John Moore & Son of Clerkenwell (which has recently been repaired); and the siting on a semicircular portico of unfluted Ionic columns is in the middle of the south wall and not at the west end. The portico is impressive but the Bath and Portland stone of which it is built does not contrast well with the stock brick of the rest of the church.

Interior

Galleries carry tall Doric columns of wood with iron filling supporting a gently curved elliptical ceiling which has been recently restored after storm damage with epoxy resin. The sanctuary is flanked by vestries. A 1914–18 Memorial Chapel lies at the east end of the north aisle.

Furnishings

Organ A fine Harrison organ which is also used for recitals and concerts.

St Mary's, Bryanston Square

Font An octagonal font in the south-west corner.

Pulpit The large pulpit is supported on eight grey upward-tapering Corinthian columns embellished with ironwork.

Stained glass A pleasant grey-gold window in the north aisle, together with a window from the demolished St Paul's, Great Portland Street but not much else.

General

This is a dignified place of worship, suffering like many other London parishes from diminishing congregations due to residents moving out, and with increasing financial needs for necessary repair work.

In 1977, however, work was started on a precinct in order to commemorate the Queen's Silver Jubilee. This was completed in 1986, providing a setting for the church which greatly enhances its visual impact, especially at night when fully floodlit.

22 St Matthew's, Westminster

History

The original church, comprising a five-bay arcaded nave with three side aisles, entered through a sturdy short tower, was built in 1849–51 by Gilbert Scott with later work by Bodley, Kemp, Tower and (notably) Comper, whose upstairs Lady Chapel (1892) contains the first 'English altar' to be erected since the Reformation. The gilded wood altar and fittings in the south aisle, designed by Comper's pupil Martin Travers, were added in 1928 as a memorial to Frank Weston, Bishop of Zanzibar (1871–1924) a revered Anglo-Catholic leader, with a lifelong association with the church.

In May 1977 the church was severely damaged by a fire which destroyed most of the roof, the west gallery, and much of the furnishing, including a fine 18th century Italian baroque confessional, the organ and choir gallery, and Bodley's rood screen and surmounting loft.

Permission was granted to restore the church on a more modest scale: keeping only the tower, chancel, eastmost bay of the nave and Comper chapel, on condition that the cost be covered by the sale of the rest of the site (now the Lord Chancellor's Office). An ingenious and sensitive scheme was devised by Donald Buttress, subsequently Surveyor of Westminster Abbey, whereby the old chancel and east bay would constitute the body of the new church (its orientation being

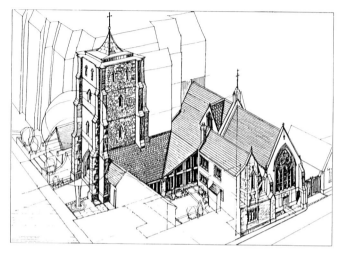

St Matthew's, Westminster

reversed to comply with fire regulations), to be joined to the tower entrance by a broad narthex with wide windows looking on to a small garth, and containing the staircase to the Lady Chapel, and the tower entrance to include the furnishings of the Weston chapel.

The new church was consecrated in 1984.

Exterior
Nothing is to be seen from the street except the tower and the (liturgical) west façade.

Interior
Despite the fire, many of the furnishings were saved, and skilful restoration and refurbishment have transformed the interior into a riot of light, colour and splendour, leading up to the regilded reredos of 1922 by Kempe and Company. Stained glass of this firm which survived the fire was reused, especially in the narthex and in the new east window. Other notable objects from the old church include the altar, the iron screen between sanctuary and side chapel, together with images of SS Matthew, Michael, George and Edward the Confessor – all by Bodley, a 15th century Spanish lectern, the oak pulpit of 1698,

and iron standard candlesticks from Seville Cathedral. In the narthex
are the bas-relief stone Stations of the Cross by Eric Gill's pupil,
Joseph Cribb; and in the inside narthex a bronze statue of Our Lady,
Queen of Peace executed in 1984 by Mother Concordia OSB.
Lady Chapel Although normally kept locked, it is well worth procuring
the key to visit Comper's Lady Chapel, brilliantly recreated by Peter
Larkworthy.

23 St Paul's, Covent Garden

Covent Garden
This was the garden of Westminster Abbey or Convent.

History
The garden was made over at the Dissolution to the Russell family.
Francis Russell, the fourth Earl of Bedford, obtained permission from
Charles I to develop his estate, one of the earliest property
developments in London outside the City and Westminster*. He
engaged Inigo Jones as architect for a splendid piazza with a church
building as 'the focal climax of the whole design'. All three being men
of taste, this must have been a notable sight. Inigo Jones however, was
kept on a shoe-string as regards the church and the Earl told him that
he would not have it much better than a barn. The architect's reply
'Well then, you shall have the handsomest barn in England' has passed
into the annals of architectural history.

Following Tudor extravagance in domestic design, Inigo Jones
determined to work to strict classical proportions and St Paul's was to
become the first classical church – and the last for a good many years –
in England. It was also, apart from St Katharine Cree in the City, the
first place of worship to be built in London after the Reformation, a
period of almost 100 years. Work was begun on 5th July 1631 and
completed in 1633, consecration, however, not taking place until 27th
September 1638. At first a chapel of ease to St Martin-in-the-Fields, St
Paul's became a parish church in 1645.

The great portico on the east front was destined never to serve as
principal entrance, for Bishop Laud insisted on the altar being placed
against the east wall.

In 1788 the architect, Thomas Hardwick, carried out a major

* As it then was.

renovation and re-fronted the church in Portland stone but only seven years later it was destroyed by fire except for the walls, portico and south-east chapel. A faithful reconstruction was carried out by Hardwick, and St Paul's was reconsecrated on Ist August 1798.

In 1871 William Butterfield, the Victorian architect, raised the chancel, also making changes in the position of the pulpit to suit current taste.

The original piazza in which the market-gardeners sold their own fruit and vegetables developed into the huge wholesale fruit market with massive buildings we knew as Covent Garden until it moved to Nine Elms, Battersea.

Exterior
This has been likened to a box with a big lid on it, not unlike a large version of a Swiss chalet. Originally, the effect would not have been so strong, as there were two cupolas on the roof and the eastern portico had wings. The proportions of the building were stated to be those of Solomon's temple in Jerusalem. The portico and the very wide eaves are the dominating features; it is supported by pillars at the corners with two Tuscan columns between.

The western end is the main entrance. Here, too, is a massive pediment with deep eaves. The side walls have simple arched windows each with its own frame. An attractive small garden makes a pleasant frontispiece.

Interior
A 'perfectly plain parallelogram' (Pevsner); there are no aisles. The dimensions, 100 × 50 feet, make it a double square. The altar is enclosed with columns from the north and south galleries which were dismantled by Butterfield. The west gallery is borne on Roman Doric columns. The ceiling, originally painted by Matthew Goodrich, is an attractive feature although now plain, and may be in the form planned by Inigo Jones himself.

Furnishings
Pulpit A two-decker pulpit and lectern in oak of the early 19th century with good carving.
Organ Built by Henry Bevington in 1861, incorporating part of the case designed by Hardwick in 1795. Restored by Noel Mander in 1967.
Stained glass East windows, dating from 1968–9, by Brian Thomas.

Monuments
There are two by the notable sculptor, Flaxman:
   John Bellamy (died 1794) known as the 'Father of the Whig Club'.
   Edward Hall (died 1798) in a Grecian style.

Associations
St Paul's is rich in associations with the stage and will long be
remembered as the opening scene of Shaw's *Pygmalion* afterwards
made into the musical *My Fair Lady*. Here also Samuel Pepys watched
a Punch and Judy show on 9th May 1662.
   Ellen Terry The ashes of Ellen Terry are kept in a casket on the
south wall in an ornamental niche.
   Charles Macklin On the same wall is a tablet commemorating the
actor, Charles Macklin, reputed to have lived to the age of 107
although his coffin plate says only 97; this gruesome monument recalls
his stabbing a fellow actor in the eye.
   20th century stage personalities Panels on the screen at the west of the
church commemorate more recent stage personalities, including Charles
B. Cochran, Ivor Novello, Leslie Henson and Bransby Williams.
   J. M. W. Turner The great painter's parents were married here on 29th
August 1773 and he himself was baptised in the church on 14th May 1775.
   W. S. Gilbert, of Gilbert and Sullivan fame, was baptised here on 11th
January 1837.
   Burials Many actors were buried in the vaults and precincts.
Amongst other people are Sir Peter Lely – court painter (1680) Samuel
Butler – author (1680), William Wycherley – dramatist (1715),
Grinling Gibbons – the great carver in wood (1721), Thomas
Rowlandson – caricaturist (1827).
   Royal Naval Division The colours of this Division, created by
Winston Churchill during the 1914–18 War, are laid up in the
northeast chapel. Celebrated members were Rupert Brooke, A. P.
Herbert and Lord Freyberg, VC.
   Hustings The portico was used in the past for election hustings,
including a poll in the 18th century between Charles James Fox and Sir
Cecil Wray which was the scene of a bitter struggle and lasted for forty
days.

General
This unique Inigo Jones place of worship is a thriving parish church
and continues to be the headquarters and spiritual centre of the
Actors' Church Union.

An Inigo Jones style entrance way has been erected on the north side of the portico into the churchyard and it is hoped that a similar gateway can be built on the south side.

24 St Peter's, Eaton Square

History
St Peter's was built early in the last century to serve the developing district of Belgravia. A Grecian plan submitted by Henry Hakewill was adopted, building started in September 1824 and consecration took place on 20 July 1827.

A serious fire in December 1836 was made good by the architect's son, J. H. H. Hakewill who kept to his father's tasteful design.

In the 1870s, Sir Arthur Blomfield interfered with this design by adding a chancel in the Byzantine/Romanesque style and later altering the nave.

In September 1904 a faculty was granted to erect a screen and pulpit and to form a south chapel.

This interior was destroyed by fire in 1987. The new interior returns the church to the original Georgian proportions, building a new east wall with access to the Victorian extensions, now converted to other uses on three floors.

Exterior
A fine portico of six Ionic columns raised on steps provides a dignified entrance but for some reason the church is not aligned with the square.

The tower rises above a large attic story over the west bay of the nave and the yellow brick walls have tall round-headed windows.

Interior
The interior is chaste and simple, relieved of the Blomfield incongruities, with four pairs of columns on their original crypt piers and a coffered ceiling. The floor is of French grey limestone with the principal altar placed forward to enable a westward-facing celebration.

Behind this altar is an apse of gold mosaic within which is a rear altar and the reserved Sacrament.

Evidence of the previous Byzantine work can be seen in the sacristy behind the apse.

Furnishings
East window The former Clayton & Bell east window has been
replaced by one designed and made by Lord Cardross of Goddard &
Gibbs.
  Organ On the west wall there is a magnificent mechanical action
tracker organ of four manuals and sixty-five stops.

General
The restoration after the disastrous 1987 fire has brought lightness and
grace to this important church.

25 St Peter's, Vere Street

Originally known as the Marybone and later the Oxford Chapel, St
Peter's was commissioned by Edward Harley, Earl of Oxford. It was
built between 1721 and 1724 and opened on Easter Day, 1724, as a
proprietary chapel to serve the residents of the new estate which he
and his wife, Lady Henrietta Cavendish-Holles, were developing
around Cavendish Square. The Earl chose as his architect James
Gibbs, who already had St Mary-le-Strand to his credit and was at the
time working on St Martin-in-the-Fields. Gibbs was thus able to use
the same carpenters and builders for the Chapel which was to be a 'St
Martin's' in miniature.

  In 1832 there was extensive restoration and the Chapel was then
dedicated to St Peter. Fairly gently treated by J. K. Colling in 1881, it
remained unspoilt.

Exterior
A plain rectangle of brick is set off by large pediments at each end,
stone doorcases and quoins, and completed with a charming little
cupola at the west end, the whole knit together with modillion
cornices. The cupola is set upon a square brick base with original clock
and consists of two octagonal open lanterns one above the other
capped by a little dome. Below the cupola at ground level is a Tuscan
portico with metope frieze and smaller pediment; it is flanked by stone
doorcases and, above these, round-headed windows.

  At the sides are two tiers of windows with red surrounds, round-
headed above and segmental below, and, at the east end, the pediment
rises above a stone Venetian window.

St Peter's, Vere Street. Drawing of 1908

Interior

There has been a transformation of the interior to serve new purposes. Although no alterations of a permanent nature have taken place the interior now serves as a church for Sunday use (by the Chinese Church) and an international study centre on weekdays.

The curved ceiling and the lively, delicate work of the famous plasterers, Artari and Bagutti, are well in evidence, as are the galleries that run round three sides, supported on the north and south by large columns.

The small open chancel remains intact, given emphasis by the generous arch decorated with rosettes in the soffit. Chairs and desks, however, can be brought into the chancel area for lecture sessions whilst the side aisles beneath the galleries have been adapted to accommodate offices. The galleries themselves now house a kitchen, a cafeteria and an extensive theological library.

The adaptations have been imaginatively undertaken with the way left clearly open for any future reversion of the building to a purely worship use.

Above the sanctuary are four theatre-like boxes used by the Herley family and other favoured people with fine wrought-iron work.

St Peter's, Vere Street. Interior looking west

The organ has been given to another church. The original organ was a Shrider instrument and the first organist was Joseph Centlivre, at one time principal cook to Queen Anne. In 1773, the year in which he was elected a Fellow of the Rural Society, Dr Charles Burney, a friend of Samuel Johnson, David Garrick, Joshua Reynolds and Edmund Burke, was appointed organist.

Furnishings
Stained glass The east window depicting Christ with the Samaritan woman at the well was designed by Sir Edward Burne-Jones and executed by William Morris. There are two other Burne-Jones windows at the sides.

General
St Peter's is a charming survival of an estate chapel and a pleasant surprise amongst the shop-windows of the big stores. It was in 1983 that St Peter's Church became the home of the London Institute for Contempory Christianity attracting many from Britain and overseas to its courses and seminars with the development of the Christian mind as its declared objective.

26 Savoy Chapel
(full name The Queen's Chapel of the Savoy)

Savoy
The land covered by what came to be known as the Precinct of the Savoy was given in 1246 by Henry III to his wife's uncle, Peter of Savoy, after whom the locality was named.

History
Since that time, the area has had a chequered history. The Manor passed through various royal hands until it came to John of Gaunt; during his tenure it was plundered and burnt in Wat Tyler's rebellion of 1381.

Since the reign of Henry IV (John of Gaunt's son), the Chapel has been the Chapel of the Duchy of Lancaster and, in right of her being the Duke, is a private chapel of the Queen, who appoints the Chaplain.

At the beginning of the 16th century, Henry VII founded the Hospital of the Savoy, completed after his death in 1509 when the original of the present chapel was built. The Hospital provided a night's lodging, food and clothing for 100 poor men but was suppressed in Edward VI's reign. Revived under Mary Tudor, it drifted on for another 150 years with its original aims forgotten being used successively as a military hospital, barracks and prison. In William III's time, the district, being outside normal jurisdictions, became a disreputable quarter and the Hospital was finally dissolved in 1702.

Many foreign communities, French Protestants, German Calvinists, and Lutherans, had chapels in the Savoy.

The old Hospital buildings were not cleared away until the early 19th century.

A chapel is known to have existed at the end of the 14th century but the present building is all that is left of three chapels built for the Hospital and probably consecrated in 1515. It not only served the Hospital and those living within the Precinct but also worshippers from St Mary-le-Strand, who had been unceremoniously deprived of their church by Protector Somerset when he built his house in the Strand in 1548. This lasted for over 150 years until their new church was consecrated in 1723.

The chapel had its usual share of 19th century repairs and alterations, aggravated by a fire in 1843 and culminating in a rebuilding after being almost completely burnt out in 1864. The architects involved were Robert and his brother Sydney Smirke (Robert was the architect of the British Museum).

Just before the 1939–45 War, in 1937, King George VI put this chapel at the disposal of the Royal Victorian Order, founded by Queen Victoria in 1896 to provide recognition for those who had rendered signal service to the Sovereign. Further alterations by Malcolm Matts were made to fit it for this purpose.

Happily, the fires of the mid-19th century were not repeated during the War and, although the chapel was damaged six times, the ill-effects were limited to the windows

In 1957–8, the dignified and spacious Antechapel was built along the east side including a new Royal Robing Room and Chaplain's Room. The architect was A. B. Knapp-Fisher.

Exterior

The simple rectangle of grey stone with belfry at the west end lies in the south-west corner of a comparatively large churchyard but dwarfed by the massive hotels and offices surrounding it. The chapel is without buttresses and runs north and south.

Interior

The rather sad exterior is soon forgotten when one sees the opulent interior. The Antechapel, which is reached by steps in the left-hand corner, makes an imposing and gracious introduction to the chapel itself. What is seen is the reconstruction by Sydney Smirke in 1864–6 which followed the pattern of the old Tudor Perpendicular building. The aisleless nave is of five bays and the eye is immediately drawn to the roof which, although only a 19th century copy, recalls the spectacular Tudor roof with its 88 quatrefoils interspersed with 14 shields of kings and queens, dukes and earls connected with the chapel.

There is panelling around the walls and the 16 stalls at the south end were placed there for the Royal Victorian Order.

Furnishings

The furnishings are unusual in that there is no pulpit (removed in 1939), although there is an old hour-glass. The chaplain's preaching desk takes its place.

Reredos Designed by Sydney Smirke and erected in 1864, it has twelve double panels with cusped and crocketed pinnacles and finials. At the sides are figures of SS Peter and Paul in decorated tabernacles. The centre painting of the Madonna and Child is 14th century work.

Lectern The rather grand lectern by Gilbert Bayes in the Antechapel is in memory of Laurence, son of Henry Irving the famous actor and his wife who were drowned when the *Empress of Ireland* foundered in 1919. It is of bronze and enamel. No longer in use, it stands on public view in the Antechapel.

Piscina The piscina, a relic from the Tudor chapel, was discovered behind a monument after the 1864 fire. The head of Christ is Florentine work of about 1520, formerly in the master's lodging.

Needlework panel The panel dating from 1600 on the south side of the chancel was given by Sir Harold Wernher of Luton Hoo as a contribution to the furnishings of the Victorian Order. It shows the Garden of Eden complete with camel, elephant and unicorn and the background includes a castle, windmill and other buildings.

Stained glass All the windows except the last four towards the south end were destroyed by the bombing. The survivors include one on the east side to Richard D'Oyly Carte, who staged the Gilbert and Sullivan operas, showing a procession of angelic musicians. The last window but one on the west side looking north commemorates the safe-keeping of the altar plate during the 1939–45 War in the Cathedral of St John the

Divine, New York. The arms of the Cathedral and also those of
Washington Cathedral are included.

In the vestry is a patchwork of 13th and 14th century glass collected
by Dr F. J. Grayling and given to the Chapel by his stepson's children
in accordance with their father's desire.

Monuments
Alicia Stewart and Nicola Murray. There are no monuments of note
but in the chancel on corbels are two figures from earlier monuments
in the shape of kneeling figures, one to Alicia Stewart who died in 1573
and the other to Nicola Murray who died in 1612.

Plaque
Dr Archibald Cameron On the floor of the sanctuary next to the
altar, a brass plaque commemorates Dr Archibald Cameron who, after
escaping to France following the Battle of Culloden, returned to
Scotland where he was arrested and executed in 1753.

Brass
Thomas Halsey and Gavin Douglas The oldest memorial is the brass
in the chancel commemorating two bishops, Thomas Halsey and Gavin
Douglas, both of whom died of the plague. It dates from 1522.

Thomas Britton Facing the churchyard on the east wall is a stone
commemorating Thomas Britton, who died in 1839 at the age of 101.

Associations
From April to July 1661 the Prayer Book Conference held in the
Hospital master's lodgings – tried unsuccessfully to reconcile
Dissenters and Low Churchmen to the doctrine and liturgy of the
Church of England as expressed in the Book of Common Prayer.
Although abortive, it led indirectly to the Revised Prayer Book of 1662
still used today.

The window on the east side, which is blank, was by Sir Edward
Burne-Jones, and formerly commemorated Dr Archibald Cameron of
Lochiel who was executed at Tyburn on 7th May 1753 for his part in
the 1745 Jacobite Rebellion.

John Wilkinson, who was minister from 1728 to 1756, celebrated
illegal marriages in the Chapel and was sentenced to transportation. In
1755; he married 1190 couples. He died at Plymouth two years later
before he was due to be transported.

Geoffrey Chaucer and John Wycliffe were followers of John of
Gaunt and must have known the Savoy well.

General

This little chapel is packed with associations and is of especial interest because of its links with Royalty.

27 St Stephen's, Rochester Row

History

Concern at the lack of churches, as voiced in Parliament in 1839 by the Whig statesman, Lord John Russell, led to more places of worship being built in the Metropolis during the following ten years than at any time since the reign of Queen Anne.

Amongst these and built to serve a slum area of Westminster, was St Stephen's, Rochester Row. It was financed entirely by the Baroness Burdett Coutts as a memorial to her father, from whom she had inherited a fortune, and erected on a site chosen for her by Charles Dickens, the houses on which were so verminous that the start of building was held up for two years.

The Baroness laid the foundation stone in 1847 and St Stephen's was consecrated in 1849. The architect was Benjamin Ferrey.

Exterior

The combination of Bargate stone from Godalming, Surrey for the main fabric and Morpeth, Northumberland sandstone for the dressings gives this church a distinctive appearance but led to structural problems which caused the spire to lean dangerously out of true so that it had to be truncated twice (in 1901 and in 1964). A new spire (built in a lighter structure with aluminium and man-made materials) was erected in 1994.

Interior

The church was built at a time when the views of the newly-formed Camden Society on worship and its setting, as publicised in the *Ecclesiologist*, held sway. St Stephen's was, therefore, built in the prescribed Middle Pointed or Decorated style considered at the time as the highest form of Gothic architecture.

The tall nave arcades with clerestory above, built of Caen stone, provide a spacious and well-lit interior. The finely carved capitals are by G. P. White, who later worked at Rochester, Salisbury and Wells Cathedrals. The capital nearest to the pulpit is interesting in that it contains portraits of twelve noteworthy people connected with the church at the time of its construction, including Queen Victoria and the then Bishop of London.

Furnishings
Pulpit Also of Caen stone with fine tracery in front.
  Stained glass Of the original windows by W. Wailes, only one remains; this is in the south aisle. In the same aisle is a Burne-Jones window with his usual strong reds, blues and greens.

Monument
The large monument to William Brown, died 1855, by G. G. Adams records in the epitaph that he was buried in the chancel; this was despite the fact that, by Order in Council, no one was to be buried in the church except Baroness Coutts and Mrs Brown 'who were to be embedded in a layer of powdered charcoal, and entombed in brickwork well cemented' (Basil Clarke). The Baroness was, in fact, buried in Westminster Abbey.

General
The high level of the interior stonework gives St Stephen's an air of quality and the unusual mixture of building stones a distinctive external appearance.

Camden

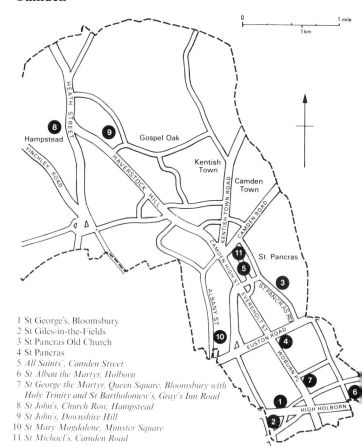

1 St George's, Bloomsbury
2 St Giles-in-the-Fields
3 St Pancras Old Church
4 St Pancras
5 *All Saints', Camden Street*
6 *St Alban the Martyr, Holborn*
7 *St George the Martyr, Queen Square, Bloomsbury with Holy Trinity and St Bartholomew's, Gray's Inn Road*
8 *St John's, Church Row, Hampstead*
9 *St John's, Downshire Hill*
10 *St Mary Magdalene, Munster Square*
11 *St Michael's, Camden Road*

Camden

1 St George's, Bloomsbury

Dedication
St George, the patron saint of England, was born of Christian parents in Cappadocia. He was martyred during the Diocletian persecution in AD 303.

History
Before New Oxford Street was cut through the area in 1847 parishioners attending St Giles-in-the-Fields from the northern part of the parish had to pass through one of the most squalid districts of London, known locally as the 'Rookery' and the scene of Hogarth's 'Gin Lane'. They petitioned the Commissioners of the 1711 Act for a new church and, although the proposed site was only a short distance from St Giles', were successful in their application.

Nicholas Hawksmoor, the architect, was commissioned, work was completed in 1730, and St George's was consecrated in January of the following year.

Except for interior rearrangements in 1791, the church has come down to us largely as built and, like Hawksmoor's other London ecclesiastical edifices, is unusual and conceived on a grand scale.

Exterior
A magnificent hexastyle portico of six Corinthian columns, two deep with coffered ceiling and modelled on the Pantheon portico in Rome, leads into the church from the south side. Plain pediment and a flight of steps complete this entrance piece.

An extraordinary steeple rises from the ground to the west and, in this position, avoids any conflict with the portico. A tall, square base with large belfry openings rising to a short stage with many columns then proceeds to a stepped pyramid modelled on a free rendering of Pliny's description of the Mausoleum of Halicarnassus. At the top, George I attired in Roman dress, representing the saint and standing on a Roman altar with arm raised, surveys the scene. This statue, donated by a local brewer, gave rise to the epigram:

> When Henry the Eighth left the Pope in the lurch
> The protestants made him the head of the church;

> But George's good subjects, the Bloomsbury people,
> Instead of the Church, made him head of the steeple.'

Sir Robert Walpole, the great Whig Prime Minister, considered it 'a masterpiece of absurdity' as no doubt many would have agreed when a couple of lions contended with two unicorns on the angles of the pyramid for possession of the Crown. The beasts were removed in 1871.

However one may feel about it, this facade is perhaps the most grandiose of any amongst London's 18th century churches.

The north façade (ritual east) facing Little Russell Street is also worth inspection. A large pediment rises above five bays of two storeys with pilastered blank arches on the ground and columned arched windows on the first floor. There is a delicate cornice.

Interior
Almost a cube, with a small clerestory but given direction by the differing treatment of each of the four sides. Hawksmoor's design provided for the altar being in the small eastern apse so that the church was aligned west/east along the short axis with an entrance on the western side under the tower. The parishioners found this inconvenient and, in 1791, the interior was rearranged with the altar on the north; the gallery on this side was removed and the altar niche appears to have been transferred to the new position. This materially changed the original effect but had the advantage of no longer directing those entering by the main portico to the side of the church but to the long axis from south to north. The ceiling mouldings have been arranged to form rectangles in line with both axes.

One might ask why the coupled Corinthian columns and segmental arch are impressively repeated at the north end if it was not the altar end from the beginning; this was probably done either for architectural balance or mere decoration.

Similar coupled columns are to be seen below a gallery at the southern or entrance end.

This is one of the liveliest of Hawksmoor's interiors. It has been tastefully redecorated with much attention to correct colour tones.

Furnishings
Some of the furnishings came from St John's Church, Red Lion Square, nearby, which was demolished after bomb damage in the Second World War.

Monument
Charles Grant In the west chapel, the monument to Charles Grant shows him 'obviously exhausted' (Pevsner) with a figure of Faith bending over him.

General
St George's is a handsome stranger in the Bloomsbury scene and its magnificent entrance front is a fine architectural addition to this part of London. Situated as the church is, near London University, it was for a few years the Anglican Chaplaincy to the University. It has now reverted to being a parish church with special attention to the visual arts and the art colleges in London.

2 St Giles-in-the-Fields

Dedication
According to tradition, St Giles lived as a hermit in a cave in France. The story that a wounded hind took refuge with him and was protected from his hunters or, as another version has it, that St Giles himself was wounded, making him lame thereafter, has established him as the patron saint of the disabled. This was extended to cover various unfortunates with whom this church has had particularly close associations (see *Association*).

History
Although there is evidence that in late Saxon times a church existed on the present site, serving a village on the old Roman road from the City to the West (now St Giles High Street), there is no reference to a church until the Scottish-born Queen Matilda, wife of Henry I, founded her monastic Leper Hospital of St Giles in the fields around the church, following her marriage in 1100. In the second Charter, dated between 1175 and 1189, it is stated that the hospital had been founded 'where John of good memory used to minister'.

The 'parish of St Giles' is mentioned as early as 1200 and the hospital held the advowson of the church, its clergy ministering to the parishioners until Henry VIII dissolved it in 1539 when the church became known as 'St Giles-in-the-Fields' and, from 1547, had a rector.

The earliest illustration shows a building with a round tower capped by a dome; this was replaced by a larger steeple in 1617 but shortly afterwards the church was considered ruinous and a Gothic brick building took its place between 1623 and 1630. This was largely paid for by Dame Alicia Dudley, daughter-in-law of Elizabeth's favourite, the Earl of Leicester; it was consecrated by Bishop Laud.

Less than 100 years later, the new church was itself in a bad state from damp, probably caused by the large number of plague victim burials, and parishioners petitioned the Commissioners of the 1711 Act for another place of worship. At first they refused because it was not a new foundation but eventually allocated £8,000 towards it. Although the well-known Nicholas Hawksmoor drew a design, the comparatively unknown Henry Flitcroft, son of William III's gardener, was preferred as architect and erected between 1730 and 1734 a building in the Wren/Gibbs tradition which possesses one of London's 'best-loved' steeples. His model for the church is to be seen in the rotunda at the west end.

The ever-busy Blomfield and Butterfield made alterations in 1875 and 1896 but there was not too much interference with the fittings.

St Giles's mercifully escaped the worst of the war bombing which merely removed most of the Victorian glass and, after a beautiful restoration and redecoration in 1952–3 by architects Gordon Jackson and Norman Haines, and the rector himself, we are able to enjoy this interesting and attractive place of worship very much as Flitcroft left it.

Exterior
An unusually dominant position for Central London, even the egregious eyesore of Centre Point does not smother it (see plate (p.000). The main façade is the north side which has a rusticated base and two tiers of windows, round-headed above and small rectangular below. At the east end a Venetian window flanked by pilasters projects, as also do vestries at the north-east and south-east corners. The churchyard to the east and south is now a public garden leased to Camden Council.

In front of the west end where the architect's name appears prominently on the main frieze is the interesting feature of a stone 'lych-gate' dating from 1804 which incorporates a crowded replica bas-relief of the Resurrection dating from 1687 and said to be based upon Michelangelo's *Last Judgement* in the Sistine Chapel at Rome. The wooden original is now inside the church in the south porch.

The relatively plain body with a green copper roof is offset by the striking 160-foot-high steeple, very similar to that of St Martin-in-the-Fields but which, instead of rising awkwardly on the portico, mounts straight out of the façade. The bell storey with coupled pilasters is

St Giles-in-the-Fields. From south

succeeded by a pretty clock stage, followed by a tall octagonal lantern with attached columns and balustrade above, and finally an obelisk with raised bands which is surmounted by a gilded ball and vane.

Interior

The interior is a well-proportioned Georgian design with square piers supporting galleries from which rise circular stone Ionic columns carrying the elliptical barrel ceiling with a design of transverse arches and panels picked out with rich gilded plaster decoration. There is no clerestory. The east end is in two stages with Ionic pilasters and a pediment above the window.

The groined aisle vaults spring from elegant gilded corbels on the walls which are partially panelled. The only stained glass is the east window depicting the Transfiguration.

Furnishings

Font This is a furnishing put back in 1952 after being taken to West Street Chapel near Cambridge Circus in 1875. It is attributed to Sir John Soane who was a vestryman and parishioner. Circular on a tapering octagonal shaft, it has honeysuckle and Greek key decoration. It dates from 1810. Its attractive wooden cover was made in 1952.

Organ This was originally installed by Father Smith in 1671 and retains all his original work but has since been much restored. The Royal Arms on the gallery are those of George 11.

Pulpit This was once a three-decker. What remains is a beautiful inlaid furnishing of oak with marquetry panels. It was given by a former rector, John Sharp, who became Archbishop of York, and dates from 1676. Flitcroft insisted on it being retained.

Another pulpit, very plain by comparison, at the east end of the north aisle, was also once in the West Street Chapel and, when there, the brothers Wesley preached regularly from it between 1742 and 1791. It has a green base, is cream above and was formerly also a three-decker.

Chandeliers The four brass chandeliers are mainly 18th century but the largest probably dates from 1680.

Mayoral Chair In the north aisle is a mayoral chair (formerly in Holborn Town Hall) with the arms of the Duke of Bedford on top, presented by Camden Borough Council.

Altar-piece This pleasing feature comprises a central framed panel with the Ten Commandments and a scrolled pediment framing surmounted by a pelican, and two side panels of Moses and Aaron painted by Francisco Vieira, court painter to the King of Portugal.

In the south porch not always open to the public are:

Iron Chest of 1630 and probably foreign with camels' feet.

Mosaic by G. F. Watts, formerly in St Giles' School and erected here in 1974.

White Ensign Worn in Tokyo Bay by the aircraft carrier HMS *Indefatigable* at the Japanese surrender in August 1945, the ensign is now hoisted in the south porch.

Monuments

George Chapman At the west end of the north aisle is a monument to George Chapman, Elizabethan dramatist (d. 1624) in the form of a Roman altar said to be by his friend, Inigo Jones. It is not well preserved, having formerly stood outside in the churchyard.

Lady Frances Kniveton Next to the Chapman memorial is a monument to Lady Frances Kniveton, daughter of Alicia, Duchess Dudley, who was a great benefactor to the Church. It is in the form of an effigy in a shroud.

John Barnfather (d. 1793) At the east end of the north aisle, this monument is oval in shape with a feminine figure beside an urn.

John Flaxman A memorial was placed in the vestibule in 1930 by the Royal Academy to John Flaxman the sculptor, who died in 1826. It is a bronze cast of one of his own works at Micheldever Church, Hampshire, depicting a figure battling with devils and helped by angels ('Deliver us from Evil').

Andrew Marvell, the poet, and *Luke Hansard*, printer of the House of Commons journals, are commemorated by tablets.

Mary Chilton, who died in 1828, is commemorated by a very fine bas-relief by William Pitts; it is situated by the chapel altar.

In the south porch is the tombstone of *Richard Pendrell* (Penderel) who died in 1671. One of the most courageous acts in the escape of Prince Charles (later to become Charles II) after the battle of Worcester in 1651 was the hiding of the Prince in the Boscobel oak-tree and the concealment of him by the Pendrell brothers in their house where they dressed him as a woodcutter. In January 1922 the slab was removed from the courtyard where the table tomb can still be seen.

Associations

The church of St Giles seems to have had more experience of human misery than most. The frightful horror of the Great Plague started in the parish and, as with its namesake at Cripplegate, many victims were buried in the churchyard. As many as 3,216 persons died in St Giles's parish.

In addition, condemned prisoners passed St Giles' on their way from Newgate to Tyburn for execution and scores of these unfortunates were also buried here. They received the last refreshment of a bowl of ale ('St Giles Bowl') and the sexton tolled the great bell when they were passing. Claude Duval, the highwayman, and a hangman, Edward Dennis, were also buried in the churchyard.

Among other victims were Oliver Plunket, Archbishop of Armagh, condemned for high treason in 1681 and canonised in 1975 who, together with five now beatified Jesuit priests who had also been executed and a further eight beatified Roman Catholic martyrs, were buried in the churchyard. Oliver Plunket, however, was later exhumed.

Sir John Oldcastle, the Lollard, was hanged in chains over a slow fire near the church in 1417.

Among less untimely deaths associated with Giles' were the following:

Cecil, Lord Baltimore, initial proprietor of the State of Maryland in the USA who fitted out the ships which took the first Maryland colonists in 1633, died in St Giles' parish in 1675 and was buried in the churchyard although he was a Roman Catholic. Four Calverts related to him were buried in the churchyard before 1711 and thus St Giles' is Maryland's chief London connection. A request has now (1994) been received for a memorial to be erected in the church.

Dr William Balmain, co-founder of New South Wales after whom a suburb of Sydney is named, was buried in the churchyard in 1803. He was a surgeon with the First Fleet.

Arthur William Devis, painter of large historical canvases, such as 'The Death of Nelson', was buried here and has a tablet in the north aisle.

David Garrick, the famous actor, was married here in 1749.

The baptisms include:

J. C. Patteson, murdered bishop, baptised here in 1827 (tablet in south aisle).

William and Clara Shelley (3rd and 4th children of the poet) and *Clara Allegra Clairmont* (Byron's illegitimate daughter) baptised here in joint ceremony 1818.

John Milton's daughter, Mary, baptised here in 1647.

Admiral Lord Rodney, baptised here in 1719.

General

St Giles', one of Camden's three 'borough churches', can justifiably claim to be a most interesting London church, both architecturally and historically.

3 St Pancras Old Church

Dedication

St Pancras, the boy of 14 who was martyred in AD 304, not only gave his name to a well-known railway station and to two churches nearby but to a whole Borough. He is the patron of youth and the avenger of false oaths.

History

St Pancras Old Church has had a long history and a travel-writer in 1700 stated that the first building even took precedence in age and seniority over St John Lateran of Rome which carries us back to AD 314, only ten years after St Pancras was put to death. The site – a small hillock above where the River Fleet used to run – is still older and, according to one expert, was a pre-Christian rural shrine.

First reliable mention, however, of St Pancras-in-the-Fyldes, as it was once called, is in the second half of the 12th century and the present place of worship was probably rebuilt about 1350 to serve a parish which extended from Ken Wood in Highgate to the boundary mark still to be seen on the shop-front of Heal's in Tottenham Court Road.

In Elizabeth's reign, although the Marian incumbent was apparently allowed to stay on, the church fell on bad times and John Norden writing in 1593 records that it 'standeth all alone as utterly forsaken, old and wether-beaten'. By 1642 it was deserted and Parliament ordered that it 'bee disposed of unto lodgings for fifty Troupers'. Services were resumed later but between 1675 and 1689 the vicar was arrested for debt and imprisoned.

By the early part of the 19th century, the vicar at that time was distinguished enough to become first Bishop of Calcutta and Primate of all India. In 1847–8, the church suffered a drastic restoration under A. D. Gough. It was given an almost complete neo-Norman casing, the old tower with its quaint bell-shaped cap was taken down to allow the nave to be lengthened by 30 feet and a new tower erected on the south side (at one time higher than it is now) with a top resembling a dovecote. Galleries were added round the interior.

With the completion of the new St Pancras church nearby in the Euston Road in 1822, the old church became a chapel of ease to it but was reinstated as a parish church in 1863.

Restorations took place in 1871 and again in 1888, the latter by Sir A. W. Blomfield. In 1925 the roof timbers were exposed and the side galleries taken down; after the War, during which it had been badly damaged, the church was repaired and restored. A major interior restoration took place in 1978 under the direction of Quinlan Terry. This involved the removal of two screens and the pulpit, and a glazed screen was placed beneath the organ gallery, to form a parish room.

During the night of 3rd January 1985 the church was broken into and vandalised by Satanists. They caused much desecration.

In 1956, the benefice was combined with that of St Matthew's, Oakley Square, although, because of it being unsafe, the church was pulled down in 1977. In 1987, the parish was united with that of St Mary's, Somers Town.

Exterior

Despite the almost completely early Victorian exterior, St Pancras' still retains, owing to its setting in what is now a public garden, a rustic appearance (see plate opposite).

The entrance is through attractive gates. The west door and the wheel window above were part of the 1847–8 alterations. Part of the Norman wall with Roman tiles remains on the north side and the north and south doors are recognizable as being of that period.

The churchyard, to which an extension of St Giles-in-the-Fields churchyard had been added earlier was made into a public garden in 1877.

Interior

The interior has even more of the village atmosphere and is larger than one might expect. Access is under a large western gallery still retaining early 18th century scroll work on the panelling. The nave, long and narrow, is closed by a light iron screen installed by Blomfield, beyond which is a flat-roofed chancel without stalls but with many monuments. Part of a 13th century lancet window suggests that it was altered at that time.

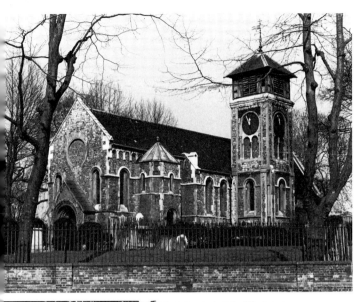

St Pancras Old Church   St Pancras Old Church and Soane monument in churchyard

Furnishings

Font The attractive font cover dates from about 1700.

   Piscina and sedile The piscina is 13th and the sedile 15th century but both are much restored.

   Reredos A 'Blomfield' furnishing. The high altar table contains panels from the old pulpit.

   *Altar-stone The most exciting item. The altar-stone was found buried under the old tower during the 1847–8 alterations. It is incised with five consecration crosses, the form of which gives reason to believe that it dates from the 6th century.

Monuments

Amongst many monuments are:

   Mary Beresford A brass of 1588 in the chancel is to Mary, wife of John Beresford.

   Robert and Lawrentia Eve On the north wall is the upper part of an early 16th century table tomb from the north side of the altar with a canopy and the matrices of kneeling brass figures. There is no inscription.

   Philadelphia Woolaston, who died in 1616, is commemorated by a monument in the form of a semi-reclining effigy with figures standing on each side.

   John and Elizabeth Offley and family. North-west of the chancel is a tablet to the Offley family with an ornamental epltaph of the 1670s.

   William and Mary Platt Next door to the Offley tablet is a large monument to William Platt who died in 1637 and his wife who died 50 years later in 1687. They are shown as frontal busts in two oval recesses. The monument was removed from Highgate Chapel in 1833 and restored by St John's College, Cambridge.

   Samuel and Christina Cowper Samuel Cowper, the miniature painter, who died in 1672, and his wife in 1693, are commemorated by a small cartouche in the chancel with palette and pencil.

   Richard Draper, who died in 1756, is remembered by a monument in the shape of a tall column with an urn on top.

Churchyard

Blackmailers, murderers, pimps, duellers, a highwayman, a forger and a spy, together with suicides, all found their last resting-place in Old St Pancras churchyard. But there had been notable people too – distinguished emigrés from the French Revolution and the Corsican patriot, Pasquale de Paoli, whose bones were returned to their native land when the Midland Railway encroached upon the churchyard. Thomas Hardy, the author, worked as an architect's apprentice in supervising the reburial of other remains in a pit and it may have been this experience which gave him his preoccupation with churchyards in his novels. The burial ground was the scene of the mock funeral and attempted body-snatching in Charles Dickens' *Tale of Two Cities*.

Many of the old headstones are arranged radially round a tree.

Amongst those buried in Old St Pancras churchyard are:

Johann Christian Bach ('the English Bach') in January 1782.

Chevalier d'Eon in May 1910. The Chevalier dressed as a woman when engaged on some of Louis XV of France's missions and continued to dress in this way so that his sex was debated until his death.

The last survivor of the Black Hole of Calcutta, aged 90

Members of the Rhodes family The family graves were restored by Cecil Rhodes in 1890.

Former St Giles-in-the-Fields churchyard

Although the St Giles-in-the-Fields extension (see *Exterior*) was quite separate from, but contiguous to, Old St Pancras' churchyard when they were used as burial grounds, the main interest of what is now one public garden is the:

Soane Monument (see plate p. 277) This monument north-east of the church was erected by the architect Sir John Soane to his wife who died in 1815. It is enclosed in a canopy carried on pillars with pierced pediments on each side and a little knob on the top. The tomb is surrounded by stone railings decorated with typical Soane carved blocks (acroteria).

Soane himself was buried here in 1837.

Also buried in the St Giles cemetery was *John Flaxman*, the sculptor, in December 1826.

Associations

Joseph Grimaldi, the famous clown, married his second wife at St Pancras Old Church in 1801.

P. B. Shelley, who lodged nearby, first saw and fell in love with Mary Godwin when she was visiting her mother's grave in the churchyard. The mother's remains were moved to Bournemouth in 1851.

General

At times neglected, deserted, its ministers even held in contempt, but also the recipient of loving care, St Pancras Old Church – looking perhaps a little wistful today – survives, despite severe restoration, as an extraordinarily countrified, almost village church, sandwiched between the bustle and noise of the main railway line behind and one of London's busy roads in front.

N.B. Not normally open.

4 St Pancras

Dedication
Pancratius (Pancras in English), the boy martyr, was born in Phrygia, Asia Minor, of noble and wealthy parents who died when he was young. Entrusted to the care of his uncle, they went to Rome where they were converted to Christianity. During the Diocletian persecution, Pancratius refused to give up his beliefs and was beheaded on the Aurelian Way on 12th May 304 at the age of 14.

History
The spread of London made the village church of St Pancras, holding about 150 people, inadequate and, despite opposition from the parish on economic grounds, a new church was authorised by Act of Parliament on 31st May 1816. In 1818, a site was acquired alongside the New (later Euston) Road and a design, submitted by a local surveyor William Inwood and his son Henry William was accepted; in the following year Henry William travelled to Greece for the purpose of making drawings to complete the design.

The first stone was laid by the Prince Regent's brother on 1st July 1819 and the new St Pancras church consecrated three years later on 7th May 1822. Built of brick faced with Portland stone in neo-Grecian style, it was the most expensive church erected in London since St Paul's Cathedral, costing about £90,000.

In 1880, the interior was redecorated in dark colours but the restoration in 1952–3 partially corrected this. The chancel was reconstructed in 1889.

Exterior
The Greek influence is apparent wherever one looks. The 156-ft high tower is a highly successful adaptation of the Temple of the Winds at Athens and the fine hexastyle portico of six fluted Ionic columns is

St Pancras

St Pancras. Projecting wing with caryatides

based on the Acropolis Erectheum on which the building is largely
modelled.

The tower rises in receding octagonal stages, the two lower ones
enclosed with eight columns, and terminates in a simple finial and
cross. The portico leads up to three entrance doors which, in the same
way as the windows of the sides, all taper upwards in Egyptian fashion.
The inner façade is decorated with much elegant detail, egg and dart,
acanthus, rosettes and bobbins, whilst the centre door has a projecting
lintel.

The north and south sides are plain except for more egg and dart
adornment and a lively motif of acanthus leaves along the top of the
wall. The windows are in two tiers, in the upper storey twice as large.

At the east end, the designer has placed two projecting wings copied from the Hall of Caryatides, containing almost detached vestries, and entrances to the burial vaults. The terracotta caryatides, demurely draped and modelled around cast-iron stanchions, were designed by Charles Rossi; he made them too tall and a slice had to be taken out of their middles in order to fit. The east end wall is curved into an apse and enclosed in Ionic columns.

Interior

Behind the portico is a vestibule with chambers at the sides containing staircases. This leads into the open and undivided hall interior which has galleries at the sides and west end supported on slender columns with lotus leaf capitals copied from the Elgin marbles. The west gallery supports the organ.

Until 1889 there was no chancel and the pews went right up to the Communion rail at one level; it was then that the floor was raised, choir stalls inserted, gilded screen provided and a marble wall built, separating the chancel from the nave. Behind the chancel, the sanctuary rises dramatically to create a splendid focal point. The screen of unfluted Ionic columns stands clear of the walls and is made of scagliola (composition of marble chippings, paste and glue); the bases and capitals are copied from the Temple of Minerva.

A flat, coffered unsupported ceiling covers the interior in one large span of 60 feet.

In the south-east corner, a Lady Chapel – dedicated in 1914 – houses the original altar and marble railing from the chancel. The chapel apse is decorated with gold acanthus leaf on a blue background and the walls with plaster frieze are panelled in brown marble.

There is another chapel on the other side, dedicated by the Bishop of Edmonton in September 1970. This is a memorial to a former assistant curate, provided by his sister. Its screen was designed by Cecil Brown.

Furnishings

Royal Arms The Royal Arms displayed on the front of the west gallery are those in use at the time the church was built.

Organ casing This is a noteworthy feature.

Font The alabaster font is octagonal. Decorated with the Star of Bethlehem, it is mounted on a plain base.

Stained glass All the glass is by Clayton & Bell, one of the better Victorian glass-makers. The east windows date from 1860–6, the 26

All Saints', Camden Street

north and south windows from 1891–2. The latter are divided into 14 large windows above gallery level, illustrating the Te Deum by depicting Apostles, Prophets and Martyrs, and 12 smaller ones below, based on sentences of the Litany referring to the Life and Passion of Jesus Christ. Deep reds, greens and gold together with white predominate whilst the large borders are brown.

Pulpit The wooden octagonal pulpit raised on four Ionic columns with a delicately curving staircase was made from the famous Fairlop Oak of Hainault Forest. It is a fine feature.

General
This notable neo-Grecian building with its elegant detail was naturally hateful to the Gothic Revivalists but perhaps they felt that there was not much they could do about it. Apart from the stained glass and the raising of the chancel which have not detracted from the general

St Alban the Martyr, Holborn. Bodley and Garner reredos (destroyed in war)

St Michael's, Camden Road. Interior looking east

character, and the darkening of the interior (later corrected), they left it largely alone.

Other Churches in Camden

The Borough of Camden which includes Hampstead has many other churches of interest.

   All Saints', Camden Street (5) – built in 1822–4 by the Inwood brothers (designers of St Pancras) and now made over to the Cypriot Community – has a splendid, broad, semicircular Ionic portico parts of which came from an Ionion temple and which carries a slender, circular steeple.

   Two saints dear to the English – St Alban, the first English martyr and St George, whose white banner with its red cross became the basis of the Union Jack – are commemorated at churches in Holborn and Bloomsbury. Despite its cramped site, **St Alban the Martyr, Holborn** (6) is an impressive Butterfield building but altered by Adrian Scott after war damage. **St George the Martyr, Queen Square** (7) dates back to 1706, when it started as a chapel to serve a 'genteel neighboourhood'. It was drastically recast by Teulon in the 19th century.

   St John's, Hampstead (8) is an 18th-century building with the unusual arrangement of the tower at the east and the chancel at the west end. It has many artistic associations – John Constable is buried with his family in the south-east corner of the old churchyard and there is a fine bust to John Keats on the west wall of the north aisle. Towards Belsize Park, **St John's, Downshire Hill** (9) is a rare survival of a proprietary chapel with a charming and well-restored interior of box-pews and galleries.

   St Mary Magdalene in Munster Square (10), designed by the promising architect Richard Carpenter who died young, was a pioneer church of the Gothic Revival and, in its unspoilt and uncluttered state, is of great interest both architecturally and liturgically.

   Bodley and Garner, two other Victorian architects, are represented at **St Michael's, Camden Road** (11) in a church with an elegant and well-proportioned interior.

Greenwich

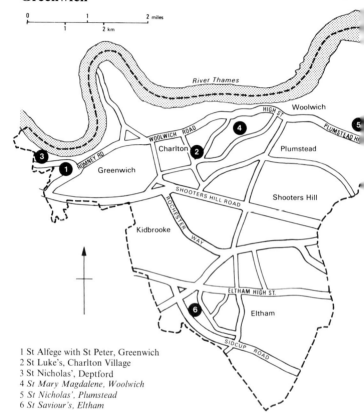

1 St Alfege with St Peter, Greenwich
2 St Luke's, Charlton Village
3 St Nicholas', Deptford
4 *St Mary Magdalene, Woolwich*
5 *St Nicholas', Plumstead*
6 *St Saviour's, Eltham*

Greenwich

1 St Alfege with St Peter, Greenwich

Dedication

St Alfege was Archbishop of Canterbury and met a violent death.
Appointed in 1006, he courageously refused to allow a ransom to be
paid to the invading Danes for his release from capture and was
martyred on 19th April, 1012 on ground where the church now stands.
St Peter's, which used to be situated nearby, was destroyed during the
1939–45 War and the parish was then united with that of St Alfege.

History

There was a church in Greenwich in AD 964 but the first one on this
site, in the area originally known as East Greenwich (Deptford being
West), may have been erected soon after the martyrdom, the second
church was probably a rebuilding in the 13th century. Little is known
of it but John Morton, who later became Henry VII's Chancellor and a
Cardinal, was Vicar here from 1444 to 1454 and, owing to the
proximity of the royal palace, the church in Tudor times was the scene
of many great occasions. Henry VIII was baptised here and his sister,
Mary, was married at St Alfege to Thomas Brandon, Duke of Suffolk,
in 1514. The tower was rebuilt in 1617 and reconstructed after a storm
in 1813. A painting by Vosterman of about 1680 shows it to have been
tall and plain with a cupola on top rising above a low-roofed fabric.

In 1710, a severe storm led to the collapse of the roof, due it was
thought, to one of the supporting piers having been undermined by
numerous burial excavations. The building was considered beyond
repair and the parish successfully applied for funds to reconstruct it.
The application probably led to the 1711 Act, although this applied
mainly to new places of worship. Nicholas Hawksmoor was the chosen
architect and, in the short time of two years (1712–14) the third church
of St Alfege, was built, being the first of the churches to be completed
under the Act. Consecration was, however, delayed because the
parishioners objected to the stipulation that a Royal Box should be
provided. Eventually this was installed in the west gallery and the
ceremony took place on 29th September, 1718.

Hawksmoor had included a tower in his design but, owing to
shortage of funds, it was never erected. Instead, the old tower was re-
cased by a local architect, John James, this being completed in 1730.

Victorian restoration was gentle and no attempt was made to Gothicise the building but in 1941 incendiaries caused extensive damage. A most careful restoration by Professor Richardson, who retrieved as much as he could of the old material, brought back the church as closely as possible to its former state.

Exterior
As at St Botolph's, Bishopsgate, the main façade, which faces the street, is the eastern one. The portico here has a deep, heavy pediment, supported by giant Tuscan columns, with a frieze broken in the centre to allow an arch to rise up into the pediment.

The frieze is carried round the sides which are decorated with large pilasters. Projecting vestibules approached by open staircases are centrally positioned in each wall.

The tower rises unconvincingly from the pedimented west end. John James provided a square base above which is the clock stage leading to a circular section surrounded by columns and capped by a small dome with diminutive spirelet.

Interior
Diagonally projecting pairs of giant columns flank the reredos and east window which lie in a shallow apse with depressed vault and trompe l'oeil coffering. The oval ceiling rises from corbels and is suspended from tie-beams. Light-toned galleries on three sides are replacements of the original ones, which had carving attributed to Grinling Gibbons. They are supported on thin legs but have fine ironwork.

At the east end of the north aisle is a Lady Chapel dedicated to the Virgin Mary. The murals behind the altar are by August Lunn.

A spacious vestibule with vestries leading off completes the west end.

Furnishings
The 1941 bombing destroyed all the fine furnishings except the reredos, one window and the wrought-iron work.

Pulpit A copy of the original but without the Grinling Gibbons carving.

Iron-work The wrought-iron work of the altar and gallery rails in Jean Tijou style is original (Jean Tijou was the most famous smith of the Wren period and worked at St Paul's Cathedral and Hampton Court).

Royal Pew The Royal Pew, which caused so much trouble during

St Alfege with St Peter, Greenwich

building, has been removed to the south side from the west gallery
where it interfered with the siting of the organ. The Stuart Royal Arms
in front were copied after the bombing.

Stained glass The only window to survive is a small 19th century one
in the south-east corner of the vestibule; this represents Cardinal
Morton. All the other windows are post-war work by Francis Spear,
representing various scenes from the history of the church (e.g.
baptism of Henry VIII) and, at the east end, Christ in Glory with the
emblems of the Passion below.

Painting The original painting at the east end was by Sir James
Thornhill, famous for the painted Dining Hall in Greenwich Hospital.
With the aid of parts that remained, it has been most expertly restored
by Glyn Jones who did, however, have to improvise for the sanctuary
ceiling.

Organ The console was popularly but erroneously believed to have
been used by Thomas Tallis, Gentleman of the Royal Chapel from
1530 to 1585. He is regarded as the founder and composed some of the
finest of our church music including Tallis's Canon which is the setting
for the hymn 'Glory to Thee, my God, this night.' He played at
St Alfrege on the former organ which dated from 1552, many of the
pipes from which were salvaged and used in the 1706 black-keyed,
three-manual organ encased on the south-west side.

Tallis (d. 1585) is buried with his wife in the church. A reproduction
of the original brass is near the south aisle east window and, at the
west end of the same aisle, there is a window in memory of him.

Monuments/Associations
There are no memorials of note.

General James Wolfe, the victor of the Heights of Abraham battle in
Canada against the French, is buried in the family vault and
commemorated by a tablet and the replica of his coffin plate is let into
the floor.

General Gordon of Khartoum fame was baptised in the church in
1833.

General
St Alfege does not reach the heights of other Hawksmoor churches,
partly because he was not allowed to build his tower, but the royal
and other associations make this skilfully restored church of much
interest.

2 St Luke's, Charlton Village

'Charlton'
Settlement of free husbandmen or churls (churl-ton).

History
The Manor of Charlton is mentioned in the Domesday Book and reference is made to a church even earlier in 1077. Little is known of the latter apart from its being made of chalk and flint, that it acquired several altars and shrines and that it came under the Abbey of Bermondsey. At the Dissolution, the Manor passed into secular ownership and was purchased by Sir Adam Newton in 1607. It is to him that we largely owe the present church erected about 1630 with money left by him and incorporating some of the old walls. The north aisle was added in 1639 with contributions from various families and it may have been then or later in the century that the tower top was added (very similar to the one at St Nicholas', Plumstead erected 1662–4).

19th-century alterations consisted of an extension to the chancel in 1840, and rearrangements in 1874. The tower was repaired in 1934.

St Luke's suffered considerably from blast damage in the 1939–45 War, involving extensive work on the roof; modern vestries were added in the north-east corner.

Two daughter churches, St Mary's and St Richard's, were built in St Luke's parish with the aid of a War Damage Commission grant in 1956 to cater for the growth of population to some 15,000 people.

The latest improvement has been the clearance of the churchyard in 1972.

Exterior
The area near the church which was only developed recently is still called 'The Village' and the homely brick exterior lying close to the handsome Jacobean Charlton House (now taken over by the Greenwich Borough Council) gives some substance to the illusion. St Luke's presents a charming rural appearance with its Dutch gabled south porch and simple tower in which the clasping buttresses are carried up to form turrets, the whole crown being crenellated. The simple Y-tracery belfry windows are also of brick and above is a strong modillion cornice encircling the tower and following the line of the turrets.

The sundial was placed on the south wall in 1934 and is an exact replica of one that had been there for 300 years.

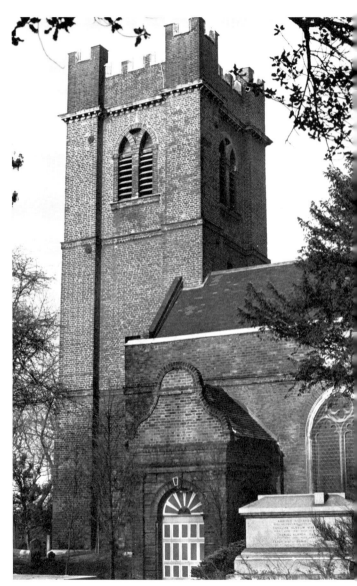

St Luke's, Charlton. Tower and south porch

Interior

A curious mixture of styles with a nave of two bays separated from the north aisle by round-headed arches and by a square pier. The arches presumably reflected Renaissance influences but in fact look early Norman, and the pier has slim attached diagonal shafts. The old chancel is also of two bays. The windows have Gothic tracery and the south chancel window could be 15th century. All is whitewashed under a wagon roof (the nave roof reconstructed in the 17th century and the one in the chancel 20th century). Three unequally spaced tie-beams are exposed at the west end.

The chapel in the north aisle was installed in 1927.

The various internal alterations have left the interior rather inconvenient for modern needs because of the difficulty of seeing and hearing clearly from all parts but it is nevertheless full of interest to the visitor.

Furnishings

Font Dated by Pevsner as 'later 17th century', it is of wineglass shape on a baluster stem with four scallops on a shallow round bowl, three turned inwards and one outwards. There is also drapery carving. The cover is of oak, carved with fruit and flowers and is probably contemporary with the font.

Hatchment On the west wall of the north aisle is a hatchment with quartering of various families.

Royal Arms On the same wall in a gilt frame are the Royal Arms of Queen Anne.

Pulpit The pulpit dates from mid-17th century with restrained carving of cherubs' heads and scroll decoration and bearing the arms of Sir David Cunningham. Under the tower is a pulpit sounding-board.

North chapel altar Originally made for the Chapel of St James in Charlton House and consecrated in 1616, it was given to St Luke's when the house was taken over by the Council.

Stained glass The north window with 17th century heraldic glass was removed for safety during the war and replaced afterwards.

Choir-stalls and communion rails Recent additions.

Monuments

Amongst the many monuments the following, proceeding from the south door, are of particular note:

*Sir Adam, died 1630, and *Lady Newton* Near the entrance door

is this fine monument by Nicholas Stone who was influenced by Inigo Jones. It is in black and white marble with broken segmental pediment and coat-of-arms. The inscription was composed by Sir Adam himself.

Lady Grace, Viscountess of Ardmagh, died 1700. Similar but with broken pediment curved. At the side are winged angels and there is attractive carving on the front panel. It is in the baptistery.

Edward Wilkinson, died 1567. On the south wall is a square sandstone memorial to Edward Wilkinson, Master Cook to Queen Elizabeth and 'Yeoman of the Mouth' to King Henry VIII, Anne Boleyn and King Edward VI. It is Dutch in style, an early example, decorated with a helm, strapwork, shields and rather agitated foliage.

Rt Hon Spencer Perceval, assassinated in the House of Commons on 11th May 1812. On the west wall of the north aisle is a tablet commemorating this distinguished and much respected statesman and above, a beautifully modelled portrait bust by Sir Francis Chantrey.

Brigadier Michael Richards, died 1721. Surveyor general of the Ordnance to George I. The monument on the wall near the chancel shows him free-standing in armour.

Elizabeth Thompson, died 1759. Frontal bust.

General Morrison, died 1799. Female figure bent over an urn by Charles Regnart.

Brasses Brasses on the wall near the Edward Wilkinson monument are 16th century. A later one dated 1669 commemorates D. Katherine Pickering.

Associations

Charles Edward Drummond Another victim of assassination; he was killed by a madman in mistake for Sir Robert Peel at a time when his brother was rector of Charlton, and is buried in the rector's vault.

General Gordon The brass candlestick on a triangular stand in the north chapel was at one time in the English church at Khartoum where General Gordon must have worshipped before being murdered. It was rescued from the Mahdi's tomb at Omdurman in September 1898.

Flagpole Because St Luke's was a landmark from the River Thames and used as a navigational aid by naval cadets and for Admiralty chartings as from the early part of the 18th century, the church was thereafter authorised to fly from the tower on St George's and St Luke's days the British Ensign, the naval flag of the time. This is still done from the front of the church.

General
This is one of the most rural churches in the area covered by this book, erected in Charles I's reign when very few places of worship were being built.

N.B. Not normally open except during services.

3 St Nicholas', Deptford

Dedication
St Nicholas was Bishop of Myra in the early 4th century. Little is known of him historically but there are many legends, including his saving of three small boys from being pickled in a barrel and the rescue from the threat of slavery of three daughters of a nobleman unable to pay their dowries by casting three bags of gold through a window, the origin of the golden balls of the pawnbroker. St Nicholas is beloved by children as Santa Claus and is the patron saint of travellers and sailors.

St Nicholas', Deptford

History

Except for its tower, the mediaeval church was rebuilt by Charley
Stanton (cf St Mary Magdalene, Bermondsey) to accommodate the
growing population of shipwrights and chandlers engaged in the
shipbuilding activities started by Henry VIII when he made Deptford a
naval dockyard. In less than twenty years however, on the plea that the
tower was in a dangerous state, a petition was submitted to the
Commissioners of the Fifty New Churches for money to help finance
another place of worship. Not unnaturally this was turned down and
instead the building 'was Oblig'd to be supported by a thorough repair
and strap'd with Iron. The Charge being near £400 AD 1716'. It lasted
with this first-aid treatment until the 1939–45 War.

   Towards the end of the 18th century it was decided to whitewash the
church and organ, and that it should be 'decently ornamented' (Basil
Clarke). The building was largely left alone in the 19th century but in
1901 the upper part of the tower was destroyed in a gale. This was
restored in 1903–4. Gutted in the 1939–45 War, an admirable
restoration was carried out by Thomas Ford and Partners enabling
St Nicholas' to be reopened for worship on 14th February 1958;
structural changes were made by cutting off the eastern bay and
sanctuary to provide a hall and other amenities.

Exterior

Approach is through an iron gate, the pillars of which are crowned
with gruesome and much worn death's-head skulls, but these are
encircled with wreaths symbolising victory over death. The former
charnel house (now a craft workshop) lies to the south in the
churchyard, which is enclosed in brick walls. (see plate p. 297)

   Except for the top, the tower of Kentish ragstone is mediaeval and
dates from about 1500. The rest of the church is brick with stone
quoins and dressings. The Dutch high-pointed gables on the north and
south sides are rather old-fashioned in style for their date. (see plate
p. 299)

Interior

The post-war alterations have left an almost square interior with the
centre bays made into short transepts. Tuscan columns support the
entablature. Scrolled metal ties appear more decorative than
structural. The large areas of clear glass make a bright and cheerful
interior.

   At the west end open steps lead down into the base of the tower.

St Nicholas', Deptford. Gateway with death's-head skulls

Furnishings

The main furnishings, including the reredos and pulpit which were moved to safety during the War, add considerably to the attraction of the church.

Royal Arms On the west wall is a nicely coloured Royal Arms.

Pulpit A lavishly decorated furnishing with staircase of twisted balusters. The six sides have small rectangular panels at the base and elaborate centre sections consisting of fluted tapering pilasters at the corners with console brackets above and below, and in the middle trompe l'oeil arches capped with turrets. The richly ornamented top projects.

Painting The painting of Queen Anne on the east wall, restored in 1957, is by Kneller.

Reredos Like the pulpit, a fine furnishing. The curved pediment is surmounted by a royal arms and delicate finial-type adornment. Fluted

St Nicholas', Deptford. Ezekiel carving

St Nicholas', Deptford. Roger Boyle monument and tablet to Sir Edward Fenton

Corinthian columns enclose panels of the Decalogue and figures of Moses and Aaron. The reredos is distinguished by the carvings above the side-pieces of Ezekiel (see plate p. 300) and the Valley of Bones (the latter once being over the door of the charnel house) and is attributed to Grinling Gibbons.

Altar-rails Of twisted baluster type on two sides of table.

Organ The organ is now in the hall but a charming organ case with trumpeting angel above and gilt cherubs' heads below has been opened out into the church on the east wall.

Doorcase A handsome doorcase with a small segmental pediment leads to the hall.

Monuments
A number of monuments, mainly 18th century, have survived.

Roger Boyle An earlier one, dating from 1615, of golden-brown alabaster, commemorates Roger Boyle who is shown praying in a tent with curtain drawn back by a cherub. A skull and dog are also included. The memorial is on the east wall below the Queen Anne painting. (see plate no. 301)

Sir Edward Fenton Below the Boyle monument, a tablet flanked by coats-of-arms commemorates Sir Edward Fenton, one of Raleigh's captains, who died in 1603.

Associations
Christopher Marlowe, the Elizabethan dramatist, was buried in the churchyard on 30th May 1593 after being killed nearby (as recorded on the west wall) in a tavern brawl. There is also a tablet in the churchyard.

Deptford Power Station A tablet on the south-east pew commemorates the men of Deptford Power Station who lost their lives as a result of enemy action in the 1939–45 War.

General
This interesting church situated in a relatively quiet residential part of busy Deptford affords a complete contrast to the baroque St Paul's. It has been fortunate in its post-war restoration and is well worth visiting.

N.B. Not normally open except during services.

Other Churches in Greenwich
Woolwich's parish church is **St Mary Magdalene** (4), dating back to the 18th century. Built of stock brick, it is a bit of a 'plain Jane' outside,

St Nicholas', Plumstead. Lithograph by W. J. Estherby

but the late 19th century chancel and raised sanctuary are delicately coloured. To the right is the Lady Chapel containing the old altar-piece with fine carving.

The parish church **St Nicholas'** (5) of Plumstead, which may be derived from plums or plumes of feathers, is, like St Mary Magdalene at Woolwich, set slightly apart from the main town centre. In its long chequered history it has suffered many vicissitudes and it was much enlarged in 1907–8. Externally, the most noticeable feature is the plum-coloured brick tower of 1662–4 with buttresses rising up into tall battlemented turrets; pleasing details within are the wellcarved kneeling angels (plate p. 304) on the choir stalls at the west end.

Although not much old work remains, this church retains a mediaeval atmosphere; it is not difficult to recall its former isolation on the edge of the marshes (plate above) and even capture something of

St Nicholas', Plumstead. Kneeling angel on stall

St Saviour's, Eltham

an East Anglian atmosphere with its stone floors, long oblique vistas and comparative absence of seating.

St Saviour's, Eltham (6), although rather chunky and graceless outside, is a good example of 20th century architecture, built in 1932–3. Brick and concrete are used to advantage inside (plate above), both in the structure and in the furnishings, which include a striking reredos in concrete.

Hackney

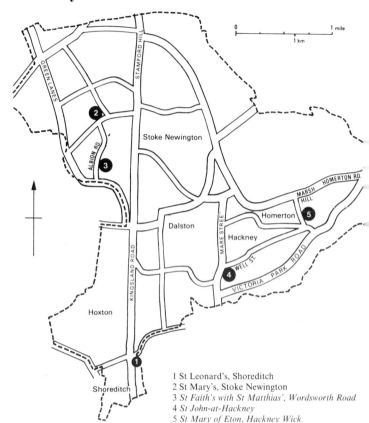

1 St Leonard's, Shoreditch
2 St Mary's, Stoke Newington
3 *St Faith's with St Matthias', Wordsworth Road*
4 *St John-at-Hackney*
5 *St Mary of Eton, Hackney Wick*

Hackney

1 St Leonard's, Shoreditch

Dedication

St Leonard was a companion of Clovis, first King of the Franks, but left his service to become a monk, then a hermit and itinerant preacher. He gained fame as a healer, and for his work on behalf of prisoners and captives, ultimately becoming Bishop of Limoges. He died in AD 570.

'Shoreditch' has many suggested derivations; 'shore' might come from 'sor' or 'scoer', meaning sewer

History

There is a tradition of a Saxon church but the first historical evidence does not go further back than a document dated between 1141 and 1149 granting St Leonard's to the Priory of Holy Trinity, Aldgate. For a time, it came under royal control but was allocated by King John to the Precentorship of St Paul's Cathedral, from which the living passed to the Archdeacon of London where it still rests.

The old church had four aisles of which the north one was a Chantry Chapel added by Sir John Elrington in 1782 for himself and his family. By the number of monuments to eminent people, it would seem that Shoreditch, despite its name, was a fashionable quarter.

Like many of the City churches that survived the Fire (St Leonard's is, of course, outside the City), it lapsed into decay – so much so that bits would fall from the fabric during Divine Service; on 23rd December 1716 part of the tower fell with a great crack causing panic amongst the congregation. Also, being below the level of the pavement, it was unhealthy. Unsuccessful attempts were made to get money from the Commissioners of the Fifty New Churches and it was not until 1736 that it was possible to make a start on a new building. George Dance the Elder was chosen as architect and the first service was held on 23rd August 1740.

Repaired, altered and restored many times, including an intervention by Butterfield in 1870, St Leonard's lost its north and south galleries in 1857 (T. E. Knightley). In 1944, a flying bomb removed most of the roof and damaged the organ and windows; the repairs took from 1946 until 1955. There was a thorough redecoration in 1968.

The church was the first to be lit by gaslight in London (1817).

During 1995/6, plans provide for the church being restored to its original Georgian layout.

Exterior

The building is prominently placed at cross-roads in an area where the 192 foot high steeple is still dominant. The main façade is approached by four steps (there used to be ten) to a portico with four giant Tuscan columns. Above, awkwardly placed in relation to the portico as at many London churches, the tower rises with attached piers at the angles, carrying an elongated cupola, small lantern and square section obelisk spire. All of this fine frontispiece to Shoreditch High Street is in Portland stone.

The steeple bears a family likeness to that of St Mary-le-Bow and inevitably suffers by comparison, but taken by itself it is a notable and original composition.

The rest of the fabric is built of red brick with stone dressings, the sides having two tiers of round-headed windows. A frieze and balcony encircle the top.

Interior

The interior is spacious and lofty, made to appear larger by the removal of the galleries. Large Tuscan columns, each with its own entablature and frieze, support arches high up, on which rests the clerestory of small segment-headed windows.

The west gallery housing the organ has arches at the sides and circular blocked windows above. A similar pattern is followed at the east end except that the arches are also blocked, giving horizontal emphasis to a mainly longitudinal design. The chancel projects slightly and the ceiling is flat and panelled.

Furnishings

Royal Arms The Royal Arms above the west door are those of George II.

Organ Built by Richard Bridge in 1756 and still retaining the original console with ebony naturals and ivory sharps. The fine case is of mahogany. The instrument was rebuilt in 1913, and repaired and restored including regilding of the front pipes by Noel Mander in 1950 after serious war damage.

*Clock Surround The finest of the furnishings, it has an exquisitely carved gilt case attributed to Chippendale (see plate p. 310).

St Leonard's, Shoreditch. Interior looking west

St Leonard's, Shoreditch. Carved clock case

Font The stone font, made from a single block of marble, with massive but elegantly-shaped stem and nicely carved cover, admirably following the lines of the fluted bowl, dates from 1740.

Bread Cupboards On the side walls are exceptionally interesting bread cupboards with pediments, metope friezes and unusual lozenge openings in the doors. Fifty loaves used to be distributed every Sunday but this practice was discontinued about 100 years ago.

Pulpit Contemporary with the building of the church, it has a sounding board on two fine fluted Ionic columns. In 1857, it went through the usual Victorian process of being lowered. It is enriched with delicate and intricate pierced carving at the base. John Wesley preached from it.

Lectern The oak lectern commemorates Henry Wilton, for nearly sixty years Deputy Clerk and Sexton of the parish.

Rood Beam The blue rood over the chancel step was set up as a War Memorial in 1923.

Stained Glass A grievous loss from the bombing was an early 17th century Flemish window at the east end depicting the Last Supper. It was replaced in 1955 by a window by A. K. Nicholson Studios representing the 'Te Deum', a memorial to those from the parish who suffered and died during the 1939–45 War.

Benefactions Boards On the east wall are interesting boards recording benefactions by former parishioners, including the gift of loaves, presumably those distributed from the bread cupboards.

Monuments

The Austens This came from the old church and still retains its colour. Thomas Austen and his sons, Thomas and John (both members of Lincoln's Inn) were buried by the old Communion Table.

Dr James Parkinson (1755–1824) The doctor (who first described the shaking palsy disease named after him) lived all his life in Shoreditch and was a member of St Leonard's congregation. He was baptised and married in the church, and buried in the churchyard. His memorial on the north wall was erected by the nursing staff of St Leonard's Hospital.

Francis and Sarah Clerke By the west door is another memorial from the old church, to Francis and Sarah Clerke. He was a former vicar.

*Elizabeth Benson The most outstanding memorial – also from the old church – is by Francis Bird to Elizabeth Benson on the southeast wall. Two skeletons are pulling hard on the branches of an uprooted oak-tree – the Tree of Life – over which is hooked a shroud upon which the inscription is written. It is frighteningly realistic. The inscription states that she was 'sprung paternally from the ancestral Kings of Pannonia (Hungary)' and that 'in her 90th year the threads of her life were not spun to the full but snapped 17th December 1710'

Bells Although not normally noted in this book, the bells of Shoreditch which, according to the old nursery rhyme, said 'When I grow rich', were twelve in number until 1963 when a thirteenth donated by the Haberdashers' Company was added.

Associations

Keats The three brothers of John Keats were baptised here in 1801.

Shoreditch Battalion Beside the south wall is the 1914–18 War Memorial of the 20th (Shoreditch) Battalion of the Middlesex Regiment and below, in a large case, are the drums of the Battalion.

St Leonard's, Shoreditch. Elizabeth Benson memorial

Actors' Memorial In 1913 the London Shakespeare League erected a memorial to 'the players, musicians, and other men of this Church'. These included William Somers, Court Jester to Henry VIII, and members of the Burbage family, of whom Cuthbert built the Globe Playhouse in Southwark.

Before the Globe was built, there were two playhouses in Shoreditch, the Court and the Theatre, thus making this the first parish to have a theatre in London. This was the reason for actors living in

the area so that St Leonard's became known as the Actors' Church in
Elizabethan times.

Thomas Cam In the burial register is a record that Thomas Cam
died in 1588, aged 207 (sic!).

Stocks and Whipping Post Under a thatched roof, north-west of the
church, are the parish stocks and whipping post.

General
St Leonard's is a landmark for some distance in an area not
overblessed with fine buildings. The splendid steeple is in need of
much money to cope with crumbling stone, but the interior has been
beautifully redecorated and the blue carpeting presented by Kenneth
White the architect during the 1968 restoration gives a warm and fresh
atmosphere to this interesting place of worship.

Open Mondays to Fridays, 12 noon to 2 p.m.

2 St Mary's, Stoke Newington

Stoke Newington
Probably means the new town in the wood ('stoc' is Anglo-Saxon for
'wood').

(a) Old Church

History
According to tradition, the Manor of Stoke Newington was one of
many in and around London granted by King Athelstan to the Canons
of St Paul's Cathedral and in the Domesday Book (1086) the Canons
appear as Lords of the Manor. Little is known of the mediaeval church
but it was probably a typical village place of worship lying under the
shadow of the Manor. Thomas de London (1313) is the earliest rector
to be recorded.

By the middle of the 16th century, the condition of the building was
'ruinous' and, in Elizabeth's reign – a rare time for the erection of
churches (this is the only example in London) – William Patten who
was leasing the Manor had it rebuilt.

Although little has come down to us today, the building being
frequently altered and restored in both the 18th and 19th centuries, its
village character has not been lost and, in fact, has been increased by

some of the changes and especially by the contrast with the large Victorian church on the opposite side of the road. The old church is still surrounded by trees and lies in a park-like setting.

A major restoration was carried out by Sir Charles Barry, architect with Augustus Pugin of the House of Commons, between 1826 and 1829. A report at the time stated that 'the building is generally leaning towards the north, the beams are rotten . . . and the coffins floating'. Sir Charles added another north aisle to the one constructed in 1716, provided galleries on the north and west sides, plastered and painted the interior, built a clerestory and erected the timber spire which so much enhances the rural effect.

Old St Mary's was in danger of disappearing when the new place of worship (described later) was built across the road in the 1850s but the parishioners rallied to its rescue, although it ceased to be the parish church in 1858. By this time, the village was starting to be swallowed up by London.

The spire was rebuilt in the 1920s, and plaster was removed from the south aisle to reveal the old brickwork. Both churches were damaged in the 1939–45 War and, while it lasted, services were only held in the less badly damaged old church. After the War, both were restored. In the case of Old St Mary's, Barry's north aisle which had received the impact of the bomb was scrapped and the north side rebuilt.

Today, after further repairs, the old place of worship stands out fresh and bright, and acts as a splendid foil to its imposing Victorian neighbour. [Old church] (see plate opposite)

Exterior

The main impression is of the extraordinary village character of this church. With its shingled spire, although this was only added in 1829 and rebuilt 100 years later, it might be a country church in the Cotswolds.

The later brickwork of the clerestory blends well with the original brick of the Tudor south aisle. Over one doorway is William Patten's motto and date of rebuilding ('1563 Ab alto') and over the adjacent entrance his initials and the family arms plus the word 'Prospice' (Look forward).

The replacement cement rendering does not so far spoil the effect and gives St Mary's a well-laundered look.

The windows are in late Perpendicular style.

St Mary's, Stoke Newington. Old church

Interior
The interior is of a piece with the exterior, having box-pews, double galleries at the west end, blue panelled roof, and low polygonal brick piers and arches. Curious features are the transverse walls and niches in the south aisle, known as Queen Elizabeth's chapel.

The north arcade has slender piers without capitals.

Furnishings
These are generally also in keeping.

Font A small font mounted on a pedestal dating from 1953 is placed under the west galleries.

Pulpit By Sir Charles Barry and dating from 1829. It has a spiral canopy.

Altar-piece The altar-piece is panelled and is in light gold and brown tones. A vine-trail is carried along the top.

Stained glass Fragments of 16th century glass have been pieced together in the east window.

Monuments
These are a noteworthy feature.

John and Elizabeth Dudley and 6-year-old daughter This typical Jacobean alabaster and marble monument with two kneeling figures facing one another is on the south wall of the chancel.

Elizabeth married as her second husband Thomas Sutton, founder of Charterhouse School, and the tomb was repaired in 1808 at the expense of 'several prelates and other persons educated at Charterhouse School'.

Jane Anne Chalmers A rather charming marble tablet at the west end depicts Jane Anne Chalmers (died 1913) seated on the ground and caressing a child; there is an urn with grapes at the bottom lefthand corner.

Joseph Hurlock On the east wall, a monument commemorates Joseph Hurlock, died 1793, and wife. It is in the form of a woman bent over a large urn.

Associations
St Mary's is mentioned by Edgar Allen Poe in 'William Wilson', one of his *Tales of Imagination and Fancy*. He spent five years at school in Church Street.

St Mary's, Stoke Newington. New church

(b) New Church

History

In the middle 1850s, the preaching of the rector, the Revd Thomas Jackson, drew huge crowds from all over London and these were more than the old church could accommodate. It was, therefore, decided to build a new church in the garden of the old Rectory on the other side of Church Street. Started in 1854, it was consecrated on 25th June 1858, the architect being Sir George Gilbert Scott.

There was only enough money to build the lower part of the steeple and this was not completed until 1890 by the architect's son, John Oldrid Scott.

The war damage was made good by yet another member of the family, Charles Marriott Scott, and the church rededicated on 2nd May 1957.

Exterior

The exterior is dominated by the steeple, the upper parts built of Doulting (Somerset) stone and the lower of Kentish ragstone. It is one of the highest in London of a parish church and is understood to be a reduced facsimile of Salisbury Cathedral spire. There, however, the comparison ends for it is not a particularly notable construction and inferior to the rest of the church.

Interior

The new St Mary's is a grandiose building with wide spacious nave and aisles, and lofty arcades with circular marble pillars. These continue past the transepts. The capitals are profusely carved with leaves. [New church] (plate p. 317)

The chancel has the unusual embellishment for a parish church of having its own aisles. Marble steps and brass rails were added in 1890 leading to the sanctuary, which was, until damaged in the War, decorated with mosaics and enclosed in a polygonal apse.

Furnishings

The furnishings generally are showy. They include a massive *pulpit* with grey-green marble columns outside and shorter pink ones within, and a *font* with four short columns at the corners supporting winged angels and a larger central column. There have been no fewer than four *organs*: the first by Gray and Davidson cost £1,200: the next by Wm. Hill & Co. £1,550 (installed 1907): the third by Rushworth &

St Mary of Eton, Hackney Wick. East side

Draper £2,500 (installed in the 1930s): and the present one after the War by Noel Mander & Co. £4,500.

The *stained glass window* in the north transept, with predominantly blue, green and gold colours, was installed in 1960. Amongst many items depicted can be seen radio isotopes, Greenwich Observatory and Jodrell Bank.

General
Although this is a rather insensitive church, can there be anywhere else in London with the contrast of a basically Tudor village church and a high Victorian town church standing so close together and both still ministering to the needs of a single parish?

Other Churches in Hackney

St Faith's with St Matthias', Wordsworth Road (3) a Butterfield church of the mid-1850s, is distinctive externally for its tall saddleback tower and internally for its feeling of spaciousness. St Faith's was pulled down after the 1939–45 War.

St John-at-Hackney (4) is a vast building of the last decade of the 18th century set in an ample leafy churchyard and conspicuous by its strange steeple erected some years later. The mediaeval tower from an earlier church remains.

Inside, there are many monuments from the old church, notably the reconstructed tomb-chest with recumbent alabaster effigy of Lady Latimer (d. 1583). After a serious fire in 1955, the interior, plain but made interesting by a large horseshoe gallery supported on blue fluted Doric columns, was reduced in size.

St Mary of Eton (5) in Hackney Wick was built in the early 1890s with funds provided by Eton College, who used to run a mission in the area; they are still the patrons. The church is a notable work of the eminent Victorian architect, G. F. Bodley, but the unusual gatetower which helps to give such an interesting skyline to the elevation facing Eastway was built later in 1911–2 by Cecil Hare

The open nave is lofty and wide with plain arches supported on massive square piers; there is a Lady Chapel in the south-east corner. This dignified interior is enhanced by the ceilings and the attractive furnishings and fittings.

Hammersmith

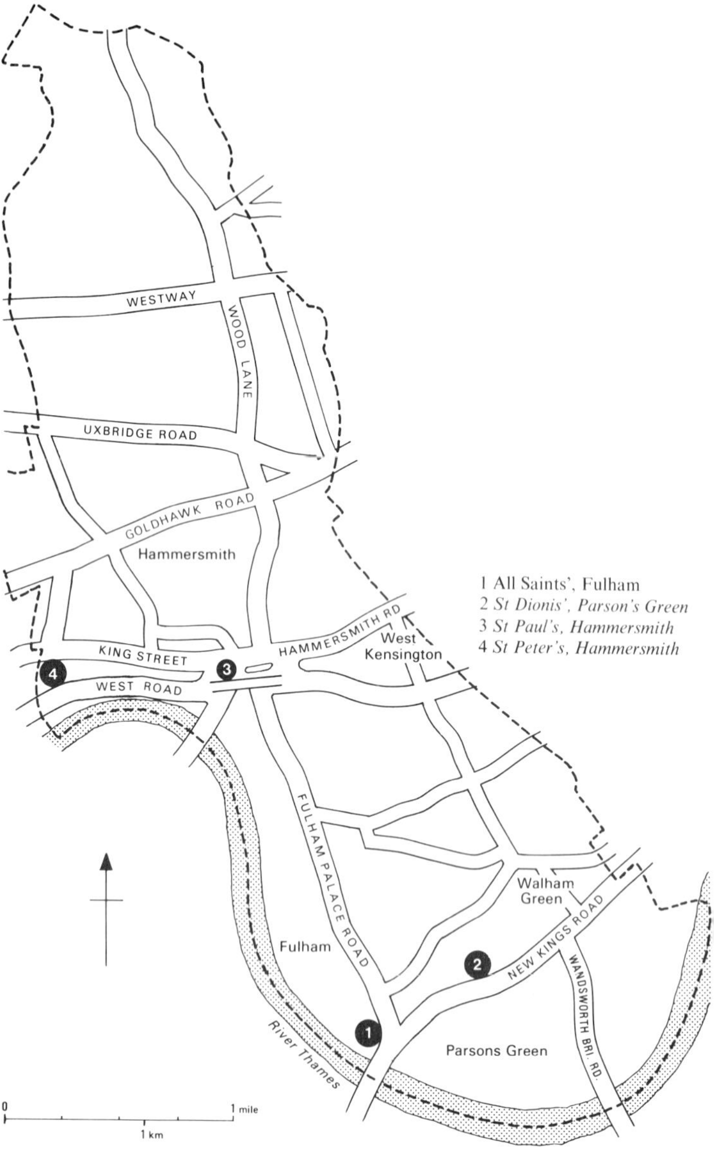

1 All Saints', Fulham
2 *St Dionis', Parson's Green*
3 *St Paul's, Hammersmith*
4 *St Peter's, Hammersmith*

WESTWAY

WOOD LANE

UXBRIDGE ROAD

GOLDHAWK ROAD

Hammersmith

KING STREET

HAMMERSMITH RD

West Kensington

WEST ROAD

FULHAM PALACE ROAD

Fulham

Walham Green

NEW KINGS ROAD

WANDSWORTH BRI. RD

River Thames

Parsons Green

0   1 mile
1 km

Hammersmith

1 All Saints', Fulham

Fulham

'Fulham' may be derived from a personal name such as Fulla (akin to Old German 'vullo'). 'Ham' is almost certainly 'hamm', describing an angle of land in the bend of a river. The dedication of All Saints was first referred to in 1445.

History

History goes back to a charter of AD 704–9 granting the tenure of land to Waldhere, Bishop of London. This land later became the Manor of Fulham and was the start of the long connection between Fulham and the Bishops of London, going back as far as 1141 when the then Bishop, Robert de Sigillo, had a manor at Fulham.

First mention of a church is in 1154 in connection with a dispute over tithes but there is little reliable evidence about the fabric until the 15th century when work was in progress on the tower. The church that existed then was added to here and there but by the 19th century it had become inadequate for the continuously growing population and, although at first it was decided not to rebuild, this later proved necessary because of the fabric becoming unsafe. With a floor level three feet below that of the present church, flooding at high tide occurred frequently and, on one occasion, the appropriately named Revd Fisher caught a stickleback in the central aisle. The old church was therefore pulled down and a completely new place of worship (except for the tower) erected by Sir Arthur Blomfield, son of a former Bishop of London, in 1880–1, just before the present bridge across the River Thames on an alignment much closer to the church, replaced the old wooden bridge dating from 1729.

By this time the parish, which at one time covered the whole of the Borough of Hammersmith, was no longer the quiet riverside area it had been. In 1834 Hammersmith had been made a separate parish and later as many as twenty-five parishes were carved out of the ancient Fulham area.

Damage was caused to the north transept and the vestry by a fire in 1923 but All Saints' was fortunate to escape all but minor damage in the 1939–45 War.

A major restoration has recently been undertaken.

Exterior

The church makes a fine picture as one crosses Putney Bridge, acting as counterpoise to St Mary's, Putney (gutted by fire, alas, at the time of writing in 1976 but now attractively rebuilt).

The Blomfield rebuilding in the Perpendicular style blends well with the old tower and is battlemented, including the large north porch added in 1880–1. There are tall clerestories and the roofs are of slate. The building material of the main fabric is Kentish ragstone with Bath stone dressings; a document of 1440 specifically exempts from requisition stone from Maidstone required for the tower. It was signed by the Secretary of Henry VI who at that time was building Eton College Chapel. The four-stage tower with stair-turret at the south-west angle was given new battlements in 1797 and was re-faced in 1845, at which time the thin wooden spire was removed. There was further extensive re-facing after the 1939–45 War. The tower is 96 feet high at the battlements.

Interior

There are typical Perpendicular arcades with slender columns of alternate shafts and hollows, aisles, tall clerestory, transepts and chancel. Most of the clerestory glass was blown out in the War. All is of 1880–1 but seemly and dignified.

The south transept is arranged as a Lady Chapel.

Furnishings

The only old furnishings are the fonts, the organ and the altar-rails but All Saints' has a collection of monuments only rivalled in the outer parts of London by those of Chelsea Old Church.

Painting In the ringing chamber of the tower is a painting of John Hudnott, beadle and sexton, in red coat with quart pot and churchwarden's pipe, dated 1690.

Fonts The main font is octagonal and panelled. The moulded bowl of black marble bears the inscription – 'this font was erected at the charge of Tho. Hyll churchwarden 1622'. The stem is of painted freestone, whilst the upper panels are carved with roses and the lower have cusped heads.

In the tower chapel is an older font, which was found buried close to the other when the old church was demolished. It is of early mediaeval type.

Organ Originally built by Benjamin Jordan of Fulham in 1732 but rebuilt more than once since, the last time in 1930 to the designs of the

All Saints', Fulham

then organist, Livingstone Hurst. It retains its original case with carved scroll work, cherubs' heads and moulded cornices, but wings have been added. The screen of the organist's seat is formed from carved upper panels taken from the three-decker pulpit that used to be in the old church.

Stained glass The greater part was made in 1880 by Heaton Butler and Bayne and presented by members of the congregation. The window next to the north door shows Christ blessing the children, one of whom is a likeness of a child of the vicar at that time. The west window below the tower has representations of heraldic shields and in the upper tracery are fragments of German or Swiss glass of the 16th or 17th century, mostly heraldic. There is also some old glass of this type in the north porch.

Altar-rails A shortened form of the old Jacobean rails made of oak with round balusters, moulded rail and sill, and panelled standards. The carving is in high relief.

Reredos screen Made by Heaton, Butler and Bayne in 1885 but

All Saints', Fulham. Margaret Legh monument

restored in 1967. The figures, painted on zinc, are those of Moses
David, Isaiah and Aaron.

Bells The bells are worthy of special mention in that – as at St
George the Martyr, Southwark – they are a complete peal of ten from
the foundry of Abraham Rudhall of Gloucester.

Monuments

Amongst the wealth of mainly 17th century monuments, and taking
them in order of walking clockwise round the church starting from the
west end, are the following:

Sir William Butts, died 1545. He was Chief Physician to Henry VIII.
This is in the north aisle.

Katharine Hart, who died in 1605. She is shown kneeling with her
two sons and two daughters. In the north transept.

Sir Thomas Smith, died 1608. This is an elaborate wall monument of
various kinds of marbles. In the chancel.

*Lady Margaret Legh The outstanding memorial. She is depicted in
stiff Elizabethan costume and holds an infant in a chrysom (plate
opposite). On a pedestal to the right is another child similarly attired
and on the left an hour-glass, which at one time was on top of the
monument. She was married when she was sixteen, bore seven sons
and two daughters, and died in 1603 at the age of thirty-three. Also in
the chancel.

Margaret Svanders, died 1529. A lozenge-shaped Flemish brass on
the east wall of the south aisle shows the head and shoulders of a
woman in a shroud with angels on either side engraved above an
inscription and a coat-of-arms.

Viscount Mordaunt This is a Baroque monument by John Bushnell
showing the Viscount in a toga and holding a baton. He died in 1675.
The monument is in the Tower Chapel.

Lady Dorothy Clarke, died 1695 and *Dr Samuel Barrow*, died 1682.
This white-veined marble wall monument is by Grinling Gibbons.
Dr Barrow was Lady Clarke's second husband, whom she married
after her first husband had been killed in a naval engagement against
the Dutch.

Associations

The main associations are with Bishops of London, eight of whom
were buried in the churchyard at the east end of the church and two
more, including Sir Arthur Blomfield's father, in the north-eastern
part. Bishop Henchman was buried in the church itself.

St Dionis', Parsons Green. Font and font-cover

General
Although very little is left from mediaeval times, Sir Arthur Blomfield
has provided a church worthy of its fine river situation and its
episcopal links.

Other Churches in Hammersmith
St Dionis', Parsons Green (2) is named after a City church demolished
in 1878 and was built and endowed with the proceeds from the sale of
the site and materials of that church. The new St Dionis', constructed
of red brick, was erected in 1884–5 (tower 1895–6). It contains the
17th century pulpit and font/font-cover (plate opposite) of the City
place of worship, the former approached by a staircase with delicately
twisted balusters and the latter completed with a delightful cover
representing the old tower.

    St Paul's (3), near the Broadway and enclosed in through-roads,
took the place of an old chapel of ease which had been consecrated by
Laud in 1631 and which had become a parish church in 1834. It was
built of pink Mansfield stone in the 1880s and is distinctive externally
for the outsize pinnacles on the tall north-east tower and the narrow
lancet windows.

    *The well-proportioned and lofty interior has columns of Belgian
marble. The church is especially noteworthy for its two excellent late-
17th century monuments, to James and Sarah Smith (north wall of
chancel – plate p. 331) and to Sir Nicholas Crispe (west wall of north
aisle). The latter carries a splendid bronze bust of King Charles I
(plate p. 330), probably by Le Sueur, the sculptor of the outstanding
equestrian statue of this monarch near Trafalgar Square. The pleasing
Wren-period pulpit came from All Hallows the Great, Thames Street.

    St Peter's (4), beside the Great West Road, became a parish church
in 1836. It was a Commissioners' building, constructed in 1827–9 of
Suffolk brick with details in Bath stone. This unassuming and rather
appealing little Greek-style church, set in a pleasant square, has a
somewhat original tower, octagonal at the base rising to a tall circular
stage (plate p. 332). The low plain galleried interior is brightened by
the use of Pompeian red on the pews.

St Paul's, Hammersmith. Sir Nicholas Crispe monument – bust of Charles I

St Paul's, Hammersmith. James and Sarah Smith monument

St Peter's, Hammersmith

Islington

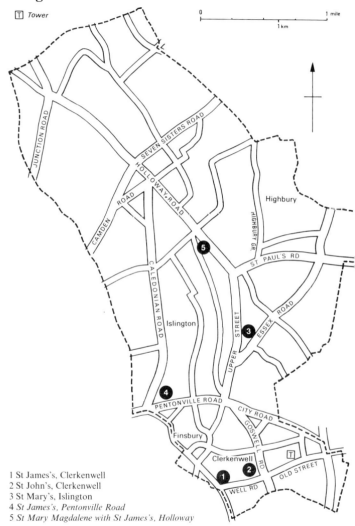

T Tower

1 St James's, Clerkenwell
2 St John's, Clerkenwell
3 St Mary's, Islington
4 *St James's, Pentonville Road*
5 *St Mary Magdalene with St James's, Holloway*

Islington

1 St James's, Clerkenwell, and St John's with St Peter's

Dedication

The Apostle James became the patron saint of Spain after what was presumed to be his body was found in a marble coffin by a Galician peasant during the year AD 816; his shrine at Santiago de Compostela became a leading centre of mediaeval pilgrimage.

'Clerkenwell' refers to the springs of pure water near the place where, in the early Middle Ages, the parish clerks used to perform mystery plays, 'en' being an Anglo-Saxon plural.

History

Although William Kent maintains that a Papal Bull of 1486 shows that St James's was a separate and at that time new church, others aver that it formed part of the convent of St Mary (possibly only a small chapel for residents). Whatever still existed passed into private hands at the Dissolution, where it remained until taken over by the parish in 1656. Partially rebuilt earlier in 1625, it subsequently lapsed into increasing decay until the building became positively unsafe. Eventually after attempts had been made in 1718 to get money from the Commissioners of the Fifty New Churches, it was rebuilt by a notable Palladian architect, James Carr, and reconsecrated on 10th July 1792.

The tower and spire were reconstructed to the old design in 1849 and the church as a whole gently treated by Blomfield in 1882, when the central pulpit and box-pews were removed and choir stalls introduced.

St James's escaped bomb damage during the War but was redecorated in 1967.

A strange circumstance of this church was that, unlike most livings, the parish retained control of it at the 1660 Restoration until the beginning of the present century. This gave rise to unseemly electoral rivalry and a strong Evangelical tradition. One of the most famous vicars, chosen in the 1850s after a particularly stormy and exciting election, was the Rev Robert Maguire, a prolific writer of Protestant pamphlets, who carried out much work on the fabric and furnishings of the church. The patrons of the living are now the Parish Church Council and the Church Patronage Society jointly.

Exterior

Raised on an undercroft, St James's is well sited on what was at one time a pleasant green. Apart from the steeple, the exterior is severely plain stock brick, relieved with classical doorways in the first and last bays (which have stone quoins) on the south side, a balustrade, and a Venetian window at the east end. The steeple has a large square stone base, terminating in a balustrade with urns, above which is an open polygonal stage and a spire on a concave base. It is strongly reminiscent of St Martin's and St Giles-in-the-Fields and therefore, a bit old-fashioned for the end of the 18th century.

Interior

A well-mannered interior with ceiling decoration, organ case, reredos, Communion table and rails all contemporary with the building of the church. Although basically a 'preaching box', it is made interesting by the curves introduced at the west end noticeably in the galleries which come round to embrace the north and south sides.

Winding round the staircases leading to the galleries on the north and south sides are so-called 'modesty' boards. This interesting feature consists of metal sheets reaching down almost to the floor and designed to prevent any view of ladies' ankles as they mounted the stairs. These sheets are 18 inches high – quite inadequate to preserve modesty with today's fashions!

There is a theatrical resemblance in that, right up under the ceiling, a gallery with iron railings was introduced in 1822 by the Clerkenwell Parochial School to provide accommodation for school children, for which this church still pays £1 a year rent; charity children were pushed back to the rear of the Upper Circle into what were called 'glove boxes'. Below, on the other hand, are imposing boxes for the 'Church Officers' and the 'Corporation Officers'. Otherwise, the building is rectangular with a charming flat plaster ceiling painted in Wedgwood blue and white. The west galleries, which are still double, are reached by two graceful circular staircases situated in rooms north and south of the tower.

Furnishings

Royal Arms The Arms over the west door dating from 1792 are those of George III and are of Coade stone, an artificial material made according to a secret patent – now lost – in Lambeth.

Font Dates from 1850.

Organ Built in 1792, rebuilt in 1877 and enlarged in 1926. The decoration of the Spanish mahogany case with carved drapery over the pipes is notable.

Wooden figure of St James A wooden figure of St James which used to stand over the poor-box in the former church is now placed above the main doorway to the nave.

Communion table and wrought-iron rails are part of the original furnishings and both are curved towards the west. The altar table is of mahogany, inlaid with box-wood, and is decorated with carved plumes of feathers and a dove.

Reredos This Doric altar-piece is also contemporary with the building of the church.

Stained glass The rather garish glass with large figures in the east window depicts the Ascension of Christ and dates from 1863; it is by Heaton, Butler and Bayne.

Vestry In the vestry a chairman's tall chair and another of the 18th century are to be found. There is also a large-scale wooden model of the steeple containing a clock which still works.

Monuments

Elizabeth, Dowager Countess of Exeter A large wall tablet with armorials at the east end of the south aisle commemorates this granddaughter by marriage of Elizabeth I's great minister, William Cecil, Lord Burleigh.

Mico Wagstaff By way of showing that all are equal before God in death, next to the Countess lies Mico Wagstaff, Ironmonger.

John Bell, Bishop of Worcester 1539–43, who lived in retirement in Clerkenwell, is remembered by a brass. This was stolen and brought back in 1884. He was buried in the old church in 1556.

Gilbert Burnet, Bishop of Salisbury, died 1714. This well-known preacher and writer has a floor slab under the Communion table commemorating him and a large monument in the vestibule with a long Latin verse.

Henry Penton, who had developed the area known as Pentonville, has a memorial in the porch. He died in 1714 and there is an epitaph with gracefully ornamented obelisk.

Thomas Crosse, who died in 1729, is commemorated with his wife by a large wall monument with two busts.

Associations

Smithfield Martyrs On the south wall is a well-carved wooden tablet commemorating those who suffered in the fires at Smithfield. These include not only the Marian Martyrs but earlier victims (probably in one case a Lollard) ranging in date from 1400–1558.

'Sir' William Wood Adjacent is a memorial to 'Sir' William Wood, author of *Bowman's Glory*, with appropriate lines to this famous archer, erected at the expense of the Toxophilite Society. Three flights of arrows were discharged over his grave at the funeral.

Izaak Walton Two of his children were buried in the old churchyard.

Victims of Fenian outrage In the porch is a tablet to the victims of a Fenian bombing outrage on Friday 13th December 1867. The deaths occurred in houses in the immediate neighbourhood of the Clerkenwell House of Detention.

General

Thanks to sensitive restoration, St James's has kept its 18th century atmosphere. The parish now includes St John's, Clerkenwell, carved out of it in 1721 and reunited in 1931, whose church has become the chapel of the Hospital of St John of Jerusalem. It also includes the Smithfield Martyrs Memorial Church of St Peter's in Clerkenwell, established in 1869, which was pulled down in 1955 after being bombed in the War.

N.B. The church is open between 11 a.m. and 3 p.m. each weekday for commuters attended by a verger.

2 St John's, Clerkenwell

Order of St John

The Order had its origins in a band of soldier-monks who staffed a Hospital in Jerusalem, becoming known as Knights Hospitaller, and who, with the members of other Orders, helped to defend Jerusalem together with the other Latin principalities and territories in the Holy Land against Saracen attacks. Gradually forced back, first to Acre in Israel, then to Cyprus and Rhodes, they came to Malta, where after withstanding a savage siege in 1565, they settled peaceably until surrendering to Napoleon in 1798. The capital of Malta, Valletta, is named after the Grand Master of the Order, Jean de la Vallette.

The English Langue (as the national divisions were called) was revived in 1831, St John's Ambulance being formed in 1877.

History

Land was granted to the Order in Clerkenwell around the year 1145 and the first church, circular as customary with churches of this Order

St John's, Clerkenwell. Etching dated 1818

after the pattern of the Holy Sepulchre Church in Jerusalem, with a rectangular choir, and crypt underneath, was consecrated in the year 1185 by Heraclius, the Patriarch of Jerusalem, who had come over to try and persuade King Henry II to embark upon a Crusade. (He consecrated the Temple Church in the same year.)

This building was attacked by the peasants in the 1381 revolt and the prior murdered. Reconstructed in rectangular form, it was enlarged and the tower rebuilt by Prior Docwra in the early 16th century. He added the gatehouse in 1504.

At the Dissolution, the church fell on evil times. The nave was blown up during the reign of Edward VI to provide stone for Protector Somerset's new Palace in the Strand, and the Great Hall may have been used as the office of the Master of the Revels. It was rescued by Lady Burleigh, wife of the grandson of William Cecil, Lord Burleigh – Elizabeth's great Lord High Treasurer – to whom ownership had passed, and it was reopened for worship in 1623 as a private chapel, coming later into the possession of the Earl of Aylesbury, who used the crypt as a wine-cellar.

In 1706, the church became a Presbyterian meeting-house and was unfortunate enough to become the butt for a second time of an angry mob who, during the Sacheverell Riots, gutted it and burnt the contents in St John's Square.

Rescued on this occasion by two local people, Simon and Charity Michel in 1721, they sold it two years later to the Commissioners of the Fifty New Churches, who made it into a parish church which it continued to be for 200 years.

With a reduction in the number of residents, the parish was absorbed by St James's, Clerkenwell, and St John's Church given to the Order; so that despite all its vicissitudes the wheel had come full circle and it is once more the Grand Priory Church of the Order of St John.

But its misfortunes were not over because it was burnt out by enemy bombs in 1941 and it remained a shell until it was rebuilt by Lord Mottistone, using the surviving outer walls, and rededicated in 1958.

Exterior

This presents a plain red-brick elevation of no particular architectural interest but alongside there is a war memorial garden on the site of the cloister of the old Priory Church. The Crucifixion sculpture is by Cecil Thomas.

The outline of the original round church is marked in cobbles on the pavement outside.

Interior

By contrast, the interior is a blaze of scarlet from the seat coverings, further enhanced by the bright new banners of the senior officers of the Order and of the Priories and Commanderies. It is used for the main services and for investitures.

The chief magnet, however, for any outside visitor must be the rib-vaulted crypt which has come through all the burnings and desecration unscathed. It is a rare London example of 12th century work, the three western bays being Norman (1140) and the two eastern ones, together with the flanking chapels, Transitional work (1185), in which the ribs of the vault rise to a point, springing from low clustered shafts. The earlier work is plain with only simple chamfers but the later construction is more elegant with many mouldings.

Smaller services are held in the crypt, the Almoner Chapel on the south being used for memorial purposes and the chapels on the north as the vestry.

Monuments

Juan Ruyz de Vergara, Proctor of the Langue of Castile. This superb monument was purchased from Valladolid Cathedral in Spain during rebuilding in the 19th century. Of alabaster and dating from 1575, it is in the form of a recumbent effigy with a sleeping boy alongside. The Proctor wears the eight-pointed cross of the Order of St John over his breast plate. The monument, by Esteban Jordan, is described by Pevsher as being 'of a quality unsurpassed in London or England'.

Sir William Weston, the last Prior of the Order who, it is said, died of a broken heart in 1540 after hearing of the Dissolution of the Order. The canopy and upper part are lost. He is shown as an emaciated corpse wrapped in a shroud and placed on a rush mat.

Associations

John Wilkes, the 'scandalous' champion of popular rights against the royal rule of George III, was married in the church in 1747.

Duke of Cambridge Against the wishes of Queen Victoria, her cousin the second Duke of Cambridge, who was grandson of George III, was married here on 8th January 1847 to Sarah Fairbrother, an actress.

General

The crypt which, together with the gateway on the other side of the road, is the last remaining part of a Priory, providing in its heyday

St John's, Clerkenwell. Ruyz de Vergara monument
St John's, Clerkenwell. Sir William Weston monument

accommodation and entertainment for royalty, should be better known than it is and a visit is strongly recommended.

The gateway is the only gateway of any age in London.

N.B. Application to visit should be made to the Curator of the nearby Library and Museum at St John's Gate. Telephone 0171-253 6644.

3 St Mary's, Islington

Islington
Referred to in the Domesday Book as 'Isendone' and also 'Iseldone', the name of the borough may come from words meaning lower town or fortress, as opposed to a higher one at Highbury; or it may be derived from 'Giseldine' – used about AD 1000 – meaning 'Gisla's Hill'.

History
Recorded history starts with a dispute between 1125 and 1141 between the Dean of St Paul's Cathedral and the nuns of Bromley-by-Bow as to the patronage of St Mary's. The nuns won and they retained the patronage until the dissolution of their convent in 1545.

Although there is an exposed Norman carved foundation stone visible in the crypt, nothing reliable is known about the building until the middle of the 15th Century when it was replaced with a new church made of a rough kind of masonry called 'boulder' with three aisles and a robust, battlemented north-west tower with a little bell cupola on top.

In 1710, a school – one of the first Church of England schools- – was set up in a room over the west porch but a few years later, the building being considered inadequate for the parish's needs, a petition was made to the Commissioners of the Fifty New Churches for a new church but, as so often happened, it was turned down. Eventually in 1750, an enabling bill was passed through Parliament and a local master joiner, Launcelot Dowbiggin, chosen as architect. Work started in 1751 and was completed in 1754.

Fears of lightning led to an extraordinary wickerwork scaffolding being erected around the spire by a local basketmaker in 1787; he was able to make money by charging an entrance fee of 6d. to see the enclosed spire.

In 1902 health hazards caused by the coffins in the crypt led to the church being closed. The following year the chancel was opened out and the three-decker pulpit which stood right in front of the altar removed. At the same time the round portico on four Tuscan columns provided by Dowbiggin was replaced with the present broad porch supported on a line of Ionic columns. The church was reopened in 1904.

All but the reinforced steeple of Dowbiggin's church was destroyed by a bomb which landed on the east end on 9th September 1940. Reconstruction to a very different design, but incorporating the old steeple, was carried out by Lord Mottistone and Paul Paget, and St Mary's was re-hallowed on 17th December 1956.

The spiritual history is even more interesting than the architectural record because, after the Reformation, Islington became a centre of extreme Protestants, many of whom suffered grievously under the Marian Persecution, from which has stemmed the Evangelical tradition which is so strong today. John and Charles Wesley started their preaching in the church and George Whitefield, not being licensed, in the churchyard outside, whilst in January 1827 Dr Daniel Wilson, who became Bishop of Calcutta and Metropolitan of India, gathered twelve clergy friends at his vicarage to discuss prayer. This was the first of the Islington Clerical Meetings and was the seed of the Islington Conference now no longer held. On the lay side, the Church Pastoral Aid Society was formed by laymen in 1836 to encourage the recruitment of extra clergy and also of lay-helpers.

Exterior

It was stated in the *Gentleman's Magazine* of February 1825 that Dowbiggin had attempted to combine the virtues of the steeples of St Bride's, St Mary-le-Bow, and St Leonard's, Shoreditch in the one he built at Islington; but, whilst there is no question of this eclectic approach producing an architectural masterpiece, one cannot help admiring the vigour and rustic originality of his steeple. Starting from a three-stage square brick tower with broad stone quoins, topped with an octagonal balustrade and four corner urns, there is an open stage with rusticated colonettes on an octagonal base, followed by a conical bulging dome with large openings and completed with a 'weird' (Pevsner) rusticated obelisk spire. Portland stone is used for the upper stages.

The broad porch of 1903 remains but the rest is post-war reconstruction in red brick by Mottistone and Paget, with tall rectangular windows and short transepts at the east end.

Opportunity is being taken of the roof needing replacement to restore the original shaped pitch roof.

Interior
A design of striking originality with large glass doors dividing the vestibule with a chapel for private prayer from the main body of the church. The interior is completely open, with a spacious sanctuary rising impressively at the east end, separated by slender black fluted pillars with lotus-leaf capitals and abacus-like rails from the transepts.

A group of eight murals with a cross as the central feature depicting Christ in His various roles as Saviour, Healer, The Son of God, etc. over the Communion words beneath – 'This do in Remembrance of Me' – close the view eastwards.

In the west wall are some of the oak Tuscan pillars which supported the old gallery.

Organ and choir are kept at the west end so that the congregation have an uninterrupted view of pulpit and lectern, well suited to the church's evangelical traditions.

Furnishings
Font The original and very elegant font of veined marble was fortunately preserved by being replaced and stored away during the 1902–4 restorations. It is situated below the lectern.

Pews Contributed by various lovers of the church, including two from passers-by.

Pulpit and Lectern These stately modern furnishings are of like design and on either side of the sanctuary under large canopies. The eagle lectern was brought in during the modernisation at the beginning of the century.

Royal Arms Beside the pulpit are the Royal Arms of George II, unveiled by the Archbishop of Sydney (see *Incumbents*) in March 1959.

Murals (see *Interior*) There is another mural by Brian Thomas at the west end showing Christ as the Judge.

Brasses Two brasses salvaged from the old church to Robert and Alice Fowler (1540) and Henry and Margaret Savill (1546) are in the Prayer Chapel on the floor of the sanctuary.

Associations
Duel Sir George Wharton and Sir James Steward (a godson of James I) fought a duel at Islington with sword and dagger in James's

reign. Both were killed and, at the King's request, were buried in one grave.

Sir Richard Cloudesley, a great benefactor of Islington, was buried in the church and his tomb is in the churchyard.

Sir Edward Elgar's parents (his father was a piano-tuner) were married at St Mary's in 1848.

Incumbents Apart from Dr Daniel Wilson, who started the great Evangelical tradition which has made the Islington Conference of world-wide significance, St Mary's has had many other famous vicars and curates. Dr George Strahan (vicar from 1772 to 1824) was a friend of and frequently visited by Samuel Johnson. Dr William Barlow (vicar from 1887 to 1901) helped to set up several Evangelical theological colleges and was involved with the work of St John's Hall, Highbury, later to be the London College of Divinity and now St John's College, Nottingham. The Rev Hugh Gough (curate 1928–31 and vicar 1946–8) became Archbishop of Sydney, and the present (1994) Archbishop of Canterbury, Dr George Carey, and a former Archbishop, Dr Donald Coggan, were curates at St Mary's. Another curate, the Revd David Sheppard, is now Bishop of Liverpool. The Revd Maurice Wood (vicar from 1952 to 1961) was Bishop of Norwich.

General

This is a church which has played and continues to play a big part in the life of the Anglican Church and the blend of Dowbiggin's steeple and Mottistone and Paget's new building symbolises how its present ministry in a heavily-populated built-up area is linked with its significant past when Islington was a quiet country village.

Other Churches in Islington

St James's, Pentonville Road (4), built in 1787 and consecrated in 1791, started as a chapel of ease to St James's, Clerkenwell. In a deprived area and looking rather shabby and neglected, the church nevertheless still makes an attractive picture with its slightly Adam-like façade and pretty cupola capped by a copper dome.

For many years, circus clowns used to hold their annual service at St James's and the most famous of them – Joseph Grimaldi, whose grave with rose tree growing out of it beside the south wall is still carefully tended (plate opposite) was buried here. Richard Bonington, the talented landscape and historical painter who died at the age of 26, was also buried at St James's.

St James's, Pentonville Road. Grave of Joseph Grimaldi

St Mary Magdalene with St James's, Holloway (5) was built in 1812–4. Set in a large open space, the exterior has a rugged solidity relieved by a short sturdy tower which is not without appeal. The tower, which is in the east end position, is capped with a stone balustrade enlivened by merry little urns at the corners. Although a 19th century church, St Mary Magdalene has a typical and agreeably unspoilt 18th century interior with galleries and a coved gently-curving ceiling.

St James's, Chillingworth Road was built in 1837–8 and later enlarged. After being bombed in 1944, the church was converted into a church hall for St Mary Magdalene.

Kensington and Chelsea

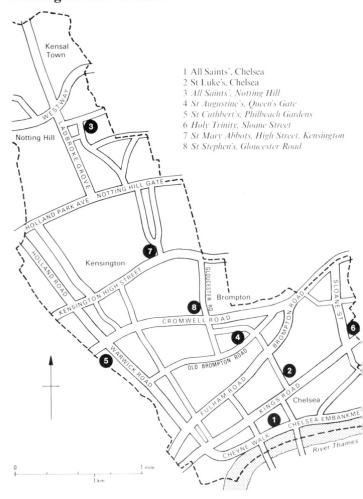

1 All Saints', Chelsea
2 St Luke's, Chelsea
3 *All Saints', Notting Hill*
4 *St Augustine's, Queen's Gate*
5 *St Cuthbert's, Philbeach Gardens*
6 *Holy Trinity, Sloane Street*
7 *St Mary Abbots, High Street, Kensington*
8 *St Stephen's, Gloucester Road*

Kensington and Chelsea

All Saints', Chelsea

Known as Chelsea Old Church 'Chelsea' is probably derived from Caelchythe, chalk wharf.

History

Until the late 18th century, Chelsea was a river village quite separate from London. It was at one time called 'the village of Palaces' as many notable people had fine mansions there standing in their own grounds. Chelsea's most famous citizen was Sir Thomas More, who lived with his family at Beaufort House.

It is likely that a place of worship existed on the site of All Saints' Church from the earliest days. The chancel is thought to date from the 13th century and the north and south chapels, which existed as proprietary chapels until the 1870s, were built in 1325. The tower, which bore a cupola until 1915, and the nave were erected between 1667 and 1670.

Towards the end of the 18th century as Chelsea expanded, London spread towards it, until by the Victorian period they were fused together into one urban concentration.

On the night of 16th/17th April 1941, two land mines released from a German bomber floated down on to All Saints' and the resultant explosion left a scene of devastation from which it seemed that little could be salvaged. Closer inspection, however, showed that by great good fortune the important More Chapel was less seriously damaged than the rest of the church. After long and sometimes difficult negotiations, it was finally decided to rebuild All Saints' as a parish church and today, after a superlative restoration by W. H. Godfrey, Chelsea Old Church (as it is more familiarly known) is once more in full use with its numerous grand monuments, although bearing the scars of war, restored to their former magnificence.

Exterior

The church presents a homely brick exterior with its south side facing the river. The simple, rectangular nave has been rebuilt to the old design, also the massive tower with its strong clasping buttresses and these, with the older parts which survived, are set in a pretty little garden. In the south-east corner is the memorial to Sir Hans Sloane with the charming inscription 'President of the Royal Society and of

the College of Physicians who, in the year of our Lord 1753 the 92nd
year of his age, without the least pain of body, and with a conscious
serenity of mind, ended a virtuous and beneficent life'. (see plate
opposite)

Interior

Attention is immediately drawn towards the east end and the wealth of
impressive monuments. The nave, wider than it is long, is an
unassuming and faithful copy of that which was destroyed, although
the light tone of the oak contrasts strongly with the darker tone of the
pulpit and the furnishings of the chancel although the pews and gallery
are mellowing with age. A screen of three arches separates the new
from the old and the monuments are grouped round the walls of the
chancel and chapels, except for two in the nave.

The Lawrence Chapel to the north-east originally belonged to the
Lords of the Manor – who apart from the Lawrence family included
Lord Bray and Sir Hans Sloane. The bombing exposed a window in
the chapel which previously had been hidden.

*The More Chapel, entered from the aisle through a depressed arch,
is to the south-east. It was rebuilt by Sir Thomas More himself in 1528
– the date can be seen on one of the capitals of the pillars leading to
the chancel – and is undoubtedly the most interesting part structurally
of the church. The capitals – by some attributed to Holbein, a friend of
More, although Basil Clarke thinks that they were probably the work
of French masons – are of national importance, being early and very
fine examples of the new Renaissance style coming in at that time; the
decoration symbolises the offices in Church and State held by Sir
Thomas and includes Tudor head-dress, holy-water stoup and brush,
bunch of tapers and acolyte's candles. It is interesting, in view of the
derivation of the name Chelsea, to see the use of chalkstone in this
chapel. An extraordinary survivor of the bombs is the wooden roof of
the chapel most of which but not all is original; the timber framing at
the west end, which had been plastered over, was revealed by the
bombing and has been left uncovered.

Furnishings

Royal Arms They are the Royal Arms of Elizabeth II.

Font Made of marble, the top part is original and dates from 1673.
The cover is a reproduction of the one destroyed.

Chained books The chained books in the south aisle, the gift of Sir
Hans Sloane, are the only chained books in any London church. They

All Saints', Chelsea

consist of the *Vinegar Bible* (1717), two volumes of Foxe's *Book of Martyrs* (1684), a *Prayer Book* (1723) and *Homilies* (1683).

Stained glass Pieces of German or Flemish 16th/17th century glass are dotted around the interior.

Pulpit Originally a three-decker, dating from the 17th century. The present one is a copy, incorporating original carving, door and one panel from the old pulpit. It is in dark wood, elevated on a pedestal with a graceful staircase containing twisted balusters.

Altar and altar-rails These date from the 17th century and the rails comply with the regulations of the Bishop of Norwich that they should be 'neer one yarde in height, so thick with pillars that dogges may not gett in'. The curtain behind the altar is a replacement made five years ago in 1990 of one from Westminster Abbey which had become faded.

Monuments

Chelsea Old Church possesses one of the finest sets of Tudor monuments outside the central area of London. These were scattered by the bombing and for the rest of the War were stored in the crypt of St Luke's, Chelsea. They were most skilfully replaced and reassembled by the architect Walter H. Godfrey who restored the church, and are now once more an ornament to it and one of its chief features of interest. Seven of the ten major ones are 16th century. Viewing them in an anti-clockwise direction starting from the south side, we come first to the grandest of them:

Nave

Gregory Fiennes, Lord Dacre of the South died 1594, his wife Ann Sackville who died a year later and one child.

Ascribed to Nicholas Johnson, it shows the main figures recumbent with hands upraised in prayer under an arch flanked by Corinthian columns with an inscription and strapwork decoration on the back. Above is a superstructure supporting a large coat of arms, two achievements and two obelisks capped with balls.

This is a sumptuous memorial and a fine example of Elizabethan sculpture.

More Chapel

Jane Guildford, Duchess of Northumberland, died 1555. She was mother-in-law of Lady Jane Grey, mother of Queen Elizabeth's favourite the Earl of Leicester and grandmother of Sir Philip Sidney. It is recessed with diapered shafts supporting a canopy enriched with fan-tracery, but was badly damaged. There is a brass against the back wall.

Chancel

On the south wall is the memorial to *Sir Thomas More*, beheaded 1535, and his first wife. Recessed, it was erected in 1532 for his wife, for whom Sir Thomas composed the inscription.

Sir Reginald Bray, died 1539. Also recessed. A tomb-chest with lozenge-shaped panels and shields.

Thomas Hungerford, died 1591 and wife. They are shown in the typical kneeling posture of the time with small figures facing one another.

Lawrence Chapel

Sir Thomas Lawrence, died 1593. Similar to the Hungerford memorial.

Sir Robert Stanley, died 1632. He was the son-in-law of Sir Arthur Gorges whose brass is on the north wall of the More Chapel. This is a large standing wall memorial with a bust of himself and the figures of his children placed before the pedestals with large urns on top of a sarcophagus. The absence of an enclosing arch gives the memorial an unfinished look.

Sir John Lawrence, died 1638. A memorial to another member of the Lawrence family on the north wall of the chapel.

*Sara Colvile, died 1631. Daughter of Sir Thomas Lawrence. A most interesting and notable memorial artistically, erected at a time when there was beginning to be strong emphasis on the resurrection of the body and showing her rising from the tomb in her shroud with eyes and hands directed upwards; it follows the style of one of the same date by Nicholas Stone to Dr John Donne in St Paul's Cathedral and is strongly reminiscent of a later memorial at Egham (1638) to Sir John Denham.

Richard Jervoise, died 1563. Under the western arch of the Lawrence Chapel is a free-standing memorial to Richard Jervoise, son-in-law of Sir Thomas More, in the form of a Roman triumphal arch. The altar-tomb that used to be there was removed years later in order to provide room for pews. The underside of the arch is decorated with rough strapwork.

Nave

Lady Jane Cheyne, who was daughter of the Duke of Newcastle and a great benefactress to the village and the church (she provided the interior roofing). Situated on the north wall, it is a standing monument designed in 1672 with a curved front. Lady Jane is shown semi-reclining on a sarcophagus with hand on heart in a niche framed by large columns and under a segmental pediment. According to the Rev. H.S. Stewart's guide book, this was designed by Paolo Bernini, a kinsman of the celebrated Bernini and was sculpted by Antonio Raggi.

There is also a wealth of wall cartouches and tablets which are too many to enumerate.

Associations
Ashburnham Bell A bell, presented in 1679 by the Hon William Ashburnham as a thank-offering for being saved from drowning, hangs in the porch.

Robert Henry Davies, who lived from 1821 to 1908, was incumbent here for over fifty years. It was he who purchased the More and Lawrence Chapels with his own money for the general use of the church.

General
Despite being engulfed by London, the area around Chelsea Old Church still retains some of its old riverside atmosphere. The red brick building, with memories of its great figures of the past, tells us much of what Chelsea was like in their lifetime when All Saints' was their parish church. Today we are reminded even more forcibly of its most heroic figure by the bronze statue outside, to Sir Thomas More, unveiled in 1969.

2 St Luke's, Chelsea

History
As Chelsea developed north of the King's Road towards Kensington a need was felt for a larger church than Chelsea Old Church and, under the powerful impetus of the Hon and Revd Gerald Valerian Wellesley, DD, Rector of Chelsea and brother of the Duke of Wellington, a new place of worship was authorised by Act of Parliament in 1819.

The design submitted to the Board of Works by the chosen architect, James Savage, provided for a building vaulted throughout with panelled stone west wall and, externally, flying buttresses,

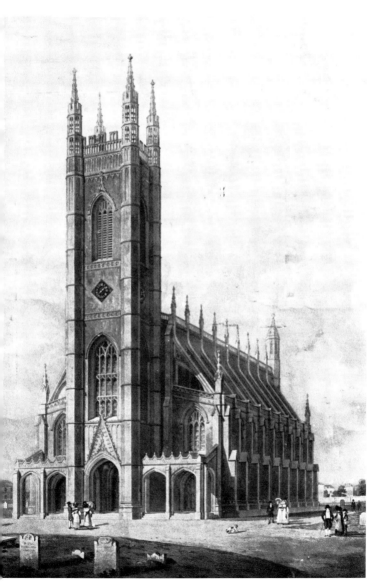

St Luke's, Chelsea. Original architect's drawing

something which had not been attempted since the Reformation. Despite the misgivings of the Board's architects, which included Nash and Soane, Savage went ahead with his design and succeeded in producing, in expensive Bath stone, the first thoroughgoing Gothic Revival church in England.

The new building was consecrated on 18th October 1824 – St Luke's Day – by Dr Howley, Bishop of London who later, as Archbishop of Canterbury, was to crown Queen Victoria.

Substantial alterations, which included the raising of the chancel and sanctuary floors and the provision of many of the furnishings, were made towards the end of the 19th century but, since then, the only major change has been the provision of a new east window for the one damaged during the 1939–45 War.

Exterior (See plate p. 355)
Surrounded by open spaces, including a wide playground, St Luke's can be viewed easily from all angles. The most arresting feature is the 142 ft-high tower. Battlemented, it has octagonal turrets capped with tapering open pinnacles and is divided by nine stringcourses placed at equal intervals. This handsome tower rises from a five-bay porch extending the full width of the building.

The stress of the roof is carried via flying buttresses to the wall buttresses with set-offs half-way down giving the building a rather taut appearance and accentuating the long and narrow lines. Small domed turrets surmount the east end.

Interior
The interior space follows the pattern used in the Commissioners' churches of the time in that it sets out to provide plenty of accommodation. Each element of the design was aimed to serve a functional purpose. The stone-vaulted nave is 60 feet high – the loftiest of any parish church in London – and has a triforium as well as a clerestory integrated into one composition both of which extend into the chancel. Wooden galleries are fitted in between the piers.

Eastwards the view is dominated by the raised chancel/sanctuary and the high seven-light east window. The altar and reredos are flanked by elaborate empty niches.

The original box pews were removed in the late 19th century, leaving the plinths of the nave columns exposed.

Blind panelling decorates the west end wall, above which is placed the organ casing; the console is at the east end.

In the south-east angle a chapel has been attractively fitted out as a memorial to the Punjab Frontier Force Association (PFFA). A framed description tells how the link with St Luke's arose and a book records the names of those members whose memorial brasses are kept in the crypt. The Garter banner of Lord Ismay, former President of the Association, hangs on the south wall.

There is a labyrinth of vaults below the church transformed into a Parish Office and a Sanctum for the PFFA.

Furnishings

Organ One of the finest in London. It was rebuilt in 1932 by John Compton but much of the casework and some of the pipework comes from the 1824 Nicholls organ. Amongst famous organists were John Goss, who later became organist at St Paul's Cathedral, and from 1904 to 1926 the composer John Ireland. Goss wrote many well-known hymn tunes including 'Praise my soul, the King of Heaven'.

Royal Arms The organ-case bears the Royal Arms of George IV.

Stalls At the west end under the organ are two sets of six stalls, with canopies, for wardens and guardians, dating from 1824.

Font This is a dignified and chaste octagonal example of marble. It is placed in the usual position near the main entrance but was originally at the east end. It dates from 1826.

Pulpit A massive and rather showy Victorian furnishing dating from 1893. It is elevated and adorned with marble panels. Round the tall stem and under the base are cherubs' heads.

Lectern A remarkable modern piece on a base resembling large coiled springs.

Stained glass The east window is by Hugh Easton and depicts the Trinity and saints of the church. A key to the symbols is on the pillar nearest the font.

Reredos painting Above the altar is a painting by James Northcote of the Entombment.

Monuments

Lt Col Henry Cadogan A memorial to Lt Col Henry Cadogan, killed in 1813 at the battle of Vitoria in the Peninsular War against Napoleon, shows two mourning soldiers contemplating a coffin. It is on the east wall of the north gallery.

Luke Thomas Flood, died 1860. A relief on the commemorative tablet shows an angel calling him to heaven.

Associations

Charles Dickens Charles Dickens was married to Christine Hogarth at
St Luke's in 1826.

Jerome K. Jerome was also married here.

Charles Kingsley, author of *The Water Babies* and *Westward Ho* was
a curate here for a time during the period from 1836 to 1860 when his
father was rector.

General

Despite the large sum of money (£40,000), all raised by subscription,
spent on the church and the great technical competence displayed by
the architect, St Luke's has a somewhat cold and machine-made look
about it and is not artistically a success. Nevertheless, this church will
always be notable for its important place in the 19th century Gothic
Revival and for the care and architectural skill which has gone into it.

Other Churches in Kensington and Chelsea

As the population of this favoured residential area grew in the 19th
century, in part as a result of the Great Exhibition, the building of the
museums and the founding of the Imperial Institute, many churches of
note were erected. Others were built in less well-off parts of the
Borough. The following are of especial interest: **All Saints', Notting
Hill** (3) was built in 1852–5, with young William White (nephew of
Gilbert White, who wrote *The Natural History of Selborne*) as
architect. The main external feature is the unusually tall,
slender west tower of four stages, with an octagonal top built of
coloured stones. The interior was restored after bombing in the
1939–45 War, and All Saints' has been fortunate in its post-war
craftsmen. Much of the glass, including the large east window and the
north transept rose window, is by Gerald Smith of A. K. Studios; other
glass and furnishings, including the Lady Chapel with its striking
reredos which depicts the Mysteries of the Rosary, are by Sir Ninian
Comper.

St Augustine's, Queen's Gate (4). Built in 1871–6, this is one of
Butterfield's characteristic London churches, designed in his highly
individual manner without regard to adjacent buildings and presenting
a west front of typical bands of stone and red brick (his 'streaky bacon'
effect) and an aggressive bellcote. The well-proportioned interior is a
good example of his skilled use of contrasts of colour and materials,
including the unusual decorative treatment of black slate inlay in the

All Saints', Notting Hill. Tower

chancel. Much of the effect was nullified by subsequent distempering and by new furnishings, especially the huge Baroque reredos introduced by Martin Travers but as far as possible the original colour contrasts have been restored.

St Cuthbert's, Philbeach Gardens (5) The dedication is due to the church having relics of St Cuthbert; the foundation stone came from Holy Island. It was built in 1884–7 of red brick with copper flèche and roof. St Cuthbert's is noted for its furnishings by W. Bainbridge Reynolds in the Arts and Crafts tradition. The vast reredos was the work of the Rev E. Geldart and was made in 1914.

Holy Trinity, Sloane Street (6). The present building of 1888–90, designed by John Dando Sedding who did not live to see it completed, took the place of a Commissioners' church of 1828–31 by James Savage, architect of St Luke's, Chelsea. Many artists, including Sir Edward Burne-Jones, planned the furnishing and decoration and made Holy Trinity into the finest exposition of Arts and Crafts work in a London church.

St Mary Abbots, Kensington (7). As its name implies, this church has a long history; in mediaeval times, it was linked with the important Abbey of Abingdon. The predecessor of the present place of worship, erected in 1697, was reported in 1866 to be in a bad state and Sir George Gilbert Scott was engaged to build a new church which, to be worthy of the Lord, was to be 'truly magnifical'. The main fabric was erected in 1869–72, the 278-ft high tower and spire (the tallest in London) in 1879 and the south porch with vaulted cloister in 1889–93.

The interior does not match up to the proud exterior and the furnishings, apart from the Wren-period pulpit from the old church which some say was given to the church by William III who spent much time at nearby Kensington Palace, are of minor interest.

St Stephen's, Gloucester Road (once called Hogmire Lane) (8). The main interest of this church, built in 1866–7, is the east end of the interior which was largely the work of G. F. Bodley, carried out in 1903–4, with its massive reredos neatly set against a circular window filled with glass of rich, glowing blues.

T. S. Eliot, poet and dramatist, was churchwarden at St Stephen's for 25 years, as is recorded on a tablet on the south wall.

Lambeth

1 Holy Trinity, Clapham
2 St Peter's, Kennington Lane, Vauxhall
3 St Mark's, Kennington
4 St Matthew's, Brixton
5 Christ Church, Streatham
6 St Leonard's, Streatham
7 St Mary's, Lambeth
8 St Paul's, Clapham
9 St John the Divine, Kennington
10 All Saints, West Dulwich
11 St John the Evangelist, Upper Norwood

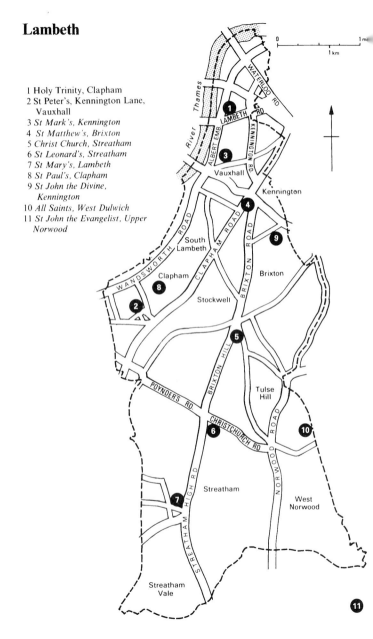

Lambeth

1 St Mary's, Lambeth

History

One of four riverside churches in the Metropolitan area dedicated to
St Mary, the others being at Rotherhithe, Battersea and Putney,
St Mary's Lambeth had been disused since 1972 although it was the
parish church of Lambeth.

After a lean period, it was rescued in 1979 by the Tradescant Trust
and most 'imaginatively restored as a Museum of Garden History,
turning a depressing interior into a beautiful place to visit and study
garden history. This use is particularly appropriate because three
generations of Tradescants are buried in the churchyard. The elder
John Tradescant (d. 1638) was Charles I's gardener and both he and
his son were distinguished botanical travellers.

Architecturally, St Mary's has much to offer. The tower and the
body of the church date from the 1370s, although the chancel chapels
were added in the early 16th century. Other 16th century alterations
were largely removed by P. C. Hardwick's restoration of 1851/2 which
gave back to the church its earlier form.

Exterior

The view from Lambeth Bridge of St Mary's nudging up against the
gateway of Lambeth Palace is one of London's most charming
mediaeval vignettes. The south-west tower, dating from 1370, is built
of ragstone with diagonal buttresses and a polygonal stair-turret; the
top storey was renewed in 1834.

Interior

The removal of the early 16th century alterations has left a 'nobly
proportioned' (Pevsner) interior of the 1370s. There are five bays in
the nave which consists of tall octagonal piers; the clerestory has threelight windows.

At the west end is a rare example of an immersion font which was
installed as a memorial to Archbishop Benson (d. 1896); it is
semicircular, faced in marble with a moulded kerb.

Furnishings

Stained glass A recent addition since the church was transformed into
the Museum of Garden History is an excellent window at the west end

designed by Lawrence Lee, one of the foremost stained glass artists in the country. It is called 'The Gardeners' Window', starting with Adam and Eve and ending with the Tradescants.

Monuments

There are many busts, cartouches and other monuments. They include at the east end two tomb-chests:

Hugh Peyntwyn (d. 1504), an archdeacon of Canterbury, on the north wall.

John Mompesson (d. 1524), master of the Canterbury registry.

Brass

Lady Katherine Howard (d. 1535). Her husband's half-sister was Anne Boleyn's mother.

Lady Howard is shown wearing a magnificent heraldic mantle.

Churchyard

This has been laid out as a garden planted with flowers introduced by the Tradescants to England and other plants of the 17th century.

There are two sarcophagi of considerable interest:

The Tradescants. This was erected by the widow of John the younger in 1662 and recarved in 1853. The unusual design has reliefs on four sides including trees at the angles, a crocodile, a hydra and ruined buildings.

William Bligh (d. 1817). This was Bligh of the *Bounty* who was cast adrift in an open boat by mutineers. He is described as 'Vice-Admiral of the Blue, the celebrated navigator who first transplanted the bread fruit tree from Otaheite to the West Indies, bravely fought the battles of his country and died, beloved, respected and lamented on the 7th day of October, 1817, aged 64.' (Actually 63). No mention is made of the Mutiny. (See illustration opposite.)

General

All concerned are to be congratulated on transforming a forlorn place of worship into a building full of light and beauty, thus creating a major tourist attraction.

2 Holy Trinity, Clapham

History

In the middle of the 18th century the old church at Clapham had become ruinous and it was decided not to spend more on it but it was

SACRED
TO THE MEMORY OF
WILLIAM BLIGH, ESQUIRE, F.R.S.
VICE ADMIRAL OF THE BLUE
THE CELEBRATED NAVIGATOR
WHO FIRST TRANSPLANTED THE BREAD FRUIT TREE
FROM OTAHEITE TO THE WEST INDIES,
BRAVELY FOUGHT THE BATTLES OF HIS COUNTRY
AND DIED BELOVED, RESPECTED, AND LAMENTED,
ON THE 7TH DAY OF DECEMBER 1817,
AGED 64.

St Mary's, Lambeth. Bligh tomb

Holy Trinity, Clapham

some years later, in 1774, that Parliament passed a Bill for a church to
be built on a new site on the north side of the Common which was
then being developed. Kenton Couse, a pupil of Henry Flitcroft who
designed St Giles-in-the-Fields near Tottenham Court Road, was
entrusted with the work. Difficulties were encountered with the
foundations because of the wet state of the ground but the new church
was consecrated on 9th June 1776.

In 1812 a porch designed by Francis Hurlbatt was added and in 1902

A. Beresford Pite substituted a chancel for the apse. In the meantime the Victorians cut down the pews in 1865 and dismantled the three-decker pulpit in 1875, retaining only the pulpit and moving it from the centre to the north side of the nave.

Holy Trinity was a late casualty from a rocket in 1945 and was restored under Thomas Ford, who had already carried out repairs in the 1920s. Other repairs were put in hand later.

Since 1986, a major programme of restoration and development has been carried out. The development work, undertaken between 1991 and 1993, included the erection of a screen under the west gallery to create a meeting area and a small chapel, called the Thornton Chapel. It also covered the conversion of the Lady Chapel (part of A. Beresford Pite's 1902/3 addition) into the Wilberforce Centre for community use. The architects for this work, except for that carried out on the bells, were the firm of Purcell Miller Tritton.

Exterior
The church is extremely fortunate in its setting on the Common, being one of the most open in London. It is a plain brick rectangle with stone quoins and a stone turret surmounted by a large octagonal domed cupola at the west end. The cupola has been described as 'awkward' but the exterior would be rather featureless without it.

Interior
The interior is plain, still retaining its galleries, and has been described as a large, harmonious brick box.

Furnishing
Pulpit This is contemporary with the building of the church and originally stood in the middle, which no doubt suited the Evangelicals who gathered there. Until 1875 it was a tall three-decker with a canopy supported on two pillars.

Communion table This was the gift of a parishioner in 1776.

General
Holy Trinity is chiefly remembered for its associations with the Evangelical Clapham Sect, men of importance in the City and in Parliament who worshipped there and who secured the living for their nominee. They included such names as the great family of Zachary Macaulay (Sir Charles Trevelyan's father-in-law), the Thorntons and the Venns (father and son, respectively curate and Rector). William Wilberforce and the Clapham Sect were moving forces in the abolition

of the slave trade in 1807; abolition of the institution of slavery fell to others later.

A plaque on the south side commemorates the group and, in 1983, the year of the 150th anniversary of the death of Wilberforce, the GLC placed a blue plaque on the west wall under the porch, commemorating him and the Clapham Sect (a rare, if not unique, example of an official London blue plaque on a church).

3 St Peter's, Kennington Lane, Vauxhall

'Vauxhall' (Fauxhall) is derived from Falkes de Breauté, second husband of Margaret, widow of Baldwin de Redvers.

History

In 1761 when Vauxhall Gardens were at the height of their popularity as a place of lively entertainment, Vauxhall or South Lambeth was a village; by 1861 Lambeth had a population of 162,000, mostly poorly housed, and St Peter's Church was built in 1863–4 to help cater for their spiritual needs.

The new church was consecrated on 28th June 1864 and is a notable example of J. L. Pearson's work, despite the fact that it was not completed as originally designed. In particular, and as so often occurred with places of worship erected in the second half of the 19th century, the planned tower and spire did not materialise; in addition only one of the four turrets was built and the decoration of the west front was never executed.

On the other hand, St Peter's escaped subsequent interference and survived the 1939–45 War. Today, like so many in the Inner London area, the parish suffers from a dwindling number of residents.

Exterior

The absence of the vertical accents which the steeple and the extra turrets would have provided detracts from the over-all impact but the church rises commandingly above the surrounding buildings including some which were constructed by Pearson and show touches of his style, as for instance the 'tourelle' of the adjoining school.

Opinions on the west front vary from 'insignificant' (Pevsner) to 'most impressive' (Clarke) but it can at least be said that it is powerful with its three-arched porch abutting right on to the pavement of Kennington Lane and its three massive buttresses. The latter enclose large plate-traceried windows, whilst above in the gable there is a circular window with similar type of tracery.

Interior

Entering through the narthex the visitor sees a fine example of 19th century architecture. Vaulted throughout and with an apsidal chancel the interior is dignified, spacious and refreshingly free of obtrusive detail.

It consists of a five-bay nave and one-bay chancel, aisles and Lady Chapel, with nave and chancel of equal height without an intervening arch. The cylindrical columns are shafted on the aisle sides only and have large elaborate capitals each differently carved, including one on the south side (next to the chancel) with small figures under arches.

At triforium level the blank walling is divided into panels by vaulting shafts and string-courses above and below; from this level the wall slopes steeply back to the plate-traceried windows of the clerestory. Round the apse the triforium consists of open arcades with small windows behind, the clerestory windows become lancets.

London grime has cast a sombre tone over the brickwork but the Lady Chapel, which extends along the chancel and part of the nave has been cleaned revealing the colour contrast between the yellow stock and red brick of which the church is built. The stone work has also been cleaned up to string-course level whilst the wall-paintings in the apse and above the west door have been restored.

The capitals in the chancel are separately carved, one being of the Byzantine basket type but with figures of Fortitude, Justice, Prudence and Temperance added.

Furnishings

The furnishings are appropriate to the architecture.

Font Distinguished by its large pyramidal cover painted gold and pink with a decorative window on each side; it is believed to be by Pearson. The baptistery is in the south-west corner.

Pulpit A run-of-the-mill Victorian furnishing supported on round columns and decorated with biblical scenes, containing large mosaic pieces.

Screens Attractive arched parclose screens of iron separate the chancel from the organ on the south side and from the Lady Chapel on the north side. There is further iron work above the low marble chancel wall.

Sedilia The most richly decorated of the furnishings with much dog-tooth carved on the four arches and elaborate capitals. The fourth opening is used as a credence table. Curved attractively round the apse.

Altars The main altar is on the site of the Neptune Fountain which used to be in Vauxhall Gardens. There are two other altars one in front of the chancel steps is gilded like the main altar and has the same type of filigree decoration so that it may be original although it came only recently from a Hertfordshire nunnery which used to be in Vauxhall; the other altar – in the Lady Chapel – is decorated in front with panels of beaten pewter.

Sanctuary lamps The seven lamps in the sanctuary represent the seven early churches of Asia.

Christ Church, Streatham

Reredos The pedimented reredos is adorned with circular motifs and a mosaic centre-piece. This is another agreeable furnishing and suited to its focal position.

Stained glass The triforium glass round the apse with its rich reds is by Clayton & Bell.

Association
Edward Denny, the second vicar, was a Labour county councillor for London. One of his sons, Sir Michael Denny, was 3rd Sea Lord.

General
St Peter's is a church of distinction by one of the best Victorian architects, where everything – to quote Basil Clarke is 'simple solid and, as the ecclesiologists would have said, real'.

It is interesting to note that the area between the church and the railway lines which used to be occupied by Vauxhall Gardens is again being developed as an open space, although hardly likely to have the attractions which were such a draw to 18th century society.

N.B. Open Tuesdays to Fridays 10.30 a.m. to 4.30 p.m.

Other Churches in Lambeth
The Borough of Lambeth has much to offer to the lover of churches besides the two described in detail.

In the 1820s, four Commissioners' buildings were erected to cater for the needs of an increasing population. Dedicated to the four Evangelists (St John, St Luke, St Mark and St Matthew), two (St John's, Waterloo Road and St Mark's, Kennington) were severely damaged in the 1939–45 War but have been restored, **St Mark's** (4) near the Oval Cricket ground almost entirely due to the efforts of Wallace Bird, who persuaded the Bishop to appoint him to the living in 1947. The Wren-period pulpit came from St Michael's, Wood Street in the City.

Of these four churches, the outstanding one architecturally is **St Matthew's, Brixton** (5) where the perennial problem of the steeple riding on the roof when placed above a west end portico has been overcome by siting the steeple at the east end, leaving the handsome portico to answer for itself. The interior has been cleared to provide space for a community centre but an adequate area for worship will be provided. St Luke's, the fourth church, is situated in Norwood. Other places of worship of particular interest are: **St Luke's** (6) **Christ Church, Streatham** (7) beside the South Circular Road. Built in 1840–1 this was the work of a highly talented architect of only 29, John

Wild, who erected a building of refreshingly crisp design in Italian basilican style. A campanile rises sheer to a height of 113 feet in the south-east corner and the excellent brickwork has many refinements of cut and colour. The interior, apart from the apse which is decorated with three mosaic murals, has been stripped of most of its decoration by war damage and is drained of colour, but there is some good modern glass.

St Leonard's, Streatham (8), with a long history, is effectively a Victorian church of the mid-19th century which has recently been restored after a disastrous fire in May 1975. It nevertheless retains its links with the days when Streatham was a sought-after village and a centre of polite society, including the circle of distinguished people, such as Burke, Garrick, Goldsmith, Reynolds, Dr Johnson and Boswell, who gathered at the home of the Thrales. Even a certain mediaeval atmosphere lingers on. At the end of the north aisle are three memorials to the Thrale family on two of which Dr Johnson composed the Latin inscriptions.

St Paul's, Clapham (9) was erected in 1815 as a chapel of ease to Holy Trinity. Although it would not draw the visitor for any architectural virtues, it contains one feature of great interest. This is the monument to Sir Richard Atkins (d. 1689), his wife Lady Rebecca (d. 1711) and their three children, all of whom died before the parents; this monument, which now lies in the Lady Chapel, was once in the mediaeval church dedicated to Holy Trinity situated where St Paul's now stands. The craftsmanship is of a high order; particularly charming is the standing figure of Rebecca, the youngest child who died in 1661 at the age of 8; she holds a skull in her hand.

St John the Divine, Vassall Road, Kennington (10) was built in 1871–4 to the designs of G. E. Street. It is fortunate in that there were enough funds to add in 1888–9 the fine tower and spire, unlike many others (e.g. St Peter's, Kennington Lane) with steeples planned for them which were never built. Despite extensive war damage, St John the Divine has been fully restored at a cost of £140,000 by H. S. Goodhart-Rendel. This is a large and notable Victorian church. The last bay of the nave is canted inwards to the narrower chancel.

All Saints, West Dulwich (11) is an impressive church of brick set up high on a sloping site and dominating Rosendale Road, built between 1888 and 1891 by G. H. Fellowes Prynne. The nave is in 13th and the eastern apsed end in 14th century style. It is mainly distinctive by its canted bays at the end of the nave and the screen, characteristic of the architect, filling the whole of the chancel arch. There are ambulatories round the apse and the Lady Chapel – also with apse to the north. The west end is

St John the Evangelist, Upper Norwood

incomplete and the projected tower was never built; a flèche erected over the junction between nave and chancel had to be taken down.

St John the Evangelist, Upper Norwood (12). Just beyond the boundaries of the Borough of Lambeth is this outstanding J. L. Pearson church, built over the years 1881–7. Tall clerestory lancets and a high-pitched roof impart a strong vertical emphasis despite the fact that the spire planned above the tower never materialised. The interior (plate above) is a fine work in Pearson's mature Early English style, full of subtleties and exciting oblique vistas, beautifully proportioned with clean lines, vaulted throughout and restrained in decoration. The plain yellow stock brick provides a neutral-toned background for the stone detail.

Lewisham

1 St Paul's, Deptford
2 *All Saints', Sydenham*
3 *Church of the Ascension, Blackheath*
4 *St Laurence, Catford*
5 *St Mary's, Lewisham*

Lewisham

1 St Paul's, Deptford

Deptford
Probably derived from 'deep ford'.

History
One of four major churches erected in the east and south-east of
London under the 1711 Act to meet the needs of a growing district,
St Paul's was created out of the older St Nicholas' parish in what used
to be known as West Greenwich.

The architect was Thomas Archer, our most Baroque architect.

Building began in 1712 but, as with the other three churches,
proceeded slowly and consecration did not take place until 30th June,
1730.

The area later lost its wealth, which may have saved St Paul's from
intensive Victorianisation, for the repairs carried out in 1856 and a
rearrangement in 1883 left it little altered. It was also fortunate in a
careful restoration carried out during the 1930s.

Today, as a result of substantial contributions from local authorities
and a great self-effort within the parish, much excellent restoration at a
cost of over £100,000 has been completed. More remains to be done
but the church – bright and fresh – is a joy to visit.

Exterior
This is one of the major architectural thrills of London. Set well back
at an angle to the beautifully kept and spacious churchyard which fans
out as the church is approached, and open on the east side, this
dazzling white building of great distinction makes a powerful impact.
Thomas Archer succeeded in overcoming the problem of the awkward
relationship between portico and steeple 'riding on the roof' by
making the tower circular and letting it project into a semicircular
portico around which he wrapped a wide radial staircase.

The portico has large Tuscan columns and is crowned by a
balustrade; the steeple derived from St Mary-le-Bow recedes in
diminishing circular stages with pilasters, urns below and spiral scrolls
above, culminating in a rather attenuated spire.

On the north and south sides there are also projecting porticos but the staircases, instead of being semicircular, emerge at right angles to the wall and then turn to run parallel with it.

At the east end, a curved apse echoes the semicircular west front. A Venetian window and the pediment above follow the curve.

The whole of this grand exterior is set on a raised platform which adds further stateliness.

Interior

The basically square interior is canted at the angles, behind which are vestries and staircases leading up to small galleries projecting far in front and looking like outsize theatre boxes. Above these are large windows. Giant Corinthian columns with capitals picked out in gold and a pastel shade of blue knit the composition together into one harmonious whole. The ceiling has deep panelled recesses.

The chancel, which is enclosed within a frame of pilasters flanked by Doric columns, lies in a shallow apse and is the least interesting feature.

Furnishings

Many fittings are of Dutch oak and their brown tone accords well with this bright interior. The pews are plain.

Font The Victorian font in Norman style came from Rochester Cathedral, the original having been sent to a mission church overseas. It is out of keeping.

Chandelier A fine chandelier which is a focal point adds further dignity to the interior.

Pulpit The pulpit, S in shape, has an iron staircase.

Communion rails The same material is used for the rails.

Reredos This extends on all three sides of the apse.

Stained glass The north-west window contains good 18th century glass, depicting a saint. The east windows are in Pre-Raphaelite style.

Monuments

John Harrison A tablet commemorates John Harrison, died 1753, who was founder of and first surgeon at the London Hospital. This is in the body of the church on the right-hand side near the statue of St Joseph.

Dr Charles Burney The profile of Dr Burney, brother of the novelist and letter-writer Fanny Burney, is shown against an obelisk which is in relief. There is also a bust to him. A rector of St Paul's, he died in 1917.

Matthew and Maria Finch Two separate monuments to Matthew and

St Paul's, Deptford. View from west

Maria Finch, who both died in 1745, are in the form of a standing wall monument with sarcophagus and an urn against an obelisk respectively. They are to the right of the sanctuary.

Admiral John Sayer The monument by Nollekens to the left of the sanctuary is an epitaph with large trophy. The Admiral died in 1776.

Margaret Hawtrees, a midwife, is recorded by an inscription on a monument which reads:

'She was an indulgent mother, and the best of wives.

She brought into this world more than three thousand lives.' The monument is to the left of the High Altar.

Obelisk in churchyard The obelisk dating from 1807 in the churchyard commemorates the Stone family.

General

However controversial Thomas Archer's other London church – St John's, Smith Square – may be and despite the Victorians' description of St Paul's as 'pagan and pompous', there can be no doubt today about its merits. Many would rate it as the finest 18th century parish church in London and some, going even further, as, externally, the most outstanding in the Metropolis of any period. With its parish life transformed during recent years and the church a focal point of the community, St Paul's – beautified and restored – is an inspiration to all who have the future of the Church at heart.

Other Churches in Lewisham

In addition to the thrill of St Paul's, Deptford, the Borough of Lewisham has other more modest architectural pleasures to enjoy in its churches.

The unpromising exterior of **All Saints', Trewsbury Road, Sydenham** (2), an Edwardian church of 1901–3, hides an attractive but incomplete interior. Three bays of tall, octagonal piers have arches which die into them without capitals, all of brick banded with stone, and a large, traceried stone screen which fills the whole of the chancel arch. This is a feature characteristic of the architect, G. H. Fellowes Prynne, also seen in his churches at All Saints, West Dulwich (see Borough of Lambeth) and Holy Trinity, Roehampton in the Borough of Wandsworth.

The Church of the Ascension, Dartmouth Row, Blackheath (3) was founded as a proprietary chapel in the 1690s and retains from that time a charming coffered apse framed in coupled columns/piers with gilded capitals. Most of the rest was rebuilt in 1824. After the 1939–45 War, the galleries were removed except for the western one which was cut back; this is supported on slender columns of iron encased in plaster and carries a modern Baroque organ, the apse was redecorated at this time. The exterior is enhanced with an attractive cupola. The chapel became a parish church in 1883.

A most original design is that of **St Laurence, Bromley Road, Catford** (4), built as recently as 1967–8 by Ralph Covell. The church is circular with clerestory of modern, thick glass set in concrete and has appropriate furnishings following the shape of the structure. The starkly simple Lady Chapel, predominantly blue, which has been likened to a Crusader's tent, contains a most graphic carving in jacaranda wood of the martyrdom of St Laurence by Samuel Wanjau, a noted artist of Kenya, which expresses the human face in great pain but with the body in an attitude of prayer. The exterior of the church which is less pleasing has an open-work spire set above the Lady Chapel and is surmounted by a crown with balls on the points reminiscent of the crown of Christ but looking rather like a ducal coronet.

St Mary's, Lewisham (5) is set effectively at an angle to the main thoroughfare. The tower dates back to 1471 but the church, built of an attractive greenish-golden stone, was mainly constructed in the 1770s by George Gibson who added the elegant crown to the tower capped by four balls at the corners. An unusual feature is the broad south porch with four columns and pediment.

The interior suffered a particularly insensitive Victorian restoration and the main points of interest are four monuments which are of considerable merit, to Anne and Margaret Petrie, Mary Lushington and John Thackeray.

Southwark

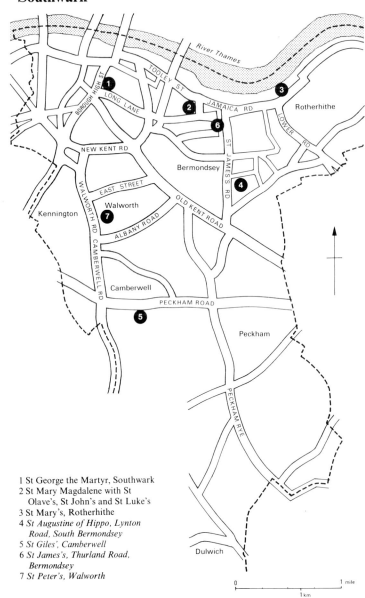

1 St George the Martyr, Southwark
2 St Mary Magdalene with St
   Olave's, St John's and St Luke's
3 St Mary's, Rotherhithe
4 *St Augustine of Hippo, Lynton
   Road, South Bermondsey*
5 St Giles', Camberwell
6 St James's, Thurland Road,
   Bermondsey
7 St Peter's, Walworth

Southwark

1 St George the Martyr, Southwark

Dedication

This was the only church in pre-18th century London to bear this dedication. St George was born of Christian parents in Cappadocia (southern central Turkey). His father was martyred and, after being tortured during the Diocletian persecution, St George suffered a similar fate in AD 303.

He became the patron saint of England and his white banner with red cross forms the basis of the Union Jack. The saint is usually shown as trampling upon a fiery dragon but, in the east window of this church, the edict of the Roman Emperor Diocletian against Christianity takes the dragon's place.

'Southwark' refers to the southern bastion of the City of London's defences.

History

There have been at least three churches on this site. In 1122, the living was given to Bermondsey Priory. There was a rebuilding in the 14th century and, prior to the Reformation, the Brotherhood of St George and the Company of Leathersellers maintained chantries in the church.

'Repaired and beautified' in 1629 and the south 'Ile' enlarged, there were further repairs in 1682 and 1705 (to the steeple) but a few years later the church was in such a poor state that a petition was put in to the Commissioners of the Fifty New Churches requesting a grant for repairs. No progress, however, could be made until a Bill was passed through Parliament in 1732 authorising a rebuilding, against the cost of which the Commissioners were prepared to allocate £6,000.

The work by John Price – started in 1734 and completed in 1736 – appears to have been badly done as frequent repairs were needed and in 1807–8 a major restoration. At the end of the 19th century, the architect Basil Champneys, who had reported very unfavourably on the fabric, carried out various alterations including the new ceiling.

Work on the south wall in 1939 helped to protect the church during the War and the damage was made good by T. F. Ford in 1951.

Exterior

St George's is splendidly placed on an island site visible from all sides. Built of brick with Portland stone dressings and possessing a City-like

St George the Martyr, Southwark. From north-east

steeple, it bears a family resemblance to St James's, Clerkenwell and
St Mary's, Rotherhithe. The steeple – also of Portland stone – is a
sturdy structure with diminishing octagonal upper stages and an almost
solid spire. The clock – illuminated on three sides only – lies under
elegant curved moulds. A balustrade and urns complete the tower.

The main entrance at the west end is placed between engaged Ionic
columns supporting a segmental pediment. Side windows are in two
tiers and, at the east end, there is a Venetian window decorated with a
cartouche and garlands above.

Interior

A typical 18th century interior with galleries and low box-pews, and an
open chancel and sanctuary. The galleries, which are on slender iron
pillars enclosed in oak panelling, were lowered in 1742.

The dominant feature is the flat Basil Champneys ceiling, badly
damaged during the War but skilfully restored by T. F. Ford in 1951.
The design consists of cherubs amongst clouds carrying scrolls upon
which are written words from the Te Deum and Benedicite, the oval
plaster decoration now being delicately tinged with pink, blue and gold.

Furnishings

Organ This was transferred from the old building but was given a new
case. It still contains Father Smith and Renatus Harris pipes.

Font The present font is modelled on an earlier one dating from the
time of Henry VIII which was used in the local workhouse for beating
oakum. It was rescued and is now in the chapel of the Old Palace
School at Croydon.

Lead cistern It is rare to find one of these 18th century receptacles
for water inside a church. This one, dating from 1738, is now used
hopefully for alms.

Royal Arms This finely carved Stuart example once formed part of
the reredos of St Michael's, Wood Street.

*Pulpit A delightful free-standing example, one of the tallest in
London. It is supported on four Ionic columns.

Communion rails These graceful rails are of iron.

Bells Worthy of mention in that they are one of the very few existing
complete peals in the country from the foundry of Abraham Rudhal of
Gloucester. They were recast in 1718.

Stained glass The east window is a post-war replacement by
D. Marion Grant of the one lost in the War but the treatment of the
Ascended Christ is different. Pilgrims with scallop shells are to be seen

in the centre light whilst Dickens' 'Little Dorrit' is a small figure with poke bonnet in the left panel. Elsewhere St George and other saints appear. There is an interesting detailed description in the guide.

Stained glass on the south side also depicts St George and came from a nearby school after it was closed down in 1930.

Monuments
There are two small brasses on either side of the chancel arch.

Associations
Nahum Tate, the author of the carol 'While Shepherds watched their Flocks by night' was buried here in 1715.

Bishop Bonner, of London in Queen Mary's reign, was consigned to the Marshalsea prison when her sister Elizabeth succeeded to the throne and was probably buried here secretly in 1569.

General Monk, instrumental in restoring Charles II to the throne, was married here in 1653.

Anne Digwid According to the registers, Anne Digwid died at the age of 101 in 1654, having had seven husbands.

Charles Dickens lived as a boy of 12 in nearby Lant Street whilst his father was in the Marshalsea prison for debt. His experience led to his casting the area as the scene of events in his novels. Little Dorrit was born in the Marshalsea, found shelter as a waif in St George's vestry and was married in it, so that it has come to be known as 'Little Dorrit Vestry'. The workhouse in *Oliver Twist* was inspired by the parish workhouse in Mint Street.

General
In mediaeval times, Southwark was the exit from London to the Continent and there were many, like Henry V on 26th April 1417, who stopped at St George's to offer up a prayer and make an offering before embarking upon some enterprise. Nearby at the Tabard Inn, Chaucer set the scene for the start of his pilgrims' journey to Canterbury whilst opposite lay Brandon Palace where Philip of Spain and Mary stopped after their marriage at Winchester.

Later, never having reached full civic status, Southwark lapsed into becoming the centre of activities such as bear-baiting, and of places like play-houses, prisons and even thieves' kitchens not wanted in the City. In the 18th century, St George's Fields was the scene of the Gordon Riots and in 1856 the then rector drew a grim picture of life in the Borough.

Now, things are better but through all these changes a church has

St George the Martyr, Southwark. Pulpit

existed on the present site providing help and comfort to the
unfortunates around and still exercising an active ministry amongst the
more fortunate of today.

2 St Mary Magdalene with St Olave's, St John's and St Luke's

Bermondsey
Probably 'Beormund's Eye', the islet (Eye is Saxon for islet) of
Beormund, a personal name. There was at one time a low eminence
above the riverside marshy ground.

History
The mediaeval history of the area is dominated by the great Cluniac
Priory of St Saviour, founded before the Conquest, which had
considerable influence until it was dissolved in 1537. It became an
abbey in 1399, after severance of its connection with the parent abbey
of Cluny 25 years earlier. Here at Bermondsey two Queens of England
died: Margaret de Valois, widow of Henry V and later wife of Owen
Tudor, and Elizabeth Woodville, the upstart widow of Edward IV.

St Mary Magdalene Church was built beside the Priory for their
'servants and tenants' (compare St Margaret's, Westminster and St
Katharine Cree Church in the City) and is first recorded in 1296 as
belonging to the monastery. No trace of the first church remains and,
apart from the lower part of the tower, a window concealed behind the
organ and some dressed stonework, the same applies to its successor.

After the dissolution of the Abbey, the church became parochial.
Enlarged in 1610 by the widening of the south aisle and altered in
1621, it nevertheless became unsafe by the latter part of the century
and was pulled down. The influx of rich merchants and others from the
City after the Plague and the Fire may have affected the decision to
build a new church.

This was constructed between 1675 and 1677 by Charley Stanton to
the designs of an architect who is not known, retaining the old tower
and perhaps part of the north aisle. In 1793 galleries were inserted and
the tower may have been heightened about this time. If so, this was
probably the cause of the trouble it gave in 1830 when the top stage
was removed and the present gabled structure substituted; the west
front was then re-done in 'Gothick style', all this work being carried
out by George Porter, a Bermondsey architect.

Repairs in 1852 were followed by a lengthening of the chancel for choir stalls in 1883 and the provision of new furnishings and the north-east vestry.

Since then the church has been left alone, apart from necessary repairs after 1939–45 war damage and a fire in 1971.

St Olave's, the oldest church in Bermondsey, was founded before 1066. The last church on the site was erected soon after 1734 but closed, due to fall in population, in 1918 and pulled down in 1926. St John's, Horsleydown was one of the places of worship built under the 1711 Act for Fifty New Churches but was not rebuilt after war damage. St Luke's was built in 1884 and demolished in 1965.

Exterior
The west front of St Mary Magdalene is practically all the rather amateur 1830 effort of George Porter in what Pevsner describes as 'playful Gothic' with stucco and the projecting aisles ending at the west end in castellated lean-to roofs. The tower has pinnacles, and the gabled top stage is capped with a diminutive lantern. Stucco was also applied to the other walls.

On the south side, there is a large window under a semicircular gable.

Interior
By contrast, the interior is basically late 17th century plus the galleries and the extended chancel.

Tuscan columns support an entablature which turns outwards at the west end of the nave to form a rudimentary crossing. The later galleries are not integrated with this, being supported on separate spindly columns and set close to those on the north side but further back on the south; they also cut across the transepts formed at the crossing and, on the south side, do not go beyond the aisle, which is wider than the north aisle.

The elliptical ceiling of the nave is irregularly groin-vaulted to conform with this pattern whilst the aisle and chancel vaults are depressed, the latter being of the coffered barrel type.

In the north-west corner is a blocked-up doorway leading at one time to and from a school which until the 1830 alterations was above the porch.

Furnishings
Organ Originally a Christopher Schrider instrument but replaced by Joseph Walker in 1853 and restored after war damage and the 1971 fire. The case was made in 1750.

Font Marble bowl with cherubs' heads of Wren period on stem of 1808. In the south aisle.

Churchwardens pew A large rectangular furnishing with seating all round and a four-sided reading desk enabling the pew to be used as an office as well as for worship.

Hatchments The hatchments on the south wall are of the Gaitskell family.

Candelabra The two fine candelabra of Dutch type date from 1698 and 1703 respectively.

Altar at end of south aisle This was rescued from St John's, Horsleydown, after the bombing, to which church it came in 1926 from St Olave's after the latter was demolished. This is a fine example of the celebrated smith Tijou's work but, although restored, it lost its marble top in the bombing.

Reredos This was reconstructed in 1907 using the old panels of the Ten Commandments, Creed and Lord's Prayer and the paintings of Moses and Aaron from the original reredos.

Stained glass The east window dates from 1883 and depicts the washing of Christ's feet, apparently set in the house of Lazarus, Mary and Martha.

Monuments

There are interesting memorials to *William Casteil*, died 1691, who is commemorated with an elegant and fairly large epitaph and to William Steavans, died 1712–13.

Associations

Maypole A Puritan rector cut down, chopped up and burnt the church maypole in 1611, rather on the pattern of what the parishioners at St Andrew Undershaft had done about 60 years earlier in the City.

Sermon Another Puritan rector preached a sermon of 69 pages, ending 'one hundred and twenty-seventhly'.

James Harriott is recorded in the register as having 40 children.

General

It is strange that, apart from a stone bearing a consecration mark in a local garage, a pair of hinge pins from the south gate at No. 8 Grange Walk and possibly a couple of capitals in the church, the Abbey of Bermondsey has completely disappeared. St Mary Magdalene maintains the link with this great monastic institution which was the centre of life in Bermondsey in mediaeval times and where Queens of England ended their days.

3 St Mary's, Rotherhithe

Rotherhithe

'Rotherhithe' may be derived from 'Aetheredes Hyth' (mentioned in a charter of 1898) or 'rethra' (mariner) 'hythe' (haven).

History

Whatever the derivation, St Mary's has the closest links with ships and the sea, and is only separated from the River Thames by empty warehouses opposite. The mediaeval church was lower in the ground and the foundations were frequently flooded.

St Mary's has a long history, going back at least to the 13th century and possibly earlier. In mediaeval times, the Patron was the Abbey of Bermondsey. It must have kept itself out of the limelight, for one incumbent, John Fayrwall, who was rector from 1537 to 1562, managed to survive the Reformation and another, Thomas Gataker (who was rector from 1611 to 1654), the Civil War.

The old church was repaired in 1687 but, not long afterwards, the flooding had so weakened it and the accommodation was so limited that the parishioners petitioned the Commissioners of the 1711 Act for a new one; they refer to themselves as 'being chiefly seamen and Watermen who venture their lives in fetching those coals from Newcastle which pay for the Rebuilding of the Churches of London and parts adjacent' (there was a tax on coal for this purpose); they asked to be allowed to 'Use duty laid on Coals' after it was no longer required for St Paul's Cathedral.

The petition was turned down and the parishioners were thrown back on their own resources. As a result, work did not start until 1714 but the new church was open in 1715. The steeple did not follow until much later and was not completed until 1747; it was built by Launcelot Dowbiggin who also built the very odd one at St Mary's, Islington. The spire portion was rebuilt in 1861.

Later, the architect Butterfield went through the usual process of removing galleries, lowering the pulpit and making a space for a choir but without too much harm to the simple Georgian interior.

Exterior

St Mary's lies in a quiet leafy corner, forming a pleasant group with the old Charity school (stone children outside) and the rectory opposite without being so overshadowed by warehouses as churches on the other bank of the river so often are.

This homely and friendly building is of brick (yellow with red dressings). Stone is used for the quoins and as trim for the windows, which at the sides are in two tiers, five round-headed above and three segmental-headed below. At the east end which projects there is one large window under a pediment. The whole is completed with the steeple and a neat parapet with modillion cornice.

The steeple consists of a plain brick tower with stone quoins and a stone spire, divided into a circular lower stage enclosed in Corinthian columns and an obelisk spire above. The spire looks somewhat of an afterthought.

Interior

The largely 18th century interior provides constant reminders in its furnishings and monuments of sailors and ships.

The Ionic nave columns are of oak, cased in thin plaster shells. They form three unequal bays. The north and south galleries were taken down but the west gallery, supported on thin wrought-iron stanchions and cast iron columns, remains. There is a shallow-vaulted ceiling with panelled ribs.

At the east end, Butterfield introduced wrought-iron railings made from 18th century hat pegs to enclose the chancel but these are no disfigurement. Otherwise, contemporary furnishings maintain the 18th century atmosphere.

Furnishings

Organ The organ is still the original Byfield instrument dating from 1764. It is adorned with musical instruments and, at the top, angels blowing trumpets.

Reredos The reredos contains fine original carving which, as the pea-pod occurs in a number of places, has inevitably been attributed to Grinling Gibbons. In fact, it was carved by Joseph Wade.

Chapel altar-table This was made of timber from the '*Fighting Témeraire*', the famous 104-gun man of war which was at the Battle of Trafalgar. Built in 1798, it will long be remembered from Turner's painting showing it being towed to the breaker's yard at Rotherhithe.

Sanctuary chairs They were also made from '*Témeraire*' timber and are an attractive pair with trefoil-pierced pointed backs.

Chancel stalls Some of the carving from the former north and south galleries has been used for the chancel stalls.

Pulpit Part of an old three-decker, it is hexagonal, inlaid and panelled, and has fluted angles.

St Mary's, Rotherhithe

Altar-rails The high altar-rails are by Butterfield.
Sanctuary panels These were painted in 1925.
Chandelier An attractive furnishing.
Royal Arms There is a finely carved Royal Arms of Queen
Victoria's time.

Monuments
*John Wade On the south wall, there is an outstanding cartouche,
commemorating John Wade, 'King's Carver in his Majesty's Yards at
Deptford and Woolwich', described by Pevsner as 'delicious'. He died
in 1743. The monument is crowned by a playful cherub. On the sides, a
cherub's head on the left is set against a skull on the right, all with
most delicate carving.

Captain Anthony Wood This is a monument almost contemporary
with the sailing of the *Mayflower* depicting in high relief a ship in full
sail very like it. Captain Wood died in 1625. Christopher Jones, the
master of the *Mayflower*, was buried in Rotherhithe and a 250th
anniversary commemoration plaque to mark this is recorded below the
monument.

Prince Lee Boo On the north wall, there is a plaque to the memory
of this Pacific Island Prince, whose father was reputed to be a cannibal.
The Prince befriended shipwrecked British sailors in 1783 and, out of
gratitude, was brought to England, where he promptly died of
smallpox at the age of 20. 'The barbarous people showed us no little
kindness.' A poignant memorial.

General
This appealing church is an interesting survival, like St Mary's,
Battersea, of a riverside village church. It contains most evocative
reminders of our maritime past, and still maintains a strong community
life.

Other Churches in Southwark
The Borough of Southwark which embraces the oldest parts of
London south of the river and where the great Priory of Bermondsey
(see St Mary Magdalene) exercised its sway, offers a wide variety in its
churches. Amongst those not described in detail there are three 19th
century places of worship deserving of special mention: **St Augustine
of Hippo, Lynton Road,** South Bermondsey (4) has a rare dedication
to the North African saint who, after a wayward youth, became one of

St Augustine of Hippo, Lynton Road, South Bermondsey

St Giles', Camberwell

the leading influences in the thinking of the Church. The future of this little-known building is uncertain but architecturally it is a product of merit, completed in 1882–3. The interior presents a wide spaciousness in the Early English lancet style. A striking feature is the pink-coloured Dumfries sandstone used for the arcades, and the tall white Portland stone stiff-leaf capitals which are richly carved.

St Giles', Camberwell (5) is the South London equivalent of St Mary's, Stoke Newington, being designed by the same architect, Sir George Gilbert Scott, although a slightly earlier building. The central tower with broach spire rises to a height of 210 ft, but is restless in outline and is not improved by the fussy dormers. The interior (plate, opposite) benefits from a notable east window of five lights – rich in blues, reds, yellows and greens – designed on the basis of a study of 13th century glass at Chartres and Rheims. On the south wall of the chancel, the sedilia and piscina from the mediaeval church dating from 1300 have been reinstalled and there is a set of brasses, dating from 1492 to 1637, on a panel under the south transept window.

St James's, Thurland Road, Bermondsey (6), one of the finest and most expensive of the 'Waterloo' churches, was designed by James Savage, architect of St Luke's, Chelsea, and was built in 1827–9. After a long period of uncertainty following war damage, this handsome place of worship, described by H. S. Goodhart-Rendel as having 'a design of great dignity and good sense' was restored and reopened for worship in 1966. St James's is distinctive for its impressive steeple terminating in a magnificent golden dragon, and for its nobly-proportioned interior with deeply-coffered nave ceiling contrasting with the shallow-coffered arched chancel ceiling.

The ten bells were cast from cannon captured at the Battle of Waterloo; and an association which has found its way into the Guinness Book of Records is the celebration at St James's on 21st June 1883 of a marriage which turned out to be the longest in Britain (82 years).

St Peter's, Walworth (7), another Commissioners' building, is the first and architecturally the most interesting of Sir John Soane's three London churches; built in 1823–5, it has a typical Ionic portico of four giant columns above which is a stone steeple, containing a very attenuated pepper-pot drum encircled with nine columns and terminating in a beehive stone dome and vane.

The galleried interior is open and light with thin arches at each end. The font (plate p. 397) has a large round top on an elegantly-shaped stem and base, all of marble.

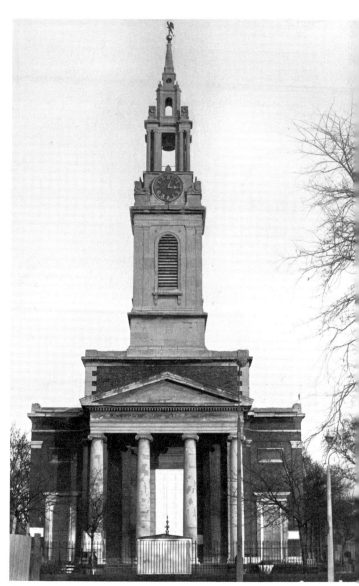

St James's, Thurland Road, Bermondsey

St Peter's, Walworth. Font

Tower Hamlets

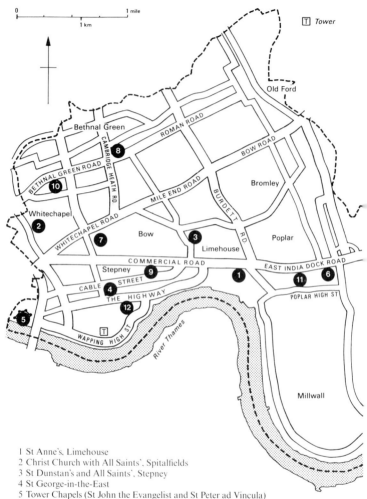

0   1 mile
1 km

T *Tower*

Old Ford

Bethnal Green

CAMBRIDGE HEATH RD.

ROMAN ROAD

BOW ROAD

Bromley

BETHNAL GREEN ROAD

Whitechapel

WHITECHAPEL ROAD

MILE END ROAD

BURDETT RD.

Poplar

Bow

Limehouse

COMMERCIAL ROAD

EAST INDIA DOCK ROAD

Stepney

CABLE STREET

THE HIGHWAY

POPLAR HIGH ST.

T

WAPPING HIGH ST.

River Thames

Millwall

1 St Anne's, Limehouse
2 Christ Church with All Saints', Spitalfields
3 St Dunstan's and All Saints', Stepney
4 St George-in-the-East
5 Tower Chapels (St John the Evangelist and St Peter ad Vincula)
6 *All Saints', Poplar*
7 *St Augustine's with St Philip's, Stepney*
8 *St John on Bethnal Green*
9 *St Mary's, Cable Street*
10 *St Matthew's, Bethnal Green*
11 *St Matthias', Poplar*
12 *St Paul's, Shadwell*

Tower Hamlets

1 St Anne's, Limehouse

Dedication

It is not known whether the St Anne to whom this church is dedicated
was the mother of the Virgin Mary or one of the other St Annes, but it
seems probable that a saint of this name was chosen because of Queen
Anne's concern for the welfare of the Church and in particular
because of her giving the money annexed to the Crown by Henry VIII
from certain mediaeval dues to form a fund, called Queen Anne's
Bounty, for augmenting the stipends of the poorer clergy.

History

At the beginning of the 18th century, the hamlet of Limehouse was
part of the large parish of Stepney but, with increasing population, a
need was felt for a separate church and, under the 1711 Act for the
creation of 'fifty new churches in and around the Cities of London and
Westminster and the suburbs thereof', work on a new place of worship
was entrusted to Nicholas Hawksmoor. This was to be the first of three
grand churches to be built in Stepney by this highly individual
architect.

Construction started in 1714 and progress was steady until financial
problems slowed it down; it was not before 1724 that the fabric was
completed, after which another five years was to elapse before a
sufficient endowment for the rector could be raised. Because of these
difficulties, Limehouse did not become a separate parish until May
1729 and consecration could not take place until four months later in
September of that year.

In 1850, on Good Friday, St Anne's was gutted by fire and major
reconstruction work was carried out by P. C. Hardwick between 1851
and 1853. The cost of this would have been much more than the actual
figure had it not been for the foresight of a Dissenter who, much
against his will, had been appointed a churchwarden. He had
persuaded the Vestry to take out insurance cover shortly before the
fire.

In 1891, Sir Arthur Blomfield, a pupil of P. C. Hardwick, rearranged
the sanctuary and provided choir-stalls.

The church survived the 1939–1945 bombing but lack of funds
allowed the building to fall into a bad state of repair and it was not

St Anne's, Limehouse. Watercolour of *c*. 1840

until 1985–1990 that generous grants from the London Docklands Development Corporation (LDDC) and English Heritage together with money-raising activities of 'Care for St Anne's', a committee of church members, specialist advisers and local residents, enabled the exterior to be restored and worship to be resumed in 1987. The completion of this admirable work by restoring the interior (estimated to cost £500,000) and the west end of the church (estimated to cost £75,000) remains a daunting task and the parish is seeking to build up a large group of Friends of St Anne's who, recognising the impossibility of such a task for an East London church, will help in this work. Already, the American millionaire philanthropist Paul Getty has made a grant.

Exterior

Despite the increased height of surrounding buildings, this church is still one of the most conspicuous landmarks in the East End. From whichever way one looks at it, St Anne's is an impressive sight but particularly from the little lane leading to the west end. The tower with its top stages set at different angles and surmounted by a pinnacled octagonal lantern rises up spectacularly with the lower part made broader by buttresses and attic storeys built above flanking vestibules. The clock, by the makers of Big Ben, is the highest church clock in London. The outer half of a tall circular porch projects from the centre.

By comparison the north and south sides are relatively restrained.

Mystery surrounds the pyramid on the west side of the churchyard but, at the eastern end of the building, there are two square pedestals and an artist's drawing exists which shows a pyramid on each of them. The suggestion is that they were never erected because of shortage of money but that one was supplied and after remaining in the churchyard for some time was used as a tombstone. It may well have commemorated a number of sea captains.

Interior

The restoration by Hardwick has retained the spacious grandeur of the original building and, despite the need for redecoration and repair, the interior is a forceful piece of architecture. Giant Corinthian columns break up the rectangular space and an extra nave bay provides longitudinal emphasis. The oval plastered ceiling of the nave contrasts with the segmental arch leading into the vaulted chancel. There are galleries on three sides and colour is afforded by the large east window which, framed in coupled Corinthian columns, takes the place of a reredos.

Furnishings

Font Dates from 1853 and was designed in marble by Morris and Hardwick.

Pulpit of oak designed by A. W. Blomfield, one of the first works of this well-known Victorian architect, and carved by William Gibbs Roger, it is contemporary with the font.

Organ Made by Gray and Davison, it gained a prize at the Hyde Park Great Exhibition of 1851. It was installed after the fire of 1850 and is in the west gallery. Still in regular use, it is one of the most magnificent and least altered Victorian organs in the country.

Stained glass The subject of the east window is the Crucifixion which is depicted in great detail including even the dice cast for Christ's garments. The technique, rarely used in the 19th century, is the application of coloured enamels to white glass. The designer was Clutterbuck.

Associations
St Anne's has associations with the Maoris and a Maori Ngapuhi chief Kamariera Te Hautakiri Wharepapa, was married here in 1864 to Elizabeth Reid of Marylebone.

General
Now the centre of a growing congregation supported by 'Care of St Anne's', and the parish church of Canary Wharf and environs, the future of St Anne's is secure.

N.B. Church key can be obtained on application to the rector at 5 Newell St., London E14 7HP (0171–987–1502).

2 Christ Church with All Saints', Spitalfields

Spitalfields
The name comes from the Priory of St Mary, Spittle (Hospital) which lay where Spital Square is now situated. Sermons, known as Spital sermons, and attended by the Aldermen, Sheriffs and occasionally the Sovereign, were preached after the Dissolution until 1642 from a cross within the hospital churchyard.

History
Christ Church is one of the three vast churches built by Nicholas Hawksmoor under the 1711 Act to meet the needs of parts of Stepney which, by the beginning of the 18th century, had become populous. Protestant refugees (Huguenots) from France had settled in Spitalfields in large numbers and their hand-weaving of silk brought prosperity to the area. Work on the foundations started in July 1714 but, as at St Anne's, Limehouse, financial problems were to hold up construction; this came to a complete standstill and Christ Church was not consecrated until 5th July 1729.

The Industrial Revolution dealt a death-blow to the hand-weaving and the character both of Spitalfields and of Christ Church entered

into a long period of decline from which it is now happily being
rescued. The area has always been associated with immigration and the
attendant problems of 'sweat shop' labour and deprivation. The
French Huguenots were replaced by Jewish immigrants and from
about 1950 by Bangladeshi immigrants working in the 'rag trade' and
leather industries whilst, since about 1970, City workers have found it
convenient and attractive to restore the 18th century houses and live
close to their place of work.

In the case of Christ Church, the process started in 1965 with the
expenditure of £50,000 on the roof and ceiling, which came from the
proceeds of the sale of the gutted remains of St John's, Smith Square,
and the formation of 'The Friends of Christ Church Spitalfields' in
1976. They have made safe the chancel beam, reopened the south door
to the churchyard and repaired, cleaned and reroofed the portico,
cleared the crypt, refurbished the old Vestry Room and repositioned
memorials in preparation for the reinstatement of the side galleries.
The front steps and forecourt have been renovated, the side windows
(altered in 1866) restored to Hawksmoor's designs and the whole
building reglazed.

As a result of all the Friends' efforts, Christ Church was reopened
for worship in 1987. They also began the Spitalfields Festival, now a
separate Charity which runs an annual Music Festival in June. The
church is also used for concerts, opera and theatre at other times
throughout the year.

Part of the crypt is used as a rehabilitation centre for homeless
alcoholic men.

All Saints, consecrated in 1839, was damaged in the 1939–45 War
and closed in 1951 when the parish was united to that of Christ
Church. The building was demolished shortly afterwards.

Exterior

From whatever direction one approaches but especially from the west,
this is an overpowering building. The tower and spire rise dramatically
to a height of 225 ft, the tower appearing as wide as the imposing
portico below. The portico, raised on steps, has four Tuscan columns
with a semicircular arch in the middle. Niches are inserted into a tower
face and projecting cornices give horizontal emphasis. The spire at one
time was crocketed and had spire-lights but it was altered in 1822 and,
after a fire in the tower in 1836 or possibly damage by lightning in
1841, smoothed to the plain brooch spire we see today.

Turning to the sides, which are plainer, it can be seen that the width of the tower is a deception created by the use of very deep buttresses with concave hollows between which are pierced by windows.

At the west end, a Venetian window placed high up is flanked by round-headed and porthole windows. There is also a line of the latter below and they appear in the north and south walls.

Interior

The interior, which has been described by Sir John Betjeman as 'massive, simple and gigantic', is a rectangle divided by giant Composite columns into aisle bays with tunnel vaults. At the east end an architrave, with two extra columns in the middle to support it, is carried right across the nave to create a chancel. The coffered ceiling is of wide span and flat.

Repairs and restoration were carried out from time to time in the 19th century (on one occasion after the church had been struck by lightning in 1841) and, in 1866, interior and exterior were radically altered by the architect Ewan Christian who has been said to have tried, in accordance with the ecclesiastical and architectural fashions of that time, to turn the classical building into a Gothic one. The north and south galleries were removed together with the wooden panelling above and below them, thus upsetting the proportions of Hawksmoor's church, and pedestals of the columns were destroyed. Parts of the side galleries were reassembled to form two tiers of galleries either side of the organ at the west end.

A vestibule under the tower separates the portico from the nave.

Furnishings

Organ The 1735 organ by Richard Bridge, the most celebrated organ builder of the time and favourite of Handel, was the largest organ in England for over a century but has been out of use for many years and awaits restoration. The walnut casing, however, is to be seen at the west end and is arguably the richest surviving example of its type.

Royal Arms There is a Royal Arms perched on the chancel beam which is a replacement in Coade stone installed in 1822.

General

Christ Church is a sombre and grandiose building. The 20th century reappraisal and appreciation of Nicholas Hawksmoor owe much to the architectural historian, H. S. Goodhart-Rendel, who says in his book *Hawksmoor* published in 1924: 'It remains doubtful whether, of its date and type, there is any finer church than this in Europe.'

It is refreshing, therefore, that the prospects of complete restoration are a great deal better than when the author wrote about the church in 1976. In September 1994 a major appeal was launched to raise approximately £3 million for this purpose and to carry out extensive repairs and the introduction of modern services to support the revived church and other public uses of the building.

N.B. Open lunchtime every Wednesday and for Sunday services. Enquiries about opening times, services, events and the restoration are welcome by the Friends of Christ Church. Tel. 0171–247–0165.

3 St Dunstan's and All Saints', Stepney

Dedication
Originally called 'All Saints', the name of St Dunstan was added to the dedication of the parish church of Stepney (probably derived from Stebba's Hithe or landing-place) after his canonisation in 1029.

History
Dunstan, Bishop of London in 959 and thereby Lord of the vast Manor of Stepney covering all that we know now as the East End, may have rebuilt or enlarged a small Saxon church. In the 13th century, a further reconstruction (at least partial) took place, of which the outer chancel walls remain, but what we see today is largely 15th century.

The church owes its mediaeval character to the fact that, unlike many others in London, it was not pulled down in the 18th century to make way for a larger place of worship. Instead, the rising population of Stepney was accommodated in new parish churches. It was, however, found necessary to increase seating at St Dunstan's by adding galleries. These were gradually removed as congregations changed and dwindled and finally, at the end of the 19th century, they were taken away altogether.

Numerous Victorian restorations have left their mark. The north and south porches and the large north-east octagonal vestry are from this period and, in 1871–2, the exterior was refaced with Kentish ragstone.

Extensive damage caused by a fire which broke out in the organ-loft in October, 1901 and by a V.1. bomb which exploded in the churchyard in January, 1945, has been made good and St Dunstan's has survived as a mediaeval church of much interest.

Exterior

The large, leafy churchyard park, where many plague and cholera victims are buried, imparts a village atmosphere and the open space around has been made larger by adding recreation grounds etc. to the churchyard on three sides, providing a most agreeable oasis. From the south-west all looks mediaeval and is probably similar to many London churches as they must at one time have been. It consists of a battlemented tower with angle buttresses and pinnacles, and a long, low body with small clerestory windows.

A staircase at one time giving access to the rood-loft projects from the south wall; it is crowned by a beacon tower – a navigational aid for shipping coming to the great mediaeval port of Ratcliff.

Interior

The dominating impression is of the long, low lines of the nave and chancel. The chancel arch was removed in the 15th century and the chancel set further back so that the nave and two aisles with their two-light clerestory windows stretch for seven bays. The total length is 150 ft, considerable for a village church as it was for so many years

The situation of the former chancel arch is indicated by the door in the south wall to the rood-loft and by the change in design of the roof (of keel type with cambered tie-beams).

Nave pillars, from which the 18th century paintwork was removed in 1871–2, are standard 15th century work with four attached shafts and concave hollows in the diagonals. The east window (see *Stained glass*) was dedicated in 1949.

A notable feature of the chancel is the triple sedilia with coupled columns in the south-east wall; this was part of the 13th century church.

In the south aisle wall there is a stone from the walls of Carthage inserted in 1663 with the words 'Time consumes all; it spares none'.

A squint is to be seen in the north wall of the chancel.

Furnishings

Rood A precious survival from the Saxon church (one of only two Saxon features to be found in London churches) is the rood placed above the altar-table. It depicts the Crucifixion with Our Lord in an attitude of suffering, attended by the Virgin Mary and St John. It is of great sensitivity, recalling the swaying figures of contemporary manuscript paintings. A border of rosettes surrounds the figures. (see plate p. 408)

St Dunstan's, Stepney

The rood at St Dunstan's, Stepney

Stained glass The muscular portrayal of Christ in the east window and its bad sense of colour, by Hugh Easton, are mitigated by the charming little scenes at the base. Other windows in the north and south aisles are also by Hugh Easton.

Panel
The appealing Panel of the Annunciation in the chancel dates from the 14th century.
Coffin lid A coffin lid with tapering sides and carved cross is 13th century.

Monuments
Sir Henry Colet A memorial in the chancel commemorates Sir Henry Colet, Lord Mayor of London in 1486 and 1495, who died in 1510. It is in the form of a tomb-chest in a recess, the back of which has blank panelling, the top, cusped arches and quatrefoil parapet.

Robert Clarke (died 1610) and daughter, and Elizabeth Startute (died 1620) are portrayed as kneeling figures in the usual style of the times.

Mary Leybourne (died 1731) A tablet records 'She wanted not spirit nor wit or a just knowledge of her selfe'.

Charrington family The Charrington family of brewers have memorials in the north aisle.

Associations
John Colet, the son of Sir Henry (see *Monuments*) and founder of St Paul's School, was vicar here in 1485.

Thomas Spert, founder of Trinity House, is buried in the churchyard.

Stephen Segrave, a rector in the 14th century, became Archbishop of Armagh.

Richard Foxe, rector in the 15th century and founder of Corpus Christi College, Oxford, became Bishop of Winchester.

George Appleton (curate 1925–27) became Archbishop of Perth (1963–69) and Archbishop of Jerusalem (1969–74).

Colin James (curate 1952–55) became Bishop of Winchester (1985–95).

General
Mediaeval churches are rare in London. For many years, St Dunstan's was the only parish church in the vast area of Stepney, which was

largely rural, but since the 14th century, 66 other parishes and churches have been created out of mediaeval Stepney in the area now known as Tower Hamlets. 'For more than 1,000 years' – as the board outside the west door reads – 'the people of God have met here to offer prayer and worship to God, and have gone out from here to love and serve their neighbourhood'. Even today, despite all that has happened, the much restored church of St Dunstan's manages to hold on to its mediaeval character.

4 St George-in-the-East

History

In the 17th and 18th centuries, the vast parish of Stepney was being broken up into smaller units and the area of Upper Wapping qualified under the 1711 Act for a new church. On a site 'in pleasantly wooded fields' beside where the once notorious Ratcliff Highway now runs, gradually arose one of Nicholas Hawksmoor's strangest flights of fancy; this was to serve a riverside parish inhabited by people who owned and sailed ships. As with his two other monumental East End churches (St Anne's, Limehouse, with which it was almost contemporary, and Christ Church, Spitalfields) building, beset by financial difficulties, took a long time; work, started in 1714, was not completed until 1726. Even then, another three years was to elapse before sufficient endowment for the incumbent could be found and the church consecrated.

In the 1850s, some of the most disgraceful scenes of modern times to take place in a Christian church occurred in St George's. The rector, the Rev Bryan King, and his curate, C. F. Lowder, were High Churchmen who introduced a very moderate form of ritual, wearing surplices instead of the generally used black gown. The Bishop who had appointed King and who favoured surplices was succeeded by a man, born a Presbyterian, determined to stamp out High Church practices; he nominated a militant Low Churchman, Hugh Allen, vicar of a neighbouring parish, to be afternoon lecturer at St George's. This led to organized disruption whenever King or Lowder tried to conduct a service: pelting the altar with garbage, catcalls, jeers: men still wearing their hats and smoking their pipes; even trombones were blown and, on one occasion, dogs drugged to make them howl were brought into the church. Press reports led to hooligans coming from other parts of London to add their quota to the

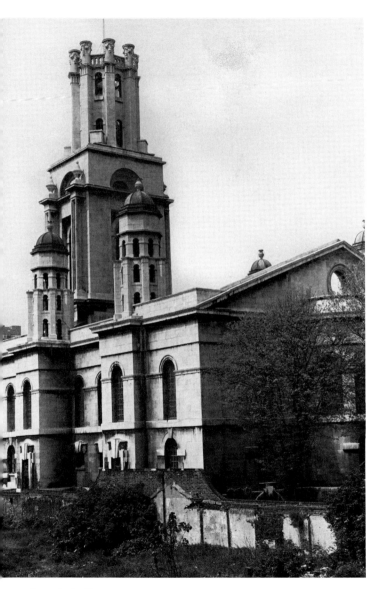

St George-in-the-East

disorder, whilst magistrates, influenced by Low Church members of the Vestry, did little to help. The matter was only resolved by the Rector being persuaded to hand over to a locum after his health had given way.

The position was aggravated by the deterioration of this once respectable area into a terrible slum with narrow, dirty streets, unsavoury houses and much violence.

Victorian changes to the church were mild; apart from the removal of the reredos and the decoration of the apse with Venetian glass mosaics in 1880, the rather dark Georgian interior was retained until it was swept away by incendiary bombs in May 1941. The east windows were designed by Sir Joshua Reynolds.

For nineteen years St George's lay a gaunt, silent ruin on the Highway but, in 1960, Arthur Bailey, an architect, worked out an ingenious scheme for rebuilding. It consisted of repairing the walls and tower: erecting a smaller, modern place of worship in the eastern part of the old nave: transforming the space between the west end of the new church and the old into an open courtyard and converting the area formerly occupied by the galleries into residential flats. Below, the old vaults would be cleared and a splendid new parish hall would take their place.

This plan was carried out between 1960 and 1964, and the church reconsecrated on April 26th, 1964, thus grafting a modern element on to the old roots.

Exterior

The gleaming white exterior of Portland stone gives little hint of the changes within and we can again stare in wonder or dismay at this strange building. Each Hawksmoor church is unlike any other and St George's is no exception, the closest resemblance being to St Anne's, Limehouse.

A massive 160 foot high tower with tall rectangular openings and deeply recessed windows rises dramatically at the west end, made to look even wider by the grooved piers at the sides. The crown is an open octagonal lantern with eight rectangular buttresses topped with Roman altars, the whole looking like a little castle.

Tall turrets, also with eight buttresses, are surmounted by copper roofed cupolas. Resembling a profusion of pepper-pots, these contained staircases to the galleries. Projections at the west and east ends mark where the transepts used to be, forming a double Greek cross.

At the east end, an apse projects from the middle of a flat wall with large pediment.

Since 1966, the houses which obscured the view from the south and which Hawksmoor failed to get moved have disappeared, giving a much finer aspect from this side.

Interior
A spacious and lofty portico leads into the courtyard beyond which glass doors give access to the new church.

No attempt, other than restoring the mosaics dating from 1880 and replacing five panels in the ceiling of the apse, has been made to reconstitute what was there before and we see today a bright, modern interior suited to contemporary needs.

Furnishings
Font The stone font in the north aisle is the only furnishing which has survived the bombing. It came from the City church of St Benet's, Gracechurch Street (pulled down in 1867 for road-widening) and was first used at St George's in 1877.

General
Although views differ as to whether over £100,000 should have been spent to build a church in a district where four exist already, there would have been even less reason for rebuilding the huge church that was destroyed by the bombs. The new hall and church are in constant use as a theatre and concert hall, in this way developing as an Arts Centre, and many of the young actors and musicians who come here are attracted by the modern church to take part in services of worship, thus extending its mission well beyond the confines of the parish.

5 Chapels of St John the Evangelist and St Peter ad Vincula, Tower of London

Situation
In the White Tower and the north-west corner of Inner Ward respectively.

Dedication
St Peter ad Vincula – St Peter in chains.

History

The Chapel of St John the Evangelist was built at the same time as the
White Tower and is the oldest surviving example of Norman
ecclesiastical architecture in London and one of the oldest in England.
It was the private chapel of William the Conqueror and, after his
death, continued for a time to serve as the Sovereign's personal place
of worship.

In 1391, the mild Sudbury, Archbishop of Canterbury, was dragged
away from the chapel whilst at his prayers by the furious mob in the
Peasants' Revolt. He was later executed on Tower Hill amidst
'ferocious yells of triumph'.

The body of Henry VI, after his murder whilst he knelt in the
oratory of the Wakefield Tower on 21 st May, 1471, is said to have
been placed in the chapel before being removed to Chertsey Abbey in
Surrey for burial – secretly 'without priest, clerk, torch or taper,
singing or saying'.

Elizabeth of York, wife of Henry VII, lay here in state after her
death in 1503, whilst 50 years later in 1553 the unfortunate girl queen –
Lady Jane Grey – used it for prayer in the nine days of her
imprisonment before execution. The rightful queen, Mary, was
betrothed by proxy in the same chapel to Philip of Spain in the
following year.

From the 17th to 19th centuries, St John's Chapel was used to store
records, but worship was resumed later and it was restored in 1968.

St Peter ad Vincula was rebuilt in 1513 and is not the first chapel on
the site. The original building was demolished by Edward I in 1286 and
a new one erected between 17th June of that year and 6th April, 1287.
This lasted until 1512 when it was severely damaged by fire, thus
leading to the construction of the present place of worship.

But, although built at the end of the mediaeval period, its
associations are no less tragic. The scaffold that faced it on the Green
was the scene of the execution, amongst others, of two of Henry VIII's
wives and of Lady Jane Grey. Their bodies were thrown hugger-
mugger into the ground below the nave, only to receive decent burial
during a restoration in 1876. They now lie under the chancel floor
beneath stones which carry their coats-of-arms. St Peter's is also
the burial-place of two martyrs, Sir Thomas More and John Fisher,
who were executed for refusing to acknowledge the king as head
of the Church. Macaulay has said of St Peter's chapel 'in truth there
is no sadder spot on earth' but today, after another restoration in
1971, with its clear glass windows and delicate architecture, St Peter's

is a place of light and the memory of these grisly associations is
dimmed.

Architecture

These two buildings, so different in style, mark the beginning and
end of the mediaeval period. St John's shows the Norman style at its
most uncompromising and seems almost hewn out of the solid rock
like an Indian rock-temple. There is little in the way of decoration
but the way in which the nave and the gallery above are carried round
in the form of an apse and the starkness itself impart a rugged
strength which makes it a compelling piece of architecture. The nave
has a tunnel vault – a rarity in England. Being completely enclosed
by the encircling rooms there is an air of impenetrability about
it which, however, did not save the unlucky Sudbury (mentioned
earlier).

St Peter's is in a much lighter style, with slender columns. Being
detached from the adjoining buildings it stands out clearly. The west
end is crowned with a small brick tower and an attractive lantern. The
church consists of nave and shorter aisle with a flat roof.

Furnishings

The furnishings of St Peter's include the following:

Font The original Tudor font was broken into four pieces during the
Commonwealth period and secreted by the chaplain in the
Cholmondeley tomb. Later the chaplain was caught and executed by
Cromwellian soldiery and it was not until the 1876 restoration that it
was rediscovered and restored to its rightful place.

Organ One of the oldest in the City of London. It was built in 1679
by Father Smith – a famous maker of organs – for the chapel of the
Palace of Whitehall, and the wooden carvings of cherubs are ascribed
to Grinling Gibbons. Some of the original pipes are still in place. The
organ was moved to St Peter's in 1890 and restored in 1953.

Pulpit The pulpit of English oak is modern with a glass frontispiece
depicting the Crown of the King of Kings and surrounding flames
which symbolise the seven gifts of the Holy Spirit.

Monuments

The oldest is the memorial to *John Holland*, Duke of Exeter, moved to
St Peter's from Regent's Park Royal Foundation in 1949. It lies in the
north-west corner. The stone used is a very white chalkstone and the
crisp, curly, cusped arch, elaborated with trumpeting angels, gives an

All Saints', Poplar. Baldacchino

almost sugar-icing effect, perhaps a shade too sweet. It dates from 1447.

The Cholmondeley memorial lies under the second nave arch from the west and dates from 1544. Sir Richard was at one time Lieutenant of the Tower but later moved away and was eventually buried elsewhere, thus leaving the tomb empty and providing space for the font (see earlier).

On the north of the chancel is a standing wall monument to *Sir Richard and Sir Michael Blount*, dating from 1620. These two men – father and son – were also Lieutenants of the Tower. There are groups of kneelers, a typical Jacobean feature, and the materials used are alabaster and marble. The skull in the hand of one wife and the cap string blown over the head of the other indicated widowhood.

Opposite is a curious memorial to *George Payler*, his wife and their children showing the family in four separate ovals with the one at the foot flanked by putti.

Other monuments are to Captain Valentine Pyne, dating from 1677, with cannon and a ship in relief, Sir John More (1679) and Captain William Bridges (1716).

Associations
Henry VI Each year on 21st May, the anniversary of the assassination of King Henry VI, representatives of Eton College and King's College, Cambridge which he founded, lay lilies and roses on the spot where his body was discovered (see *History*).

General
These two chapels, so tranquil today, are standing monuments to the barbarities of the mediaeval age.

Regular services are held at St Peter's and Choral Evensong is celebrated at St John's on the first Sunday of the summer months.

Other Churches in Tower Hamlets
Although the East End is not well-to-do, it is one of the richest areas in London for fine churches.

All Saints', Poplar (6). This imposing building, constructed in 1821–3 of Portland stone and set off by an impressive tower and spire reflects the ambition of the residents to have a church which they felt would be worthy of them, and is a landmark in the Poplar townscape. Internally,

St John on Bethnal Green

the most striking features are the baldacchino (plate p. 416) and the western organ-gallery.

St Augustine's with St Philip's, Stepney (7). This, the largest church in the East End, was built in 1888–92 by Arthur Cawston largely at the expense of the first vicar, the Revd Sidney Vacher, who was determined to have something better than the dilapidated chapel which existed before. The red brick exterior rises to a great height and, if the western tower had been completed, would have been striking. One need have no reservations, however, about the pale yellow stock brick interior, for it is vaulted throughout, has double aisles with apsed chancel and Lady Chapel, transepts, clerestory and a richly-moulded triforium of double twin arcades above the nave bays.

St John on Bethnal Green (8). This was a Commissioners' building and the second of Sir John Soane's London churches, built in 1825–8, but extensively remodelled in 1871 after a fire. The excellent siting at

St Matthew's, Bethnal Green

St Paul's, Shadwell

the end of Bethnal Green Road has been largely spoiled by the main railway line which cuts across the western façade (plate p. 418); this is surmounted by a tower crowned with a small stone cupola. The best part of the interior is the vestibule which has exciting vistas through the arches opening to the basement under the tower.

St Mary's, Cable Street (9). This is another church which was the inspiration of one man, in this case the Revd William Quekett who gave much selfless service in the East End. Built of stone in 1849–50 it is plain externally with a south-east tower. The main feature of the interior, which is nicely uncluttered, is the lectern.

St Matthew's, Bethnal Green (10). This church was built by George

Dance the Elder in 1743–6 and rebuilt after a fire in 1859. Externally with its plain brick it looks like a cousin of the two St Mary Magdalenes at Holloway and Woolwich, but internally it owes much to the gaily coloured redecoration after it was gutted in the 1939–45 War. Of many attractive features perhaps the most beautiful are the Stations of the Cross in varying colours by Donald Potter.

St Matthias', Poplar (11). This church started in 1654 as a private East India Company chapel but, after being rebuilt in 1776, suffered much from an insensitive restoration by Samuel S. Teulon, who recast the exterior in the second half of the 19th century. Internally, however, it has retained what might be described as a quarter-deck appearance because of its width and openness, heightened by the use of timber for all but one of its columns (reputedly made from the masts of East India merchantmen). There is a notable memorial to George Steevens by Flaxman dating from 1800.

St Matthias' was closed in 1977 and has since suffered from serious vandalism.

St Paul's, Shadwell (12). This is another church which started life in the Cromwellian period, being built in 1656 as a chapel of ease to St Dunstan's, Stepney. The present church is a 'Waterloo' church consecrated in 1820. The steeple, which is set in a spacious, leafy churchyard, is similar in design to that of St Leonard's, Shoreditch (plate opposite). The modest, galleried interior with columns mostly of scagliola (composition of marble chippings, paste and glue) is rather dark. It contains original font and pulpit, and charming lectern. The church is often referred to as the Church of the Sea Captains. More than 175 names of commanders and their wives appear in the register between 1730 and 1790, including Captain James Cook whose son was baptised here in 1763. The mother of Thomas Jefferson, third President of the USA, was also baptised in the old St Paul's.

The future of this place of worship is uncertain.

Wandsworth

1 All Saints', Tooting Graveney
2 St Mary's, Battersea
3 *St Mary's Putney*
4 *All Saints', Wandsworth*
5 *St Anne's, Wandsworth*

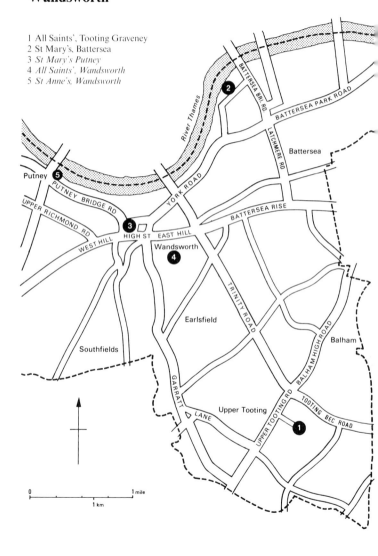

Wandsworth

1 All Saints', Tooting Graveney

Tooting Bec/Tooting Graveney
'Tooting' may indicate the settlement ('ing') of the people of Tota.
'Graveney' is the name of a local river; 'Bec' recalls the ancient
connection with the Abbey of Bec Hellouin in Normandy, from which
the great Archbishops Lanfranc and Anselm came in early Norman
times.

History
All Saints was built out of funds bequeathed by Lady Augusta
Georgiana Sophia Brudenell-Bruce in memory of her husband, the son
of the Ist Marquess of Ailesbury (Aylesbury), who died in 1897. The
architect was L. Temple Moore and the foundation stone was laid in
October 1904, consecration taking place in July 1906.

Exterior
The exterior of yellow stock brick is fairly plain and the elevations of
the sides are broken by the gables of the aisles pointing outwards away
from the main building. The south-west battlemented tower has two
belfry windows on each side and angle buttresses terminating at the
belfry stage. There is a square-ended (Lady) Chapel beyond the
chancel.

Interior
The exterior gives little hint of the beautifully proportioned and
distinguished seven-bay interior within, which has the luxury of double
aisles to the nave and single aisles to the chancel, providing many and
varied vistas. The aisles are roofed in gold-painted timber and the
shafts between the aisles support arches which separate the bays
transversely. The nave is roofed in green-painted timber.

   The chancel opens out into the Lady Chapel through an arcade of
three bays; a similar arcade at the west end opens out into the
vestibule.

Furnishings
Many of the furnishings were collected by the first vicar, Canon
Stephens, from Italy and France, and date back to the Renaissance

All Saints'. Tooting Graveney

period. These have been adapted by the interior designer, Walter Tapper, who added further fittings of his own and introduced the olive green and gold colour scheme. All this admirably blends in with the architecture and suits the atmosphere of the church.

Memorial plaque and bust Behind the font on the west wall is a memorial plaque and bust to Lord Charles Brudenell-Bruce.

Organ and organ-case The richly gilded organ-case, designed by Tapper, houses a fine Harrison 3-manual instrument which has not been altered tonally. It was restored in 1990.

Font The marble font and wooden cover are also by Tapper.

Pulpit The disproportionately small green panelled pulpit with octagonal stone base was probably designed by Temple Moore.

Lectern This is a copy of the fine 18th century lectern brought by Canon Stephens from Italy to St Oswald's Church, Blankney, Lincolnshire, which was his living before he came to All Saints'.

Candlesticks The very large wooden candlesticks standing ten feet high came from Florence.

Iron grille Came from a church near Lake Como and is thought to be the oldest fitting in the whole building.

Reredos The *pièce de résistance* is the Baroque reredos from Bologna with broken segmental pediment and gilt and fluted pilasters/columns. The painting above the finely carved and gilded high altar is a copy by Raoul Maria of Velazquez' 'Crucifixion' in the Prado Gallery at Madrid.

Choir stalls, credence table, tester canopy and preacher's chair came from Bologna. The stalls are panelled and decorated with urns and acanthus cresting.

Chapel altar-piece Origin and date uncertain, but thought to be German and may be 16th century. The carved Crucifixion above the altar could be as early as 14th century.

Stained glass The stained glass in the east window is by Victor Milner and represents bishops of the diocese in which Tooting Graveney has been situated over the years i.e. Canterbury, London, Rochester and Dorchester (transferred to Winchester). The 20th century is represented by two windows installed in 1956 of Bishop Talbot of Rochester and Bishop Simpson of Southwark.

General

This is the finest and probably the largest church in South London. In addition to being a place of worship, the church is used for musical recordings by famous orchestras.

2 St Mary's, Battersea

Battersea

In AD 693 Battersea was referred to as 'Batrices Ege' or 'Badrices Ege – probably Badric's isle – but there were at least 77 variants of the place name. In Domesday it is called 'Patricesey'. The site on which the village was built was in fact a gravel island bounded on the north by the river and surrounded by misty marshland.

History

William the Conqueror granted the Manor to Westminster Abbey in 1067. The English Pope, Nicholas Breakspear (Adrian IV) confirmed the Abbey in their ownership including the church in 1157.

As a result of this connection, St Mary's enjoyed work from the shop of the great mason, Henry Yevele, who constructed the nave of the Abbey. From his workshop came the east window, the shape of which survives in the present one. There were many alterations between the 15th and 17th centuries and by the 18th century the building had a miscellany of windows in different styles, a long staircase on the south side giving entry at the first floor, various dormers and a quite imposing battlemented tower, rebuilt 1639, with clasping octagonal buttresses.

Like other mediaeval London churches which lingered on into the second half of the 18th century, the building became dilapidated and hardly suited to the fashionable residential suburb which Battersea had become, said to have the 'second best carriage congregation in London'.

Joseph Dixon, churchwarden and local architect, therefore submitted plans for a new church which were accepted; Richard Dixon was the builder. The frame of the east window and its glass and tracery were kept but otherwise the fabric was entirely rebuilt, although following almost exactly the ground line of the old building. Work began in July 1775 and the church reopened in November 1777.

In 1876–8, extensive reconstruction and repairs were carried out by Sir Arthur Blomfield during which he made space for a choir and provided new seating.

There was some war damage but this has been made good.

Exterior

An unassuming rectangle of pleasant yellow brick with an attractive portico of Tuscan columns plus plain pediment, and appealing steeple with stone quoins and green copper spire. An endearing oriel window peeps out behind the columns. The side windows are in the usual two tiers for galleried interiors. (plate opposite)

Interior

A simple and largely unaltered 18th century interior fitted with seemly pews, and galleries on three sides having unusual supporting brackets in front with benefactions written on them. The ceiling is flat with a scalloped motif and garlands in the centre. There is no chancel and the nave opens out into the panelled curve of the sanctuary with its arresting east window and roundels on each side. At the end of the south aisle is a side-chapel with interesting modern triptych (see *Altarpiece*).

There is much to enjoy and there are many fine monuments.

St Mary's, Battersea

St Mary's, Battersea. Memorial to Sir John Fleet

Furnishings

Font Of white marble and coming from the earlier church. The existing large bowl was added by Blomfield in 1878 and placed on top of the original basin.

Pulpit Once part of a three-decker and still very high; the lower parts now serve as sidesmen's pews in the west corners of the church. The decoration is Victorian.

Lectern One of the lecterns came from the studio of Holman Hunt the artist, who painted 'The Light of the World'.

Organ The organ in the south-east corner of the side-chapel at the end of the south aisle was rebuilt by Saxon Aldred in 1991.

Sanctuary rails Dating from 18th century, they are made of a combination of lead and iron. They were re-erected in 1938, replacing a Victorian rail.

Altar-piece The side chapel altar-piece, painted by John Napper, shows Gospel scenes in 'Battersea' terms (e.g. the Annunciation in the centre is set against a background of Battersea Park and Power Station).

Turner's chair The chair on which the artist J. M. Turner sat to contemplate his riverside sunsets and cloud effects is in the northwest of the sanctuary.

Candlesticks Made in 1938 of wood from the old roof which was rebuilt at that time.

Chandelier A nice modern example.

*Stained glass The east window is the most striking feature of the church, glowing with yellow and gold. Probably by Bernard van Linge, it was installed in 1631 by Sir John St John after his succession to the Manor. At the base are medallions of Henry VII, Margaret Beauchamp and Elizabeth I and, in the middle, heraldic shields, all advertising Sir John's royal antecedents and his connections with distinguished families by marriage.

*The delightful circular transparencies of the Dove and the Lamb at the sides, which blend so well with the window, were the work of James Pearson in 1796. The Dove roundel was shattered by a bomb in 1944 but has been skilfully restored by Miss Joan Howson.

New stained glass windows by John Hayward have been inserted in one of the lower windows of the church as memorials to General Benedict Arnold (see *Monuments*), Joseph Turner, William Blake and William Curtis.

Royal Arms
Royal Arms of Elizabeth I and of George IV are on the north and
south walls of the apse.

Monuments
Nicholas Stone, Roubiliac and Scheemakers are all represented in
memorials to the St Johns, Battersea's most famous family. Other
important ones are in the galleries. Taking them in a clockwise
direction, there are:
North side gallery
Sir Oliver St John, Viscount Grandison, died 1630 and his wife *Joan
Holcrofte* by Nicholas Stone, master mason to James I and Charles I.
Two frontal busts under a heavy segmental pediment and between
columns.

   *Henry St John, Viscount Bolingbroke died 1751 and his second wife
Mary Clara des Champs de Marcilly, Marchioness of Villette, died
1750. He was Secretary of War in Queen Anne's reign and the most
famous of the St Johns; the Marchioness was a niece of Madame de
Maintenon, Louis XIV's wife. The epitaphs were written by
Bolingbroke himself. The monument in green, white and grey marble
is by Roubiliac and of excellent quality with two portrait medallions to
the left and right of the apron and, above, an urn under heavy drapery.

   *Sir John Fleet, died 1712. He was Lord Mayor of the City in 1693
and a member of the Grocers' Company who repaired the memorial in
1891. A wall cartouche with shields, cherubs' heads at top and bottom
and very rich flower and fruit carving. Drawn curtains with prominent
tassels enclose the inscription. A fine monument.

South side gallery
Sir Edward Wynter, died 1686. A relatively plain memorial recording
in the inscription his more improbable exploits such as crushing a tiger
to death and taking on single-handed 60 mounted Moors. A relief on
the apron shows two of his feats.

   Holles St John, died 1738, half brother of Bolingbroke (above). An
urn with foliage trails set between two smaller urns. It is of grey and
white marble and is by the Antwerp sculptor, Peter Scheemakers.

   John Camden, died 1780 and his daughter, *Elizabeth Nield*, died
1791. In the form of a tall nymph standing beside a pedestal with an
urn and constructed of the well-known artificial Coade stone once
made at Lambeth to a formula now lost. The monument is signed by
Coade with date 1792.

Crypt

Benedict. Arnold, American general. A memorial records that he, his wife and daughter were buried here between 1801 and 1828 and the inscription records that he was 'Sometime General in the Army of George Washington' and that 'The two nations whom he served in turn in the years of their enmity have united in this memorial as a token of their enduring friendship'.

Associations

St Mary's is also rich in associations and many of its vicars were outstanding men.

William Blake, poet, artist and mystic, and writer of the wellknown hymn 'Jerusalem', was married here in 1782 to Catherine Boucher, daughter of a Battersea market gardener. She signed the marriage certificate with an X.

Edward Hyde, later Earl of Clarendon and Charles II's great minister, who steered the Restoration on to a firm course, married Anne Ayliffe, his first wife who was a cousin of Sir Walter St John in the church in 1631 .

Edward Adrian Wilson, one of Scott's gallant companions on the ill-fated expedition to the South Pole, lived in the former vicarage and worked at a boys' club in the district. There is a plaque on his old home nearby.

General

Much as Battersea has changed and although sandwiched between Lots Road, Chelsea and Fulham power stations, the area round the church is still a riverside oasis and the atmosphere is extraordinarily peaceful.

3 St Mary's, Putney

History

Originally a chapel of ease to Wimbledon, St Mary's was first mentioned in 1292. It is not known whether an earlier church existed. For many years until 1846 the parish was a 'peculiar' of the See of Canterbury, the Archbishop being Lord of the Manor.

The church was substantially rebuilt in 1836/7 by E. Lapidge but was the victim of a devastating fire in 1973. An imaginative and comprehensive restoration was completed in 1982 by Ronald Sims; the sanctuary and altar were moved to the north side with seats facing it in a half-hexagon.

The fire fortunately spared the early 16th century Bishop West Chantry Chapel, an outstanding feature which had been moved from the south to the north side of the church during the 1836/7 restoration. It has two finely fan-vaulted bays and two panelled arches open to the chancel. It also has two notable bosses with the Bishop's coat of arms.

Exterior
The tower, although restored, is mediaeval. At one time, it had a cap. There is a new south-west porch set at an angle.

Interior
The four-bay nave and four-centred arches with shafts and hollows are partly of mediaeval material but, in the 1836/7 rebuilding, the nave was widened and extended eastwards. What was left of the chancel is now the Cromwell room.

Furnishings
Organ This splendid instrument, built by the Danish firm of Marcussen & Son, was installed in 1982 in a gallery in front of the inner face of the tower.

Altar-table, stained glass window over the sanctuary and portable font are modern

Light fittings and corona over the altar Ronald Sims introduced black metal hanging lamps and a corona over the altar supported by the beams remaining from the 19th century gallery.

Monuments
Memorials under the tower include:

Richard Lussher (d. 1615) Architectural surround with a broken segmental pediment over a frame with strap and ribbon work. There are obelisks at the sides.

Catherine Palmer (d. 1619) Inscription framed by a good cartouche and two columns with broken pediment.

Sir Thomas Dawes (d. 1655) It consists only of a skull on a bracket.

Leicester Burdet (D. 1691))

Thomas Payne (d. 1698) Two animated cartouches commemorate them.

All Saints', Wandsworth

Associations
Putney Debates of 1647 A slate plaque on the south wall of the nave
commemorates the Putney Debates of 1647. During the Civil War, the
headquarters of Cromwell's army was briefly located at Putney and,
between 27th August and 13th November, meetings of the Army
Council were held in the then chancel. The discussions on the future
government of the country were published in the 'Putney Debates'.
Cromwell and his generals sat round the communion table with their
hats on.

  Bishop Nicholas West, after whom the Chapel is named, was born in
Putney in 1461 and educated at Eton and Cambridge. He rose to

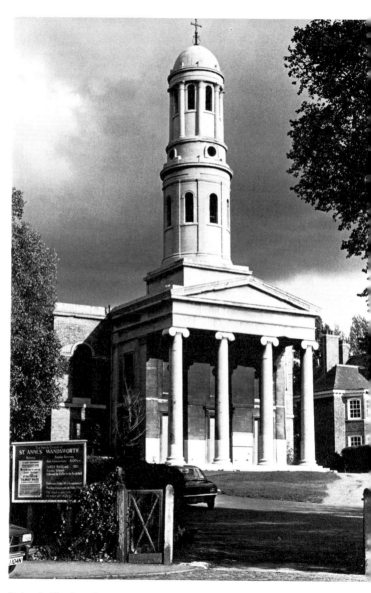

St Anne's, Wandsworth

become Bishop of Ely in 1515 but fell out of favour with Henry VIII by siding with Catherine of Aragon. The bishop died in 1533.

Thomas Cromwell, Henry VIII's agent in the Dissolution of the Monasteries, was also born in Putney, the year being 1485. He was executed in 1540 for his part in arranging the marriage of the King with Anne of Cleves.

Edward Gibbon the historian, was baptised at St Mary's in 1737.

Samuel Pepys mentions St Mary's in his diary for 1667 when he attended a service and 'good sermon' and where 'I saw girls of the school few of which pretty.'

Charles Dickens made Putney Church the setting for David Copperfield's marriage to Dora Spenlow.

General

St Mary's makes an effective counterpoise to All Saints', Fulham at the other end of Putney Bridge but is a completely separate parish and in a different borough.

Other Churches in Wandsworth

At the beginning of the 19th century much of Wandsworth was semi-rural.

All Saints' (4), with a long history, is a modest unassuming church of which parts of the chancel, the porch and the north aisle date back to the 18th century; the tower dates from 1630 but was raised a storey in 1841 (plate p. 433). The galleried interior has a roomy square churchwardens' pew and two good monuments including one to Henry Smyth (d. 1627), noted for his benefactions to Surrey towns.

St Anne's (5), a Commissioners' building of 1822–4, is well sited in a commanding position. It has a disproportionately tall round stone pepper-pot tower which is almost a carbon copy of that at St Mary's, Bryanston Square by the same architect. The open and spacious galleried interior is well lit by clear glass.

Roehampton

The parish church of Roehampton is Holy Trinity built 1896–8 by G. H. Fellowes Prynne. It has his characteristic traceried screen filling the whole of the chancel arch. The spire is 200 feet high.

ATKINSON, THOMAS D., *Local style in English Architecture* (Batsford, 1947).

BARNES, GORDON, *Stepney Churches* (The Faith Press for the Ecclesiological Society, 1967).

BETJEMAN, SIR JOHN, *The City of London Churches* (Pitkin Pictorials, 1969).

BUMPUS, T. FRANCIS, *Ancient London Churches* (T. Werner Laurie, 1908).

CLARKE, BASIL F. L., *Parish Churches of London* (Batsford, 1966).

CLIFTON-TAYLOR, ALEC, *English Parish Churches as Works of Art* (Batsford, 1974).

COBB, GERALD, *The Old Churches of London* (Batsford, 1942).
N.B. This has now been brought up to date in a new edition called *London City Churches* published by Batsford in 1976.

COLVIN, H. M., *A Biographical Dictionary of English Architects. 1660–1840.* (John Murray, 1954).

ELLEN, R. G., *A London Steeplechase* (City Press, 1972).

GUNNIS, RUPERT, *Dictionary of British Sculptors, 1660–1851* (Odhams Press, 1953).

KENT, WILLIAM, *An Encyclopaedia of London* (J. M. Dent & Sons, 1970, *revised by Godfrey Thompson*).

NAIRN, IAN, *Nairn's London* (Penguin Books, 1967 reprint).

PEVSNER, SIR NIKOLAUS, *The Buildings of England* (Penguin Books).
1. London—except the Cities of London and Westminster (1952, hardback 1969) 2. London—The Cities of London and Westminster (1957, later editions 1962 and 1973).

STOW, JOHN, *Survey of London* (Everyman Edition) (J. M. Dent & Sons, 1970 reprint).

YOUNG, ELIZABETH AND WAYLAND, *Old London Churches* (Faber & Faber, 1956).

Glossary

Acroteria Foliage-carved stone blocks.

Ambulatory Semicircular or polygonal aisle.

Apse Semicircular or polygonal termination to chancel.

Apse, Dalmeny, Linlithgowshire, c 1150

Architrave Lowest of three main components of entablature: surrounds (e.g. jambs, lintels) of a door or window.

Ashlar Hewn or squared stone.

Atrium Entrance hall or inner court of a Roman house, sometimes open to the sky.

Aumbry A receptacle, usually a recessed cupboard, for sacred Communion vessels.

Baldacchino (baldaquin) Canopy supported on columns.

Ball-flower

Ball-flower Form of 14th century decoration—globular flower with three incurved petals.

Baluster A small pillar usually circular: a column swelling in the middle or towards the base.

Barrel-vault See **Vault**.

Boss Projecting ornament placed at intersection of ceiling ribs.

Chapter-house, Oxford Cathedral, c 1220

Cartouche Tablet with ornate frame usually enclosing an inscription.

Caryatid Human figure used as column.

Chamfer Angle pared off.

Chrysom Robe confined in long swaddling bands worn by infant after baptism until churching of mother.

Clerestory Upper storey of nave or chancel wall pierced by row of windows.

Coade stone Artificial stone made in Lambeth by Coade and

Seely to a formula now lost.

Coffering Panels sunk in ceiling for decorative purposes.

Console Bracket or corbel frequently in form of letter S used in classical architecture to support cornices etc.

Corbel Stone bracket.

Hereford Cathedral, c 1250

Broadwater, Sussex, c 1250

Kidlington, Oxfordshire, c 1350

St Benedict's Church, Lincoln, c 1350

Credence table Small table beside altar upon which the bread and wine are placed before being consecrated: a shelf over a piscina.

Crenellate To embattle a parapet with notches or embrasures.

Crocket Leaf-shaped projection.

Choir, Lincoln Cathedral, c 1200

Litcham, Norfolk, c 1450

King's College, Cambridge

Diaper Surface decoration, incised or in low relief, consisting of squares or diamonds.

Dog-tooth Early English decoration in form of raised stars, resembling row of teeth.

Easter Sepulchre Recess with tomb-chest for holding the sacrament between Good Friday and Easter Day on north side of chancel, usually in sanctuary.

English bond The method of laying bricks in alternate courses of headers (bricks laid endwise) and stretchers (bricks laid lengthwise) as opposed to Flemish bond where headers and stretchers are laid alternately in the same course.

Entablature Horizontal structure lying upon columns in classical architecture, consisting of architrave, frieze and cornice.

Finial Foliage-shaped decorative termination to spire, pinnacle, gable, etc.

Flambeau A flaming torch.

Groined-vault See **Vault**.

Hammerbeam Beam projecting at right angles, usually from top of wall, to provide support for vertical member or arched brace of a roof.

Hatchment Arms of deceased person within a black lozenge-shaped wooden frame.

Hexastyle Having six columns.

Hood-mould Projecting moulding above arch or window to throw off water.

Iconostasis Screen of icons separating sanctuary from rest of church.

Intaglio A figure cut into any substance.

Label stop Ornamental head or other shape at end of hood-mould.

Lierne See **Vault**.

Lucarne Spire-light.

Lunette An arched opening in a vault often for a window.

Metope The space, frequently decorated, between triglyphs (three vertical grooves) in a classical frieze (see **Entablature**).

Modillion Small projecting bracket under a cornice.

Narthex Enclosed portico or vestibule at western end of church between entrance and nave.

Ogee Partly convex and partly concave shape.

Quirked Ogee, Arch of Constantine, Rome

Orders The various classical styles applying to combination of base, column, capital and entablature.

Pier Free-standing solid support, frequently square, between arches.

Pilaster Shallow pier attached to and projecting from wall.

Piscina Shallow basin with drain usually to south of altar.

Crowmarsh, c 1150

Warmington

Prie-dieu A praying-desk or chair.

Putti Small naked boys often used in Renaissance art.

Queen-post One of two vertical posts in a roof placed on a tie- or collar-beam.

Quoin Dressed stone at angle.

Rere-arch Arch supporting the inner part of wall as in front of a window.

Reredos Wall or screen behind altar usually ornamented.

Reveal Side surface of an opening in a wall for doorway or window.

Rood A cross or crucifix.

Rood-loft Means of access for cleaning, lighting and decking rood and sometimes acting as a base for it. The loft also provided accommodation for choir and instrumentalists.

Rotunda A round building especially when domed.

Rusticated Built of stone with joints greatly emphasised.

Sacrament-house An elaborate receptacle for reservation of the Sacrament.

Saddleback Shaped like a timber gable and applied to tower roof.

Sarcophagus A stone coffin or tomb elaborately carved.

Sedilia Recessed stone seats in chancel for priest and assistants.

Segmental In the form of a segment or arc of a circle.

Soffit Undersurface of an arch.

Spandrel Triangular wall surface between two arches.

St Alban's Abbey Church, c 1400

Stanchion An upright iron support.

Stock brick Term originally used for bricks made on a special board called a 'stock' but later associated with brownish-yellow colour of bricks made in London area.

Strapwork Ornamentation popular in late Tudor and Jacobean period of crossed and interlaced bands similar to those of cut leather.

String-course Projecting horizontal band or moulding on surface of wall.

Lincoln Cathedral, c 1220

Swag Festoon in the form of carved cloth suspended at both ends.

Tesselated A mosaic of small coloured pieces of brick, stone, marble etc. fitted into cement and made up into varied ornamental designs.

Tessera The small coloured piece (see **Tesselated**) used in tesselation.

Tetrastyle Having four columns.

Three-decker Pulpit with clerk's stall and reading-desk below.

Tourelle Turret with conical cap seen in French chateaux.

Tracery Decorative treatment of upper part of windows also used on walls, screens, vaults, etc. (a) *Plate* Early form of tracery in which shapes are cut out of solid stone of window head. (b) *Bar* Tracery consisting of curved and intersecting slender shafts which follow lines of mullions. (c) *Geometrical* Tracery consisting mainly of circles, often foiled. (d) *Y* Tracery in which central mullion of window divides into two forming a Y shape. (e)

Intersecting Development of Y
tracery in which more than
one mullion divides into two
and the branches intersect. (f)
Reticulated Tracery composed
of ogee shapes producing
net-like pattern. (g)
Perpendicular Tracery of
rectilinear form in which
mullions carry up into head of
window.

Transom A bar dividing a
window horizontally.

Triforium Arcaded wall passage
or blank arcading above
nave/chancel and below
clerestory.

Triptych A set of three painted
panels hinged together and often
used to adorn altars.

Tympanum of Doorway, Essendine, c
1130

(b) *Fan-vault* A type of vault
in which the length and
curvature of the ribs, which
spring from the same point, are
similar.

(c) *Groined-vault* The vault
obtained when two barrel vaults
intersect.

(d) *Lierne-vault* A vault
incorporating decorative short,
subsidiary ribs (liernes).

(e) *Rib-vault* A vault with
diagonal ribs projecting along
the groin.

Volute Spiral scroll.

Vitruvian Scroll

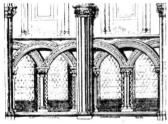

Triforium, St Cross, Hampshire, c 1200

Trompe l'oeil Architectural or
painting effect—often to give
three-dimensional appearance to
a plane surface—which 'deceives
the eye'.

Tympanum Space in head of
doorway arch.

Vault Arched roof of stone.

(a) *Barrel-vault* A simple
round vault like a tunnel.

Volute

Voussoir Wedge-shaped stone
of an arch.

Wagon-roof A curved wooden
roof resembling the canvas
awning over a wagon.

Wind-brace Inclined curved
timber placed lengthwise along
roof to strengthen it.

By the same author

Parish churches of England in colour (Blandford Press 1974)
Cathedrals (Blandford Press 1980)

A guide to London's churches